Refiguring
ENGLISH
STUDIES

Refiguring English Studies provides a forum for scholarship on English Studies as a discipline, a profession, and a vocation. To that end, the series publishes historical work that considers the ways in which English Studies has constructed itself and its objects of study; investigations of the relationships among its constituent parts as conceived in both disciplinary and institutional terms; and examinations of the role the discipline has played or should play in the larger society and public policy. In addition, the series seeks to feature studies that, by their form or focus, challenge our notions about how the written "work" of English can or should be done and to feature writings that represent the professional lives of the discipline's members in both traditional and nontraditional settings. The series also includes scholarship that considers the discipline's possible futures or that draws upon work in other disciplines to shed light on developments in English Studies.

OTHER VOLUMES IN THE SERIES

DAVID B. DOWNING, editor, *Changing Classroom Practices: Resources for Literary and Cultural Studies* (1994)

JED RASULA, *The American Poetry Wax Museum: Reality Effects, 1940–1990* (1995)

JAMES A. BERLIN, *Rhetorics, Poetics, and Cultures: Refiguring College English Studies* (1996)

ROBIN VARNUM, *Fencing with Words: A History of Writing Instruction at Amherst College during the Era of Theodore Baird, 1938–1966* (1996)

JANE MAHER, *Mina P. Shaughnessy: Her Life and Work* (1997)

MICHAEL BLITZ AND C. MARK HURLBERT, *Letters for the Living: Teaching Writing in a Violent Age* (1998)

Writing and Healing

Toward an Informed Practice

Edited by

Charles M. Anderson
University of Arkansas at Little Rock

Marian M. MacCurdy
Ithaca College

National Council of Teachers of English
1111 W. Kenyon Road, Urbana, Illinois 61801-1096

Manuscript Editor: Bob Heister
Prepress Services: G & S Typesetters, Inc.
Production Editor: Rita D. Disroe
Cover Design: Pat Mayer
Cover Photo: © Tony Stone Images
Interior Design: Jenny Jensen Greenleaf

NCTE Stock Number 58609-3050
ISSN 1073-9637

Library of Congress Cataloging-in-Publication Data

Writing and healing : toward an informed practice / edited by Charles M. Anderson, Marian M. MacCurdy.
    p.   cm. — (Refiguring English studies)
  Includes bibliographical references and index.
  ISBN 0-8141-5860-9
  1. Creative writing—Therapeutic use. 2. Psychotherapy. I. Anderson, Charles M. II. MacCurdy, Marian M. III. Series.

RC489.W75 W756 1999
615.8′515—dc21

                 99-048921

This collection is dedicated to the students, colleagues, friends, and other voyagers whose courage and grace in the face of trauma help us all to transform it.

CONTENTS

PERMISSIONS

We gratefully acknowledge the publishers who generously gave us permission to reproduce the following materials:

"Weeds and Peonies" from *Without* by Donald Hall. Copyright © 1998 by Donald Hall. Reprinted by permission of Houghton Mifflin Company. All rights reserved.

"So Not to Be Mottled," by Bernice Zamora, from *Infinite Divisions: An Anthology of Chicana Literature.* Ed. Tey Diana Rebolledo and Eliana S. Rivero. Tucson: U of Arizona P, 1993. 78. Reprinted by permission of Bilingual Press/Editorial Bilingüe, Arizona State University, Tempe Arizona.

"Plot," by Pat Mora, from *Infinite Divisions: An Anthology of Chicana Literature.* Ed. Tey Diana Rebolledo and Eliana S. Rivero. Tucson: U of Arizona P, 1993. 144. Reprinted with permission from the publisher of *Chants* (Houston: Arte Público Press, University of Houston, 1985).

"Doper's Dream" and "Eagle in the Land of Oz," by Donald Receveur, from *Winning Hearts and Minds: War Poems by Vietnam Veterans.* Ed. Larry Rottman, Jan Barry, and Basil Paquet. Coventry: First Casualty Press, 1972. 49, 99. Reprinted by permission of the author.

"Rape," by Marla Humphress. Reprinted by permission of the author.

Figure 8.1 taken from M. S. Gazzaniga, D. Steen, and B. Wolpe, *Functional Neuroscience*, p. 61. Copyright © 1979 by Harper & Row Publishers, Inc. Reprinted by permission of Michael S. Gazzaniga.

Figure 8.2 taken from Mishkin, Mortimer, and Tim Appenzeller. "The Anatomy of Memory." *Scientific American*, 256, 6 (June 1987): 80–89. Copyright © 1987 by Carol Donner. Reprinted by permission.

ACKNOWLEDGMENTS

We wish to thank Steve North, whose early enthusiasm for this project helped us believe it could be done. We also wish to recognize the anonymous reviewer of the first version of our book who understood it and supported it, part and whole.

Weeds and Peonies

Your peonies burst out, white as snow squalls,
with red flecks at their shaggy centers,
in your border of prodigies by the porch.
I carry one magnanimous blossom inside
to float in a glass bowl, as you used to do.

Ordinary happiness, remembered in sorrow,
blows like snow into the abandoned garden
overcoming the daisies. Your blue coat
vanishes down Pond Road into imagined snowflakes
with Gus at your side, his great tail swinging,

but you will not return, tired and satisfied,
and grief's repeated particles suffuse the air—
like the dog yipping through the entire night,
or the cat stretching awake, then curling
as if to dream of her mother's milky nipples.

A raccoon dislodges a geranium from its pot.
Flowers, roots, and dirt lie upended
in the back garden, where lilies begin
their daily excursions above the stone walls
in the season of old roses. I pace beside weeds

and snowy peonies, staring at Mount Kearsarge
where you climbed wearing purple hiking boots.
"Hurry back. Be careful, climbing down."
Your peonies lean their vast heads westward
as if they might topple. Some topple.

DONALD HALL, *Without* (1998)
(with permission of Houghton Mifflin)

PREFACE

I first heard Donald Hall's "Weeds and Peonies" on the radio as I was driving home from work one day. He began by speaking of the illness and subsequent death of his wife, poet Jane Kenyon. By the time he got to reading "Weeds and Peonies," the first poem he wrote after his wife's death, I had arrived home and was continuing to sit in my car in my driveway so as not to miss a single word. I looked out to my ten peony plants with their heavy pink heads in luscious bloom that greeted me along the walkway, the plants I dug up from the garden at the old farmhouse that I lived in with my husband and children, the house I thought we would die living in. He did; I didn't. So I brought my two young children and those peonies, the only artifacts from my old life, to this new house, new town, new job, new life.

Listening to Donald Hall read that poem, I knew that he and I—and anyone who had ever been bereaved—were part of a common but relatively silent community. We expect poets to write of loss, because poets, after all, have license to do such things, but others become quiet, even at times mute, and need help to speak of their grief.

A week after my husband died, I returned to teaching to face a "Professional Writing" class whose empathy for me bled out of their eyes. I knew as soon as I walked into the room that I had to do something, say something, and soon, or they would dissolve and then so would I. I forced myself to look at them, smiled, and said, "So tell me, what's it like being single in the eighties?" Our laughter protected us from nearly falling through one of those holes in the universe, and we could begin to talk. We talked about grief in the workplace and how unprepared our culture is to handle it. We talked about what to say to the bereaved, what not to say. We talked about our cultural silences. We talked. The next class was "Women and Writing." When I walked in they just looked at me and said, "Thank you for coming back to us." Then the questions came. They wanted to know how I was dealing with this sudden, catastrophic loss. They wanted to know who I was becoming. So we wrote and we shared our work. Toward the end of the semester, I read them the first poem I wrote after my husband's death, and they—students from physical therapy, health sciences, biology, cinema studies—offered the stories of their lives. As one of my students wrote a few years later:

> In that forum, Marian shared with us a small piece of her grief and love. . . . We learned along with her how trauma is healed through writing. . . . Marian had been unable to write since her husband's death, and here in late December she had finally broken through. It was that breakthrough piece that she shared with us, and the thought of that moment moves me still. By sharing her work and emotions with us, she became one of us. . . . Cloaked in that strength and comfort she helped create, we not only wrote about our difficult topics, but were able to share our work with each other and for each other.

My grief gave my students permission to tell the truth, to me, to themselves, to each other. They taught me how to integrate public and private, and our class became a healing community for them and for me.

This communal participation in the collective truths that make us whole is, for me, the genesis of *Writing and Healing: Toward an Informed Practice.* Donald Hall had the courage to express the truth of his grief to the community, a truth that found a response in me. That response immediately entered my professional as well as my personal life. We expect poets to do this. We do not expect our students to do this. The history of our profession and the positions of those among us with the greatest power and prestige have, in fact, encouraged us in our writing, in our speaking, and in our teaching, to cut our students and ourselves off from the healing resources of poets, peonies, weeds, and grief. The purpose of this book is to recover that loss.

MARIAN M. MacCURDY
Ithaca College

CHAPTER ONE

Introduction

CHARLES M. ANDERSON
University of Arkansas at Little Rock

MARIAN M. MacCURDY
Ithaca College

When we entered the teaching profession in the mid-seventies, one of us in a large, northeastern, private, research institution and the other in a large, southern, public research institution, the students in our classes were very different from the ones who fill them today. In one institution, nearly all the students entering the university were eighteen years old, mostly white, mostly male, and middle-class. Relatively few minority students appeared, and those who did often had been recruited to play one sport or another. In the other university, more nontraditional students and persons of color were present, but in far fewer numbers than in today's population. However, even with these significant demographic differences, what was common to our experience was that we assumed students arrived at college ready to engage in the intellectual mission of higher education. Our universities, despite the upheaval of the sixties and the economics of rising interest and inflation rates, represented for them and for us the doorway through which they would eventually step into adulthood after preparation for the good, permanent jobs and middle-class lives that awaited them on the other side of graduation. Our primary concern as teachers of writing was to develop the intellectual capacities, skills, and abilities of our students, and we assumed that only their academic preparation and personal motivation could affect their ultimate success in life beyond the university. But that was then, and this is now.

In a speech to the 1996 annual conference of the National Association for Poetry Therapy in Columbia, Maryland, poet Lucille Clifton, speaking of children raised in the inner city, said, "every day some of those children are bearing something you could not bear. . . . Every day something has tried to kill [them] and has failed" (Clifton). Of course, the effects of such trauma are not limited to the inner city. Students in suburban and even rural settings must deal with traumatic events ranging from fist fights to drive-by shootings, as well as the less-directed but equally destructive effects of addictive drugs, sexually transmitted diseases, neglect, economic indulgence, and poverty. Even family structures are no protection from traumatic experiences. Today we know that the number of children damaged by sexual, physical, and emotional abuse, even within the family, far exceeds our expectations. Their faces confront us every day, as we pour milk over our morning cereal, as we witness their broken bodies being "found" almost every week on the evening news.

Most recently, new levels of trauma resulting from children randomly attacking others at schools across the country have entered our cultural consciousness. Photographs and film from Edinboro, Pennsylvania; Jonesboro, Arkansas; Springfield, Oregon; Littleton, Colorado; Granada Hills, California; and other places across the nation graphically demonstrate that schools are not sanctuaries for the pursuit of matters purely academic. Saturation coverage of such events engenders a growing discourse of frustration and anger directed at a society unable to deal adequately or fairly with such acts and their human consequences.

Children who survive these and other kinds of overt and covert traumas become young adults, and many find their way into our classes, where the writing they do about what they have experienced challenges our practical, political, and theoretical assumptions about the power, place, and purposes of writing. The general inclination of our profession has long been to marginalize such disturbing texts in favor of safer, more controlled discourses of the academy. To do so necessarily marginalizes, isolates, and alienates the writers who create those texts, valorizing our own illusions of academic sanctuary over their invitations to engage in the complex material, cultural, and socio-personal worlds of actual and virtual experience that dominate the lives of late-twentieth-century human beings. We and those who have contributed to this book have chosen a different stance. We believe texts about traumatic experiences constitute legitimate sites at which the work of writing can be done both in and out of the academy. We believe this work, difficult, scary, and messy, is important and worth doing. We believe the benefits are substantial. *Writing and Healing: Toward an Informed Practice* is our attempt to help writing teachers who feel as we do understand the dynamics and consequences of their students' efforts and learn to respond to those efforts in appropriate ways. In the pages that follow, we examine the verbal and relational consequences of a wide variety of trauma-producing experiences, and argue that writing has the potential to help survivors deal with these events in a way that mitigates their traumatic consequences.

Trauma, Writing, and Healing

In 1980, the *Diagnostic and Statistical Manual of Mental Disorders*, third edition (DSMIII), the standard reference for medically acceptable diagnoses depended upon by medical providers and insurance companies, included a new diagnostic category of emotional/mental disorders—post-traumatic stress disorder (PTSD). This diagnosis was a response to the Vietnam War veterans who had recently returned from the most unpopular war in our history, emotionally and physically battered by battle, only to discover that their communities, unlike those of previous wars and military actions, did not welcome them home as heroes. Used and discarded by the military, vilified or ignored by the public, and haunted by sights and sounds no one wanted to know about, these men and women suffered from what we now recognize as typical symptoms of PTSD—nightmares, dissociation, inability to form close relationships, mistrust often bordering on paranoia, dysfunction at work, etc. These classic sufferers of PTSD had had personal bodily and psychic control ripped away and were attempting to regain that control, sometimes in destructive ways. Finding themselves in a culture that could not or would not understand or accept them, veterans' symptoms only intensified. As difficult as it was for Vietnam War veterans, their sheer numbers forced the development of a more effective treatment than the "shell shock" model developed during World War I had allowed. The DSMIII diagnosis enabled veterans to name their condition, to take control of it, and to form communities to help each other.

Experience with Vietnam veterans has taught us a great deal about trauma at every level and in every aspect of human experience. We now know, for example, that no one can experience traumatic moments without serious effects, that PTSD is more likely to occur when survivors are isolated by cultural or individual denial, and most important, that one's recovery from PTSD is directly related to the response of the community to the sufferer. PTSD isolates people, makes survivors feel like victims, freaks, pariahs that others cannot encounter because, having stepped outside the "normal," they have seen, experienced, and have come to know things that others do not. Trauma survivors are usually very careful to protect others from what they know. They keep silences because they fear that others will be broken by what survivors have to tell them. Unfortunately, PTSD festers in just such an environment of silence; its symptoms intensify when survivors are and feel isolated from their communities. Support groups help trauma survivors speak, but as helpful as they can be, support groups have the ambient effect of "ghettoizing" their members, creating the modern equivalent of the leper colony, an effect that is antithetical to trauma recovery.

The medical diagnosis of PTSD has had another, even more profound effect: We now know that every instance of trauma has the potential for grave psychic harm and that even witnesses to disasters can be susceptible to the effects of PTSD. This has helped us to understand and to begin addressing damage done by the host of traumatic events that comprise life in the twentieth century: two world wars, one involving nuclear weapons; two major genocides and countless others around the world; routinized physical, sexual, and verbal abuse; assassinations of political leaders; entrapment of minority populations in dying inner cities; the concentration of wealth in the hands of smaller and smaller percentages of the population; the proliferation of deadly microorganisms including HIV, Ebola, and resistant strains of tuberculosis and pneumonia; a shrinking economy and social safety net; the visual representation of Los Angeles policemen beating and kicking an African American man; the explosion of the space shuttle Challenger; and the bombing of the federal building in Oklahoma City. The list goes on and on and on. And because we are all witnesses to, perhaps participants in, this apparently endless succession of virtual and actual encounters with great traumatic potential, PTSD has become a central, material fact of our time. We are all survivors.

As trauma survivors, we share one very important characteristic: We feel powerless, taken over by alien experiences we could not anticipate and did not choose. Healing depends upon gaining control over that which has engulfed us. We cannot go back and change the past. The adult who was sexually abused as a child of five is permanently altered by that experience. But she can recognize the truth of her past and confront it with all the knowledge, anger, and understanding of the adult she has become. Alice Miller, in her tiny but significant book, *The Drama of the Gifted Child,* argues that children are quick to discover what their environments want of them and how to mirror that behavior. Children are remarkably fast learners. That abused five-year-old may not tell her parents of her abuse if she knows that they will have great trouble dealing with it. Miller asserts that when parents do not attempt to view their children's worlds empathetically, children must defer to their parents' view of reality, suppressing their lived experience in the process. The locus of control shifts from the child to the environment, and personal agency is lost. Silence is easier than confrontation, particularly for a child. She hides her experience from them, but she will remember it in that dark place where nightmares live because only memory can protect her from the frightening, relentless, uncontrollable, and inevitable effects of the truth surfacing at some point in the future, perhaps when she loses one she loves, or she is mugged on the street, or she goes away to college and finds herself confronted by young men who see her as a sexual target.

Healing arises from just such confusion and psychic pain, never from peace. It is when we are overloaded with past and present trauma that we are motivated to take on the difficult work of healing. When past and present selves collide, often precipitated by a single incident or a crisis that calls up past traumas, business as usual cannot continue, and the survivor is motivated to delve into the past to see what was left behind in an attempt to make sense of the present. This sense of something missing, of loss and grief, characterizes all trauma survivors. And, as Judith Herman writes in her groundbreaking book, *Trauma and Recovery,* "all of the classic writings ultimately recognize the necessity of mourning and reconstruction in the resolution of traumatic life events. Failure to complete the normal process of grieving perpetuates the traumatic reaction" (70). Grieving and the healing that accompanies it allow the survivor to reclaim the self and its agency, to develop a representation of the self that is congruent with the experience of the survivor, and to integrate both the self and its representation into a larger community of understanding. However, such recovery is complicated by the fact that traumatic events are isolated by pain and, often, by shame, and by the fact that our culture provides few opportunities for survivors to incorporate their experiences into the realm of the "normal," or the real, which Jacques Lacan describes as "that which always comes back to the same place" (42).

Traumatic events, because they do not occur within the parameters of "normal" reality, do not fit into the structure and flow of time. Instead, they are imprisoned within the psyche as discrete moments, frozen, isolated from normal memories. Because they are not connected to the normal, linear flow of time-bound memory, these moments emerge into consciousness at any point, bringing the force of the traumatic event with them. To free these moments requires what Dori Laub calls *"re-externalizing the event"*:

> Re-externalization of the event can occur and take effect only when one can articulate and *transmit* the story, literally transfer it to another outside oneself and then take it back again. Telling thus entails a reassertion of the hegemony of reality and a re-externalization of the evil that affected and contaminated the trauma victim. (Felman and Laub 69)

While there are numerous techniques by which persons can engage this process, many survivors find writing to be a powerful and appropriate site for work of this sort to take place. As Laub puts it, survivors need "to tell their story in order to survive. There is, in each survivor, an imperative need to tell and thus to come to know one's story, unimpeded by ghosts from the past against which one has to protect oneself. One has to know one's buried truth in order to be able to live one's life" (78). By writing about traumatic experiences, we discover and rediscover them, move them out of the ephemeral flow and space of talk onto the more permanent surface of the page, where they can be considered, reconsidered, left, and taken up again. Through the dual possibilities of permanence and revision, the chief healing effect of writing is thus to recover and to exert a measure of control over that which we can never control—the past.

As we manipulate the words on the page, as we articulate to ourselves and to others the emotional truth of our pasts, we become agents for our own healing, and if those to whom we write receive what we have to say and respond to it as we write and rewrite, we create a community that can accept, contest, gloss, inform, invent, and help us discover, deepen, and change who we have become as a consequence of the trauma we have experienced. This is a natural, non-utopian discursive process that integrates the personal and the social and depends upon the community's capacity to be both supportive and critical. It is, by definition, a site at which the social and discursive practices of the individual, the community, and the larger culture are interrogated and from which they may be effectively altered. The work of healing, as we and the theorists and practitioners we have cited above conceive of it, depends upon this process. The crucial assertion we want to emphasize here and throughout this collection is that healing is neither a return to some former state of perfection nor the discovery or restoration of some mythic autonomous self. Healing, as we understand it, is precisely the opposite. It is change from a singular self, frozen in time by a moment of unspeakable experience, to a more fluid, more narratively able, more socially integrated self. Students seek out the writing classroom for this kind of work because the very process of writing and rewriting invites them to tell their stories, to listen to what their stories tell them, to hear and to be heard by others engaged in similar work, and it supports the healing those stories make possible.

This being the case, those of us whose professional lives are defined by the writing classroom often find ourselves reading essays that contain the traumatic life stories of our students, even when such stories are not the focus of the class or of the assignments we give. Such essays open a discursive space in our classrooms in which the lives of our students and the multiple cultures, events, and discourses that produce, support, and impinge upon those lives enter the university in ways no textbook, collection of essays, or journal article can hope to make available. When we choose to allow and to occupy this space, we demonstrate that the academy is not a place of alienation, an "Other" to "the real world," or an ivory tower. We transform it into a locus of connection where the hard, personal, and social work of understanding the lived realities of experience can happen. Out of this transformation, we believe, may come human agents capable of generating real and lasting social action.

But we must be absolutely clear on one point: *We are not arguing that writing teachers should require such stories or that writing classrooms must focus on them.* In fact, no essay in this book mandates writing assignments about painful or traumatic experiences. Many contributors are careful to describe the safeguards necessary to prevent abuses and circumvent the real dangers that can arise from such writing. We know that conversations among writing professionals have been intense and heated in the area of such personal writing. Teachers are understandably nervous about inviting students to engage in work that seems more the purview of therapists than writing teachers. Articles in the *Chronicle of Higher Education* and a variety of writing journals, talks at conventions, and discussions among faculty across the country attest to the concern we all have that the line between therapy and writing instruction be kept clear and that we not put our students, ourselves, or others in harm's way. We know that many teachers and even more writers will choose not to engage in such writing. We believe these choices must be respected and honored.

We are, however, arguing what we know to be true—stories about painful, traumatic events in the lives of students do appear in our classrooms, they have always appeared, and they will continue to appear, not because we want or don't want them to, but because writing is quite simply the medium in which, for many people, the deepest, most effective, and most profound healing can take place. While teachers can respond in any number of ways to such stories, our conversations with peers and our own experience lead us to see four general response categories, each with its own particular set of consequences:

1. Teachers can reject the essays outright, refusing to accept them as legitimate classroom projects.

2. Teachers can engage the stories and their writers in inappropriate ways, becoming overly sympathetic, taking sides, and losing sight of the writing as writing.

3. Teachers can take over the stories, substituting their own voices, experience, politics, or values for those of the student.

4. Teachers can approach the stories as sites or occasions for making sense of experience, using their expertise as writing professionals, writers, and human beings to help students create texts that embody their lived experience, the clearest expression of it, and whatever understanding of that experience is available to the student and the community within which the student lives and writes at the time of the writing.

Our choice and the choice of those who have contributed to this collection is obviously the fourth one, and it is our intention, through the essays in this book, to help teachers wishing to make the same choice develop the knowledge necessary to respond appropriately to the healing narratives their students write.

While we are not mandating that teachers deal with narratives of trauma, we do know that the choices we make, as individual teachers and as a profession, regarding the nature and quality of our response to these texts are not innocent or neutral. They are highly consequential. The choices we face place us in a situation analogous to the one that Freud faced nearly a century ago. When he observed behaviors among what he termed "hysterics," women who suffered psychosomatic illnesses, Freud postulated that their illnesses were caused by the trauma associated with sexual abuse. He abandoned this position, which he called his "seduction theory," for a variety of reasons, not the least of which was his inability to convince both himself and his colleagues that his culture could produce so many victims of sexual abuse. Freud's decision to abandon his seduction theory turned the therapeutic focus of psychoanalysis away from the experience and back to the survivor. Instead of recognizing that trauma could produce deleterious symptoms, Freud placed the agency of and responsibility for psychic pain directly onto the "victim," resulting in a psychoanalytic school that saw repression of unconscious desires as the primary cause of psychic pain. Had Freud not abandoned his seduction theory, we might have had more appropriate methods for treating trauma survivors throughout the twentieth century: soldiers in two world wars and the Korean and Vietnam wars, victims of the Armenian genocide and the Holocaust, and millions of men, women, and children affected by domestic and criminal violence. By choosing to treat trauma as a problem only of the individual sufferer rather than a site of individual and collective interaction, an occasion for a critique of communal values, and an opportunity for significant social change, psychoanalytic approaches to trauma have intensified the feelings of individual powerlessness and sense of isolation arising from traumatic experience, particularly in the case of women.

The most famous example is Freud's case of Dora, which has been commented upon at length by psychoanalysts, feminists, Marxists, and others, and by scholars as wide ranging as Lacan, Jeffrey Masson, and Phyllis Chesler. However, as Robin Lakoff and James Coyne argue in their book, *Father Knows Best: The Use and Abuse of Power in Freud's Case of Dora*, "Cavalier dismissal of feminist criticism of analytic theory from within the profession . . . shows that this criticism has been neither integrated into current analytical thinking nor fully understood. Superficial acceptance into theory of feminist critique has much the same effect" (7). Indeed, as late as 1974, the profession generated the following comment by Kurt Lewin in an article published in *Psychoanalytic Review*: "One could well imagine such a girl [as Dora] leading men on, frustrating them, and finally destroying them altogether. . . . Hell hath no fury like a woman scorned" (521–22). The traditional psychoanalytic model, according to Lakoff and Coyne, provided a Catch-22 for trauma survivors who were not believed—particularly women:

> Women, as analysts or patients, were bullied into becoming advocates for their detractors' methods. It was a classic double

bind. If women agreed with psychoanalysis that they were stupider, weaker, and less moral than men, then at least those individuals who agreed could be exalted as "honorary men," women who had risen high enough above their baseness to appreciate that baseness. But a woman who was not convinced of the reality of penis envy and its concomitants thereby demonstrated her inability to think rationally and scientifically, as well as her moral corruptibility. Arguments of this sort, however delicately phrased, continue into the present. (9)

The point is that the actualities of individual experience, no matter how compelling, were and continue to be made secondary to the constructed reality promoted by the larger psychoanalytic community and the culture of which it is a part, a reality that serves the interests not of those in need, but of domination. Across much of our profession, a similarly consequential sacrificing of the personal to the professional has taken place.

The Struggle for the Self

For many compositionists, the individual self (and its experience) as a functioning, believable entity has become so problematic that they no longer claim a generative, central place in writing pedagogy (Bruffee). In fact, the self, if it exists at all, exists not in the lived experience of the writer but in the context within which that experience takes place, in the discourses of political and economic communities whose ideologies, with or without the writer's knowledge or assent, construct the writer's subjectivity, effectively removing him or her from the agent position, most often replacing agency, especially collective agency, with crass consumerism (Berlin). Raising students' critical consciousness so they can recognize their own constructed nature, resist the hegemonic ideological forces that drive that construction, and finally, effect progressive social action have become the chief goals of much instruction. With the support of a host of European and American rhetoricians, philosophers, and critics, this has led to a potentially dominant model of writing in which attention to the self is not simply problematic but ultimately dangerous to writers, communities, and to culture itself. In the words of Wayne Pounds, pedagogies dealing with the self teach the student "to blame herself because she accepts the ideology which locates the source of all action and value in the individual self. . . . History [in this view] is only personal history, which exists without any capacity to bring about change in the objective world. Public or social history is impossible" (Pounds 47). For Kathleen Pfeiffer, personal or expressive writing, our most common terms for writing about the self, creates a "weepy world of confessions and revelations" that teaches students "only to look inward and cry" and constitutes a "radical destruction of community and communication" (Pfeiffer 671). David Bartholomae, in "Writing with Teachers: A Conversation with Peter Elbow," sums up such positions in the following way:

> I don't think I need to teach sentimental realism, even though I know my students could be better at it than they are. I don't think I need to because I don't think I should. I find it a corrupt, if extraordinarily tempting genre. I don't want my students to celebrate what would then become the natural and inevitable details of their lives. I think the composition course should be part of the general critique of traditional humanism. (71)

Such dismissive comments encourage us to imagine that our business can be about community and culture but not those who live there, about the public but not the private, about what students think but not what they feel, about how all these terms are different but not how they inform each other. The consequences of such dichotomies are real. Student experience is limited or dismissed by them (Spellmeyer, "Out of the Fashion Industry"); our classrooms and our professional discourse are made oppositional and unyielding (Bauer; France; O'Donnell); and the academic culture of which we are a part becomes increasingly adversarial as various factions and ideologies battle for control (Ebert; "Interchanges"). The "conversations" staged at the Conference on College Composition and Communication in 1989 and 1991 between David Bartholomae and Peter Elbow and the *College Composition and Communication* articles that followed in 1995 provide ample evidence in support of this point (Bartholomae; Elbow).

As Freud's own limitations and the limitations of his professional community rendered him unable to assert the consequential relationship of self and cultural environment, so may our own professional discourse and its history render us unable to recognize that our students' public and private worlds are inextricably connected. For them (and for us, too, if we are truly honest about it), the pain of divorce, the loss of a loved one, the memory of an attack on a dark street are the sites at which the dissonance of lived experience creates authentic opportunities for significant political and personal change. When teachers exclude lived experience in favor of more abstract or distanced concepts, concerns, and representations of reality, they rob students of genuine opportunities to engage in the very individual and collective work such teachers expect them to do. When students resist separating public from private, personal from political *as they understand these terms* or when they assert themselves by refusing to identify with the teacher's political position, they get blamed for the failure, labeled immature, unprepared, unmotivated, or the helpless dupes of a system of oppression only the teacher can discern. If they object to such manipulation, their very objections become proof of the legitimacy of the teacher's position. Dale M. Bauer, for example, after ascribing students' objections to what they saw as an overemphasis on feminist politics in the classroom to "indoctrination" asks, "How do we move ourselves out of this political impasse and resistance in order to get our students to identify with the political agenda of feminism?" (387).[1] In effect, such teaching, no matter how well-intended, makes the decision Freud made—it blames the victims created by the limitations of its own discursive practices.[2] Meanwhile, writing teachers find themselves more and more alienated from students who seem less and less attentive and more resistant to the increasingly abstract benefits of academic literacy, which students experience as increasingly removed from the circumstances of their particular histories. In the end, if teachers are not careful, they become the very thing they most despise, agents not of change but of dominance, personal glorification, and hegemony (Spellmeyer, "After Theory"; Horner; Anderson).

We do not intend to set ourselves in absolute opposition to the concerns of our profession. Social action as our profession has articulated it is indeed a good thing. Nor do we intend to disregard the contributions of social constructionist theory, feminist critique, culture studies, postmodern perspectives, and critical theory in general to writing and the teaching of writing. Without the important work of scholars and teachers influenced by these movements, we might still be treating our students in the way we described at the beginning of this introduction, and clearly, without the knowledge their efforts have generated, the essays in this book could never have been written. But we believe that the strong forms of such perspectives—by contesting and too often marginalizing the lived experience of students in favor of political and ideological concerns of individual practitioners and the profession in general—have created classrooms hostile to the very persons they are supposed to serve. In these classrooms traumatic experience similar to what many students have suffered outside the academy becomes everyday educational policy. As Virginia Anderson, in her recent sympathetic critique of confrontational teaching puts it, "We believe we can simply tell students that their world is so rotten it will crumble before aggressive challenge, that all their truths are unstable, that their lives are a mishmash of fabrications, and that their worlds must be yielded up to exactly the kind of corrective exposure that Susan Miller, for example, decries" (207). To choose this option is to use authority to silence the experience of students, which, as Kurt Spellmeyer puts it, is "to silence much more than the person, not only everyone from whom the speaker learned his words, but also everything these words have made real" ("Too Little Care" 269).

Fortunately, as even a cursory survey of our professional literature will show, there are other options. Colleagues such as Lynn Bloom, Jane Tompkins, Richard Miller, Chris Anderson, Donald McQuade, Nancy Sommers, and many others now tell us stories in which the public and the private are essential components of the professional text. Such stories often focus on trauma and its aftermath and are not significantly different from the ones that appear in our writing classrooms. An entire issue of *College Composition and Communication* in 1992 focused on "personal and innovative writing" and included essays dealing with the trauma of a loved one's death (McQuade) and on the consequences of giving away ones' voice to an authoritative other (Sommers). Such essays open both their writers and our profession to the richness and the healing potential of the interplay of personal and public discourses. They allow us to witness what Min-Zhan Lu and Bruce Horner have recently called a problematizing and deepening of the term "experience" to include that of the teacher as well as the student, a deepening that at once brings greater risk and greater hope to the work we do (Lu and Horner).

As our eyes and ears open to the potential of our colleagues' and our own lived experience to inform our professional work, so may we begin to see that potential in the writing of students and others who live, work, and suffer in realities not so very far from those we inhabit. The identification necessarily issuing from this revelation allows the classroom and other sites where writing takes place to change. Richard E. Miller puts it this way:

> I conceive of the work of the classroom as an ongoing project where I learn how to hear what my students are saying. Learning to do this helps me to find a way to speak that they can hear. It also makes it possible for them to learn how to hear what I, as a representative of the academy, am saying and how to speak, read, and write in ways that I can hear. This is the only approach I know of for making the classroom a possible resource for hope and it is the only mechanism I've found for transforming recitations and revelations of personal experience into moments for reflection and revision about the complex, conflicted, and contradictory ways that culture makes its presence known in the day-to-day workings of one's life. (R. Miller 283)

Miller's classroom depends upon "first learning to listen to others" (285) and encourages teachers and students "to construct alternatives to the lives we have been living" (284). It becomes "a place to see and re-see the components and possible trajectories of one's lived experience and to situate and re-situate that experience within a world of other thoughts and other embodied reactions," a place where writing can "generate material for constructing a more humane and hospitable life-world by providing the very thing the academy is currently most in need of: a technology for producing and sustaining the hope that tomorrow will be better than today and that it is worth the effort to see that such hopes aren't unfounded" (285). Speaking even more directly to the point of this introduction and the essays that follow is Miller's description of his lived experience of the importance and difficulty of his and our project:

> Sitting in my father's room on the psychiatric ward, holding his shaking hands, paring his fingernails so he won't cut himself, I see just how difficult such an imaginative transformation of reality is. He is afraid, he tells me, of everything: of being locked away for good this time, of his decaying body, of what his doctor is going to think, of things innumerable and unnamable. It is as if he were physically trapped inside his own fears. As I listen to him struggle to find some way to relax, I sense that he is making his way back from the madness, battling a set of internal and external systems that had made the decision to live untenable once again. He understands this time that just medicating the body is insufficient; he must also learn a new language, learn how to tell the stories that he has never told in order to escape the terrible power they have over him. (284–85)

More than twenty years of work with students and other writers have taught us that this is exactly the power which writing about trauma brings to the teaching and learning relationship. It transforms stories that have never been told into texts that bear witness to lived experience; it opens confusion and pain to the possibilities of wholeness; and it encourages victims to become agents for personal and public healing.

We have chosen the phrase "informed practice" to describe the various practices we hope will issue from careful reading of the essays in this book. It is derived from the classical rhetorical term "techne," which means neither theory nor praxis, but a melding of the two into a single entity in such a way that each supports and extends the other, and both are equally and fully realized (Tiles; Byrum). Informed practice, like techne, has a strong ethical dimension. It demands both a technical skill and a deep concern for the right use of that skill, embracing the process of working with writers to produce texts, the production of those texts, the texts themselves, and the healing effects, often ambient, of the whole encounter. Informed practice leads us to value both the writing and the writer, the individual and the community, the public and the private, to see ourselves in the work of those with whom we write and to see them in what we do and who we are. This complex, ambiguous, sometimes painful dialogue between self and other is what it means to be whole, a term we use not to suggest a romantic or Edenic condition from which writers have fallen but an ongoing, recursive process in which self and community challenge, affirm, serve, and extend each other in the drama of personal and public history.

Shape and Substance of *Writing and Healing: Toward an Informed Practice*

We have divided the essays that follow into four sections: "Finding Our Way In"; "Traditions and Extensions"; "Writing and Healing in the Classroom"; and "Writing and Healing in the World." In the first section we have placed essays that seemed to us to address issues of how teachers and theorists have come to experience writing as healing and how they have come to practice it. Anne Ruggles Gere brings the personal and the public together by telling the story of finding her voice and tracing the political and professional consequences of that discovery. Tilly Warnock describes ways in which the writing of Kenneth Burke helps her to understand that revision is and always has been a life-making, life-preserving skill. Charles Anderson, Karen Holt, and Patty McGady explore the ways in which writing allows writers to negotiate the personal and the public when the stakes for doing so are as high as they can possibly be. Their essay shows us how to resist and how to negotiate the pressure to be what the Other might have us be.

In "Traditions and Extensions," we have included essays that seem to us important both for what they teach us about classrooms and for the connections they help us make with areas inside and outside our own profession as well as with the past. T. R. Johnson provides a remarkable look at the tradition through which therapeutic writing has made its way to our time. Johnson locates and articulates resolutions for a number of serious differences between postmodernists and expressivists, discovering not conflict but continuity in the ways they view the self. Michelle Payne examines the discursive traditions that allow writers in her classrooms to explore issues of sexual abuse, drawing on eighteenth-century American court records and journals as well as contemporary feminist, postmodernist, and writing theories. She challenges postmodernist teachers to see the healed self not as a romantic, immutable entity, but as a locus of multiple discourses engaged in the past and present work of being and becoming. Marian MacCurdy examines the writing her students do through the insights of contemporary trauma theory and psychological research. Through years of classroom experience and detailed research into the neurobiology of trauma, she provides a safe and effective model for working with writing that focuses on painful life events. Alice Brand explores recent research on brain anatomy and physiology, especially as that research addresses the issues of emotion and trauma. She helps us to see the relevance of such research for the teaching of writing. Finally, Anne Hunsaker Hawkins examines a genre she calls "pathographies," or stories of sickness, in which mythic narratives help persons suffering from significant, often intractable, physical illnesses find healing in the worst of circumstances. Hawkins teaches us how we might read and understand the essays our students bring to the classroom, as well as the work those essays may be doing in the lives of the persons who write them.

"Writing and Healing in the Classroom" contains essays particularly focused on events in the classroom and on teachers of writing. Of course, the distinction here is an arbitrary one, as most essays in this collection arise from and specifically address matters of the classroom. Guy Allen's essay charts his course from literature teacher to professor and teacher of what he calls "expressive," or personal, writing. Allen conducts a series of experiments and surveys and finds that his students not only write better, more engaging prose in his classes, but that they do measurably better in other, less personal writing in the university. Jeffrey Berman and Jonathan Schiff explore the writing students do in Berman's literature class focused on texts dealing with suicide. Together they discover that "diaries" help students become stronger, more engaged readers and that they help students explore subjects that are of real and lasting importance to their lives. Jerome Bump's essay examines the relationship between the personal and the professional in the writing classroom as he describes the history of therapeutic writing in the twentieth century and of his own course at the University of Texas. Reporting on the actions of a university committee that prevented him from teaching his course, Bump details the most common arguments against teaching writing as healing as well as his own answers to those arguments. Regina Foehr examines the effects of fear on teachers in training and describes a method for helping such teachers locate and clarify values such fear touches and by which it is driven. Foehr encourages us to face our fears and to overcome them by bringing them to light where they may be examined, understood, and overcome.

The title of the final section, "Writing and Healing in the World," does not intend to duplicate the problematic separation of school from the "real world." Instead, it simply signifies writing and healing that take place outside schoolroom walls. Laura Julier's essay, for example, places before us the Clothesline Project, a public text depicting and decrying violence against women. Likening the powerful, deeply moving words and images written on the shirts to the names on the Vietnam War Memorial in Washington, D.C., and the individual squares of the Names Project, Julier sees in such displays a hope for political, social, and legal healing, not in addition to the personal but through it. Emily Nye describes results she obtained from a workshop she conducted with a group of persons suffering from HIV, AIDS, and other serious illnesses in Boulder, Colorado. Her work not only examines the interactions of the writing group itself, but also connects their writing with research and theory in composition and health care and provides a careful description of a highly effective research methodology that can be emulated by others engaging in such research. Finally, Sandra Florence provides us with a look at writing and healing in a community of abused mothers and children where the lives and words of those who teach and those who learn intersect, interact, and overlap. Using her journals and the journals of others as the primary matter of her essay, Florence invites us to see how a limited writing workshop can grow into a much larger project designed not only to heal individual traumas, but also the larger damages suffered by all persons who seek to live in community at the end of the twentieth century.

Notes

1. For a detailed critique of and response to Bauer's position and practice, see Anderson.

2. For several examples of similar choices, see Spellmeyer ("Out of the Fashion Industry"). Smith deals with some of the same concepts and practices under the faux name "illegeneracy."

Works Cited

Anderson, Virginia. "Confrontational Teaching and Rhetorical Practice." *College Composition and Communication* 48.2 (1997): 197–214.

Bartholomae, David. "Writing with Teachers: A Conversation with Peter Elbow." *College Composition and Communication* 46.1 (1995): 62–71.

Bauer, Dale M. "The Other 'F' Word: The Feminist in the Classroom." *College English* 52.4 (1990): 385–96.

Berlin, James. "Rhetoric and Ideology in the Writing Class." *College English* 50.5 (1988): 477–94.

Bruffee, Kenneth. "Collaborative Writing and the 'Conversation of Mankind'." *College English* 46.7 (1984): 635–52.

Byrum, C. Stephen. "The Greek Concept of 'Techne'." *Viewpoints* 120 (Oct. 1984). ED 251 394.

Clifton, Lucille. Keynote Address. National Association for Poetry Therapy. Columbia, MD. 5 May 1996.

Ebert, Teresa L. "For a Red Pedagogy: Feminism, Desire, and Need." *College English* 58.7 (1996): 795–819.

Elbow, Peter. "Being a Writer vs. Being an Academic: A Conflict in Goals." *College Composition and Communication* 46.1 (1995): 72–83.

Felman, Shoshana, and Dori Laub. *Testimony: Crises of Witnessing in Literature, Psychoanalysis, and History.* New York: Routledge, 1992.

France, Alan W. "Assigning Places: The Function of Introductory Composition as a Cultural Discourse." *College English* 55.6 (1993): 593–617.

Herman, Judith. *Trauma and Recovery.* New York: Basic, 1992.

Horner, Bruce. "Students, Authorship, and the Work of Composition." *College English* 59.5 (1997): 505–29.

"Interchanges: Theory, Populism, Teaching." *College Composition and Communication* 48.2 (1997): 284–96.

Lacan, Jacques. *The Four Fundamental Concepts of Psychoanalysis.* Ed. Jacques-Allain Miller. Trans. Alan Sheridan. New York: Norton, 1978.

Lakoff, Robin, and James Coyne. *Father Knows Best: The Use and Abuse of Power in Freud's Case of Dora.* New York: Teachers College Press, 1993.

Lewin, Kurt. "Dora Revisited." *Psychoanalytic Review* 60.4 (1973): 519–32.

Lu, Min-Zhan, and Bruce Horner. "The Problematic of Experience: Redefining Critical Work in Ethnography and Pedagogy. *College English* 60.3 (1998): 257–77.

McQuade, Donald. "Living In—and On—the Margins." *College Composition and Communication* 43.1 (1992): 11–22.

Miller, Alice. *The Drama of the Gifted Child: The Search for the True Self.* New York: Basic, 1997.

Miller, Richard E. "The Nervous System." *College English* 58.3 (1996): 265–86.

O'Donnell, Thomas G. "Politics and Ordinary Language: A Defense of Expressivist Rhetorics." *College English* 58.4 (1996): 423–39.

Pfeiffer, Kathleen. "Response." *College English* 55.6 (1993): 669–71.

Pounds, Wayne. "The Context of No Context: A Burkean Critique of Rogerian Argument." *Rhetoric Society Quarterly* 17.2 (1987): 45–59.

Shaughnessy, Mina. *Errors and Expectations: A Guide for the Teacher of Basic Writing.* New York: Oxford UP, 1977.

Smith, Jeff. "Against Illegeneracy: Toward a New Pedagogy of Civic Understanding." *College Composition and Communication* 45.2 (1994): 200–19.

Sommers, Nancy. "Between the Drafts." *College Composition and Communication* 43.1 (1992): 23–31.

Spellmeyer, Kurt. "After Theory: From Textuality to Attunement with the World." *College English* 58.8 (1996): 893–913.

———. "Out of the Fashion Industry: From Cultural Studies to the Anthropology of Knowledge." Review. *College Composition and Communication* 47.3 (1996): 424–36.

———. " 'Too Little Care': Language, Politics, and Embodiment in the Life-World." *College English* 55.3 (1993): 265–283.

Tiles, J. E. "*Techné* and Moral Expertise." *Philosophy* 50 (1984): 49–66.

1

FINDING OUR WAY IN

You gotta tell the truth if you wanna get well. That's part of recovery. Telling the truth is how you get better. Not telling the truth keeps you sick.

PATTY MCGADY

CHAPTER TWO

Whose Voice Is It Anyway?

ANNE RUGGLES GERE
University of Michigan

When I was a seventh grader, I wanted more than anything to be a cheerleader. I imagined that wearing a short skirt, waving a blue-and-white pompom, and doing cartwheels on the basketball court would transform my shy and awkward self into someone with sophistication and confidence. I practiced the routines, jumping up and down in front of my bedroom mirror until my mother insisted that I stop because she was afraid I would make cracks in the living-room ceiling. The great day came, and I reported for tryouts at the elementary school gym. When it was my turn to leap and twirl in front of the high school cheerleaders, I punched my arms and legs into the air, shouting "GHS, We're the best!" Watching Linda Bissett snap her gum, I knew I hadn't been impressive, and, sure enough, when the tryouts ended, my name was not on the list for the junior high squad. In a gesture of consolation, Linda said, "You did a good job on the routines, Anne. Your voice just isn't loud enough."

Linda Bissett has faded from my life, and I'm sure she never thought of herself as a teacher of mine. Yet, I hear her whenever I think about the concept of voice. Being told that my voice was too soft had as much influence on my understanding of the concept as anything I've read in professional journals. The term we use most frequently to describe voice—authentic—takes on meaning when we connect that word "authentic" with our own lives. Feeling inadequate or not powerful enough shapes one's understanding of voice just as feeling important and in control does. Connecting with one's life does not, however, mean continuing to think of voice in entirely individual terms. Many of our current discussions about voice presume a stable, coherent self while our conversations about other aspects of composition take for granted a more complicated and less unified concept of the self we call "the writer." In wanting to become a cheerleader, I sought to join other voices, and I believe that the finely textured personal and autobiographical writing now emerging in the academy leads us to public and social contexts rather than private and individualistic ones.

With the door to cheerleading closed, I looked to the window of academics and became the quintessential good student, reading the required work, writing what my teachers expected, doing well on tests, and planning my escape. I came to realize, thanks to a session with Mr. Hodge the guidance counselor, that I could get out of Gorham by earning good grades and going to college. I didn't have to spend the rest of my life with the same twenty-seven classmates I'd known since kindergarten; I could join a community where there would be others like me, people who were always voted "most respected" but never "most popular." Mr. Hodge was right. At Colby College I edited the newspaper with people who actually cared about writing, I took English courses with classmates who really enjoyed reading, and I didn't worry about not having a voice loud enough for cheerleading. During my first year of graduate school, however, the voice problem returned in a new form. In a required speech course I encountered Robert Smith, a professor who was convinced that I needed speech therapy because my voice didn't project. When I listened to a tape, I was startled. Mine was a soft voice, full of breath and hesitancy. It was my mother's voice.

Born of two immigrants who arrived at Ellis Island on June 13, 1903, my mother had an overdeveloped respect for the authority of others. Americanization projects at the turn of the century aimed to teach immigrants proper respect for their elders, their country, and authority of all sorts. They succeeded completely with my mother. Adolph Dies and Margareta Scholl, who left forever their families, familiar culture, and language, made their way to St. Louis, Missouri, where Adolph hoped to find work as a carpenter in the construction of the 1904 World's Fair. This young couple, who would raise three children, and become my grandparents, left Germany, according to family lore, because differences between Margareta's middle-class and

Adolph's working-class backgrounds prevented their marriage. Plunging into a new culture with its unfamiliar language reduced both of them to working-class status, and only my mother, the youngest of their three children, received the college education that enabled her to become—like her maternal grandfather—a teacher.

My mother's climb from her working-class beginnings to the quasi-professional status of teacher required continuing encounters with authority. First, there was her father, the stern disciplinarian who insisted that his two older children leave school after the eighth grade and take factory jobs to help support the family. Then there were the teachers, principals, and ministers who sought to regulate her literacy and her assimilation into American culture. With her marriage to a man named Ruggles from New Hampshire, she escaped the authoritative voices of the German enclave in which she grew up, but new ones awaited her in the Anglo-Saxon-ish culture to which she migrated. In a tight, white corner of northern New Hampshire, she faced sets of prohibitions and stipulations which she, the outsider, had to learn one by one. She articulated the authority of this culture as "they," and I grew up listening to the voices of the ubiquitous "they," as in "they don't wear white shoes before Easter," "they drink tea at the women's club," or "they don't give wine to children." With the zeal of the newly fluent, my mother also invoked the authority of correct English. She forbade her mother to speak when they rode the city bus together during World War II, arguing that my grandmother's accent would attract powerful anti-German sentiments, and she carefully monitored my sister's and my speech, warning us to pronounce the nearby town of *B-e-r-l-i-n* as BERlin not BerLIN, and excising all faults of usage from our spoken language. As she typed our high school papers on the old Royal left from her pre-marriage teaching days, she monitored our writing as well.

In monitoring the writing of our students, many of us, like my speech professor Robert Smith, see our students' voices as problems to be fixed. Just as Professor Smith would have dismissed my detailed explanation of how I came to have the voice he and I heard on the tape recorder, so we often consider our students' voices separate from the particular family history, significant persons, and events that helped to shape them. We forget that "authentic" means relational. To describe a voice as authentic is to put it in relationship to other voices.

Some of the voices that blend with my own echo from another moment in my past. The sun drops close enough to the mountain tops to cast a tiny shaft of pink light through the gray clouds hanging over Gorham, New Hampshire, on a March day in 1959. Hugging my books to my chest, I trudge home, past the crosswalk where Tony Dooan, the town's only police officer, stops traffic for the kids who need to cross Main Street; past the Universalist church where my mother plays the organ on the two Sundays in the summer when services are held; past Fiske's Gift Shop where Dot Nadeau, the pretty wife of the gray custodian at my school, sits at the corner of the display of shamrocks and stares unsmiling out the window; past Stone's Hardware where my father bought the gun that killed him; past Welch's Restaurant where the older kids who wear tight blue jeans smoke cigarettes and stand around the juke box in the back; and past the park where the ice-skating rink has turned slushy.

As I walk toward my house, I wonder what kind of silence I will find today. Since my father's death more than a year ago, home has become a cold and quiet place, and I have learned to distinguish the silence of grief from the silence of anger from the silence of concentration. Then I notice Helen Philbrook's blue Chrysler in the driveway and remember that this is the day when the group from the Women's Club meets at our house. A mixture of fresh brewed coffee and cigarette smoke greets my nostrils when I open the door, and I hear Helen reading something about cut glass. In response to my mother's prompting—today she smiles and talks warmly—I go into the living room to say hello and grab two cookies before I retreat to my room with my stack of books. I always bring home more books than I need, just as I take out the maximum allowed at the public library. Stacked up according to size, my books become a fortress I can hide behind. Reading protects me from people, from household chores, and from my cute and talkative younger sister Mary Jane. Writing does the same. I keep my diary locked and hidden where Mary Jane can't find it, and I write thank-you notes as I do school assignments, to avoid the talk which would come from not writing. But today I have a hard time reading because I keep hearing the voices and laughter in the living room. I'm tempted to go and sit at the top of the stairs and listen as I did in younger and happier days when my parents had parties. But I push my glasses back up my nose and try to concentrate. Helen's voice reads for a while, then another voice chimes in, then they laugh. As I stare without focusing on the page in front of me, I absorb voices that instruct me.

The voices of Helen Philbrook and the other women in my mother's group did not reject or attempt to correct me. They helped me begin to see reading and writing in new ways. I learned from them that reading didn't need to be protective coloring with which to hide or a fortress to keep others out. Reading could be a way of connecting with other people. Similarly, I began to get the idea that writing could be more than a completed assignment or something inscribed in a locked diary. I began to understand that writing and reading could be done *with* people and that the pleasure I took in writing a poem or reading a novel could be multiplied by sharing it with others. This understanding grew as I moved on to college and teaching and graduate school. I began to talk with friends about books, reading passages aloud and listening to their ideas. Perhaps more important, I began to share my writing with others. Sometimes it took the form of asking for or providing responses to a draft, but more often it meant meeting with a group of colleagues to read aloud, argue over, and suggest ideas for one another's writing. My research into writing groups grew out of these practices, and my book, *Intimate Practices: Literacy and Cultural Work in U.S. Women's Clubs, 1880–1920,* is inflected with the voices of several New Hampshire women who sat in my mother's living room drinking coffee and smoking cigarettes.

Carolyn Steedman, whose book *Landscape for a Good Woman* demonstrates how the personal and autobiographical statement leads directly to the public and social world, describes her stories as a case study which "allows the writer to enter the present into the past, allows the dream, the wish or the fantasy of the past to shape current time, and treats them as evidence in their own right. In this way, the narrative form of case-study shows what went into its writing, shows the bits and pieces from which it is made up, in the way that history refuses to do, and that fiction can't" (21). As Steedman is careful to say, the bits and pieces need interpretation, but she insists upon bringing them into the reader's view, and through them the past shapes the present.

Listening carefully to voices from the past only partly prepared me for speaking on behalf of others in the present. Among the greatest challenges of my life has been the necessity to give voice to the thoughts of two of the most significant women in my life—my daughter and my mother. My mother's descent into dementia made it impossible for her to speak for herself. She, a woman who had always expressed clear views, began to utter sentences such as "I don't read that one until the body comes back" in response to a request that she take her pill, and "I'm trying to but I couldn't get a boat down in the other section" when asked to drink her milk. Gradually, she lost her capacity to utter more than a few syllables, and I tried to speak for her, to give words to what I guessed she wanted to say. Interpreting her physical needs proved relatively easy, but I struggled to articulate what she must be feeling as her mind drifted away. At one point, when most of her language was gone, she gave me an important clue as she stood in front of a mirror and said quite clearly, "I don't recognize myself." I became increasingly grateful for our common voice as I tried to help her recognize herself with family stories and explanations of everyday events as they became more and more confusing and frightening to her. In part, I was prepared for giving voice to my mother's thoughts because I had many years of practice—albeit a different sort—with my daughter.

When Cindy came to us at age three and a half, we knew that she bore the emotional scars of moving through three families before ours, but we did not know that she suffered neurological damage because of her birth mother's alcoholism. Although she was bright and lively, we soon learned that fetal alcohol syndrome left her unable to retrieve language easily. "Use your words," we'd plead, and she tried, often resorting to convoluted syntax such as "when we have juice and cereal in the morning" because she couldn't think of the word "breakfast." Other times her searches yielded poetic results, as she described a clear, cloudless Seattle morning as a "blue-sky day," insulation as the "lining of the building," and the pattern of the fabric of her dress as "cloth paint." Her most frequent response to questions, however, was, "I cannot tell." When she could not tell, I learned to think with her, playing a sort of guessing game until we located the missing words. "What do we use it for? Do you mean the friend you met at school? Is it inside or outside?" Because I shared much of her life, I could frequently guess the words she sought. While many children manifest difficulties like these, Cindy continues to struggle with them even now that she is in her late twenties. Names of friends and common objects elude her; she writes with fractured syntax and unconventional spelling, even though she is a prize-winning painter.

Unlike speaking on behalf of my mother, helping to give voice to Cindy's ideas and experiences also means representing a larger group of persons, those afflicted with fetal alcohol syndrome. Ever since Michael Dorris's book *The Broken Cord* appeared, the diagnosis of FAS has taken on tragic proportions. Because Dorris presents with great confidence a very dark picture of his adopted son's experience with fetal alcohol syndrome, his has become the dominant image. Upon hearing that a child has FAS, adoptive parents have returned children to social service agencies, convinced by Dorris's book that nothing can be done to help them or these afflicted children. While we don't minimize the difficulties that FAS poses, Cindy and I take a different view, and we have written a memoir, *Woman of the King Salmon*, that offers a more hopeful perspective based on Cindy's successes as an artist and a college student. In writing we developed antiphonal forms of voice to construct a narrative that preserves complexity and resists easy consumption by offering the multiple truths of our shared lives. Faced with the question, "Whose voice is it anyway?" we're both likely to respond "I cannot tell." In addition to negotiating the difficult terrain of our shared lives by sorting out who has the "right" to which narratives and determining how to tell stories in ways that preserve dignity and integrity for each of us, we face the challenge of finding ways to talk back to Dorris. Can we represent our experiences so that they will get a hearing from the audience convinced of Dorris's tragic view? Linda Bissett and Robert Smith come to mind as I wonder if our relatively soft voices can be heard as we speak out for an alternative perspective on FAS, against the pessimism of the Dorris book, and with the convictions born of our experiences as mother and daughter.

It would be easy to fall into the kind of writing that "indicates such freedom of mind, such liberty of person, such confidence" that Virginia Woolf describes as a man's writing. But, as Woolf notes,

> after reading a chapter or two a shadow seemed to lie across the page. It was a straight dark bar, a shadow shaped something like the letter "I." One began dodging this way and that to catch a glimpse of the landscape behind it . . . in the shadow of the letter "I" all is shapeless as mist. Is that a tree? No, it is a woman. But . . . she has not a bone in her body. (90–100)

To write our experiences as mother and daughter, Cindy and I seek to create voices that avoid the shadow shaped something like the letter "I" and simultaneously to resist constructing ourselves as women without bones. For the past of our lives to enter the present, we cannot be shapeless as mist; we need the structure and strength of bones to support our voices.

Our students face similar challenges in their writing, particularly at a time when composition pedagogy assigns high value to autobiographical and personal writing. We have only to look at a collection like Coles and Vopat's *What Makes Writing Good* to see that writing instructors frequently equate quality with self-disclosure. As they develop their own voices, students negotiate complexities of representation similar to those Cindy and I encountered. The shadow shaped something like the letter "I" looms, threatening the kind of erasure bell hooks describes:

> No need to hear your voice when I can talk about you better than you can speak about yourself. No need to hear your voice. Only tell me about your pain. I want to know your story. And then I will tell it back to you in such a way that it has become mine, my own. Re-writing you I write myself anew. I am still author, authority. I am still colonizer, the speaking subject and you are now at the center of my talk. (152).

To avoid becoming the colonizer hooks describes, our students may try to become the woman without bones, the shapeless mist obscured by the shadow of the letter "I," and in so doing they run the risk of developing a voice that is not soft but inaudible, one that Linda Bissett and Robert Smith would not be able to hear.

A better alternative lies in the possibility Zora Neale Hurston describes in *Their Eyes Were Watching God,* when Janie says, "You can tell 'em what Ah say if you wants to. Dat's just de same as me 'cause mah tongue is in mah friend's mouf" (6). Hurston suggests that we give prominence to the relational side of voice, that we consider the ethical dimensions of voices representing one another. Janie does not authorize just anyone to give voice to her story; she authorizes her best friend, Phoeby. She trusts Phoeby to represent her to others because their long-standing relationship will make the story "just de same," as if Janie herself told it. Like the women who smoked cigarettes and drank coffee in my mother's living room, Janie and her friend Phoeby can share stories, recognizing that they are not just entertainment; they are, as Carolyn Steedman says, "evidence in their own right."

Works Cited

Coles, William E., Jr., and James Vopat. *What Makes Writing Good: A Multiperspective.* Lexington, MA: Heath, 1985.

Dorris, Michael. *The Broken Cord.* New York: Harper, 1989.

Gere, Anne Ruggles. *Intimate Practices: Literacy and Cultural Work in U.S. Women's Clubs, 1880–1920.* Urbana: U of Illinois P, 1997.

Gere, Anne Ruggles, and Cynthia Margaret Gere. *Woman of the King Salmon.* Forthcoming.

hooks, bell. *Yearning: Race, Gender and Cultural Politics.* Boston: South End, 1990.

Hurston, Zora Neale. *Their Eyes Were Watching God.* Philadelphia: Lippincott, 1937.

Steedman, Carolyn. *Landscape for a Good Woman: A Story of Two Lives.* New Brunswick, NJ: Rutgers UP, 1986.

Woolf, Virginia. *A Room of One's Own.* New York: Harcourt, 1990.

CHAPTER THREE

Language and Literature as "Equipment for Living"

Revision as a Life Skill

TILLY WARNOCK
University of Arizona

Prologue: A Revisionary View of Writing

When I first read Carolyn Heilbrun's *Writing a Woman's Life,* I realized everyone she wrote about had seamless, polished, final-copy, reader-based lives, while I, and most people I know, live rough-draft lives. We write our lives, and our lives rewrite us: The trajectory of our lives is not clearly discernible, and, when it is, it appears more like a scatter than a line and more like a series of starts and stops than a continuous progression.

Similarly, we write along, only sometimes reaching a final-copy stage, at least enough of one for long enough to send something off, but more often we just keep writing. We identify with Anne Tyler in "Still Just Writing," when she describes getting an idea for a novel but having to put it aside for children, the dog, housework, relatives, and daily matters. Interruptions are not just a stage in our writing nor a break in our lives; interruptions constitute our writing processes, products, and daily lives to such an extent that we understand interruptions as writing and living.

Most people I know live by trying to make do, and only on occasion does our writing seem just right. Some days, our writing takes the upward way, as Kenneth Burke calls the pull toward perfection, but at any moment writing takes the downward way, which may lead to revision and rebirth, that is, until the negative sets in again. Indirection is the way we find direction; only rarely do we live by the straight and narrow, travel the direct route, or know where we're going before we begin.

Ours are not single-copy, single-voice, or single-identity lives. Bernice Zamora's poem, from which the title for the anthology, *Infinite Divisions: An Anthology of Chicana Literature*, was taken, characterizes the attitude we adopt as often as we can, and in so doing, we adopt what Burke calls the "comic corrective," or the act of seeing what is and has been as what might be. Terms are performances, not references to what is true; we take other people's labels and our own words seriously because they have real consequences, but we also take them as rhetorically motivated and therefore subject to revision:

So Not to Be Mottled

You insult me
When you say I'm
Schizophrenic.
My divisions are
Infinite. (78)

Most writers I know, both in school and out, understand ourselves and our writings as rough drafts that we write, as collages that various people and experiences have written all over, and as multimedia hypertexts. We write nothing alone since we see ourselves as multiple and our texts as alive with people we know and have read, remembered, imagined.

We recognize ourselves in RuPaul's statement—"You're born naked, and the rest is drag"—at least sometimes. On other days, we feel ground to a halt by our bodily realities. We see our lives and our texts in revision, except for those rare moments of harmony and wholeness, of *kairos*, when what we write seems to fit just right. When we select from our ongoing writing to recontextualize our drafts for specific purposes, audiences, and situations, we know that what we do may not work, because writing is always a guessing game, a gamble, a judgment call. Creativity and contingency, rather than certainty, motivate us to write. Even what we take to a "final form," we admit, is not completely coherent, logical, or seamless.

While the limitations of this revisionary view of writing and living are obvious—your focus changes rapidly, your commitment is to something writing can do rather than to what it is, you take the longest way home, and you don't always finish what you start—the benefits are great: You never have to start writing because you are always writing, and you never have to stop writing because you're always working on many things at once. In addition, you're always learning, figuring, and doing rhetoric; your work is never done.

School typically teaches a more straight-arrow approach to writing or a more task-oriented revision from writer-based prose to reader-based writing. The purpose of process is to yield product; daily writings are daily waitings until something really worthwhile comes along.

William Stafford, however, argues for writing daily with faith that the writing will keep you afloat and with acceptance of what comes on the page. I imagine him in jeans and a white shirt sitting palms up, ready for what language brings. Donald Hall described how he writes one summer at the Wyoming Conference on English and, unknowingly, he gave me permission to work on many things at once and to pick up for further work and revision whatever interests me at a particular time. He released me from having to clean my plate before having dessert. Vivian Gornick makes clear how the rigor and routine of a writing life keeps her alive: "I get up every single morning at 8:00. I struggle out of bed by 8:30, and by 9:00 I'm at that desk. If I didn't do that I'd be dead" ("Interview" 124).

These definitions of writing as living, and both as revisionary, are not the only definitions of writing nor the only ways to write. Certainly, this view, with its attitudes, theories, and practices, is seldom the most efficient way to write in the short run. It works well though for the long haul, for it sustains writing as "equipment for living" and "strategies for coping," to use Kenneth Burke's terms. His rhetoric advocates seeing things other than they are in order to figure out how best they might be. For Burke, little is written in stone; words define words, and, therefore, they can be revised to equip us better to come to terms, not to war and violence.

Burke's rhetoric also demonstrates the importance in writing and living of practicing in writing what we preach. His own writing aims "to elucidate a point of view" (1931, viii), not make it "crystal clear" (1937, 86). The paradox of what he advocates motivates him to keep writing: "Aiming always at reduction, it must admonish continually against the dangers of reduction" (1945, 314). Burke encourages flexibility, pliancy, and liquidity so that we stay on our toes in the dancing of attitudes; he warns against perfection and our tendencies to drive ourselves and others "into the corner."

In general, what I advocate is a rhetorical approach to writing and living that provides "strategies for coping" and "equipment for living." We live in a world that is filled with doubt and uncertainty. Our languages, identities, relationships, and values are in flux; we must read situations critically and choose among possible actions if we are to identify with and persuade others. Our readings of the world and our choices about writing are social and ethical actions with far-reaching consequences. While we cannot act freely, for we act within the constraints of others and of situations, we can learn to act wisely, so that we use language to get along, and stay alive.

What follows practically from a rhetorical understanding of language as communication among people identified by a common goal of coming to terms, not war, is that writers recognize their own assertions as rhetorically motivated. Our arguments do not rely on claims to truth or on logical absolutes. Rather, our arguments rely on common grounds between writers and readers who are willing to give a little in order to come to terms, since that is the aim of their rhetoric. An essential but often ignored dimension of identification between writers and readers is the attitude that both writers and readers must participate in the creation of meaning, because no one can be dead certain, because airtight arguments are suffocating, because conviction comes from cooperation, and because all evidence is circumstantial.

This approach to writing invites readers to revise the text by filling in the gaps, bridging the abyss, connecting the dots, and supplying the missing links. In these actions, readers and listeners create meaning together. Readers are convinced, not by appeals to another's authority or logic, but by their own immediate experiences in making meaning. Rhetorical proof, then, is the experiential evidence of daily life.

Part I: An Autobiographical Way In and Out and Roundabout

> *"Life is good," my colleague says. I wonder. I have caught the flu John caught from his sister when she came two weeks ago Saturday when their father died. And two weeks before that, John and I were in Boston while Jane was in the hospital for a week of tests to determine whether or not she is a candidate for brain surgery. "It is," I replied, remembering that past illness there may be health, that past surgery there may be a seizure-free life, and past death our parents live on within us.*

Writing a Woman's Life clarified for me lessons about writing and living that I had learned from my family and from the digressive talk and fiction of family, friends, and writers in the South. Heilbrun's book helped me realize that I had always understood writing and reading as life skills and later, with Burke's help, as "strategies for coping" and "equipment for living." Her study helped me understand how and why I had been teaching writing as I often do in workshops, writing projects, and community literacy centers. It helped me to see that excluding life writing limits what people can do with words. And I realized that the absence of attention to *rewriting* our lives impoverishes our conceptions of writing and our possibilities for living.

My earliest lesson in living and writing was that "I" and "me" were social constructions that would be deconstructed and reconstructed again and again by others and by me. In various ways, my life was written for me. My father named me Sue Mac, an abbreviation of my mother's real name, Susie MacDonald, which was shortened by her friends to Sue Mac or Mac. My borrowed and abbreviated name was replaced for me at about age two. The story goes that I was busy sweeping with a little broom when someone called me Tilly, after Tilly the Toiler in the funny papers. Although I never saw the "real" Tilly the Toiler in the cartoon, I have been called Tilly all my life. I grew up thinking of myself from a perspective by incongruity: I was like my mother and like someone in the funny papers.

Luckily, perhaps, I was not the only person whose name and life were largely written for her and whose gender and other identities were linguistically and socially determined. Children used to shout at each other, "You better not call me a name," by which we meant a bad name, since we called each other by names and nicknames all the time. Who could believe that the name's the thing, or the person, when everyone you know is called by their nickname—Babychile, Ellie-gal, Streak, Boots, Skin, PaJim, Son, Tita, and Pinky? Even this short list makes clear how names locate, rank, and distribute power, goods, and values.

I also learned the effects of naming, re-naming, and not naming aspects of external reality. What counts as home when most people in the small southern town I lived in acted as if Fort Benning, the biggest infantry center in the world after WWII and during the Korean War, did not exist, when, in fact, it framed and populated the town? How can boundaries be anything other than arbitrary yet determinative signs when, by simply crossing the Fourth Street Bridge over the Chattahoochee River, I left Georgia and entered Alabama and passed from one time zone to the next? The power of language to reflect and deflect and to construct reality was a lesson for white children, who were taught once, implicitly and explicitly, that half of the people in their world did not exist as human beings, and taught later, explicitly and implicitly, that this view was wrong, immoral, and illegal.

The tablets distributed each month in school had "Muscogee County School District" on the cover, and yet no one ever explained the name or gave us any history of the Native Americans from whose language the name had been taken. Students similarly erased people and history as we marked out and added letters so that our tablets asked, "Must We Go to School?" We acted under erasure, knowing and not knowing, but pretending otherwise.

I knew the Muscogee County School District included Carver High School for black students and other segregated schools, but I joined in the shouting in elementary school when we sang:

"Tramp, tramp, tramp, go the feet of many children, from the mountains, rivers, and shores," who "with smiling faces take their schoolroom places with their friends and neighbors." I also knew that the town was divided into the mill sections, the white areas, the black neighborhoods, and the army grounds, all rigidly separated though inextricably connected, marked only by loose wire fences, flowering bushes, abrupt drops from paved roads to dirt ones, and turns from painted houses to unpainted ones.

I lived in a world divided by constructed differences which, out of politeness, we were supposed to ignore and accept, without question. Such ignorance required hyper-vigilance from all.

I learned early that life keeps changing and being changed by forces known and unknown. We drew invisible lines marking our property and threatened others to cross the boundary under penalty of law. We learned to evade such restrictions by standing on the sidewalk in front of someone's house and claiming, "You can't make me. This is public property." I learned to play make-believe and became Josephine Martin for years, as well as many other people; my pretend selves were as real as "Tilly" and others around me.

As we constructed imaginary boundaries and learned to heed other people's fictional restrictions, we also refused to see many of the barriers that divided us from others. Growing up southern and female meant knowing that the unstated is as important as the stated because the most fundamental rule was to sweep anything significant under the rug and make mountains out of molehills. I learned to read between the lines, to memorize the writing on the wall, and to listen for what was not said.

I also learned to see myself as an intersection of social constructions and bodily determinants. I was always taller than anyone else in my class. My mother had to verify my actual age through a handwritten note, which I carried with me for years, so that I could pay children's price for tickets at the movie. Everyone, including teachers, my friends' parents, and people on the street, thought I was responsible because I was tall. I remember standing in line to register for the second grade with all of my friends' mothers who were there to register their children. My grandfather let me drive home from Sunday school when I was ten or twelve, although, as the story goes, I was talking so much one day that I drove off the side of the road and said, "Oh, I forgot I was driving." This story was a family favorite and one which I took as evidence of my sense of responsibility and sense of humor. Less clearly, I knew that my physical self denied many constructions or stereotypes of the young southern girl.

Stories also told me who I was and was not mentally and intellectually. I learned from others' delight to enjoy this interpretation of me: "Lord, if I hadn't known her before she was born, I would've thought she was one of those twisty-headed children." While this story may not accurately reflect my intellectual capacities, it did reflect my parents' willingness to let their third child and daughter live in her own world of make-believe. I remember the warmth of my mother's palms on both sides of my face when she kneeled down to ask me one day, "You do know who you are, don't you?" At the moment, I was probably being Josephine, married to George and mother of six children in Virginia.

While life, time, history, race, class, gender, and subjectivity were always up for grabs, though seldom acknowledged to be, we were taught explicitly in school what was true, once and for all and forever. Our teachers and our textbooks were right, at least as long as we were in class or on the school grounds. I always felt as if I got through school by tilting my head slightly to the right, believing one thing and saying another and accepting one story when I knew there were many versions. I knew how to do well in school because there was little distance for me between home and school. Reading and writing were living, in school and out.

Our mother had been an English major at Sophie Newcomb College of Tulane University where she got a master's degree and wrote in longhand a thesis on brotherly love in Shakespeare's sonnets. When her mother, an elementary school principal, died at forty-two, my mother returned home to take care of her father. She taught school until she married, and then she became a member of the school board. She read whenever she could and treasured her monthly book club, The Junto. I connected the papers she wrote with the toasted anchovy and cream cheese sandwiches we helped her make the night before the club met at our house.

Our mother seemed to have taught everybody in our town, that is, everybody older and white. We never went to a store, to school, or even to the county fair that people didn't come up to her, acting like teenagers again, saying "Hello, Miss Fox. You remember me, don't you? I knew you would never forget me." They would then turn to us, her four children, to say that she was a hard English teacher, but she taught them a lot about life. Education was education for life, not for life in the academy or life in the work place, but for Life with a capital "L."

There was little separation between life inside and life outside school for me. The literature series in my high school was entitled *Literature and Life*. I grew up knowing that Carson McCullers was raised right around the corner on Stark Avenue, that Flannery O'Connor lived in Milledgeville, and that the South was filled with many famous writers, mainly women. I had the flu on the day my senior English teacher, Roberta Lawrence, took our class to visit her friend, Flannery. I knew Carson McCullers as the cousin of Mrs. Storey, the town librarian, Truman Capote as the cousin of my beautiful Sunday school teacher, and Eudora Welty as someone who also ate tomato sandwiches for lunch.

These were famous writers, but everyone told stories and made up stories. My grandfather spent many hours with his friend, Eagle Eye, talking baseball and local politics. My Aunt Susie crossed her legs, drew on her Camels, and told us stories about our family that no one else would speak. When Aunt Jane finally gave in and told us what she and our mother did as girls, we would not move for fear she would stop and instead pass around her box of Whitman Sampler Chocolates. We knew all about people we'd never met and events that happened (or didn't) long before we were born.

Our mother remained a teacher, though not a school teacher, all of her life. She served on many church, hospital, museum, and other community committees. Her friends constantly sought her advice on life, and she made clear her own positions on matters in formal and informal meetings, always without rocking the boat. To what extent she chose not to rock the boat—to keep people from falling out, to avoid conflict, or to be as persuasive as she could in that context—I do not know. Who's at the table? Who's in the boat? Who's talking to whom in the parlor room?— all remained unasked but powerfully influential questions.

"Who's absent?" was a question asked at school each day. I never spoke up to say, "All colored children." We were only supposed to count white children. Strict lines merged with blurred ones in the unbearably high humidity and heat.

What seemed stable and foundational was fragile. I noted early that our father sang joyfully in church, particularly the hymn, "I Love to Tell the Story," but he stood silent during the Lord's Prayer and the doxology. It became clear that he went to church for our mother's sake. He called her his "heaven on earth." I knew his silence did not result from the fact that he was raised Methodist, but we attended First Presbyterian; I knew he did not believe as our mother did. I also knew he and mother disagreed about racial and class issues. After she bought candy one night from an Optimist who came to the door, he refused to eat it because "people are blame fools to think someone else will take care of them."

On the Sunday our minister invited the congregation to open the doors and our hearts to blacks, I knew where my mother stood. I was not sure about our father's commitments, not until he worked as the lawyer for the school board to integrate the schools. I always knew that our mother was moved to action by faith and that he was moved by the law. Their sense of civic responsibility was powerful, changing, and challenging. Terms, beliefs, and arbitrary signs and symbols constituted and reconstituted life.

The relationships among words, things, ideas, and people were mysterious, changing, and as tangled as kudzu draped over trees alongside Georgia roads: The relationships were equally parasitic. People wrote their lives daily in talk, in actions, and on paper; with each telling, the story changed through ornate digressions, extreme qualifications, contradictions, and hilarious exaggerations. I learned to respect the potentialities and probabilities of revision, as I learned to respect the fallacy of hindsight, the truths we create with hindsight, the patterns we change by turning the kaleidoscope, the potential distortions of historical facts and horrors.

Our mother was different from many of her friends and family because she was not a storyteller, except in her writing and in her accounts of us and her grandchildren. I saw her create in her needlework, not in her talk, and I learned to translate her needlework as lessons in reading, writing, and living. I remember her working with fine linen to make handkerchiefs, underwear, pillowcases, or napkins. She often sketched patterns on paper or copied ones from books or memory. She practiced on small pieces of cloth or canvas. She ripped out stitches routinely and carefully, as if starting over and redoing were as important as the final stitching, sprinkling, and ironing. I watched carefully as she pulled one thread and effected the composition of the transparent, delicate cloth. She might then whip three threads together with a stitch to create another pattern. She sewed flowers and monograms in corners and tucked the cloth into tiny identical folds. Her stitches were even and small, yet strong. She worked *with* the materials and tools at hand. I wanted to be like her, I wanted to make things, I wanted the give and take of working with materials and with people, I wanted to enjoy creation and recreation.

From her needlework, I learned about maintaining the tension between writing life and letting life write me. Living, writing, and sewing were not only matters of finishing what you started and doing what you were supposed to do, both of which were powerful and useful guides for writing and living and sewing: Nothing is a simple as that.

Because I also wanted to be a teacher like her, and like my aunt and grandmother, I played teacher all of my life. I am told that one day I stomped my foot and told my imaginary class, "If you don't be's quiet, we're gonna have to pray to God." Gradually I learned other means of inspiration and located real students. One day, running to meet a class of younger neighborhood children in our green toolshed, I realized I didn't have a lesson plan. I leaped over the Rutledge's daylily hedge, grabbed a bud, and realized I could teach them how flowers bloom. After a painstakingly delicate demonstration, pulling apart one petal at a time, I released the class for a field trip. They were to pick as many buds as they could find in the neighborhood and bring them to the telephone pole where we played Tag-Out-of-Jail on summer nights. We gathered on the sidewalk to open each bud and then spread the drying blossoms like a colorful carpet for the big children to walk across on their way home from real school, as we watched, hidden in the bushes.

I also played teacher and became a teacher because that was what ladies did who worked. I probably also became a teacher because I was overlooked as a student in my family. My older siblings were schooled and disciplined about everything. I heard them quizzed about the sermon every Sunday by our father, as they leaned forward from the backseat and I leaned back. I learned to spell by hearing him quiz them with rhyming words like "mat," "cat," and "bat." I learned to read on my own because the people I admired most were readers. I watched them compete for attention and approval and receive it for learning.

But, again, it was more complicated than that. I remember vividly the night I walked into the living room complaining about a story problem in math in the third grade. My father looked up from what he was reading to speak: "That child doesn't need to know that." Not he, nor our mother, had ever excused any of us from anything; we were stunned into silence. Such gender limitations increased later, as my brothers, sister, and I matured.

After my son was born, my father wrote a letter which he ended by saying I had a gift for writing and that he hoped I would find time after caring for my family to write. By then I had already picked up the thread my mother dropped when, after completing her master's degree, she returned home to care for her father. I had become a teacher and someone who tried to put others first, especially family and students. I remembered that my grandmother died at forty-two, after walking home from a day at school as the elementary school principal, but I had forgotten that she had left her husband and two daughters for several summers to go to New York for an advanced degree in education. For years, I remembered not my father's encouragement about my writing, but his warning that I put family first. By identifying and untangling the threads and by retelling the stories, I can create new patterns and in part rewrite my life.

Ambiguity, hyperbole, contradictions, stories, rhymes, and lies—little white lies and the big white one about race—all were intersections of language and life. I studied literature and I wrote because language and literature were life, but not until I read the works of Kenneth Burke was I able to name and revise my early language and life lessons. Not until I read his works did I understand such matters consciously and theoretically. His scholarly works encourage me to theorize my life and to make theory life-giving. They help me define writing and reading as "strategies for coping" and "equipment for living."

Part II: Burke's Theoretical
Approach to the Actions of Life

> *Dr. Hoch asked Jane to meet with neurologists, residents, psychoneurologists, nurses, and technicians to review her case. In addition to the week-long EEG taken while she was in the hospital, the week-long video- and audiotapes, the MRI, the PET, and written observations by nurses, he needed her autobiographical account and assessment of the data. She didn't hesitate a minute. She told me afterwards on the phone that it was easier to communicate in that setting than it sometimes was with teenagers at the girls and boys club where she works. Later, I called a colleague whose work and spirit I admire greatly. I stumbled awkwardly talking to his wife about the brain tumor from which he suffers.*

What motivates Burke, and why I am drawn to his theories, is his desire to find "strategies for coping" and "equipment for living," so that people can come to terms, not to war, and so that we can experiment symbolically in order to gauge just what might work in various circumstances. In this effort, he is not always trying to find the final word or to be "pinpointingly" accurate. Sometimes, the way in becomes a way out and the best way is often circuitous:

> Frankly, we were not sufficiently aware of our procedure until we neared the end of the book (that is, we did not verbalize our implicit method into an explicit methodology). It is probably better so, since an over-exactitude of schematization, maintained throughout, would have wearied writer and reader both. (*Attitudes* 294–95)

We write not always aiming to transform writer-based to reader-based prose; we live not always to get somewhere else.

Burke's theories of symbolic action make sense of my life, and my life helps me make sense of his theories. Understanding the relationship between theory and practice as dialectical encourages ongoing revision and regeneration.

Burke defines words and symbols as abstractions from the situations of life that can help us not only to see life from a perspective by incongruity but also to act, symbolically and otherwise. With this critical edge and attitude toward action, we understand that our perceptions and actions are changeable, as our words are revisable. He never suggests that shifting, from the Frame of Acceptance to the Frame of Rejection, from a formalist approach to a historical approach, from one "occupational psychosis" to another, or from one terministic screen to another, is easy, quick, or inevitable: What he does is show readers how to keep revising: "Let us try again. (A direct hit is not likely here. The best one can do is to try different approaches towards the same center, whenever the opportunity offers.)" (*Rhetoric* 137).

Burke never loses touch with reality, although for him, terms define terms. While our language constructs us and our worlds, language and reality are not the same: "And our 'Lexicon' would not for the world make literature and life synonymous since, by comparison in such terms, the meanest life is so overwhelmingly superior to the noblest poem that illiteracy becomes almost a moral obligation" (*Counter* x).

I admire Burke's decision to choose "rhetoric" as his key term for investigation. His definition of man (revised later to become "human") as *animal symbolicum* leads him to rhetoric and to "strategies for coping." I read his wordiness as both an attempt to get things clear and an effort not to get them so clear that they are reductive and have little to do with the richness of life. Several representative anecdotes from Burke help me to see "our own lives as a kind of rough first draft that lends itself at least somewhat to revision" (*Grammar* 442) and show me how to teach revision as a life skill, as well as a textual art and an epistemology, philosophy, religion, ideology, or economy. His key term, "rhetoric," turns each of these other terms into forms of rhetoric; when defined as rhetoric, the rhetoric of ideology, for example, can be revised. Ideas and realities that appear monolithic and too weighty to move become terms to revise. And in these revisions of our words, worlds turn.

Essential to Burke's rhetoric and to the understanding of rewriting as a life skill is the "comic corrective." For Burke, words are magic in that they call people, things, and ideas into being; words entitle and say, "let there be" and "let that no longer be." The comic attitude is the attitude of poets who understand that, in emphasizing language as figurative, they allow themselves to see things "other than they are" and to entertain what is, what was, and what might possibly be.

The comic perspective keeps Burke light on his toes, flexible, liquid, and strategic; writing and reading are the "dancing of attitudes." His "cult of perhaps" and his "comic corrective" are serious business because human beings seem to be "goaded by the spirit of hierarchy" and "rotten with perfection" (*Language* 16). The Upward Way becomes the Downward Way, which can lead to rebirth. The recycling continues—if we keep ourselves rhetorically fit and flexible.

In speaking of the comic frame, Burke says that it "operates on the miso-philanthropic assumption that getting along with people is one devil of a difficult task, but that, in the last analysis, we should all want to get along with people (and do want to)" (*Attitudes* 1). If getting along is our goal, as it is Burke's main motive, rather than dominating or defeating, then our rhetoric aims at identification rather than manipulation or coercion. Burke explains: "It is not part of our contract here to make final decisions on these many matters" (*Grammar* 117). He admits candidly: "From this point on, I must admit, the perfect symmetry of our case is impaired" (*Grammar* 135). He accepts uncertainty in others: "But in any case, we can know what he was driving at, which is enough for our purpose" (*Grammar* 193). He acts bewildered: "All told, what is our point?" (*Grammar* 157). He repeatedly turns to his readers to ask: "Now, where are we?" and "All told, what are we trying to get at here?" (*Grammar* 360).

The comic perspective allows us to see ourselves critically and to risk change:

The comic frame, in making a man the student of himself, makes it possible for him to "transcend" occasions when he has been tricked or cheated, since he can readily put such discouragements in his "assets" column, under the head of "experience." Thus we "win" by subtly changing the rules of the

game—and by a mere trick of bookkeeping, like the account-
ants for big utility corporations, we make "assets" our of "li-
abilities." And can we, in our humbleness, do better than apply
in our own way the wise devices of the leviathans, thereby "de-
mocratizing" a salvation device as we encourage it to filter
from the top down?" (*Attitudes* 171)

The comic perspective is essential if the goal is to get along with
others because it helps us see and accept ourselves and others as
imperfect:

> The progress of humane enlightenment can go no further than
> in picturing people not as *vicious*, but as *mistaken*. When you
> add that people are *necessarily* mistaken, that *all* people are
> exposed to situations in which they must act as fools, that
> *every* insight contains its own special kind of blindness, you
> complete the comic circle, returning again to the lesson of hu-
> mility that underlies great tragedy. The audience, from its van-
> tage point, sees the operation of errors that the characters of
> the play cannot see; thus seeing from two angles at once, it is
> chastened by dramatic irony; it is admonished to remember
> that when intelligence means *wisdom* (in contrast with the
> modern tendency to look upon intelligence as merely a *coeffi-
> cient of power* for heightening our ability to get things, be they
> good things or bad), it requires fear, resignation, the sense of
> limits, as an important ingredient. (*Attitudes* 41–42)

Burke offers the possibility for change in our attitudes and
actions, if we develop particular attitudes and motives: "It will
thus be seen that, in playing the game of life, we have at our
command a resource whereby we can shift the rules of this game"
(*Philosophy* 130–31).

Part III: Revised Lives

*Walter asked if we'd listened to NPR. We said no, but we
heard from him and from the local paper that thirteen
teenagers overdosed on a prescription muscle relaxant at
a dance at their local girls and boys club. Ten were in
critical condition. Someone said the teenagers were
"dropping like flies" when the ambulances and police*

arrived. Drugs to revise a life? Jane gave us her version as a member of the staff at the dance. She talked mainly about what the club and the community might learn and do now. I am glad she was there along with other members of the staff. I am glad that she knows about drugs and their effects. I am glad that she is trying to make her life better by other means, aware of the risk of surgery.

What actually catapulted me from many rough drafts for this paper to a final copy was a conversation I overheard. In response to a student's discussion of her dissertation, which included chapters on the rhetoric of healing, someone leaned forward to say, "I must tell you: I don't believe in writing as therapy."

All that is life-giving, life-sustaining, and life-transforming about writing became "therapy," with connotations of help for those who can't help themselves.

I understand why, for professional reasons, a teacher might be reluctant at times to talk about writing and reading as strategies for coping. English studies has been primarily about living the good life by acquiring and cultivating particular aesthetic tastes and social conventions, not about living the good life by acknowledging and respecting who and what we and others are individually and collectively—in terms of class, gender, ethnicity, sexual orientation, and more—as a way to figure out what more we need to know and do so that everyone lives better.

The traditional focus on figures and tropes and on forms and texts in isolation seems to distance if not detach art from life. But as Burke argues convincingly in *Counter-Statement* in 1931, we can also understand forms, symbols, and words as "abstractions from situations" and "strategies for encompassing situations." With his revision, from forms as abstractions, to forms as abstracting, he revises symbolic forms into *symbolic actions*, which have consequences in the world. He explains that the symbolists argued for art-for-art's-sake in order to make their poetry appealing in the then-current scene; like all writers, they wrote to be read, and their motives were rhetorical.

Burke's lessons are not easy to learn nor to accept, for they challenge our views of reality and our own positions; many prefer terministic screens other than "rhetoric," ones that are more stable and foundational or more stable and transcendental. Despite his efforts in all of his works to redefine "symbol," so that it is understood as constructed from and as a construction of situations and cultures, many still resist this interpretation and accept the traditional one of symbols as removed from life. And despite his efforts to address the rhetorics of aesthetics, literature, history, psychology, economics, and language, many resist his rhetorical stance and prefer to address these perspectives as reflections of reality, as bodies of knowledge, or as epistemologies, philosophies, ideologies, and histories, not as forms of rhetoric that are motivated, consequential, probable, changeable, and changing.

I also understand teachers' reluctance and refusal to see or present ourselves as therapists, counselors, psychologists, or psychiatrists. As writing teachers we work with people on their writing. We keep "writing," "composition," and "rhetoric" before us as our guiding terms. Just as Burke's key term "rhetoric" defined and limited what he could do, our purposes as teachers, and the situations in which we teach, limit what we do.

But writing and reading can allow people to live other lives and to try things out symbolically, so that we can make better decisions about what we value and do. There is no guarantee, of course, that reading and writing make people act more wisely. But, writing and reading, by expanding our experience and repertoire of strategies, can provide additional possibilities from which we may choose in order to live and act effectively in specific contexts.

Another problem with the idea of teaching revision as a life skill in a school context may also emerge if we as teachers take our positions and ourselves too seriously, and shift from teachers to experts, whose persuasive authority rests on empirical facts and truths rather than rhetoric, and forget that teaching is an art of persuasion. When we shift from being people who learn in order to teach to people who have already learned, we no longer model learning and adapting what works in one context to new situations: We are no longer teaching writing and revision, and we have become "rotten with perfection" (*Language* 16).

Burke tries to be persuasive by practicing in his critical writing what he advocates. He does so by questioning his own methods and conclusions, by presenting perspective by incongruity, by tracking down terms and clusters and then dissociating them, and, perhaps most effectively, by relying on representative anecdotes, or short narratives, to convince readers who are typically persuaded in criticism by logical arguments and sound evidence. Burke relies on stories to engage his readers in a co-creation of meaning. Although his best-known representative anecdote is probably the one set in the formal parlor room, he typically writes about the rhetoric of The Scramble, The Barnyard, The Give and Take, The Wars of Nerves, The Rat Race, and The Muddle. Throughout his books, he draws from literature and life to support his arguments, and he relies on his readers to revise and adapt his stories and arguments to their own contexts.

When we read works of fiction and nonfiction, including scholarly works such as Burke's, as "equipment for living," we find strategies everywhere, and we learn what Pierre Bourdieu calls the "logic of practice," which relies on agents' capacities for action, invention, and improvisation and their "feel for the game."

With Burke's terministic screen of rhetoric, we find examples of writers and of characters within writing who rewrite their lives. *Infinite Divisions: An Anthology of Chicana Literature*, for example, offers many. In "My Name," a short prose piece, Sandra Cisneros chooses among the possible meanings of her character's name:

> In English my name means hope. In Spanish it means too many letters. It means sadness, it means waiting. It is like the number nine. A muddy color. It is the Mexican records my father plays on Sunday mornings when he is shaving, songs like sobbing. (79)

As she continues, she decides not to live one of the lives her name seems to have fated her to live:

> It was my great-grandmother's name and now it is mine. She was . . . a wild horse of a woman, so wild she wouldn't marry until my great-grandfather threw a sack over her head and carried her off. Just like that, as if she were a fancy chandelier. . . . And the story goes she never forgave him. She looked out the window all her life, the way so many women sit their sadness

on an elbow. . . . I have inherited her name, but I don't want to inherit her place by the window. (79)

Pat Mora, another poet in the anthology, presents the voice of a courageous woman determined to resist the pattern of her life and of her daughter's life:

> I won't let him hit her. I won't
> let him bruise her soft skin, her dark
> brown eyes. I'll beg her to use the ring
> snapped from a Coke can. That's my wedding
> gift for my daughter. (144)

In a collection of interviews, *Backtalk: Women Writers Speak Out*, Paula Gunn Allen responds to a question about a character in *The Woman Who Owned the Shadows*. She explains that the woman can revise her life only by reassessing it and then retelling it:

> It is only when she goes back and recognizes all that pain and that she is Indian and that she has told all these lies to herself that she discovers who she is. She has to go back and retell her stories and then she can reclaim herself. (9)

Joy Harjo's *The Spiral of Memory*, another collection of interviews, is filled with poems and stories of how she and people she knows have revised their lives. Other contemporary works that invite revision include Audre Lorde's *Zami: A New Spelling of My Name*, Linda Hogan's *The Book of Medicines*, Ofelia Zepeda's *Ocean Power: Poems from the Desert*, Jane Miller's *Working Time: Essays on Poetry, Culture, and Travel*, Alice Kaplan's *French Lessons: A Memoir*, James Galvin's *The Meadow*, and Alice Walker's *The Same River Twice: Honoring the Difficult*.

In *Approaching Eye Level*, Vivian Gornick demonstrates how feminism was constructed and revised and then deconstructed, before she shows how she again revised feminism to make it work for her: "Without change, the connection within oneself dies. As that is unbearable, life is an endlessness of 'remembering' what I already know" (69). In the first essay in her collection, "On the Street: Nobody Watches, Everyone

Performs," she again gives readers a view of her rewriting life, this time at the end of a day after walking in New York:

> I begin revising the scenes, adding dialogue here, analysis there, commentary further on. Then I find myself backing up, imagining each of them before we met up. With a start, I realize that I am writing the story of the day, lending shape and texture to the hours just behind me. They're in the room with me now, these people I brushed against today. They've become company, great company. I'd rather be here with them tonight than with anyone else I know. They return the narrative impulse to me. Let me make sense of things. Remind me to tell the story I cannot make my life tell. (28)

In *You Must Revise Your Life*, William Stafford explains how he lets the "process of writing bring about things rather than be just the writing down of things that are already brought about" (73). He explains how he teaches writing this way:

> One issue, "How the hell do you teach others to write poetry?" can be answered this way. One thing you do with others is try to encourage them, induce them and be company to them when they go ahead and follow the immediacies of experience. You tell them, "Don't be inhibited, don't be cautious, don't be correct; just go headlong into the experience." (62)

Stafford's poetry, his teaching, and his life encourage us to welcome change and make revisions in writing and in life. He also teaches us to accept the metaphor that writing is living because it is useful for both life and writing.

An Inconclusion

Jane tells me that the surgery is "penciled in for August 1." That date will be erased if further tests or events between now and then lead elsewhere; that date will be written in ink as the time arrives. We are all tending in that direction. John's mother called today, eager to get the toaster fixed. We wish we'd gotten zinc tablets to minimize the next cold. I've started a light blanket of red cotton yarn sprinkled with bright yellow, turquoise, purple, green, and blue.

In *A Lesson before Dying,* Ernest J. Gaines writes about how people—a student, a teacher, and their surrounding families and communities—educate each other to rewrite their lives, so that they identify and cooperate with each other to live better. In this book, Gaines shows how family, education, law, religion, racism, story, and language are all used—by people for various motives in different situations—to equip themselves and others to live, to die, to cope, to kill, to shame, and to celebrate. Within the constraints of particular situations, to decide what to do and how to act is what it means to be human.

In a series of entries from Jefferson's diary, Gaines shows how a young man gains his life as he contemplates his death through the act of writing to his teacher and friend. I want to close this essay as Gaines closes his chapter "Jefferson's Diary," not with an ending but with the possibility of beginning again through writing and reading:

> mr wigin you say rite somethin but i dont kno what to rite an
> you say i must be thinkin bout things i aint telin nobody an i
> order put it on paper but i dont know what to put on paper
> cause i aint never rote nothin but homework i aint never rote
> a leter in all my life cause nanan use to get other chiren to rite
> her leter an read her leter for her not me so i cant think of too
> much to say but maybe nex time (226)

> mr wigin you say you like what i got here but you say you stil
> cant give me a a jus a b cause you say i aint gone deep in me
> yet an you kno i can if i try hard an when i ax you what you
> mean deep in me you say jus say whats on my mind so one day
> you can be save an you can save the chiren and i say i don't kno
> what you mean an you say i do know what you mean an you
> look so tied sometime mr wigin i just feel like tellin you i like
> you but i dont know how to say this cause i aint never say it to
> nobody before an nobody aint never say it to me (228)

> i kno i care for nanan but i dont kno if love is care cause cut-
> tin wood and haulin water and things like that i dont if thats
> love or jus work to do an you say thats love but you say you kno
> i got mo an jus that to say an when i lay ther at nite and cant

sleep i try an think what you mean i got mo cause i aint done
this much thinkin and this much writin in all my life befor (229)

good by mr wigin tell them im strong tell them im a man good
by mr wigin im gon ax paul if he can bring you this

sincely jefferson (234)

Works Cited

Allen, Paula Gunn. Interview. *Backtalk: Women Writers Speak Out.*
Ed. Donna Perry. New Brunswick, NJ: Rutgers UP, 1993.

Bourdieu, Pierre. *The Logic of Practice.* Trans. Richard Nice. Stanford:
Stanford UP, 1990.

Burke, Kenneth. *Attitudes toward History.* 3rd ed. Berkeley: U of California P, 1937.

———. *Counter-Statement.* Berkeley: U of California P, 1931.

———. *A Grammar of Motives.* Berkeley: U of California P, 1945.

———. *Language as Symbolic Action: Essays on Life, Literature, and
Method.* Berkeley: U of California P, 1966.

———. *The Philosophy of Literary Form.* Berkeley: U of California P,
1941.

———. *A Rhetoric of Motives.* Berkeley: U of California P, 1950.

Cisneros, Sandra. "My Name." *Infinite Divisions: An Anthology of
Chicana Literature.* Ed. Tey Diana Rebolledo and Eliana S. Rivero.
Tucson: U of Arizona P, 1993. 79.

Gaines, Ernest J. *A Lesson before Dying.* New York: Vintage, 1993.

Galvin, James. *The Meadow.* New York: Henry Holt, 1992.

Gornick, Vivian. *Approaching Eye Level.* Boston: Beacon, 1996.

———. Interview. *Backtalk: Women Writers Speak Out.* Ed. Donna
Perry. New Brunswick, NJ: Rutgers UP, 1993. 105–25.

Harjo, Joy. *The Spiral of Memory: Interviews.* Ed. Laura Coltelli. Ann
Arbor: U of Michigan P, 1996.

Heilbrun, Carolyn G. *Writing a Woman's Life*. New York: Norton, 1988.

Hogan, Linda. *The Book of Medicines*. Minneapolis: Coffee House Press, 1993.

Kaplan, Alice. *French Lessons: A Memoir*. Chicago: U of Chicago P, 1993.

Lorde, Audre. *Zami: A New Spelling of My Name*. Trumansburg, NY: Crossing Press, 1982.

Miller, Jane. *Working Time: Essays on Poetry, Culture, and Travel*. Ann Arbor: U of Michigan P, 1992.

Mora, Pat. "Plot." *Infinite Divisions: An Anthology of Chicana Literature*. Ed. Tey Diana Rebolledo and Eliana S. Rivero. Tucson: U of Arizona P, 1993. 144–45.

Perry, Donna, ed. *Backtalk: Women Writers Speak Out*. New Brunswick, NJ: Rutgers UP, 1993.

Rebolledo, Tey Diana, and Eliana S. Rivero, eds. *Infinite Divisions: An Anthology of Chicana Literature*. Tucson: U of Arizona P, 1993.

Stafford, William. *You Must Revise Your Life*. Ann Arbor: U of Michigan P, 1986.

Sternburg, Janet, ed. *The Writer on Her Work*. Vol. 1. New York: Norton, 1980.

Tyler, Anne. "Still Just Writing." *The Writer on Her Work*. Ed. Janet Sternberg. New York: Norton, 1980. 3–16.

Walker, Alice. *The Same River Twice: Honoring the Difficult*. New York: Scribner, 1996.

Zamora, Bernice. "So Not To Be Mottled." *Infinite Divisions: An Anthology of Chicana Literature*. Ed. Tey Diana Rebolledo and Eliana S. Rivero. Tucson: U of Arizona P, 1993. 78.

Zepeda, Ofelia. *Ocean Power: Poems from the Desert*. Tucson: U of Arizona P, 1995.

CHAPTER FOUR

Suture, Stigma, and the Pages That Heal

CHARLES M. ANDERSON
University of Arkansas at Little Rock
with

KAREN HOLT

PATTY McGADY

This page held some space, perhaps for whole scenes, in the way that—after a loss—a great friend holds some space for you in which to grieve or find your bearings.
ANNE LAMOTT, *Bird by Bird*

"This course," I tell my advanced expository writing students on the first night of class, "is about all the essays you never got to write. I won't tell you what you have to write or what you can't write. The only restriction I place on your writing is that it must be nonfiction—what you tell us really happened, really did happen. You can't make it up."

Under these conditions, the students choose not to write academic prose or research papers or fluff. Instead, they go to the hardest places they know and write about the things they seem least able to understand—births and deaths, loves and hatreds, fears. I have witnessed writers struggling through texts of unimaginable difficulty, telling and retelling stories so harsh and broken that I have wondered how they could ever have survived the lives those stories tell me they have lived. I and the others in the class have worked with them, not on their lives, but on the stories of their lives, on the texts they bring to us, on the pages that hold the possibility of meaning and therefore of wholeness. I have watched those pages resist and submit, shift and change, grow luminous as watch dials at midnight. And I have seen writers change, come into being, and discover themselves. I have seen them get better. I have seen them healed and have come to understand that it *is* life, theirs, mine, and ours, upon which we work in the class, in my office, in small groups scattered across the campus and the city, rich, deep, and complex. I have seen that broken stories are also broken lives. And I have come to know writing as a primary symbolism, a way we are and can be in the world, the material out of which we spin what Ernst Cassirer calls "the varied threads which weave the symbolic net, the tangled web of human experience" (Cassirer 25).

For years, I knew only that writers seemed to need to tell such stories, that nothing I could do short of tying them to the train tracks would keep them from doing so and that our work with their essays seemed important and that it seemed to do some good for the writers and certainly for the writing. But I did not know how to explain such essays when my colleagues and others would give me that funny look and tell me I really ought to call the counseling service (I was never certain whether they meant the call to be on behalf of my students or myself or both). When I read Karen Holt's and Patty McGady's essays, which we will look at later in this chapter, in the context of hundreds of such essays I had received over the years and in light of other reading I happened to be doing—Lacanian theory, film criticism, an article on the work of Richard Selzer—an understanding began to emerge. That understanding, as it relates to their essays, and as it has been deepened by other reading and talk with colleagues across the country and with Karen and Patty, are what we want to share in this chapter. I begin with theory and move to its application.

Suture

It is both commonplace and accurate to say that we live our lives inside an endless network of stories. In Lacanian terms, our participation in such story networks or discourses is through the subject, which is created and maintained not by us but by the discourse of the "other," the "not us" with whom we speak. We live according to some variations of this commonplace, in a constant state of being victimized by the other, whose discourse creates, positions, and controls our subjectivity. That is, when we enter a story or a discourse, we become both subjects within that discourse and subject to its terms and its rules. According to Lacan and his commentators, such subjectivity allows us access to discursive or narrative meaning, but we can have that meaning only by giving up being. We trade who we are (or who we imagine ourselves to be) for a meaningful role in the discourse of the other. Self and all that murky term might or might not mean, is compromised, some have said, to the point of disappearance. To participate in the discourse of the other is necessarily to suffer the loss of self and to be, in a very real sense, written over or spoken out of existence.

To understand the concept, think about coming into a new discourse, for example, marrying into a family. In the discourse of this other—your spouse's family—you are not who you think you are, an individual with likes, dislikes, and a particular history, but a subject filling the position of "in-law." As an "in-law," certain attributes are dictated to you, which you cannot ignore if you expect to be a part of the discourse of the family and to be integrated, eventually, into its story. While no particular subject position necessarily dominates in your particular case (each family will be a little different in its particulars), all reduce your sense of the complexity of your actual being to that of the subject position in the story of "the son-in-law who stole my daughter" or "the daughter-in-law who can't keep a clean house or cook a decent meal."

What complicates this already complicated situation is the powerful urge, the "desire" all of us have to assume the subject position. Some film critics and Lacanian scholars and commentators call this urge "suture," a term denoting the process by which we, as viewers of a given scene or as participants in a particular discourse, move toward and are fastened into the subject position. Because meaning is essential to human beings and is dependent upon being located within the discourse of an other, the process of suturing ourselves or allowing ourselves to be sutured into the discourse of an other is all but irresistible. It is, in fact, normal and constitutes the primary movement and source of energy by which "abnormal" and "normal" are derived, defined, and sustained. As Kaja Silverman puts it, "we want suture so badly that we'll take it at any price, even with the fullest knowledge of what it entails—passive insertions into pre-existing discursive positions . . . ; threatened losses and false recoveries; and subordination" (Silverman 199).

Suture inserts us into discourses that appear to give our lives coherence, wholeness, and meaning, but in that process, they also wound and break us, separate and alienate us, pacify us, and expose us to losses so severe that we can easily cease to be. For film critics such as Silverman and for Lacanian commentators, such losses constitute a wounding and a lack that is definitive, inevitable, and irreversible.

Somewhere in all this theorizing, I recognized that the losses entailed by the suturing of persons into subject positions that controlled, violated, and silenced them were at the center of many of the most powerful and puzzling essays my advanced expository writing students brought into the class. Their essays, in fact, catalogued and probed the wounds such losses left. At some point, I understood that the essays were not the wounds themselves, but rather stories dispatched into and out of the lives of the writers by language functions that exist at the sites of pain and confusion, loss and longing, grief. They were symbolic strands attempting to connect memory and being with the larger web of human experience, its personal, social, and political dimensions. This was important, and gave me words to explain to my colleagues and others that I worked with the symbols of woundedness but not with the wounds, with the meaning of pain but not with pain, with what Old Deuteronomy in *Cats* calls "the experience in a different form" without which meaning and the self cannot exist (Really Useful).

As more and more writers worked to clarify, to name, to tell the stories behind the stories, to work over and through the dispatches, to get at what had hurt and broken them, I began to see that the losses were neither inevitable nor irreversible. In the struggle to represent, to name and rename, to revise personal and public histories, I began to see writers creating complex alternatives to the obscurely simplistic formulations of discourse, self, and world that I had been studying. I began to see that such for-mulations could be both wrong and damaging, could suture all discourse into a single subjectivity, a single sad voice having what T. R. Johnson (in his essay later in this volume) calls an "unmis-takable ring of acute morbidity, even madness. . . . [A] profound nihilism" (95).[1]

As the writers and I and the class joined together to write and rewrite, to chip away the excess and fill the empty spaces and explore the silences of essays, we discovered that the other with whom we interacted most lay not outside our speaking, but in-side the margins and across the pages. We discovered that to dis-course with the other, when the other is the fluid text out of which one's story emerges, is not to be trapped and wounded by the words of the other nor to trade being for meaning, but to be re-leased by those words, to experience a convergence of meaning and being, and to name a self not broken by discourse, but, im-mersed in it, in charge by it, empowered by it. Here is how it hap-pened for Karen.

Immediate Family

BY KAREN HOLT

"You never talk about *your* family," Joann said without warning, as I combed the thick auburn color mixture through her waist-length hair. "I mean, I've told you about mine, and I've heard all sorts of wonderful things about your mother, but you've never mentioned anything about your father."

Since our initial meeting four years ago, Joann had become one of my favorite clients. Unlike with others, a special relationship had formed and a rapport built I rarely shared with my clients. She bordered on the friendship line. I trusted and cared about her. Nevertheless, I usually maintained the client/stylist attitude regarding conversations, abiding by the sacred rule of thumb of not bombarding the client with information about myself. The attention should always be on the clients, allowing them to vent their feelings, keeping my conversations light, never focus-ing on myself. But for some reason, on this particular evening, my very intuitive and dedicated client insisted on upsetting this established order.

"He's dead," I replied without taking my eyes away from my work, meticulously ensuring the end of the hair had as much color distributed to it as did the rest. If the color wasn't evenly combed through, the ends would be lighter like the time before. And if I omitted any hairs, the color would fade faster. Combing through the strands, I realized the silence. Looking up, I saw Joann staring through the mirror, frozen by my lack of concern at her comment.

"It's okay, he's been dead for five or six years now. He had cancer." Sensing she thought my answer inclusive I added, "I hardly knew him. My mother divorced when I was two. He was an alcoholic. One day my grandmother called my mom, told her he was dead and that was it." And I realized for the first time how these lines sounded very much like something a news reporter might convey about a particular incident, no emotion, just fact.

"Joann, it's okay," I said halfway laughing, anticipating the usual look of sympathy one gets when they tell about a loved one dying. "In fact, I can't even remember the exact date of his funeral."

But really I could. September 12, 1989. Slowly the smell of heat mixed with mother's perfume filled my nostrils. "Park right there," Mom said, pointing, as I slowly pulled the Accord behind the packed limousine. We had chosen to ride in our own car, separate from the others, separate from the rest of the family. The drive itself was long: car steaming, air conditioner blasting, Mother sitting silently as if the summer humidity had sucked all the words from her. Handing me a wad of Kleenex, she checked her reflection in the visor mirror. She attempted to be strong, but I could feel her uneasiness as she blotted her coral lips and dabbed her eyes. Squeezing my hand, she silently urged me out of the car and into the sweltering day. "Let's go; they're waiting on us," she said, breathing deeply and straightening the black linen dress. Gripping my arm, she led me toward the others as they watched, carefully, with placid faces and questioning eyes. I was the forgotten child; the one no one ever knew or cared to know until now.

With everyone whispering, mother and I were led to the room behind the curtain where the immediate family members could go to mourn together in private. Taking my seat, I remember being conscious of everyone crying and was embarrassed by the dry tissues in my hand. Sensing my uneasiness, Mom squeezed my hand reassuringly, smiling through her tears, and I exchanged my dry tissues for her damp ones.

As the familiar hymns were sung and prayers read, the guests sat shaking their heads at the pitiful history of the dead. The preacher talked of a sick man with a disease that had taken over his body, but not his soul. "He was a Christian," he said, "who in his death bed asked for forgiveness." He continued by expressing how the man wanted to be forgiven for all of the pain and worry he caused the people he loved during his sickness, for hurting those close to him by never being there. As the words sank in, I tried to imagine what he would have said to me if I had been there. Would he have said he was sorry? Would he have told me he loved me?

When the eulogy was finished and the congregation dismissed, the casket was opened. "It's better to remember him the way he was," my grandmother said, as she attempted to stop me. But the only memories I had were almost forgotten. Inside the casket was a 48-year-old body that could have passed for 100. The 5'10" frame had deteriorated into almost nothing. The wrinkled cheeks were sunken, hair sparsely distributed, and the skin clung to the skeleton of a man. And without emotion, I turned away. I could hear my mother's voice saying, "He was once a beautiful, caring man, Karen."

But that was a man I never knew. The only man I knew was one with alcohol on his breath and uncertainty in his step, one who chose life without his daughter or her mother, who visited once a year, calling me his "little girl" but having the touch of a stranger, who had nothing to say, nothing except, "I love you," and who received the same empty words in return. Now, I was expected to feel a loss for this man. But unlike the rest of the guests, my loss occurred years before, when I was too young to understand, but old enough to know he wasn't there.

No one understood my dilemma. "If it weren't for your father marrying your mother you wouldn't be here," my grandmother used to say. As I got older, I understood her motivation for saying those things to me: She wanted me to appreciate the fact that I did have two parents, that my mother was not the only one who cared about me, and that her son, wherever he was, really did love me. But the man in the casket was never a father to me; he was never a part of *my* family. Nevertheless, I was supposed to react to his death like a daughter, as if he meant as much as the mother beside me.

But he *didn't*. He was nothing like her. She was a *parent*, a parent who raised her child alone with no help from anyone, not from relatives, not from him. She was a parent who worked two jobs to ensure meals because child support laws of today didn't exist then. And most of all, a parent, who despite her young age and friends' advice, sacrificed her whole life, devoting it to her child, the child who was originally two people's responsibility but ended up hers alone. This woman beside me was both mother and father who did not neglect her child, taking the place of the father who did.

And she is the reason I can feel the way I do. Although it takes a man and a woman to make a child, biology alone doesn't constitute family. It takes far more to be part of a child's life. The man and woman have to be there physically and mentally, supporting and sacrificing, sharing the everyday trials children go through growing up to be considered a part of a child or the child's life. She had no choice because he did. She made the right decision; he didn't. I am her daughter, not his.

There. I said it. The bell of the timer sounded, and I motioned for Joann to follow me to the shampoo bowl—time to rinse. Examining the hair strands, I smiled—the color was perfect. No fading this time. Sensing my discomfort, Joann had dropped the father conversation twenty minutes earlier. I decided to pick it back up.

"You know, I guess I don't talk much about my father. But it's because I never knew him. I try to stay away from the subject. Not because I don't want to talk about it, but because people usually think I'm cruel or heartless for not caring more than I do. So to answer your question, I guess I don't have anything to say about him. To me, family always meant mother. No more, no less."

And with her smile, my friend Joann told me she understood. With her silence, she offered me her respect, closing the conversation on my family and on him. Enough said. She already knew about my family; I talk about her all the time.

Karen's essay begins at the beauty shop where she earns her living working with the hair of customers like Joann, who breaks the sutures that bind her and Karen into a known, professional discourse with the opening words of the essay:

"You never talk about *your* family," Joann said without warning, as I combed the auburn color mixture through her waist-length hair. "I mean, I've told you about mine, and I've heard all sorts of wonderful things about your mother, but you've never mentioned anything about your father."

In the paragraphs that follow, Karen responds to the first of a long series of sutures that are the substance of her piece. Her client's comments about Karen's father invite Karen to participate in a conventional discourse of the conventional family—mother, father, daughter. Karen's response, while true—she hardly knew her father—disturbs her because it violates the discursive expectations of Joann's conventional conversation opener and leads Karen to doubt her position in the story of her own life—she feels like a reporter giving "no emotion, just fact," communicating none of the feeling that ought to be present in the discourse of family relationships. Understanding the cost of resisting the subject position in the conventional narrative which Joann has initiated, Karen responds with a lie and then with a move to an internal monologue, the other of which is not Joann, but the implied reader for whom Karen's essay has been written.

"Joann, it's okay," I said halfway laughing, anticipating the usual look of sympathy one gets when they tell about a loved one dying. "In fact, I can't even remember the exact date of his funeral."

But really I could. September 12, 1989. Slowly, the smell of heat mixed with mother's perfume filled my nostrils. "Park right there," Mom said, pointing as I slowly pulled the Accord behind the packed limousine. We had chosen to ride in our own car, separate from the others, separate from the rest of the family.

The shift to interior monologue effectively suspends the immediate pressure of conversation with Joann and the immediate discourse constraints of the here-and-now context of that conversation. The importance of this suspension cannot be overestimated. By suspending what Derrida might call the presence of the immediate context and turning to an explicitly written text characterized by time and place shifting and the absence of her auditor (Derrida), Karen enters a contra-contextual space in which she is free to represent and to examine her own history. The contra-discourse she creates in the textual space of her essay does not objectify and remove Karen from the sites of her experience as the discourses of family that Joann has offered threaten to. Instead, it allows her to represent, to interrogate, and to resist the sutures offered by the discourse of her father's funeral.

> Gripping my arm, she led me toward the others as they watched, carefully, with placid faces and questioning eyes. I was the forgotten child; the one no one ever knew or cared to know until now.

> With everyone whispering, mother and I were led to the room behind the curtain where the immediate family members could go to mourn together in private. Taking my seat, I remember being conscious of everyone crying and was embarrassed by the dry tissues in my hand. Sensing my uneasiness, Mom squeezed my hand reassuringly, smiling through her tears, and I exchanged my dry tissues for her damp ones.

The discursive content of the events Karen depicts is highly conventional and extremely complex, factors of which Karen is acutely aware. Because the discourse into which Karen has entered is also very powerful, she feels enormous pressure to allow herself to be sutured into an acceptable subject position. Karen is conscious of everyone's expectations, clear about who she is and is supposed to be, embarrassed by the dry tissues in her hand, relieved by her mother's exchange of damp tissues for dry ones. But she does not accept the inevitability of the suturing. Again and again, she is offered subject positions. Again and again she rejects them:

> The preacher talked of a sick man with a disease that had taken over his body, but not his soul. "He was a Christian," he said, "who, on his death bed, asked for forgiveness." He continued by expressing how the man wanted to be forgiven for all of the pain and worry he caused the people he loved during his sickness, for hurting those close to him by never being there. As the words sank in, I tried to imagine what he would have said to me if I had been there. Would he have said he was sorry? Would he have told me he loved me?

> "It's better to remember him the way he was," my grandmother said, as she attempted to stop me [from looking at the body]. But the only memories I had were almost forgotten.

> I could hear my mother's voice saying, "He was once a beautiful, caring man, Karen."
> But that was a man I never knew.

> "If it weren't for your father marrying your mother you wouldn't be here," my grandmother used to say.

> . . . I was supposed to react to his death like a daughter, as if he meant as much to me as the mother beside me.

Having rejected the "easy" subjectivities she has been offered, Karen turns from her father and focuses her attention on her mother. First in the factual past of the news report and then in the passionate present tense of the contra-discourse she has created in the textual space of her essay, Karen shakes off the force of suture and speaks her self into being, claiming the meaning of her experience, not in the absence of her father, but in the presence of an other who does not seek to subjugate her:

> He was nothing like her. She was a *parent*, a parent who raised her child alone with no help from anyone, not from relatives, not from him. She was a parent who worked two jobs to

ensure meals because child support laws of today didn't exist then. And most of all, a parent who despite her young age and friends' advice, sacrificed her whole life, devoting it to her child, the child who was originally two people's responsibility but ended up hers alone. This woman beside me was both mother and father . . .

And she is the reason I can feel the way I do. Although it takes a man and a woman to make a child, biology alone doesn't constitute family. It takes far more to be part of a child's life. The man and woman have to be there physically and mentally, supporting and sacrificing, sharing the everyday trials children go through growing up to be considered a part of a child or the child's life. She had no choice because he did. She made the right decision; he didn't. I am her daughter, not his.

In the process of asserting her independence from the suturing discourses of the funeral and her father's family, Karen discovers that she has been, in fact, the other to her own mother's life, an other who has sutured that woman into a hard, demanding subjectivity. Having seen this, she submits, not unwillingly or in a way that violates her integrity, but in a graceful series of epistemic oppositions, to the knowledge that she is her mother's, not her father's, daughter. In this no longer contra-contextual space, Karen discovers and asserts an interdependent self linked by obligation and love to the (m)other she has created. Immediately following this assertion comes a blank place in the page, signaling a return to the scene of the beauty shop where the essay began, a conventional enough transition, but with a difference. The break in this essay is not a clean one. Two short sentences transport Karen's story across the gap between the contra-contextual space of the interior text and the presence of Joann, her client:

There. I said it. The bell of the timer sounded, and I motioned for Joann to follow me to the shampoo bowl—time to rinse. Examining the hair strands, I smiled—the color was perfect. No fading this time. Sensing my discomfort, Joann had dropped the father conversation twenty minutes earlier. I decided to pick it back up.

"You know, I guess I don't talk much about my father. But it's because I never knew him. I try to stay away from the subject. Not because I don't want to talk about it, but because people usually think I'm cruel or heartless for not caring more than I do. So to answer your question, I guess I don't have anything to say about him. To me, family always meant mother. No more, no less."

And with her smile, my friend Joann told me she understood. With her silence, she offered me her respect, closing the conversation on my family and on him. Enough said. She already knew about my family; I talk about her all the time.

What might have been simply an embarrassing conversational opener, dropped as quickly as possible, has become, through the writing, revising, and sharing of this essay, a symbolic event through which Karen has emerged as a powerful discursive agent. As such an agent, she is able to recognize and respond directly to others seeking to suture her into a subject position in controlling discourses that would reduce the richness and depth of her life to "cruelty" and "heartlessness." Karen signals these consequences in the perfection of Joann's hair and in the movement of Joann from "client" to "friend," a movement that enables silence and respect to replace the pressures of conversation and suture. In the final sentence, Karen claims her history by asserting it, not to Joann, but to the others who read her piece and to the other that is her self.

In writing such as Karen's essay, the stakes are high—integrity, meaning, the building, assessing, and honoring of human relationships. In others, it is not relationships or pieces of writing that come to the red table in my office for interrogation and discovery. It is life itself.

The Swepston Table

BY PATTY MCGADY

We walked into the Arkansas Children's Hospital lobby. Bright plastic clowns, teddy bears, and Disney characters rode up and down the atrium on thin wires as the elevators moved from floor to floor. I watched through the clear glass as we traveled up to The Turn Point, the adolescent treatment program. My eyes fixed on the mechanical elves—precariously balancing as they moved back and forth the length of the room on trapezes.

My first clue something was terribly wrong had been when I walked into my fifteen-year-old daughter's bedroom and found her curled up in the closet, hugging her Teddy Bear, her face painted white, large purple circles round her eyes. Three blue tears were drawn down her cheeks, and SAD was written across her forehead in black. Though stunned, I teasingly said, "Gee Sara, you feeling sad?"

The fear faded from her eyes, and she cracked a little smile. "Oh, I was cleaning out my closet shelf and came across these old face paints, I was just playing around."

Sara had been missing school a lot. Since our move, she'd been crying almost nonstop. After attending Marshall High in a town populated by about 1,400, North Little Rock East Campus was a nightmare she woke up to each day. Pushed, shoved, and lost in a maze of people who had known one another for years, she felt as if she were writhing under a microscope.

A few weeks later, after she'd gone through another sleepless night of tears, I went in her room. She let me cradle her and stroke her hair. Sara agreed to go for some help; if nothing else, it got her out of going to school one more day.

During the hospital evaluation, she admitted she had razor blades stashed in her vanity drawer—and a plan. The true depth of her depression was revealed; she was admitted. Now, I'd known for at least a year that she was using drugs and alcohol, but this was Sara's first bottom.

Jessica, my seventeen-year-old daughter, has been using for five years and has been hospitalized three times for her depression and substance abuse issues. She's hit several bottoms.

My last bottom threw me in Benton Detox for two weeks—not exactly the silk-sheet treatment I'd gone through in the past. In Benton Detox, most people require restraints the first few days, delirium tremens are ugly, grand mal seizures an everyday occurrence. My dorm mates were often toothless, homeless women who'd REALLY hit bottom.

I guess it's kind of like in some people's families they share the same birth marks and moles. In my family it's substance abuse, trauma, and depression—generations worth. I'm one of the few who has chosen to suture the wounds and live. This is what encouraged me to sit still as my daughters confronted me in family therapy about their own scars from growing up in a dysfunctional family.

After Sara was released from the hospital, the girls went to see Pearl Jam together. They came home wasted on alcohol and crack, Sara driving without a license 'cause Jess was too drunk to drive her car. Mind you, Sara was in no better shape than her sister, but Jess had been busted for a DWI two weeks before. As they walked in the door, I took Jess's keys out of Sara's hand. Jess stomped into my room and came up behind my swivel chair where I was working on my computer. She kicked my chair and yelled, "Give me my keys!"

"No. I told you the car could be used for work only, and I was stretching my rules by letting you drive to the concert tonight. You can't have them back." It took all the peace, the Zen, the God I could pull from inside to keep me seated and calm.

She kicked my chair a few more times, then shoved me into my desk. "My life and what I do with it is none of your fucking business." As she stormed out of my room, she turned in the doorway, spit in my face, and screamed, "Fuck you."

My temper snapped. I chased her into her room and pinned her to the bed. I wanted to hurt her, hit her with all my strength, but her kicks blocked each punch I threw.

A kick to my chest drove home the realization that the only one hurting was me. Jessica was numb. Sara hid, huddled under her covers. I retreated to my own bed for another sleepless night, my heart aching for relief, my mind churning for solutions.

The next morning, I gave them each a choice, move out or enter a twenty-eight-day program for substance abuse. They chose treatment.

I know they were clean and sober for 28 days. That was the length of their stay in the hospital. Not long after that, they went back to using. Sara was suicidal again, and Jessica was telling me her life "was none of my fucking business" most every day.

Early one Sunday morning, I crawled out of bed and found the coffeepot. That, and a Marlboro, consoled me for a few minutes. Then back up the stairs, back under the covers, I thought, "Nope, just can't do it one more day. I can't do *anything* one more day."

For hours, I'd looked from the razor knife on my desk to the pills on my shelf. Razor. Pills. Razor. Pills. Wondering. Which could I do with finality?

That weekend, Dale was in town visiting her family. She's a Ph.D. student and TA at Texas Woman's University. I met Dale when I was a student at North Arkansas Community College my freshman year. She was my Composition teacher both semesters, and by the end of the year, my closest friend. She drove by my place to say good-bye before heading back home to Denton. When she came in my room and saw where I was at, she tried to talk me through it. As I said, I was hopeless, so when she asked what she could do, I said, "I want you to leave; go home."

"Are you angry with me, Patty?"

"God, no, I'm not angry. I just know you need to get home, and there's nothing you can do here. I'll be fine."

I wanted to end my life, and she was in the way. But Dale wasn't leaving till I was in a better place. She talked. I cried. I talked. She cried. Finally, I admitted I just wanted to die, or to run far away.

"Aha. That's the solution. Pack your bags and come with me."

"I could actually walk out of here? Just leave?"

"If you don't, they'll be carrying you out of here."

"What about the girls?"

"Life hard, huh?! Those girls are going to do what they want anyway, whether you're here or not."

I threw stuff in suitcases while Dale made some phone calls to let professors know I wouldn't be in for a few days. My daughters were shocked when I told them I was leaving. I gave them several phone numbers of friends in Narcotics Anonymous. Jessica and Sara rolled their eyes, and turned away as I kissed them good-bye.

The next thing we knew, my bags were loaded and I was sitting in the passenger seat of Betsy, running away to Texas.

Dale kept me moving when we got to Denton. Her place was the first stop, to unload, then the library, her office to use the copy machine, home to grade papers, then finally, we crashed and burned till morning.

Dale had a plan. "How about fixing my Swepston table?" I'm thinking she means tighten up the legs 'cause it's kind of wobbly. So I take a look at this table, and figure out what I need to tighten it up. "After your classes tomorrow, let's head to Wal-Mart and get what we need, some new screws and wood glue." It had to be right; this antique was a gift from her mom and has sentimental worth.

We get to Wal-Mart, and I pick out the hardware I need to stabilize this delicate mahogany heirloom; then Dale heads over to the paint department. Whoa. Looking through this shroud of depression, my thinking wasn't near clear. If Dale had said, "How about refinishing my table?" I would have said, "No way, I can't." Instead, she wisely took me over to the stains and asked me to help pick one out.

Well, that's all it took. Refinishing is one of my passions. I had built and refinished guitars for many years in the past, and the satisfaction gained from restoring the wood is beyond measure.

Not having my refinishing tools, sanders and whatnot, I had to do it all by hand. So the next morning I got up, and was all excited about tackling my project. Dale suggested, "If you just refinish the top, that will be good enough."

I started sanding, and sanding, and sanding. But just refinishing the top wasn't good enough for me. From the oval top, I traveled down each spindled leg to the lower shelf. Dale came and went. Each time she returned, the table was in a new stage of discovery.

By discovery, I'm talking about taking down the layers. The first layer had been water stained, marked and scratched. Once I got beneath the old finish, patterns rich with grain surfaced. Now, that's exciting. Dale marveled at how the elegant design seemed to materialize.

Here's the thing. I could relate to that table. I needed to have the imperfections, the stains, the scratches taken off me for a while. None of the marks are intentional. They just happen and then have to be dealt with.

The next day I did the final sanding and applied the stain. This brought out more of the imperfections, so back to sanding. A phone call came in from Sara's therapist as I was applying the second coat of stain.

"Patty, this is Lucy. I got the message you called; what's going on?"

"Sara's using and suicidal again. I don't know how to deal with it."

Lucy agreed Sara's depression was critical. "It looks like we'll have to search for new alternatives. You call me when you get back to Little Rock, you hear? And Patty, hang in there."

When I got back to my table, the stain had soaked in and covered all the grain. Nothing I could do about it now. Except walk away for a little while and come back tomorrow.

As I drank my first cup of coffee the next morning, I held coarse steel wool in my palm and rubbed the wood. Dale periodically came out to encourage me on. "Patty, I see it emerging again; it's so exquisite." That's all it took to keep me moving forward.

I rubbed in circular motions for many hours, expending strength and energy. Lots of energy and love getting ingrained in that Swepston table.

Finally, the finish coats. The rebuilding of a layer to protect against the elements. To strengthen and enable it to withstand future damage.

I left a few imperfections in the Swepston table. Dale and I agreed; it's important that it not be perfect.

I flew home the following Saturday, sanded, stained, clear-coated, and prepared for what might come next, able to take a stand.

I told Jessica she couldn't live another day in my home unless she stayed clean and sober. She ran at first, threatened to move out, to go her own way. Two weeks ago she started back to NA meetings and has ten days clean again.

Sara's back in the hospital. Her depression is clinical. To stay alive, it looks like she's going to have to be there until long-term residential treatment opens up.

I guess that's the thing. I can refinish a guitar. I can fix a Swepston table. I can even work on myself. But Jessica's and Sara's problems are beyond my fixing.

The first draft of Patty's essay was written several weeks after she had returned from Denton, after her daughters had entered treatment. The final draft emerged some months later. It is a retrospective in which Patty reflects upon and attempts to make sense of events that seem, to those who have never experienced addiction and the violence it brings, incomprehensible. The immediacy that dominates the piece comes from multiple revisions in which Patty moved ever closer to the central images of the events that had sent her away and the relationships that brought her back again, images that were nascent, but unacknowledged in early iterations of the essay.

Stigma

What dominates the writing and generates its most potent healing moments is Patty's response to a powerful and highly organized

set of social processes best described by sociologist Erving Goffman as "stigma":

> When a stranger is presented before us, evidence can arise of
> his possessing an attribute that makes him different from
> others in the category of persons available for him to be, and
> of a less desirable kind—in the extreme, a person who is
> quite thoroughly bad, or dangerous, or weak. He is thus
> reduced in our minds from a whole and usual person to a
> tainted, discounted one. Such an attribute is called a stigma,
> especially when its discrediting effect is very extensive. . . . (3)

Such attributes lead us to make judgments about people on the
basis of perceptions that may or may not connect with what is
true about the person in question. Skin color leads some to fear
certain young males, signs of disability lead others to adopt a
sympathetic expression and to adjust their speech to a higher
volume, unkempt appearances on city streets lead still others to
take on a stony forward stare and to clutch their wallets. This
is learned behavior, and, will we nil we, it is learned early and
thoroughly. While it may look somewhat different, stigma, in
fact, is a highly persuasive, highly organized, virtually unconscious, and socially legitimized form of suture. It is subject posi-
tioning with a vengeance.

In Patty's essay, instances of stigma include the fact that she
and her family are characters in a long-running drama of addiction, violence, and mental illness. Her daughters are depressed,
on drugs, filled with suicidal thoughts. Patty's own history is not
much different:

> My last bottom threw me in Benton Detox for two weeks—
> not exactly the silk-sheet treatment I'd gone through in the past.
> In Benton Detox, most people require restraints the first few
> days, delirium tremens are ugly, grand mal seizures an everyday
> occurrence. My dorm mates were often toothless, homeless
> women who'd REALLY hit bottom.
>
>   I guess it's kind of like in some people's families they share
> the same birth marks and moles. In my family it's substance
> abuse, trauma, and depression—generations worth.

Patty acknowledges the attributes that stigmatize her and her
family and then sets them aside by engaging in perhaps the only

socially authorized discourses in which she can remain viable, the discourses of recovery and therapy, which open a space for her experience and allow her socially and discursively approved means of acknowledging her stigma and of dealing with it: "I'm one of the few who has chosen to suture the wounds and live. This is what encouraged me to sit still as my daughters confronted me in family therapy about their own scars from growing up in a dysfunctional family." But when her daughters undergo treatment only to return to drugs and violence, it is not possible for Patty to simply sit still.[2]

> Early one Sunday morning, I crawled out of bed and found the coffeepot. That, and a Marlboro, consoled me for a few minutes. Then back up the stairs, back under the covers, I thought, "Nope, just can't do it one more day. I can't do *anything* one more day."
> For hours, I'd looked from the razor knife on my desk to the pills on my shelf. Razor. Pills. Razor. Pills. Wondering. Which could I do with finality?

What is at stake here is Patty's response to the stigma she has suffered as a member of an addicted, dysfunctional family and her own inability to function as the mother in her own addicted, dysfunctional family. As a person occupying the sutured position of mother, she is expected, by those around her and, more important, by herself, to perfectly fulfill a set of roles that include those of nurturer, adult, confidant, authority, roles that, under the present circumstances and the circumstances of her own history, simply do not make sense. Because the suture is so powerful, the discourses of recovery and therapy, while they have been helpful, finally fail her, and she is left with only one alternative, to impose an utter and everlasting silence upon the voices that speak a subjectivity into which she cannot enter.

When her friend, Dale enters the scene, Patty discovers an alternative:

> I wanted to end my life, and she was in the way. But, Dale wasn't leaving till I was in a better place. She talked. I cried. I talked. She cried. Finally, I admitted I just wanted to die, or to run far away.

"Aha. That's the solution. Pack your bags and come with me."

"I could actually walk out of here? Just leave?"

"If you don't, they'll be carrying you out of here."

"What about the girls?"

"Life hard, huh?! Those girls are going to do what they want anyway, whether you're here or not."

I threw stuff in suitcases while Dale made some phone calls to let professors know I wouldn't be in for a few days. My daughters were shocked when I told them I was leaving. I gave them several phone numbers of friends in Narcotics Anonymous. Jessica and Sara rolled their eyes, and turned away as I kissed them good-bye.

Leaving, while it seems clearly to be the only viable act, carries with it a set of stigmatizing attributes that are as difficult to accept as the ones Patty faces within her family. To leave means that she fails as a parent, that she cannot control her daughters, that she abandons them to the violence of addiction and the dangers of depression. She doesn't believe she can do it; her daughters are shocked. Nonetheless, because both Dale and the discourses of abandonment and rescue she speaks are powerful and appropriate, Patty is allowed a new, though disturbing, subjectivity—the runaway mother. The suturing here both subordinates and inserts a passive Patty into a new subjectivity, whose consequences will, in stigmatizing terms, wound and rob her of the characteristics that have defined her life. Note the passive voice: "The next thing we knew, my bags were loaded and I was sitting in the passenger seat of Betsy, running away to Texas." Ironically, as the suture stigmatizes, it also allows her the space, the absence she needs to survive the trauma she has experienced and to begin interrogating, revising, and shaping that experience into a history that may adequately anchor the self she will become as she writes her way toward the meaning of her experience over the following weeks and months:

Dale had a plan. "How about fixing my Swepston table?" I'm thinking she means tighten up the legs 'cause it's kind of wobbly. So I take a look at this table, and figure out what I need to tighten it up. "After your classes tomorrow, let's head to Wal-Mart and get what we need, some new screws and wood glue." It had to be right; this antique was a gift from her mom and has sentimental worth.

It is important here to understand that while the "plan" may have been intended to get Patty's mind off her problem, it was only in the retrospective composition and revision of her essay that refinishing the table came to have the significance and the healing power that it finally holds for her. Healing took place not because it was Dale's plan or because the table had power over Patty's health, but because refinishing the table became, in the writing and rewriting of her essay, Patty's contra-contextual metaphor for the process by which one discursive self might work intentionally upon another in order to bring into being a subjectivity imbued with significance and understanding, a subjectivity capable of healing itself by ordering, transforming, and finally overcoming stigma. By communicating her revised and deepened history to others, Patty may help them to rehistoricize their own "mother" and "family" expectations and to achieve an understanding, not of the generic subjectivity "runaway mother," but of this particular, situated mother who ran in order to be and to heal and who returned to be again, not a person occupying the normative subjectivity called "mother," but a real, here-and-now, hard-and-loving mother of *these* children. Only in such particularity of situation is wholeness possible.

I flew home the following Saturday, sanded, stained, clear-coated, and prepared for what might come next, able to take a stand.

I told Jessica she couldn't live another day in my home unless she stayed clean and sober. She ran at first, threatened to move out, to go her own way. Two weeks ago she started back to NA meetings and has ten days clean again.

Sara's back in the hospital. Her depression is clinical. To stay alive, it looks like she's going to have to be there until long-term residential treatment opens up.

I guess that's the thing. I can refinish a guitar. I can fix a Swepston table. I can even work on myself. But Jessica's and Sara's problems are beyond my fixing.

Not long ago, in a recorded conversation Karen, Patty, and I had about their work, Patty described the complex process of writing and revising her essay as well as the significance it held for her. The comments that follow are taken from that conversation. All are in Patty's own words. They need no commentary:

My life was so tumultuous. Both my daughters were addicted to crank and coke, drinking alcohol, coming from an alcoholic family, and I was trying to write an essay called "Good Ole Joe" about my dad, but the pain, watching, because of my daughters being addicted and my own, you know I'm a recovering addict, to write about my dad . . . I mean even talking about it right now is making me, you know . . . back then it was, like, too hard.

Addiction for generations, and sadness because I was in the middle of it. My son was even acting out with crank and everything, and it was real, real scary. So, I went to you [Chuck] and said, "I can't do this, you know, I just have to quit this class. I'll take it again some time." And you gently said, "No, let's write about something that's not so deep. Maybe that's what the class needs, something light." So I was going to write about refinishing the table.

I had no boundaries; my kids had no boundaries. I started the piece with, "This is how fucked up my life is." It didn't matter what I tried to write—I couldn't get anything out; it would all be depressed. You said "Write fluff." Okay, I tried to write fluff and what did I get? Another piece about addiction and depression.

I had turned all my power over at the beginning to my two teenage daughters who were addicted to drugs, and I was allowing that power to shut me down. I'm talking about Sara being in the hospital and what it was like going to visit her there. And I told you probably too much; I talked about my parents' addictions and all that and how I'd lost control, but really what the essay was about was my gaining control over my life. And so that's where I was doing a little readjusting. It started taking form by my [second] draft. By saying where was it exactly I had to let go to take charge, to heal.

In fact, what came out in this second revision is I was just a passenger. I was a passenger in life. Letting things go whatever direction it would happen. I was a passenger in Dale's vehicle even when we got to Texas. I just kind of followed her, da, da, da, whatever she wanted to do, then it was, "Okay, would you fix this table?" "All right."

I was trying to rationalize that it was okay for me to leave these kids.

I thought I was abandoning them when they needed me most. And that was real scary. When I would look at things, you know, uh, from all appearances that's what it would be, but it wasn't.

In writing this essay, I could let go of that shame because I started understanding more through this metaphor of refinishing the table, but it wasn't about shame—it was just about defense, and the defense didn't begin with me, but I had to see it visually, in the essay.

When I started refinishing that table, that was something I knew. It was something I was sure about. Everything else I just didn't. I said, Okay, I'm sure about this, I can do this process, and then the writing connected it with how to deal with [my kids], so I mean there was a lot going on in one small piece.

So, I worked it through, and refinishing the table was so much because I was suicidal. My friend came and caught me that way. I wanted her to get the hell out, you know, and I'm writing all this because that's an intro into doing this table. How did I end up in Texas, when I live in Little Rock, refinishing somebody's table? So, I'm writing all that, and then I start refinishing the table, and—layers. You have to sand down those layers. And then put a new coat on it ultimately. That's when I let go of it. I said, Okay, I can't handle it, and then when I started refinishing the table, then I could take it up. That's where the metaphor came in because in refinishing the table I was refinishing my life.

And so, through this essay, I was able to say [what Karen had said], "OK, there, I said it." Finally named it. What was this about? You know, it was about other people's shame, and perhaps a little bit of my guilt for being a part of it, but now I deserved to be respected because I was clean and sober, and I could sit here and say, "OK, watch the process." I can look back at what I had written, and this is where the healing comes in.

I mean, today, right now, today, three of my kids are in recovery because I was able to let go, I was able to stand back and say, "You're out of here." My walking away from them is what has allowed me to have them in my life today, you know, fully, because my walking away made them do it for themselves. If they were old enough to be snorting crank and getting drunk and doing the things they were doing, then they were old enough to sit there by themselves while I went away and took a breather for a week, and ultimately, I could be there for them by not being there.

I still have furniture in my carport. I've got a workbench. That's what I do to get out of other people's business and just take care of myself. I have to fix things; it's something that comes from being a small kid and growing up in the insanity. I have to fix things; why not wood? Wood's okay 'cause that's something that's appropriate.

The Pages That Heal

Patty and Karen are not unusual among the writers with whom I have worked. When I open the pages of the anthologies I have collected over the past ten years, I hear other voices: the crack junkie who says, "I will not behave like an animal ever again"; the woman who shows me the blisters her feet suffer so she can be "beautiful"; the lonely man who finds his father's finest, purest moment in the reading and understanding of tax records dating back to the fifties; the adopted child who discovers in the writing of her master's thesis that she is not afraid of finding her biological mother but of being a bad mother to her own young daughter; the wife who finds her mother, her daughter, and a world of hope and promise in black-and-white photographs and a wedding dress on the top shelf of her bedroom closet.

These writers complicate the simple binaries that underlie so much discussion of writing at our conferences and in our professional publications—academic/personal, political/solipsistic, self/other, postmodern/romantic. They invite us to look for a more complex interaction of discourse, other, act, society, history, and subject, one in which the self may or may not exist (depending on which side of which theoretical line one comes down on), but in which the *sense of self* plays a vital role. By sense of self, I mean the part that wrestles with the other, the part that feels the pressure of stigma and breaks the sutures by which it is bound to a hard subjectivity it cannot occupy if it is to survive. I mean the part that feels pain, love, joy, and grief, the part that acts, the part that speaks across the pages to bring a future where silence means respect, where people can let go and take up again, where difference is real because wholeness is possible, where personal, academic, and political are inextricably bound, and where we may all rise, phoenix-like, from the language of confusion and come to know who it is that we have become. I have seen it happen.

Notes

1. Such a discourse, in fact, characterizes many of the extreme, almost hysterical responses to assertions that writing might be a source of healing. For examples in the literature and elsewhere, see Jerome Bump's "Teaching Emotional Literacy" and Michelle Payne's "A Strange Unaccountable Something" in this volume.

2. For a good study of socially authorized discourses, see Michael Kleine's examination of the discourse of Alcoholics Anonymous, "The Rhetoric of *I Am an Alcoholic*: Three Perspectives," *Rhetoric Society Quarterly* 17.2 (1987): 151–65.

Works Cited

Carroll, Noel. "Address to the Heathen." *October* 23 (1982): 89–163.

Cassirer, Ernst. *An Essay on Man*. New Haven: Yale UP, 1974.

Derrida, Jacques. "Signature Event Context." Trans. Samuel Weber and Jeffrey Mehlman. *The Rhetorical Tradition: Readings from Classical Times to the Present*. Ed. Patricia Bizzell and Bruce Herzberger. Boston: Bedford/St. Martin's, 1990: 1168–84.

Davis, Robert Leigh. "The Art of the Suture: Richard Selzer and Medical Narrative." *Literature and Medicine* 12 (1993): 178–93.

Goffman, Erving. *Stigma: Notes on the Management of Spoiled Identity*. New York: Touchstone, 1986.

Heath, Stephen. "On Suture." *Questions of Cinema*. Bloomington: Indiana UP, 1981: 76–113.

Kleine, Michael. "The Rhetoric of *I Am an Alcoholic*: Three Perspectives." *Rhetoric Society Quarterly* 17.2 (1987): 151–65.

Lamott, Anne. *Bird by Bird: Some Instructions on Writing and Life*. New York: Anchor/Doubleday, 1995.

Miller, Jacques-Allain. "Suture." *Screen* 18 (1977/78): 234–44.

Oudart, Jean-Pierre. "Cinema and Suture." *Screen* 18 (1977/78): 235–47.

The Really Useful Company, Ltd. "The Moments of Happiness." *Cats: Complete Original Broadway Cast Recording. Act II*. Los Angeles: Geffen Records, 1983. 2 sound discs: 33⅓ rpm.; 12 in.

Silverman, Kaja. "On Suture." *Film Theory and Criticism*. 4th ed. Ed. Gerald Mast, Marshall Cohen, and Leo Braudy. New York: Oxford UP, 1992.

2

Traditions and Extensions

The pedagogical problem in the era of the post-modern is to place emotion, which has been severed from meaning, at the disposal of meaning once again and thereby to produce affective investments in forms of knowledge that will lead to empowerment and emancipation.

Lynn Worsham, *"Emotional and Pedagogic Violence"*

CHAPTER FIVE

Writing as Healing and the Rhetorical Tradition

Sorting Out Plato, Postmodernism, Writing Pedagogy, and Post-Traumatic Stress Disorder

T. R. JOHNSON
University of New Orleans

> *The mind*
> *becomes an*
> *oil-slicked pool*
> *of night time*
> *liquid,*
> *under the oil*
> *dark shapes*
> *struggle and mate,*
> *small still-born*
> *terrors*
> *rise toward the surface.*
>   DONALD RECEVEUR,
>   *"Doper's Dream"*

"Soldiers are dreamers." Thus Tim O'Brien quotes Sigfried Sassoon to open *Going after Cacciato*, his fanciful, even hallucinatory novel of the Vietnam War. Donald Receveur, the Vietnam-era veteran I've quoted above, would surely agree. As O'Brien's novel begins, a bizarre announcement works its way up the chain of command: A soldier has gone AWOL—has, in fact, decided not only to walk away from the combat zone but to walk all the way to Paris. The novel charts the process of chasing Cacciato—on foot, around the world. *The Things They Carried,*

O'Brien's next Vietnam novel, becomes self-reflexive: instead of a dream-like tall tale, it explicitly addresses the dynamic between storytelling and the author's war experience. Just as Cacciato's platoon never captures the missing soldier, O'Brien emphasizes again and again in *The Things They Carried* that no narrative can ever fully capture the truth of combat experience: The horror of war simply exceeds conventional representation. Such memories, Receveur might say, reduce the mind to an "oil-slicked pool / of night time / liquid." Moreover, what motivates the narrative— the purpose it serves—is vastly more complex than mere representational accuracy. Such war stories, fictional creations rooted in actual experiences of war, serve instead a healing purpose.

By distinguishing the goal of recovery from the goal of representation, we connect the healing dimension of composing to what, in schools, is called *creative* writing. This link carries a definite risk: Whether about memories of combat, rape, or child abuse, writing that heals is often writing in which the writer names, describes, and takes control of experiences in which the writer's powers of naming and controlling have been explicitly annihilated. To call this writing "creative" in the traditional sense of the word is to risk undermining or trivializing its extraordinary "real-life," nonfiction relevance, the truth it seeks to generate. If we intend to take the notion of healing seriously, we must problematize the easy line between "creative" writing and writing that purports to be "factual"; we must understand both more complexly. To build such an understanding, we must first sort out a long-standing, pervasive, and rather cumbersome confusion— an epistemological confusion about the self, about truth, and about the teaching, doing, and learning of writing. Only then can we more fully attune our pedagogies to the particular power of language to heal.

As far back as classical Athens, ideas about the healing power of words have been at odds with the dominant assumptions that language must either represent a reality that exists "out there" in the world or "in here" in the mind of the writer. This latter notion—that truth exists "in here" in the mind of the writer—has had a particularly confusing relation with ideas about the healing powers of language. The notion that truth exists "in here" in the mind of the writer allegedly forms the core of expressivist rhetoric, a much criticized rhetoric often associated with writing that serves a healing purpose. Critics of such writing and its rhetoric construe the healing process as one in which the writer manages to "liberate" from deep within the unconscious not just an object of representation, but an ideal self or "true self," to *express* a kind of private Platonic essence, an authentic "soul" that is absolutely unique. Writing as healing becomes an activity of "rugged individualism." Such a view misunderstands both the classical practice of logotherapy and the contemporary expressivist ideas derived from it.

For the early Greeks, language could heal not because it allowed one to discover or liberate an eternal soul or "true self," but because it enabled one to experience one's self as transformative, as an open-ended, socially engaged process that is always available for revision. Unfortunately, these ideas ran counter to the epistemology that emerged with Plato into mainstream Greek thought. They were attacked by Plato and quickly marginalized. Ironically, the contemporary attack on these ideas reverses Plato's line of attack. Instead of marginalizing writing as healing for promoting a view of the self as transformative and open to revision, as Plato did the verbal healing of his time, many today attack ideas about writing as healing for the opposite reason, for what they see as these ideas' Platonic tendencies—that is, for assuming that deep within the writer's unconscious there languishes one's "true self" or eternal soul, a kind of Platonic Ideal that the sufferer must discover and liberate.

Critics who take this line have misread expressivist rhetoric. In the essay that follows, I will argue that the ways expressivists understand the healing powers of language do not necessarily involve Platonic notions of the self. On the contrary, major sources for expressivist thought directly echo the ancient, pre-classical, anti-Platonic theory of the fluid, locally situated self. More specifically, I will show how two major sources for expressivist logotherapy—Jerome Bruner and Carl Rogers—identify the healing powers of language with the discovery of the self as transformative, as socially engaged, as open to revision. Indeed, these ur-expressivists anticipate distinctly postmodern conceptions of the self and of truth—even as they echo pre-classical Greek theory. I will thus conclude that the pre-classical, the expressivist, and the postmodern conceptions of the self and of truth imply directly analogous conceptions of writing as healing.

Such a clarified understanding of the role of writing in recovering from trauma has obvious practical significance. Indeed, for those who seem to have been paralyzed by traumatic experience and cut off from the world, writing serves as a kind of bridge back into an experience of community, a material activity of hope. For O'Brien, the "true war story," one that fulfills its aim, is one in which imagination and revision play a large part, not because one alters events, but because in the act of imagining and revising one reasserts a degree of control over one's *experience* of events. Thus, the process of tracking Cacciato to Paris is far more valuable than catching him—for with each step, the platoon enjoys greater and greater imaginative vitality and moves further and further away from a world the soldiers can only associate with pain and death and what O'Brien elsewhere calls "the kind of boredom that caused stomach disorders" (*Things* 37). As such, the novel partially allegorizes the process of recovery from traumatic experience.

We can prepare ourselves to sort out this recovery process and to discuss the Greeks, the expressivists, and the postmodernists if we specify, first, the nature of traumatic experience. In *Trauma and Recovery,* Judith Herman claims that when a human being is suddenly placed in danger, an integrated system of reactions, encompassing both mind and body, mobilizes. An adrenaline rush sends the nervous system into a state of high alert, and the human organism can become oblivious to hunger, fatigue, and even pain as it prepares for strenuous action, whether in fighting or fleeing. However, as Herman explains, when neither fighting nor fleeing is possible, the experience of abject helplessness fragments the nervous system's preparation for strenuous action. Herman's description is worth quoting at length:

> When neither resistance nor escape is possible, the human system of self-defense becomes overwhelmed and disorganized. Each component of the ordinary response to danger, having lost its utility, tends to persist in an altered and exaggerated state long after the actual danger is over. Traumatic events produce profound and lasting changes in physiological arousal, emotion, cognition, and memory. Moreover, traumatic events

may sever these normally integrated functions from one another. The traumatized person may experience intense emotion but without clear memory of the event, or may remember everything in detail without emotion. She may find herself in a constant state of vigilance and irritability without knowing why. Traumatic symptoms have a tendency to become disconnected from their source and take on a life of their own. (34)

Herman explains further that the traumatic moment becomes encoded in an unintegrated (non-narrative) form of memory, which breaks spontaneously into consciousness, both as flashbacks during waking states and as traumatic nightmares during sleep. That is, instead of being encoded into verbal, linear narratives that are assimilated into an ongoing life story, the traumatic memory takes the form of an *idée fixe*—an assemblage of vivid sensations and images that insistently and spontaneously intrude on the fabric of ordinary consciousness. Indeed, the process of recovery is, in large part, the process of weaving the raw fragments of the traumatic memory into a narrative that can then find a place in the lore—that is, in the larger fabric of narratives— that constitutes the person's life experience and sense of identity (Herman 177).[1]

Classical Logotherapy

In the centuries directly preceding the classical era, the belief in what Pedro Lain Entralgo calls the *primitive* character of disease intensified significantly (39–40). Entralgo writes, "Disease, the punishment for a personal fault, of a collective transgression, or of a crime of one's ancestors, was popularly conceived of as the contamination of the individual 'nature' of the patient by a more or less invisible *miasma* or by a god or demon" (40–41). Disease marked one's moral character, one's *ethos* or personality—and it signified the presence of some other entity, some other *ethos*, a god or demon come to punish the sufferer. As this belief intensified in the years leading to Plato, new categories of disease emerged, and various magical, cathartic, verbal therapies became more and more frequent (Entralgo 40–41). Specifically, healers used verbal charms, prayers, and incantations to drive away the invading, punishing entity and to restore the patient's public identity to one of moral purity (Entralgo xvii).

Thus, the Greeks of this era viewed all disease—not just what we now call post-traumatic stress disorder—as open to the curative powers of language. But it might be more correct to suggest that the Greeks viewed the onset of disease as a form of trauma. In other words, what Entralgo calls the "primitive" character of disease might best be understood as the *traumatic* character of disease. This pre-classical notion of illness as possession by a punishing spirit—perhaps what Receveur, in the poem quoted at the beginning of this essay, refers to as "small still-born terrors"—jibes well with the twentieth-century notion of possession by a traumatic memory or an *idée fixe*. In fact, as Herman points out, part of what makes the treatment of post-traumatic stress disorder so difficult is the stigma that attaches to its victims (7–8). And this, too, corresponds with the pre-classical Greek notion of disease as the presence of a punishing spirit, a visitation solicited by—and marking—some sort of ethical infraction. To be hounded by a demon that can be cathartically cast off by the application of special verbal charms and to re-experience compulsively a memory that can only be subdued when it is woven into the fabric of the linear narratives that constitute one's sense of self, are, in widely varying cultural contexts, two distinct ways of describing roughly analogous processes.

In the fifth century B.C.E., a different, more "scientific" medicine emerged—one that emphasized not words but diet, drugs, and surgery (Entralgo xviii). This new medicine explicitly rejected the old verbal therapy. In fact, it was identified tellingly by Virgil as the "mute art" (Entralgo xviii). In Plato's *Charmides*, however, a Thracian physician charges the newer, "silent" physicians of Greece with an insufficient grasp of the way the ailments of the body can stem from the soul (*psyche*) or from the emotions (Entralgo xviii). This point of view, of course, is not necessarily that of Plato, and elsewhere he regards the medicine of his day as an exemplary intellectual undertaking. Indeed, with Plato's blessing, the "silent art" soon supplanted language-based therapeutic practices (Entralgo 241–42).

But how exactly did language-based treatment develop in pre-classical Greece, and why was it suppressed? To sort out the

cultural shifts and mutations that generated what we have traditionally called the "Golden Age" is far too complex a task for
one work; however, both Eric Havelock and Walter Ong have
suggested that we might well account for these sudden transformations in Greek culture—in particular, the rise of a radically
magical vision of disease and medicine, and then a still more radical switch to a scientific practice—by noting that they were
both immediately preceded by a significant, widespread growth
of *literacy*. As an aid to memory, written language freed the mind
to construct longer and longer trains of thought, out of which
"abstractions" could be forged, new hypothetical vantage points
that yielded new insights, a welter of intellection that would ultimately engender *logic* as a governing or restraining principle
(Ong 130). Oral cultures, without this memory aid, must do
their thinking—and constitute themselves—in easily remembered ways. Such cultures rely on a stock of flexible proverbs
and epithets to "hold" the community's knowledge in the form
of heavily rhymed, highly alliterative, incantatory "songs" (Ong
35). As a literate mode gradually infiltrated the Greek world
and began to co-exist with the oral culture, a magical verbal
medicine emerged. Figures like Gorgias, Antiphon, and others
began to think in analytic or literate ways about the sacred
proverbs, epithets, and rhymes. They appropriated and applied
these words/spirits to create a medicine that effectively served
ailing individuals (Entralgo 53). Under various names—*epode*
or "charm," *thelkterion* or "spell"—the Greeks made increasingly wide use of verbal formulae of explicitly magical character
against the painful event of disease.

A representative healer-Sophist, Antiphon practiced medicine as the art, in particular, of playing upon the tension between
nomos and *physis*. In simplest terms, this is the tension between
discourse and the body. More particularly, *nomos* means law, society, or established convention, a way of being, an ethos, a discursive position or practice. And *physis* refers to the "natural,"
original, spontaneous, material dimension of the human being.
For Antiphon, playing upon this tension between *nomos* and *physis* with words was the essence of all medical practice. Indeed,
Entralgo summarizes Antiphon's doctrine thus: "By means of the
persuasion of the rhetorician, the patient, painfully and helplessly

situated within his own *nomos* and unable to escape from it alone, succeeds in placing himself in another" (101). In other words, illness as the mark of moral impurity and of a punishing invader was a signifier that could be altered by a steady stream of a different sort of signifier—sacred songs and chants. These words/spirits could expunge the other signifier or, by wrapping it in a new verbal context, could alter its meaning, inducing a purifying, cathartic transformation of the sufferer.

To experience the *nomos* in which one lives as capable of such transformation, one must first experience it as flexible and lax. To see a social configuration as lax is to experience a corresponding laxity in one's physical body (Douglas 103). In extreme situations, when one perceives social structures, the *nomoi,* as completely dissolved, one's physical being can become completely dissociated and a euphoric catharsis can follow (Douglas 104). Presumably, Antiphon's rhetorical performance, like that of Gorgias, arranged the sacred chants to enable precisely this hypnotic, transformative, euphoric release.

We can discern a literary version of this ancient practice in one of Donald Receveur's poems about his Vietnam experience.

Eagle in the Land of Oz

i was talking
to a friend
and i noticed
a tin
leg
        hanging on his wall
he said he
got it
        in cambodia
there had been
an air strike
on a
        n. v. a. hospital
it had been on
one
        of the bodies
i thought of the
Tin Man of Oz
        who had no heart
lions and tigers and bears.

Here, the chant or song is one that Receveur probably associates with his childhood: the "lions and tigers and bears—O my!" chant from the *Wizard of Oz*. The movie supplies Receveur, too, with an apt figure for the sort of steely technocrat who would call for an air strike on a hospital: "the Tin Man of Oz / who had no heart." This initially strange shift from the tin leg to the movie suggests perhaps a corresponding shift in perspective on his war experience, a flexibility in his point of view that produces a slightly revised sense of his cultural identity, his *nomos*. That is, by juxtaposing the fearful "lions and tigers and bears" with the heartless American military officials, Receveur suggests that this "tin man" is, like the lions and tigers and bears, a thing to be feared and despised, rather than trusted and obeyed.

Not surprisingly, a practice that enables people to see social structures as lax, even dissolved, will not sit well with those interested in solidifying and extending their authority through these structures. For example, in the dialogue called *Gorgias*, Plato seeks to strip medicine of its subversive, verbal, "magical" dimensions and turn it into a "hard science." In fact, Plato repeatedly uses the central tool of the Sophists—their radical flexibility, their immersion in the changeful particularity of local contexts, and their capacity to render these structures fluid—against them. Medicine and rhetoric are quite different, Plato argues, because "medicine rests on knowledge, [and] rhetoric does not" (qtd. in Deromilly 41). Going further, Plato, according to Deromilly, insists that medicine always seeks to provide that which is good, whereas rhetoric does not. Rhetoric can manipulate, can make the worse cause appear the better, and generally erode one's good sense and one's sense of goodness. It traffics in illusions and takes as its purpose the swaying of opinion. It has no necessary relationship with Truth or Knowledge or Goodness or Well-Being. It has no solid ground to stand upon—and therefore no legitimate claim to our attentions.

Indeed, Plato created a taxonomy of the arts that explicitly opposes rhetoric and medicine. First, Plato distinguished between the arts of the soul and those of the body. The principle art of the soul is political philosophy and the principle arts of the body are gymnastic and medicine. Rhetoric has no place whatsoever until Plato created a further distinction: He delineated a set of spurious or counterfeit arts based on flattery. That is, if the study of medicine allows us to know and to understand "healthy food," its counterfeit—the art of cooking—aims only at creating pleasurable food, which may in fact be quite bad for one's health. The counterfeit of gymnastic, the other legitimate art of the body, is cosmetics and fashion, for these only manipulate mere appearances without necessarily having a beneficial effect on one's actual being (see Deromilly 48–49). Among these spurious arts, we find rhetoric: It is the counterfeit of the principle art of the soul, "political philosophy." Deromilly writes,

> But even there it will have nothing to do with medicine. It deals with the soul, not the body; and it aims at pleasure, not the good. . . . [Rhetoric in this system is] reduced to the level of cooking and adorning one's person—lost, unscientific, dangerous, and low. [Rhetoricians] teach nothing, they aim at nothing good. (48–49)

Plato succeeded in marginalizing the study of rhetoric and all but obliterated inquiry into the therapeutic power of words. While Plato elsewhere opposed the dependency upon written texts for the transmission of information and for argumentation, his position with regard to rhetoric and medicine proved pivotal. Indeed, we can read Plato's "entire epistemology . . . [as] a programmed rejection of the old, *oral*, warm, personally interactive lifeworld" (Ong 80) of preliterate culture. As Ong puts it, "Writing separates the known from the knower and thus sets up the conditions for 'objectivity,' the sense of personal disengagement or distancing" (45–46). In an oral culture, "learning or knowing means achieving close, empathic communal identification with the known . . . 'getting with it'" (Ong 45).

This "getting with it," this "close, empathic communal identification with the known," assumes a certain flexibility in one's identity, for to know something in this way is to transgress the limits of one's previous identity, to change, to adopt/adapt a partially new identity. To borrow the terms of Receveur's "Oz" poem, one can only know in this way if one casts off the *nomos* of the tin man. Indeed, the tin man of Receveur's poem can be read not only as a symbol of heartless inflexibility, but also of the Platonic will to detachment, to unchanging idealism, to the sort of abstract reasoning that devalues both the communal and the rhetorical in favor of objectivity.

Plato, by valorizing what will eventually become the print-centered epistemology of the tin man/technocrat, endangers the possibility of "close, empathic, communal identification." He paves the way for precisely the sort of thought processes that lead to the bombing of hospitals. Consider this not atypical remark from one of Plato's more radical offspring, Descartes:

> When looking from a window and saying I see men who pass in the street, I really do not see them, but infer that what I see is men . . . And yet, what do I see from the window but hats and coats which may cover automatic machines. (qtd. in Levin 506)

Not only is Descartes not "getting with it" here, his remark has the unmistakable ring of acute morbidity, even madness. The kinds of abstraction and "distance" that literacy makes available may cross over into forms of alienation that engender very real pathologies. Indeed, David Michael Levin argues that Descartes marks, historically, the emergence of the profound nihilism that characterizes the modern era, a nihilism which engenders emotional stresses that lead to cardiovascular, neurological, metabolic, gastrointestinal, and nutritional diseases (62–74).

The healer-Sophists who opposed Plato's position constituted, in some ways, an attempt to preserve within the *nomoi* of literate culture certain crucial verbal and symbolic experiences associated with oral culture. These experiences provided then, and may provide even now, an antidote to the more damaging abstract tendencies of a text-centered, literate culture. They constitute an orality-within-literacy, which can balance, temper, and channel the power of writing so that it can become, as we have seen in the poems and novels we have examined, a servant of healing and a techne of wholeness.

Contemporary Expressivist Logotherapy

While it might seem outlandish to suggest that any rhetoric can work as a curative to Levin's list of disease categories in the preceding section, it is not outlandish to seek an alternative to the rhetoric that enables the bombing of hospitals and the reduction of human beings to overcoats, hats, and mechanical devices. This

alternative would value human interaction and empathic identification and might locate those characteristics within the realm
of written discourse as the Sophists located their healing words
within the emerging literacy of classical Greece. Expressivist rhetoric, properly understood and applied, constitutes just such an
alternative.

Although expressivist rhetoric is commonly identified with
Platonic Idealism and the isolated, even solipsized individual
(Berlin 12), James Britton's definition of the language upon which
it is based casts it as the approach to writing that values face-to-
face speech:

> So I want to define expressive language as language close to
> the self; language that is not called upon to go very far from
> the speaker. . . . I believe [expressivism] has a very important
> function. Its function in one sense is *to be with* [Britton's em-
> phasis]. To be with people. To explore the relationship. To ex-
> tend the togetherness of situations. It's the language of all
> ordinary, face-to-face speech. (96–97)

While Britton's first few remarks seem to voice the familiar individualism that so many have derided in expressivism, the latter
sentences suggest a very different expressivism, one that echoes
the orality-within-literacy upon which the old verbal medicine
was based. In particular, Britton's emphasis on "to be with"
echoes what Ong described as the close, empathic communal
identification between knower and known toward which oral
cultures precipitate their members.

Expressivist rhetoric derives in large part from the ego psychologists of the 1950s, Jerome Bruner and Carl Rogers (Berlin
146–47). Many associate Bruner and Rogers with notions about
writing for "self-actualization," and many have attacked them
for encouraging the naive search for one's "true self"—that is, a
self that exists outside of social contexts, an idealized, solipsized
"essence." This radical individualism carries with it a certain resistance to pedagogy. Since everyone is different and the purpose
of writing is to access this unique individuality, surely no one can
teach anyone else how to write; generalized truths about composing do not exist.

However, a close look at the texts of Bruner and Rogers indicates that while a certain bourgeois individualism is present

in their discussion, they ultimately define self-actualization or successful therapy as the discovery of the self-as-a-changeful-process that is always and entirely entwined with a vast multiplicity of other selves. The solipsized, detached "ideal," for Bruner and Rogers, is a source of misery, an ailment that language can heal. And they cast this discovery of the self-as-process/multiplicity in terms of euphoric catharsis. In fact, writing enables the shift from a Platonic notion of the self and of knowledge to a pluralistic, localized, "process"-based sense of self and of knowledge. Although they do not invest words with spirits or conceive illness as a form of punishing, demonic possession, the general structure of their notions of language and healing is directly analogous to that of the classical Sophist. In fact, we'll find in Bruner and Rogers something like a twentieth-century reiteration of Antiphon's thinking, a reiteration that anticipates certain key insights of postmodernism.

Jerome Bruner's "Library of Scripts"

Bruner introduced the language of cognitive psychology to education circles (Berlin 122). As a leading cognitive psychologist, Bruner directed composition research toward the inner processes of the writer's mind—misunderstood by many, unfortunately, as functioning independently of the social contexts in which composing always occurs. Typical of those who maintain this dichotomy, James Berlin, for example, places Bruner firmly on the cognitive side, opposite to the contextual vision of writing:

> [According to Bruner] the emphasis in the classroom should be on individuals coming to terms with the nature of composing—its inherent structure—on their own, without regard for social processes. . . . The individual must arrive at a unique, personal sense of the knowledge of the discipline concerned; only through this private perception is learning and composing possible. (123–24)

Berlin adds, "Bruner was not interested in relating knowledge to society" (123); again, "[for Bruner] students must learn for themselves" (123).

While typically associated with the expressivist-therapeutic pedagogies of the 1960s, considerable evidence suggests that Bruner actually theorized the self as constituted in discourse and as a multiplicity—as having the sort of flexibility upon which Antiphon based his medical practice. In the opening pages of *Toward a Theory of Instruction,* Bruner posits the first feature of intellectual growth as the child's increasing independence from the immediate stimuli of the environment, an increasing capacity to extrapolate and predict, to process and abstract ever larger expanses of information ever more quickly (5). One might interpret this idea as suggesting that intellectual development occurs as increasing "freedom" from social contexts, with the realization of some sort of solipsized, Platonic Ideal of self as the summit of development. However, one might also read Bruner here as describing the child's movement into language and the discourse norms that constitute a culture. In other words, the increasing capacity to extrapolate and predict develops as one acquires the perceptual-discursive habits of one's social surroundings. The processing of ever larger expanses of information in ever more efficient "shorthand," in this reading, constitutes precisely the opposite of solipsism and the emergence of a Platonic Ideal self. Here, the self emerges as socially constructed, as constantly engaged in practices that the child's community makes available.

Even more than in his work on pedagogy, Bruner's work in cognitive science anticipates more explicitly postmodern notions of the self—notions that mirror those of Antiphon. For example, on the nature of the self and its relation to the community, Bruner writes:

> [The community contains] a corpus of images and identities and models that provides the pattern to which growth may aspire. . . . [T]he corpus of myth [provides] a set of possible identities for the individual personality . . . a library of scripts upon which the individual may judge the play of his multiple identities. (36)

Indeed, the "images and identities and models" may be precisely the sort of thing that Antiphon sought to supply in his sacred chants and songs, the sort of thing he thought would help his patients "grow" away from the particular *idée fixe* or outworn *nomos* in which they were trapped.

Bruner's cognitive approach clearly roots itself in the discourse of the community, for he constructs the self in terms of intertextual play and intersubjectivity. For example, in writing about the popular notion of the "identity crisis" and the search for one's "true self," Bruner pointedly declares, "what complicates the search . . . is not the simple fact that identity inheres in action, but rather that action is not single in its purpose" (*Knowing* 44). Not only a lived, active process but a multiplicity of such processes constitute the self. What's more, these processes always unfold in contexts: If, for example, the environment of the developing child offers scant possibility for dialogue or for problem solving, or if it fails to reward these activities, the increased capacity for them will not develop (*Knowing* 29). Thus, the very figure who introduced cognitivist work into our field was himself fully interested in social contexts. Indeed, to link Bruner to some sort of radically autonomous bourgeois subject becomes virtually impossible, especially when one considers these remarks:

> The shape or style of a mind is, in some measure, the outcome of internalizing the functions inherent in the language we use. (*Instruction* 107)

> When we are thinking at the far reach of our capacities, we are engaged with words, even led forward by them. (*Instruction* 104)

The notion that words can lead one forward to new identities is of course the fundamental assumption of Antiphon's medical practice as well as contemporary theories of discourse. James Berlin's classification of Bruner under the expressivist heading in his taxonomy—for thinking of writing in terms of the "sheer joy of discovery . . . a process requiring intuition and the pursuit of hunches" (123)—suggests that we must understand the authorial self in expressivist-therapeutic pedagogies differently than we have in the past. In short, we should recognize Bruner—and the contemporary expressivist rhetoric to which he contributed so much—as a descendant of figures like Antiphon and Gorgias, not Plato and Descartes. And we should view his profound influence on writing pedagogies not as something to eradicate, but something to understand more accurately and to cultivate.

Carl Rogers's "Self-as-Process"

Attacks on Rogers follow the same line as the attacks on Bruner, and he can be defended in much the same way. As Kay Halasek writes, "Theorists and practitioners whose work has been associated with Rogers have been accused . . . of escapism, self-indulgence, and solipsism" (143). Many of Rogers's remarks, if not examined closely and in context, do invite precisely such attacks. For example, in *On Becoming a Person*, Rogers presents a list of what he calls "Significant Learnings" and the very first of these reads: "I have not found it helpful or effective in my relationships with other people to try to maintain a facade." Immediately following this, we read the second one: "I find I am more effective when I can . . . be myself" (17). Many have taken remarks like these as evidence that Rogers encourages an essentialist search for one's "True Self," and that he views the therapeutic quest for self-actualization as ultimately a quest for solipsism.

Wayne Pounds excoriates everyone in rhetoric and composition who has claimed to benefit from Rogers:

> Rogerian strategies try to escape the [social] gravitational field . . . by igniting the booster rocket of an intensified subjectivity, but engineer only a flight into an ahistorical inane. (45)

And later:

> In the absence of any consciousness of social conflict and the constraints of social structure, the individual—the student or the teacher—learns to personalize problems and thus is prepared for the role of the Rogerian client. Essentially, the student learns to blame herself because she accepts the ideology which locates the source of all action and value in the individual self. . . . History [in this view] is only personal history, which exists without any capacity to bring about change in the objective world. Public or social history is impossible. (47)

Similarly, M. C. Tuman, drawing on Henry Giroux, sharply condemns pedagogies that conceive writing in terms of the Rogerian themes of personal growth, inner happiness, and the dignity and autonomy of the self (qtd. in Teich 10). And M. L. Gross summarizes the immensely popular, Rogers-inspired "human growth movement" of the 1960s, in distinctly unflattering terms, as

> blatantly romantic. It insists that each of us has within us the potential for emotional stability and happiness. By calling on humanistic techniques, we not only will grow emotionally but will find our authenticity. If the individual can be self-actualized, he will in a new theological sense, be Saved. (298; qtd. in Teich 10)

"Saved," in this context, very likely means solipsized, for the words "stability" and "authenticity" suggest the arrival at a fixed point of radiant inertia, an ideal stasis. Having arrived at this end point, no interaction with new or other-ly entities need occur— no transformations or movements.

Rogers, however, encouraged precisely the opposite. That is, while Rogers repeatedly affirms the value of discovering one's "True Self," he paradoxically insists on defining this entity as a process, a fluid multiplicity, that constantly encounters and embraces that which is Other. To return to the terms of Antiphon, Rogers develops the patient's ability to cast off outworn, "diseased" *nomoi* and to enter new, more effective ones. Resistance to this process-based self generates neurosis and misery. Its acceptance generates joy. A typical remark from *On Becoming a Person* reads:

> Here is a personal description of what it seems like to accept oneself as a stream of becoming, not a finished product. It means that a person is a fluid process, not a fixed and static entity; a flowing river of change, not a block of solid material, a continually changing constellation of potentialities, not a fixed quantity of traits. (122)

A self in process, a pluralistic "constellation of potentialities," open to change and movement, must have the capacity to entertain and at least temporarily enter into new states of mind, new emotional territories, new identities that, at least at the outset, register as distinctly Other. Such a self cannot be solipsistic. On the contrary, it constantly seeks the experience of the intersubjective. Rogers, like Bruner, sponsors a vision of writing as therapy that descends not from Plato and Descartes, but from Gorgias and Antiphon—for these Sophists, the flexibility of the self and its knowledge is the key to healing, for, as we recall, catharsis means casting off outworn selves and entering into new ones.

With regard to attacks on both Bruner and Rogers, surely one must consider Nathaniel Teich's assertion that the critique of the radically autonomous bourgeois subject does not necessarily demolish cognitive science and the expressivist, therapeutic rhetorics that borrow from it; indeed such a critique must distinguish more carefully between the "ideologically contaminated notions of extreme individualism: the autonomous, aggrandizing, and rationally coherent self of capitalist, commodity society" and the "psychological theories of the self, with their clinical and pedagogical contexts" (12). To elide such differences is to impoverish our understanding.

The Problem of Knowledge in Bruner and Rogers

The second major complaint against expressivist-therapeutic rhetorics is that by privileging a radical individuality, they necessarily assume that no two writers compose in quite the same way. Ultimately, this implies that no one can teach anyone else how to write. Neither Bruner nor Rogers, however, understands the authorial self as a hermetically sealed, mystic source of writing—rather, the self develops and evolves via contact with other selves. Nonetheless, many in composition assert that Bruner and Rogers sponsor an expressivist-therapeutic rhetoric that seeks to mystify the composing process in the name of an anarchic individualism.

This point of view has not helped writing pedagogies derived from psychotherapy to gain much credibility in the academy, for it renders the teacher largely irrelevant.[2] However, a close reading of Bruner and of Rogers shows that while their theories might lend themselves to certain abuses, their epistemologies are quite defensible.

James Berlin claims that "Bruner was not interested in relating knowledge to society" (123) and that "[For Bruner] students must learn for themselves" (123). Plenty of Bruner's remarks suggest that he does sponsor precisely the antipedagogy that Berlin attacks. For example, Bruner asserts that for students to learn they must only inhabit a certain kind of environment, that the formation of such an environment marks the teacher's only responsibility, and, what's more, that this special environment resists technical understanding since "people are not machines."

However, Bruner nowhere describes this environment in terms of the "cozily permissive" or the "emotionally effusive." Instead, he specifically describes it as an environment that makes available certain symbols by which the students can signal to themselves what they have achieved or what they intend to achieve (*Instruction* 5, 28). When students come upon such symbolic means, they undergo sudden intellectual growth spurts in which they "know that they know," and these spurts register as richest pleasure (*Instruction* 27). In other words, "learning" occurs as a flash of inspiration in which the student forges from her surroundings a new means of addressing herself—a new depth, a new dignity. In short, the student accesses a new identity in the "library of scripts" available in her community, a new *nomos*—exactly what Antiphon hoped to provide with his cathartic songs and chants. Bruner further explains that if the environment fails to make such symbols available, disaster can result:

> The evidence from animal studies indicates that virtually irreversible deficits can be produced in mammals by depriving them of opportunities that challenge nascent capacities. In the last few years there have been reports showing the crippling effects of deprived human environments. . . . The principle deficits appear to be linguistic in the broadest sense—the lack of opportunity to share in dialogue, to have occasion for paraphrase, to internalize speech as a vehicle of thought. (*Instruction* 28–29)

These intellectual growth spurts or moments of creative insight occur as an experience of surprise (*Instruction* 18)—a transgression of the orderly categories of expectation by which the student formerly organized her identities and by which a technical understanding of the person-as-machine would occur. As such, it occurs as an encounter with the Other, a flash of inter-subjectivity. Writing, which proceeds as the "sheer joy of discovery," involves continual learning and surprise, and therefore it presumes the subversion of totalized, systematic knowledge. In the broadest sense, Bruner helped composition to understand writing as an ongoing subversion of totalized systems—as a *process* (Berlin 122).

In Bruner's theory, writers who become "inspired" or "self-actualized" have enabled themselves, through writing, to encounter and enter into that which is, as yet, Other or unknown and mysterious. They have, in fact, recovered something of the face-to-face character of oral discourse within the written word, a recovery that at once counters the abstractive tendencies of written discourse and connects them directly with the therapeutic practices of the Sophists. More writing will help to concretize and bring to fuller knowledge the Other, the new *nomos*. Expressivists mystify or problematize the composing process as a first step to encountering, transgressing, and entering into the Other, the unknown,[3] not as a final step in a solipsistic assertion of an essential self.

We need not understand such transgressive encounters as impossible-to-attain absolutes or as the supreme negation of our current existence. On the contrary, transgressive possibilities interweave themselves regularly among the discursive limits that shape us. In "Preface to a Transgression," Foucault writes:

> [T]ransgression is not related to the limit as black to white, the prohibited to the lawful, the outside to the inside, or the open area of a building to its enclosed spaces. Rather, their relationship takes the form of a spiral which no simple infraction can exhaust. . . . Since this [transgression's] existence is both so pure and so complicated . . . it must be liberated from the scandalous or the subversive, that is from anything aroused by negative associations. . . . It is the solar inversion of satanic denial. (35–37)

Neither impossible nor apocalyptic nor even scandalous, avenues of transgression, for Foucault, are built into the "prison-house" of culture every bit as much as the figurative steel bars. That is, the signifiers that constitute the system are always prone to excess—to multiple, even conflicting meanings, and therefore to transgressive potentials. Their solidity depends upon and necessitates a contrasting fluidity or openness. The ruling structures have gaps and absences.

Carl Rogers's commitment to ideas about the self-as-process and about the importance of an openness to transformation, to encountering and entering into Other-ness, led him to embrace nearly forty years ago ideas about knowledge similar to those I've just outlined. Rogers does not reject knowledge altogether, as some critics have asserted; rather, he insists that it must be nondogmatic, nontotalizing, nonfoundational. Knowledge, according to Rogers, must root itself in the limited (though ongoing) contexts of one's experience. One can read Rogers's use of phrases like "self-discovery," "ever-changing complexity," and "experience" as reflecting a radical suspicion of any universalizing gesture that might make possible an easy movement of knowledge, conceived as "product" or commodity, from context to context.[4] Instead, knowledge must remain flexible, local, particular, and pragmatic—that is, it must never pretend to be more than what Stephen North calls "lore," which he defines as the kind of knowledge that "is driven by a pragmatic logic: it is concerned with what has worked, is working, or might work in teaching, doing, or learning writing. . . . [I]ts structure is essentially experiential" (23), precisely the sort of knowledge expressivists seek to build (Burnham 155).

Expressivist Rhetoric and Contemporary Theory

In keeping with the readings of Bruner's and Rogers's writings on education, therapy, and knowledge outlined above and in defense of their descendants, those expressivists rooted in practitioner's knowledge, I claim for lore an intuitive poststructural and postmodern sophistication. That is, I claim for it a compatibility with the contemporary critiques of transcendental signifiers, of ultimate, a-contextual or foundational truths, of metanarratives. Whereas scientific or quasi-scientific research as well as formal dialectical philosophizing seek to pin down rigid dogma that apply across all contexts, expressivists do not seek to escape the local, nor do they pretend to isolate final, determinate truths about composing. On the contrary, immediate contexts are all that concern them, and truth is a matter of function.

Recently, the figures we associate with poststructuralism and/ or the postmodern era have delineated and celebrated precisely such an anti-Platonic epistemology. Derrida, for example, borrows the term *bricolage* from Lévi-Strauss to refer to the construction of discourse from the always only partial and borrowed knowledge to which poststructuralists must restrict themselves. According to Derrida, Lévi-Strauss sought

> to keep his analysis on the side of "primitive" thinking that would seek to interpret [cultural phenomena] on their proper terms, that is to say, by respecting mythological thought and not trying to explain it from a standpoint of enlightened reason. He uses the word *bricolage*—roughly speaking, "the ad hoc assemblage of miscellaneous materials and signifying structures"—to describe how mythologies make sense of the world in a way quite remote from our own more logical and regimented habits of thought. . . . [Levi Strauss felt that his work succeeds as] a species of applied *bricolage;* that it makes good sense at the "mytho-poetic" level and therefore has no need to claim a systematic, "totalizing" power. (Norris 134)

As resistance to the Platonic interest in ideal essences, this position echoes the kind of oralist epistemology identified with Gorgias and Antiphon, the kind that might keep specific, local selves such as O'Brien's soldiers, Receveur's Doper, and students burdened with traumatic memory flexible and thus available to the power of language to resist the totalizing *nomoi,* to promote change, and to bring about healing.

Foucault, too, praises the flexible, piecemeal "method" of knowing that sharply contrasts with the search for transcendent signifiers and absolute origins. In *Language, Counter-Memory, Practice,* he derides the alternative to *bricolage,* what he describes as the Platonic

> attempt to capture the exact essence of things, their purest possibilities, and their carefully protected identities, because this

search assumes the existence of immobile forms that precede the external world of accident and succession. This search is directed to "that which was already there," the image of primordial truth fully adequate to its nature, and it necessitates the removal of every mask to ultimately disclose an original identity. (142)

Such resistance to Platonic epistemology, again, echoes Antiphon and Carl Rogers—an attempt to dissolve the *idée fixe* of so-called eternal truth.

Similarly, Jean François Lyotard differentiates the modern past from the postmodern present by asserting that the former had full confidence in legitimating master narratives (stories about the inherent good of liberating the rational or the working subject, the accumulation of wealth, etc.) through which knowledge could be developed and circulated. In the postmodern era, on the other hand, those foundational or universal myths have largely dissolved and been replaced by radically local assemblages of lore. "Simplifying in the extreme," writes Lyotard,

> I define *postmodern* as incredulity toward metanarratives. . . . To the obsolescence of the metanarrative apparatus of legitimation corresponds, most notably, the crisis of metaphysical philosophy and of the university institution which in the past relied on it. The narrative function loses its functions, its great hero, its great dangers, its great voyages, its great goal. It is being dispersed in clouds of narrative language elements—narrative, but also denotative, prescriptive, descriptive, and so on. Conveyed within each cloud are pragmatic valences specific to its kind. Each of us lives at the intersection of many of these. However, we do not necessarily establish stable language combinations, and the properties of the ones we do establish are not necessarily communicable. (xxiv)

Compare these passages from Rogers' *On Becoming a Person:*

> I find that . . . a [successful] way of learning . . . seems to mean letting my experience carry me on, in a direction which appears to be forward, toward goals that I can only dimly define, as I try to understand at least the current of that experience. The sensation is that of floating with a complex stream of experience, with the fascinating possibility of trying to comprehend its ever-changing complexity. (276)

> Such self-discovered learning, truth that has been personally
> appropriated and assimilated in experience, cannot be directly
> communicated to another. (276)

Given that all of the theorists we have considered accept, in one way or another, the "clouds" or lore that Lyotard describes, given that "local knowledge" is the only kind of knowledge available in the postmodern or poststructural or social constructionist era, and given that local knowledge is in a modified sense "personal" knowledge as described by Rogers and developed by expressivists as lore—given all of this, we can finally understand the process of recovery from post-traumatic stress disorder as a process of moving from a Platonic sense of self into a postmodern experience of the self and of knowledge—or, more pointedly, of self-knowledge. When Herman absorbs the *idée fixe*—which has become the repressive, "eternal truth" of the one who suffers post-traumatic stress disorder—into the many narratives that constitute the self she delineates a form of healing focused on the self after, not before, trauma, the fluid self of many interwoven narratives, not the self of one, unchanging idea. This movement, perhaps in less dramatic forms, is both present in and appropriate to the writing classroom, where knowledge is constituted and reconstituted within the experience of each writer and within the context of a local culture that supports and shapes it.

Conclusion

We can now see that what the Thracian physician in Plato's dialogue lamented was not the silence of the physician, but the adoption of an epistemology that sought to locate healing in a plane of absolute, unchanging truths above and beyond the plane of lived experience. Such an epistemology loses all serious regard for the entirely local, flexible, therapeutic powers of language and for the individual sufferer, subsuming both into a rigid, totalizing master discourse rooted in the abstractive powers of literacy. By designating such a milieu of transcendent truths and, in turn, idealizing the values of "objectivity," "neutrality," and "critical distance" that literacy made possible, Plato and his followers generated an epistemology that explicitly reverses the processes of healing and recovery, as Herman describes it. Instead of dissolving the *idée fixe* by weaving it into an ongoing fabric of narratives that constitute one's ever-changing life experience, they turned the *idée fixe* into timeless, unchanging Ideals or Essences that we can but dimly perceive and that rule over us like punishing demons, marking us as secondary, weak, and hopelessly benighted. One need only check into a modern hospital with its mystifying machinery, abstract terminology, and extreme dehumanization to immediately understand the consequences.

Postmodern points of view, on the other hand, echo themes and concepts of expressivism's sources, Bruner and Rogers—figures who, in turn, echo the ideas of Gorgias and Antiphon. For these practitioners, the process of "self-actualization" or "knowing" or healing is a process of coming to a vision of one's self as flexible, as a changeful process always involved with the larger processes of evolving social contexts. What is left behind is a Platonic notion of the self—the a-social, inflexible, detached self well-figured in Receveur's tin man and in Herman's notion of the *idée fixe*. Perhaps this is what O'Brien and Sassoon mean when they say that "soldiers are dreamers." For in dreams, perhaps, we are free to manipulate symbols of various kinds to bring ourselves to a fresh imaginative vitality, a vitality that renders a sense of ourselves as processes, as changeful. Such a sense loosens us from trauma and its consequences and creates in turn a reason to *hope*. We might thus see writing that heals as writing that seeks to work in the way that dreams do—such writing helps us to recover the strength to awaken to the flux and flow, the multiplicity of the world.

This notion of writing, of course, involves experiential terrain about which scientific medicine, many compositionists, and the university in general have had little to say—areas about which writers have much to say. We need not and should not, however, associate this kind of writing exclusively with the clinic, the couch, with the jungles of Vietnam, or with writers whose books and poems about such places have made them famous. The experiences of a great many of our students have led them to this same sense of writing, despite injunctions against it and despite the fact that they do not come to writing classrooms as patients or as clients to be cured. Consider this poem by Marla Humphress.

Rape

First, rugburn:

Sandpaper passions
Leave raw burns

No reserve of aloe delight
Reduces the scarlet

Shine.
A warning mark, not a
Childish gash:

Ugly patches
Of worn skin like scraps
Of purity
Scrubbed into the ground.

Then, scabs:

Swimming like an ichthed fish
Searching for the cure

Hiding in life's lime-
Stone—Double cross

On my back.

I hold my head

Straight,
Marching gently across

Moments only
To clutch Hope's
Hand.

At first, "no reserve of aloe delight" can get rid of the marks the experience left on her. However, just as the rugburns become scabs, the writer, too, will ultimately change. By the end of the poem, the marks become an extraordinarily complex figure. No longer grimly literal, the "Double cross" on her back has a number of meanings, suggesting a multiplicity of identities—a cross she bears, a stigmatizing mark of victimhood, a reminder of having been double-crossed, of having been a figurative target sighted through the scope of a rifle. The open-endedness of this figure suggests a great deal about the writer's new sense of herself. The cross, already the intersection of two lines, is explicitly cast as double now. She may be marked or scarred as a victim, but the mark is doubled or reversed as she begins to mark herself via poems like these as a survivor. And these new marks occur in terms of the radically local, a process of "Marching gently across moments only." Such a localism suggests a dynamic flexibility, a new resiliency as she cathartically casts off the "tin" dimensions of the self. Indeed, language allows her to do what "no reserve of aloe delight" could ever do: It enables her to clutch "Hope's Hand."

Notes

1. See Marian M. MacCurdy's essay, later in this section, for a more detailed explanation of Herman's work.

2. Consider the title of one of the most popular books by the figure who many see as the leading expressivist, Peter Elbow: *Writing without Teachers*.

3. For example, Barret Mandel published a colorful description of his composing process which he aptly entitled, "The Writer Writing Is Not at Home." In it, he characterized composing as precisely a flight out of the familiar ("home"), a mysterious transgression into the terrain of the Other. Mandel's flight requires the temporary dissolution of the knowing, self-conscious ego, and he would therefore likely describe successful teaching as teaching that allows for and even encourages this "freedom," this space for transformation, this radicalization of "process" metaphors for self, writing, and learning. Mandel and Bruner, then, do not wholly deny the value of knowing something about writing—rather, they value immensely knowing how not to know, for such knowledge allows one to enter the kind of euphoric, cathartic, trance-like state that we described earlier in connection with Douglas: That is, when social structures are perceived as lax or even dissolved, a corresponding laxity can occur in the body of the individual, a laxity that can ultimately occur as euphoria, or what the French feminists have taught us to call *jouissance*.

4. Similar to Rogers, Freire derides what he calls the "banking concept of education," in which teachers deposit solid, unquestionable chunks of truth into the passive, empty minds of the students. He describes this pedagogy as "necrophiliac" to contrast it with the emphasis on lived, experiential contexts.

Works Cited

Bartholomae, David. "Inventing the University." *When a Writer Can't Write: Research on Writer's Block and Other Composing-Process Problems*. Ed. Mike Rose. New York: Guilford, 1986. 134–65.

Berlin, James. *Rhetoric and Reality: Writing Instruction in American Colleges, 1900–1985*. Carbondale: Southern Illinois UP, 1987.

Bernauer, James. "Michel Foucault's Ecstatic Thinking." *The Final Foucault*. Ed. James Bernauer and David Rasmussen. Cambridge: MIT P, 1991. 45–82.

Britton, James. *Prospect and Retrospect: Selected Essays of James Britton*. Ed. Gordon Pradl. Upper Montclair, NJ: Boynton/Cook, 1982.

Bruner, Jerome. *On Knowing: Essays for the Left Hand*. Cambridge: Belknap/Harvard UP, 1962.

———. *Toward a Theory of Instruction*. Cambridge: Belknap/Harvard UP, 1966.

Burnham, Christopher. "Expressive Rhetoric: A Source Study." *Defining the New Rhetorics*. Ed. Theresa Enos and Stuart Brown. Newbury Park, CA: Sage, 1993, 154–70.

Crowley, Sharon. *A Teacher's Introduction to Deconstruction*. Urbana, IL: NCTE, 1980.

Deromilly, Jacqueline. *Magic and Rhetoric in Ancient Greece*. Cambridge: Harvard UP, 1975.

Douglas, Mary. *Natural Symbols: Explorations in Cosmology*. New York: Vintage, 1973.

Elbow, Peter. *Writing without Teachers*. New York: Oxford UP, 1973.

Entralgo, Pedro Lain. *The Therapy of the Work in Classical Antiquity*. Trans. L. J. Rather and John Sharp. New Haven: Yale UP, 1970.

Fishman, Stephen and Lucille McCarthy. "Is Expressivism Dead? Reconsidering its Romantic Roots and Its Relation to Social Constructionism." *College English* 54.6 (1992): 647–61.

Flower, Linda. "Cognition, Context, and Theory Building." *College Composition and Communications* 40.3 (1989): 282–311.

Foucault, Michel. "Nietszche, Genealogy, History." *Language, Counter-Memory, Practice.* Ed. Donald Bouchard. Ithaca: Cornell UP, 1977. 139–64.

——. "Preface to a Transgression." *Language, Counter-Memory, Practice.* Ed. Donald Bouchard. Ithaca: Cornell UP, 1977. 29–52.

Halasek, Kay. "The Fully Functioning Person, The Fully Functioning Writer: Carl Rogers and Expressive Pedagogy." *Rogerian Perspectives: A Collaborative Rhetoric for Oral and Written Communication.* Ed. Nathaniel Teich. Norwood, NJ: Ablex, 1991. 141–58.

Havelock, Eric. *The Literate Revolution in Greece and Its Cultural Consequences.* Princeton: Princeton UP, 1982.

Herman, Judith. *Trauma and Recovery.* New York: Basic, 1992.

Humphress, Marla. "Rape." Unpublished manuscript.

Levin, David M. "Clinical Stories: A Modern Self in the Fury of Being." *Pathologies of the Modern Self: Postmodern Studies on Narcissism, Schizophrenia, and Depression.* New York: New York UP, 1987. 479–538.

Lyotard, Jean François. *The Postmodern Condition: A Report on Knowledge.* Trans. Geoff Bennington and Brian Massumi. Minneapolis: U of Minnesota P, 1989.

Mandel, Barret. "The Writer Writing Is Not at Home." *College Composition and Communication* 31.4 (1980): 371–77.

Norris, Christopher. *Derrida.* Cambridge: Harvard UP, 1987.

North, Stephen. *The Making of Knowledge in Composition: Portrait of an Emerging Field.* Upper Montclair, NJ: Boynton/Cook, 1987.

O'Brien, Tim. *Going after Cacciato.* New York: Delta/Seymour Lawrence, 1978.

——. *The Things They Carried: A Work of Fiction.* Boston: Houghton, 1990.

Ong, Walter. *Orality and Literacy.* New York: Methuen, 1982.

Pounds, Wayne. "The Context of No Context: A Burkean Critique of Rogerian Argument." *Rhetoric Society Quarterly* 17.2 (1987): 45–59.

Receveur, Donald. "Doper's Dream"; "Eagle in the Land of Oz." *Winning Hearts and Minds: War Poems by Vietnam Veterans*. Ed. Larry Rottman, Jan Barry, and Basil Paquet. Coventry: First Casualty Press, 1972. 49, 99.

Rogers, Carl. *On Becoming a Person: A Therapist's View of Therapy*. Boston: Houghton, 1961.

Spear, Karen. "Psychotherapy and Composition: Effective Teaching Beyond Methodology." *College Composition and Communication* 29.4 (1978): 372–74.

Teich, Nathaniel. "Introduction." *Rogerian Perspectives: A Collaborative Rhetoric for Oral and Written Communication*. Ed. Nathaniel Teich. Norwood, NJ: Ablex, 1991.

CHAPTER SIX

A Strange Unaccountable Something

Historicizing Sexual Abuse Essays

MICHELLE PAYNE
Boise State University

Marcia is excited about visiting her uncle. She thinks her mother doesn't want her to go. Sure, Marcia knows her uncle was an alcoholic, but when she had seen him three years before, he had been fine. Marcia is certain he hasn't gone "back to the bottle."

But he has, and though Marcia knows he is drinking, it seems only in moderate form. Marcia doesn't think she will have a problem handling it for a week. However, her visit doesn't even last two days.

Marcia's uncle obviously misses his wife. He constantly tells Marcia how much she looks like her aunt, and how beautiful she is. He offers Marcia his wife's wardrobe, which he has kept. He suggests taking Marcia to her aunt's hairdresser, to have her hair styled in the same fashion as her aunt's. And that evening, he molests her.

STEPHANIE, 1990, COLLEGE SOPHOMORE

This Weepy World of Confession

When Stephanie turned in this third-person account about being molested by her uncle, she was not the only one in the class to do so—two other women handed me drafts whose primary focus was on a family member who had either raped or molested them. That was more than six years ago. I was in my second year as a teaching assistant, and I had created a course whose focus was "Writing about Female Experience." Like the other courses I had taught up to that point, I designed this one as an investigation of the subject, a sustained class project that, through a sequence of assignments, asked students to write about that seemingly nebulous topic, "female experience." Starting from their own experiences and engaging the ideas and experiences of other writers and classmates, each assignment asked them to consider this "subject" from vastly different perspectives and then begin to draw some conclusions about what "female experience" means. The students chose the specific subjects they wanted to explore, like marriage, sexuality, independence/dependence, and then I organized readings and assignments around those interests.

In the years before "PC" was even a term, let alone a weapon used to silence discussion about such issues, the twenty-seven women and one man in the class didn't hesitate to argue with one another, to see class discussion as a way to think through, define, and pursue the implications of their ideas and what all this might mean for their writing. The course was based on a view of language and knowledge as dialectical and social, as contingent, as implicated in the ways we understand ourselves and others, as part of the process of constructing realities. Before the professional debate about "personal writing" heated up (or at least before I was aware of it), I expected and received student writing that situated the personal within larger discourses, that managed a kind of critical dialogue between "self" and "other," and that illustrated how each was implicated in the other.

Thus I have been more than surprised to hear the kinds of assumptions that colleagues often make when talking about students who write about such private and personal matters as being raped: In both private conversations and many professional texts, such essays are used as examples of some of the fundamental blindnesses of "expressivist" pedagogies. In *Fragments of Rationality*, for example, Lester Faigley questions the "selves" that are being privileged in a book such as Coles and Vopat's *What Makes Writing Good*. Faigley points out that, of the student essays represented there, thirty of them are about personal experiences, twenty are autobiographical, and several of the rest have writing about the writer. What seems to make these essays "good," Faigley argues, is the perception that the writer is being "honest," writing in an "authentic voice," and therefore both writer and text possess "integrity." Autobiographical writing, it is implied, is more "truthful" than non-autobiographical writing (120–21). In illustrating this point, Faigley focuses on an essay by Norma Bennett, a young woman who has written about the difficulties of vacationing—separately—with her divorced parents:

> I have a great deal of sympathy for students like Norma Bennett, who must cope with difficult family situations as well as the pressures of college, but why is writing about potentially embarrassing and painful aspects of one's life considered more honest than, say, the efforts of Joseph Williams's student, Greg Shaefer, who tries to figure out what Thucydides was up to in writing about the Peloponnesian War? (121)

Faigley argues that in defining such painful past experiences as more honest and thus conducive to better writing, teachers are privileging a subject position for the student that asks him or her to turn a prior self into an object of analysis. In the process, they are instructing the student in the "desired subject position she will occupy" (129). As Faigley points out, what the teachers in Coles and Vopat's collection do not explore is the institutional context within which students are revealing such personal issues. As many have argued, a different relation of power is created when a teacher receives an essay from a student that is personal and "revealing": Such an essay might set the participants up as confessor and penitent, and the teacher's role becomes one of "certifying" the truth of the student's "confession" (130). In defining effective writing as "truth telling," Faigley argues, writing teachers can imply an ability to distinguish (universal) truth, believing they are empowering students when, arguably, they are exercising institutional power, but more surreptitiously.

This is one of the primary criticisms made by Susan Swartzlander, Diana Pace, and Virginia Lee Stamler in "The Ethics of Requiring Students to Write about Their Personal Lives." In opening their article, in fact, they use sexual abuse narratives as an example of how university professors are violating their students' privacy under the auspices of teaching writing:

> Imagine a university professor asking a student to reveal in class the most intimate details of a childhood trauma like sexual or physical abuse. We would all agree that such behavior would be shockingly unprofessional. And yet, every day in college classrooms and faculty offices across the country, students receive writing assignments requiring inappropriate self-revelation. (B1)

Unfortunately, they say, compositionists only argue about whether personal writing influences how students write academically, ignoring the more important issue, the ethics of personal writing: "When the boundaries between professional and personal are blurred by turning personal revelation into course content, paternalism may thrive in the guise of professional guidance when the professor is male and the student female" (B1). They also question what students are learning about writing in revealing personal traumas, a criticism made most passionately in a recent *College English* "Response" letter. Kathleen Pfeiffer, in taking issue with Carole Deletiner's article, "Crossing Lines," asks, "How does engaging in 'true confessions' help students become better writers or thinkers?" (670):

> Throughout [Ms. Deletiner's] essay, we see powerful influences from the cult of the victim, the ethos of the twelve-step program, the mentality of the chronically dysfunctional. Ms. Deletiner *is*, in the end, teaching her students something in the classes she describes—but it is not good writing skills. It is not effective communication. It is, in fact, just the opposite. What she teaches in this weepy world of confessions and revelations is a fundamentally egocentric sort of self-absorption. Such teeth-gnashing and soul-baring might help a student recover his or her lost inner child, but it will do little in the way of developing a sophisticated communicative ability, analytical skills, or a clear-sighted understanding of the world. The purpose of the university is to look out at the world, to wonder at what we see, to understand its meaning and purpose. None of this can be accomplished when a student is taught only to look inward and cry. (671)

Just as Swartzlander, Pace, and Stamler argue, Pfeiffer clearly believes that essays about traumatic experiences threaten the purposes of the university. She figures "emotional" writing as a "radical destruction of community and communication" (671); it seems, in fact, to be so unrelated to the real work of the academy as to be laughable, worthy of caricature. Such writing is only "valid" (and yet still not valid at all) within the context of popular culture, in twelve-step programs, popular psychological understandings of the inner child, victimization, and dysfunction. It is difficult to read anything other than contempt for this culture in her response, further emphasizing the implicit hierarchy of high and low culture, the academic and the popular, reason and emotion.

When a student writes, then, about an experience the culture defines as intensely personal and emotional, that essay comes to signify a number of things: the problematic power relations inherent in institutions, the potential for that power to be exploited, the nebulous purposes of college writing instruction, and the permeable definitions of the role of a writing teacher. In these discussions of such essays is a struggle over meaning—an anxiety about the consequences of those meanings for students, teachers, academe, and culture. This suggests the extent to which essays about sexual trauma are as much about relations of power and knowledge as they are about their writer's "inner child."

Critics like those cited above often conclude that if a student writes a personally revealing essay in a class, then that class is most likely expressivist—why else would a student choose to write about something so traumatic and private unless she or he has been asked to do so within a pedagogy that values "personal voice," self-reflection, and an uncritical, nonsocial stance toward discourse? As such critics have argued, expressivist pedagogies have affirmed dominant ideologies by emphasizing the discovery of a romantic, humanist self through writing in an "authentic voice," for a teacher whose job it is to affirm these (often) white, privileged, (often) male voices. To make this argument about highly personal writing, however, constructs the personal and the emotional in rather traditional philosophical terms: a personal experience is associated with emotion, an internal, bodily, socially unmediated response to individual experience that is unstable, irrational, easily exploitable by those who have mastered reason. This understanding of emotion does not account for the recent anthropological analyses of the term which argue that emotion is socially constructed, "an idiom for communicating, not even necessarily about feelings but about such diverse matters as social conflict, . . . gender roles, . . . or the nature of the ideal or deviant person" (Lutz and Abu-Lughod 11). Nonetheless, highly personal student writing has become a trope for arguments against expressivist pedagogies. However, in the research I have done focusing on students who write about bodily violence, I have not found this argument to reflect accurately the motives of students who choose to write about these issues, or the motives of the teachers who are often surprised and sometimes confounded when they receive such essays. What I have found in the cases of ten students who wrote about their sexual abuse (defined here as rape, incest, or sexual contact deemed inappropriate by the dominant culture) is that they have written about it *regardless* of the kinds of assignments required in their first-year writing course, regardless of whether the teacher focused on personal or academic essays, or any combination of the two.

Although I cannot draw broad conclusions from my research with only ten students, I can safely argue that their work complicates some of the assumptions often made about painful personal essays and the pedagogies that engender them. Too often it is assumed that someone who has been abused sexually can only write about it as a purely emotional, psychically traumatic experience, a narrative not likely to engage in academic critique, in part, because few if any autobiographical traditions exist for doing so. In addition, a sexually abused "self" has been constructed as too emotionally vulnerable to sustain appropriate relationships with others (like authority figures) or to engage in "intellectual" work that requires a less vulnerable, more "stable" self. A survivor of rape or molestation, the argument goes, needs the stabilizing work of therapy to create a self capable of academic work. The abuse and the abuse survivor here are only knowable through this psychotherapeutic discourse, a "strateg[y] of cultural coping" Kali Tal terms "medicalization" (6). Yet, students and their written texts often disrupt these too simple dichotomies, first by the very act of writing about a private experience in a public genre, and second by doing so with both "rational" and "emotional" rhetorical practices. While some survivors may only feel comfortable writing about their abuse within a class focused on personal essays, they are not necessarily "deterred," as it were, from addressing the issue in a class focused on academic, critical, nonpersonal genres. In fact, several of these students chose to write about their abuse in a researched essay, a genre traditionally considered academic and public. Plus, over half of them structured their texts to move, either implicitly or explicitly, from often hauntingly detailed or powerfully understated narratives of the abuse to analyses of how it has affected their relationships with others and themselves, as well as generalizations about what such abuse suggests to them about families, American culture, gender, and power relations. Clearly, these students are not simply looking inward and crying, but are engaging in sophisticated analyses and critiques of the social and institutional contexts within which they live their lives.

Instead of considering their essays as sites to critique expressivism, I want to ask what it might mean for students to write these essays within a classroom informed by postmodern views of the self and how it is socially and historically constituted. This shift in focus might allow us to step away from the binaries (academic versus personal, university versus outside world, therapy versus analytical performance, talk television versus intellectual discussion) that dominate arguments between so-called expressivists and their critics and enable us to reconsider what many perceive as the greater stakes in the writing we receive: what constitutes knowledge and subjectivity, and who or what controls the dominant power structures that, through language and identity, perpetuate domination and oppression. I'll begin by situating the student essays I have studied within a historical, cultural, and political context, something a pedagogy like Susan Jarratt's would ask a student to do, "lead[ing] students to see how differences emerging from their texts and discussions have more to do with those contexts than they do with an essential and unarguable individuality" (121).[1] I want to borrow terms from Lynn Worsham to distinguish Jarratt's approach from that of other postmodern pedagogies: Arguably Jarratt employs a critical pedagogy, like Paulo Freire, Henry Giroux, and others who emphasize "experience as the medium through which the conditions of domination and subordination are articulated and resisted" (Worsham 138). Postmodern pedagogy, on the other hand, critiques the "authority of experience" and focuses instead on discourse and ideology as the means of domination and resistance (141). In the last section of this essay, as I explore in more detail how students employ various discourses to structure narratives and arguments about the "truths" of sexual abuse, I will briefly consider what it might mean for students to write within a postmodern pedagogy that seeks, in Gregory Jay's terms, to "undo the 'subject of certainty'" (Jay 789–90). I will begin, however, with a brief analysis of how various ways of speaking and writing about sexual abuse have functioned historically in American culture and been shaped by various forces. In doing so, I hope to sketch some of the "prior discourses," the cultural and discursive contexts, that have influenced how anyone might speak about sexual abuse. All discourses have histories—I've been wondering what such a discursive history might be for our students.

"Wanton and Uncivill Carridges"

Dear Miss _____,

. . . You would not realize, I know, how many troubles I have because I try hard to be cheerful and happy. Now my heart is overflowing with grief. I have brought them to Jesus and I know he will make them right for me. I am telling you so that you may understand why I cannot be with you.

I have suffered since childhood my father's abuses. He hates me for what I am. I work for him and obeyed him as much as I can even if they are unjust. . . . [Y]et he says that I am still a slave to him. I am willing to work if he gives me my freedom to do the right thing. . . .

This last month father seemed to like me for he was very kind, but no, it didn't last long. He tried to make me *sin* (emphasis added by MSPCC social worker), I wouldn't do it so he made me promise not to tell anyone, but the week before last mother found out. I told her all. How many tears were shed, I can't say. Father is very angry and hates me worse than ever. He wants revenge and he torments me in every way. . . .

Don't you think this is hard? Cruelty cannot seem to rule me, only love can so I disobeyed him last Sunday.

. . . [He] knocked me about so that my head was in a whirl. . . . He told me he would kill me with a knife, I ansered and told him I would be very glad to have him. I was ready to die, I couldn't bear it any longer. . . .

This excerpt from a letter Grace, a sixteen-year-old Chinese-born American, wrote to her Sunday school teacher in 1920 is an artifact of resistance and escape. Repeatedly raped and beaten by her father, Grace was the oldest of six children in this Chinese family. Her father consistently tried to isolate her by preventing her from attending Sunday school at a Catholic church, but she was able to write to her Catholic Sunday school teacher and begin the process of leaving her family. Her teacher took her to the Massachusetts Society for the Prevention of Cruelty to Children, where her Chinese American social worker tried to persuade her to return home. In spite of her father's threats, Grace left her family and attended a seminary, having begun this escape from physical and sexual violence by writing. Full of euphemism and asserting the authority her religious beliefs grant her to reject paternal authority (Gordon 236–39), this letter is a rhetorical act with profound personal and public consequences. Grace "used Catholicism as a route to modernization, Americanization, and escape from patriarchy" (Gordon 239), and this letter was her vehicle.

We rarely think about letters like this when it is asserted that sexual abuse has been "unspeakable." Yet court documents, child protection agency files, and even a few memoirs from the early part of American's history illustrate that such abuse *has* been spoken about, but as feminists have pointed out, in mythologized ways. These textual documents have been used to establish truths about sexual abuse that often maintain patriarchal systems, but at times they also have been used as the means to escape and resistance. Like the texts of the other women I explore in this chapter, Grace's letter demonstrates the rhetorical and emotional skills needed to construct an identity that would be visible to the authority figures she wanted to reach, as well as an awareness of the competing discourses of truth she could appropriate in representing her experience and arguing for her escape. Her letter is part of the prior discourses that have shaped how survivors of sexual violence can write about their experiences, yet rarely do survivors have access to such texts. Often not viewed as legitimate rhetorical or literary works, letters like Grace's seem to have never been written, contributing to the assumption that only in the twentieth century have women "broken silences."

Current understandings about sexual abuse come from feminist, psychological, and anthropological discourses, in addition to the growing number of autobiographical and fictional narratives of survivors, and each of these discourses is part of the "prior texts" that have shaped how students write about and understand themselves and their experiences of being abused. Although talk about sexual abuse, incest in particular, is not a new phenomenon, *how* that abuse is talked about, how it is understood and operates in American culture, might appear to be new. The feminist movement that emerged in the 1960s and 1970s is often identified as the point at which issues of sexual violence were significantly reinterpreted, analyzed not as "unnatural sexual acts" but as acts of violence supported and created by Western, patriarchal family structures. Women were encouraged to "break the silence" surrounding sexual abuse and thereby begin to disrupt the power structures that maintained the oppression of women. The personal became political, and language was its medium. Since that time, sexual abuse, whether defined as rape, molestation, or incest, seems to have become the topic of everything from the much-reviled TV talk shows to the equally reviled self-help material that lines bookstore shelves, to the focus of what Katie Roiphe argues is the newest and cheapest trope in contemporary American fiction. Autobiographical narratives of sexual abuse, written by the victims themselves, have recently been published, some of them in collections such as *I Never Told Anyone: Writings by Women Survivors of Child Sexual Abuse* (1983) and *Voices in the Night: Women Speaking about Incest* (1982). All of this attests to how well women responded to the call to talk about their lives and their stories, to "speak the unspeakable."

Feminist theorists like Judith Herman not only listened to the victims of sexual abuse, but began to formulate theories and therapies from the "subjugated knowledges" of incest survivors (Bell 174). As they emerged, accounts of survivors and feminist theories of incest not only opened up "discursive space" for the abused, but added terms to the debates about incest and its meaning that problematized the ways it had historically been interpreted. During the eighteenth century, for example, incest was defined as an unnatural sexual act because it was considered sexual activity outside of marriage and not for procreative purposes; twentieth-century feminists now argue that this construction obscures the gendered power structures in the family that make incest possible. *How* sexual abuse is interpreted—not only how family and friends respond, but how "professionals" of all kinds respond—constructs the abuse experience itself. It is thus a constructed category, not simply an act (Bell 179). These interpretations operate to define and discipline sexuality, gender, power relations, and language. When a writer chooses to describe an abusive scene, whether it is fictional or not, she or he steps into, consciously or not, all these contemporary ways of understanding sexual violence, each of which determines what can be said, how, by whom, within what context, and with what evidence. In analyzing the ways of speaking about sexual violence in two historical texts, I hope to propose a way of reading student essays that makes more visible the various discourses students employ. Attending to these discourses invites us to reflect critically on them and on the students' experiences and affects how we read seemingly personal essays and how we understand the terms of important pedagogical and philosophical debates in composition studies.

Some of the earliest accounts of sexual abuse in America date back to the colonial period and are found primarily in court records. These documents functioned to establish a number of "truths" about the alleged incidents to determine if they were "illegal" acts: who the primary actors were, as well as their respective ages, marital status, race, and class status; what physical acts occurred; who witnessed the activities. These accounts are therefore quite detailed, often slowly narrating the acts of sexual violence. Take this description from a case in Middlesex, Massachusetts, in 1660, documenting sexual intercourse between seven-year-old Elizabeth Stow and Thomas Doublet, a Native American, given by a witness, Mary How, who had been caring for the Stow's baby when this occurred:

> Elizabeth Stow says Here comes my man & the Indian says Here is my squa. [While How was getting the baby to sleep] the Indian and Elizabeth went out to the corn field out of her

hearing. He laid her down upon her backe and turned up her coats on her face & then put his finger in at the bottom of her belly and then lying upon her did with some other thing hurt her at the bottom of her belly which made her cry Oh Oh but afterward hee let her goe. . . . She [How] hath often seen & observed wanton & uncivill carridges by the aforesaid Elizabeth Stow and hath told her father who corrected her. She found signes of seed upon the childs wombe & some attempt of breaches in entering her body but not very farr. (Thompson 74)

This "testimony" was not given by Elizabeth Stow; it was not used to "break silence" about child rape, nor to illustrate Elizabeth's victimization. This document was used to establish whether Elizabeth's father had been violated, with Mary How's visual observation and the physical signs of intercourse comprising two crucial pieces of evidence. Elizabeth's version of the event, could she have articulated it at age seven, would have been irrelevant, invalid, by colonial standards. In this description, Elizabeth has no control over how she or the event is reconstructed and interpreted. She is only "visible" through Mary How's rhetorical use of seventeenth-century "truths" about sexual deviance.

In this account, How authorizes her interpretation of what happened within prevailing beliefs about girls' sexuality: In describing Elizabeth's "wanton and uncivill carridges," How casts her in the role of seductress, reflecting the predominant assumption that she is sexually aware at the age of seven and has the qualities of older women—"physically and sexually vulnerable, easily aroused, quick to succumb to flattery" (Ulrich 97). A woman's complicity usually determined whether an act of intercourse was in fact "illegal," and this was largely determined by her connections to males. In cases of rape, court documents from Massachusetts suggest that "single, adult women were often perceived as willing sexual partners": "the death penalty for rape applied only if the woman was married, engaged, or under the age of ten"—if she was, in short, considered the property of another man (D'Emilio and Freedman 31). Elizabeth's subjectivity is thus defined here by her relationship to patriarchal structures.

The result of defining sex as abusive under these conditions meant that the woman was never a "victim." The victim of Doublet's crime, for example, was ultimately not Elizabeth but her father. Because she is believed to be the property of her father, Doublet has violated that property and harmed Mr. Stow. This suggests the extent to which sex crimes were defined as and prosecuted according to gender and power relations. At the same time, these cases were adjudicated along the lines of race and class. The fact that Doublet was Native American made it even more likely he would be convicted and sentenced for this crime. In eighteenth-century Massachusetts, three of the five men actually convicted for having sex with girls under ten were either Native or African American. The same was true of rape cases during this period: Although 86 percent of the men *accused* of rape were white, three out of the five men *executed* were Native or African Americans. The other two were white laborers (D'Emilio and Freedman 31).

During the colonial period, then, written accounts of sexual abuse produced for the courts functioned to establish "truths" about the event that supported racial, class, and gender dominance. They established, in a sense, whether a threat to that dominance existed. In this way, certain sexual acts were defined as criminal. Whether gathered from witnesses or the abused themselves, these written accounts were (and still are) used to establish "truths" about sexuality and power. In contrast to the late eighteenth-century memoir I discuss below, these court documents not only defined the legal issue of abuse and limited the role of women in the courtroom, they effectively repressed the "subjugated knowledges" of the abused. No opportunity existed for a sufferer to do what Abigail Abbot Bailey does—to engage prevailing discourses in a written text, where they can interrogate, interpret, and inform each other and eventually lead to significant social action.

"I endeavored to console my afflicted heart with my pen"

In 1815, when Abigail Abbot Bailey died at the home of her son in Bath, New Hampshire, a manuscript was found among her possessions, a document that detailed her emotional and spiritual struggle to understand and eventually leave her abusive and incestuous husband. Spanning the years between 1788 and 1792, this manuscript was woven from her diary and, at the prompting of friends, was eventually published in 1815, edited by the man who had been Abigail's minister during this period. Twenty-five hundred copies were printed. *The Memoirs of Mrs. Abigail Bailey* is not the tale of an impoverished or marginally literate woman—it is the re-membering of a woman from a propertied and educated family, whose father held various political offices in town and was a founding member of the Congregational Church in Coos, New Hampshire (now Haverhill). Her husband, Asa, was also from a family of means and was a prominent figure in town. Together they had seventeen children. In the course of twenty-six years of marriage, Asa had an affair with one of their hired women, attempted to rape another, and eventually "withdr[ew his affections] from the wife of his youth" and focused them on his sixteen-year-old daughter, Phebe. When he began "courting" his daughter, Abigail was well into her fifteenth pregnancy, carrying twins. In 1792, she writes:

> Had such conduct appeared toward any young woman beside his own young daughter, I should have had no question what he intended: but as it now was, I was loth to indulge the least suspicion of base design. His daily conduct forced a conviction upon my alarmed and tortured mind, that his designs were the most vile. All his tender affections were withdrawn from the wife of his youth, the mother of his children. My room was deserted, and left lonely . . . while this one daughter engrossed all his attention. (Taves 70–71)

Unlike the case of Elizabeth Stow, the written representation of Phebe Bailey's abuse was never admitted to a court of law or used to criminalize the violence or the abuser. Written by an intimate witness, her experience is made visible through her mother's private diaries and revised into a potentially public document. At the same time, this narrative was shaped by institutional figures who had an interest in maintaining particular relations of power. Before being published, the manuscript of *The Memoirs* was surveyed, as it were, by "a minister of the Gospel and . . . another gentleman of public education" (Taves 52) to see whether it should be published. Believing that the public would be "benefitted" by it, these gentlemen agreed and then asked Reverend

Ethan Smith, one of Abigail's ministers, to transcribe and edit the text. As Smith admits, he took the liberty to "abridge some pages,—to shorten some sentences,—and to adopt a better word, where the sense designed would evidently be more perspicuous, and more forcibly expressed" (Taves 52). In addition, Smith says he added nothing to the "wickedness or cruelty" of Asa; in fact, in various (unnamed) places he has omitted some of these descriptions "not from the least apprehension of their incorrectness; but to spare the feelings of the reader" (Taves 52). Although these comments suggest Abigail may have been even more specific and direct about Asa's behavior in the earlier draft, the original manuscript does not exist to examine where Smith "improved upon" Abigail's words. The function of this "Advertisement" at the beginning of the published memoirs is to validate Abigail's truthfulness and authority, reinforcing the "proof" of Abigail's piety and devoutness given in the "Introduction" and supported with long passages from Abigail's diaries.[2] In establishing Abigail's piety, the editor maintains a separation of "normal" and "deviant" sexualities, reinforces an image of women as innocent and vulnerable to "the depravity of fallen man," and establishes the appropriate subjectivity of a Christian woman in relation to her God.

At the same time, the "Advertisement" gives readers frames of reference for understanding the purpose of the book and tells them how they should interpret it, as a morality tale and a story of God's grace and mercy:

> In her memoirs, the intelligent reader will find, strikingly exhibited, the dreadful depravity of fallen man; the abomination of intrigue and deceit; . . . the simplicity of the christian temper; the safety of confiding in God in the darkest scenes; . . . the supports afforded by the christian faith when outward means fail; and the wisdom of God in turning headlong the devices of the crafty. . . . These things . . . are singularly calculated to exhibit the detestable nature and consequences of licentiousness and vice. (52)

Although the narrative suggests more ambivalence than this, Asa is cast in the role of "fallen man" and Abigail in the role of saint, Phebe in the role of innocent victim. Speaking publicly about something so "abominable" as incest was evidently sanctioned by these religious and educated authorities because it was situated within prevailing beliefs about God's grace, the power of prayer to sustain and comfort, the ordering of the world into good and evil. Although Abigail does reinforce these beliefs, her own behaviors cast her as the formidable protector of her family, the one who is able to confront her husband with the consequences of his abuse and demand that he leave. No story of such violence is ever so simple as Smith casts it, and Abigail renders hers with painful complexity.

She begins with her marriage to Asa in 1767 when she was twenty-two. Within three years Asa has an affair with a young woman and Abigail is devastated. She turns to God for comfort, pleads with Asa to "consider the evil of his ways," and decides to preserve his public reputation by keeping quiet. This will be the pattern of her behavior throughout the memoirs, even in the face of his attempted rape of another woman and his temptation to kill Abigail, until she finally learns how "abominable" his relations were with his own daughter. She loves her husband, believes he can reform if he chooses, and wants to help him for the sake of his soul and the sanctity of their family. She believes his many promises to change and lives with him for years, in fact, after he seems "reformed," having become a political leader in the town. She repeatedly forgives him, an act that may seem the only power she has.[3]

Abigail interweaves a number of her diary entries with her reflections on this period, and they show her wavering between subtle anger at God for what has happened—"My prayer seems to be shut out from God as though he regarded not my mourning"—and then overwhelming remorse and complete trust that God has a plan:

> I can do all things through Christ, who strengthenth me. I will not fear, though the earth be removed. God will, in his own time and way, afford me the best kind of relief. . . . Wait patiently, therefore, O my soul, wait I say upon the Lord. (Taves 59)

Echoing the words and cadence of biblical text, Abigail willfully tries to both account for these new "tribulations" in her life and to find the comfort she has lost and needs. The tenets of New

England Congregationalism provide her with a way of coping with the psychic dissonance created by Asa's behavior and her initial expectations of him. As Clifford Geertz says, suffering, within a religious framework, is not about "how to avoid suffering but how to suffer, how to make of physical pain, personal loss, . . . something bearable, supportable" (104). This is in fact what Abigail realizes right before the incest occurs. She has had a dream that Asa wants to move, to sell their farm, and to take two of their sons with him, one of whom never returns, and she dreams this repeatedly, in retrospect seeing these dreams as admonitions from God to prepare her "to endure scenes of most unusual affliction" (Taves 64). Having dreamed almost all the events that come to pass, except for the details of the "strange unaccountable something" that caused them to separate forever (65), Abigail prays to be prepared for these new trials and not attached to "worldly things" (67).

In December of 1788, Mr. B. (as Abigail calls him) announces his plan to take a son and daughter to the Ohio Valley to look for land. Soon he changes his plans to include only his daughter: "He now commenced a new series of conduct in relation to this daughter, whom he selected to go with him, in order (as he pretended) to render himself pleasing and familiar to her; so that she might be willing to go with him, and feel happy . . ." (70). From this point on in the narrative, Abigail repeats how "words fail" to describe what happened, and yet she continues to try to use words to render her feelings, her fear of Asa, and the horror of his behavior. "Must I record such grievousness against the husband of my youth?" (70), she asks. Unthinkable to her before marriage, Asa's conduct is virtually unsayable during it.

The only way to say it is to do more than simply describe the specific events that took place and/or how they made Abigail feel. Just as Mary How tries to account for Elizabeth's sexual abuse by accusing the girl of being wanton, Abigail needs to "account for" Asa's behavior in terms of Christian understandings of evil, her own deservedness, her proof that she did not provoke such behavior and in fact tried to stop it.[4] She eventually casts Asa as an enemy, an evil captor, but not before describing his respectful and often loving attention to her. Because she "felt the tenderest affection for him as [her] head and husband," she agonized over his betrayal, not wanting to believe him capable. She adopts Psalm 55:12–13 to capture how much more wrenching and ambiguous it is to be under "this grievous rod" when the "cruel oppressor" is one's spouse: "It was not an enemy; then I could have borne it. Neither was it he that hated me in days past; for then I would have hid myself from him. But it was the man mine equal, my guide, my friend, my husband!" (these last two terms being substituted for "mine acquaintance") (73). One of the central themes in *The Memoirs* is the confusion and pain created by the seeming conflation of husband/lover/friend with oppressor/deceiver/abuser. Eventually Abigail reconciles these conflicting images and feelings through the framework of biblical text and Congregational interpretations.

As Asa pursues Phebe's affections, he spends more and more time with her, especially while she was spinning, and appears to ignore everyone else: "He seemed to have forgotten his age, his honor, and all decency, as well as all virtue. He would spend his time with this daughter, in telling idle stories, and foolish riddles, and singing songs to her, and sometimes before the small children" (72). Despite her suspicions that her husband was "continually plotting, to ruin this poor young daughter," Abigail "strove with all [her] might to banish it from [her] mind, and to disbelieve the possibility of such a thing" (72). At this time Abigail is pregnant with twins and unable physically to do much, even though she does try to "frustrate those abominable designs" (72). She is overcome with despair and doubts God's presence, unable to "conform" to His will in this, describing her grief as greater than all the grief of those who had lost loved ones (74). Knowing her "nature [would have] sunk under the violence of the shock," Abigail must create a friend and comforter to sustain her. She believes she must bear it all alone, but, through her writing, sees God's grace in the premonitions he gave her in order to prepare her for such sufferings. She is not then abandoned by God but benefitted by His mercy.

Once she submits herself to God and is able to believe that He has prepared her to suffer well, Abigail is able to accept what is happening and then to act on Phebe's behalf. Not yet delivered of her twins, she watches as Asa turns from a pleasant and cajoling wooer into an angry and violent one, whipping Phebe in one instance, "without mercy . . . striking over her head, hands, and back . . . her face and eyes" (76), at other times with a "beach stick, large enough for the driving of a team; and with such sternness and anger sparkling in his eyes, that his visage seemed to resemble an infernal" (75):

> He most cautiously guarded her against having any free conversation with me, or any of the family, at any time; lest she should expose him. (72)
> . . . I clearly saw that Mr. B. entertained the most vile intentions relative to his own daughter. Whatever difficulty attended the obtaining of legal proof, yet no remaining doubt existed in my mind, relative to the existence of his wickedness . . . (75)

While pitying Phebe for what she must be suffering, Abigail admits "a degree of resentment, that she would not, as she ought, expose the wickedness of her father" by agreeing to tell her mother and authorities what had been happening (76). But Abigail is well aware that Asa's "intrigues, insinuations, commands, threats, and parental influence" caused Phebe fear and shame that prevented her from speaking. We see Phebe, through her mother's eyes, trying as best she can to resist her father's advances while not disobeying him, an impossible task at best, and the very quality of the father-daughter relationship that enables incest to occur and to remain in secrecy. Like her mother, she is suspended in the dissonance between her father's socially and religiously defined role and his actual behavior, as well as between her own defined role as an obedient daughter and the religious imperative to resist evil and temptation.

Not until she gives birth to twins and watches one of them die does Abigail find the strength to confront her husband. It is at this point that Abigail, as both sufferer and witness, has arguably moved through what philosopher Alison Jaggar would call a process of critically reflecting on her "outlaw emotions," emotional responses constructed by dominant ideologies as "conventionally unacceptable" and characteristic of subordinate groups (160). Having no one else to share her emotional responses with, Abigail becomes confused and unable to name what she is experiencing; she turns to a text that helps her organize and accept these outlaw emotions, but that also provides a means of acting on them without deviating too much from her defined roles. In the following scene with Asa, Abigail's resolution is bolstered by her firmly held logic. She relies on neither emotion nor reason to the exclusion of the other, but both equally, suggesting the extent to which her spiritual diaries have become sites for engaging her emotions with other persuasive discourses, producing a change in epistemology and action.

Abigail tells Asa what she thinks of his behavior with his daughter (he had long ago stopped sleeping in his wife's room) and when he becomes angry, even though such anger had frightened her in the past, she tells him that "the business [she] had now taken in hand, was of too serious a nature . . . to be dismissed with a few angry words." She is "carried equally above fear, and above temper" (77) and asserts that she will pursue her course with whatever "wisdom and ability God might give [her]" (77). Throughout this discussion she attributes her resolve and the justness of her actions to God's will, authorizing her assertiveness in terms of direct revelation and biblical commandments. She tells him, "I would now soon adopt measures to put a stop to his abominable wickedness and cruelties. . . . And if I did it not, I should be a partaker of his sins, and should aid in bringing down the curse of God upon our family" (77):

> . . . Gladly would I have remained a kind faithful, obedient wife to him, as I had ever been. But I told Mr. B he *knew* he had violated his marriage covenant; and hence had forfeited all legal and just right and authority over me; and I should convince him that I well knew it. . . . (78)

Abigail makes it very clear that she "is not in a passion" (78) but acting on "principle and . . . long and mature consideration" (78). She has confided her deepest fears and anguish to her diary and come to a well-reasoned argument for acting independently and on behalf of her family. When Asa tries to appeal to her trust in God by offering to swear his innocence on the Bible, Abigail is undeterred, seeing clearly that "such an oath could not undo or alter real facts" (78). Asa becomes appropriately scared and repentant after awhile, even though he "denies the charges of incest."

Asa's repentance does not last long, however. Within a month he resumes his relationship with his daughter and conceives a sixteenth child with Abigail. Abigail confronts Asa again, pleads unsuccessfully with Phebe to "become evidence against him" (82), and eventually separates from Asa after finding that "none of my dreadful apprehensions concerning Mr. B's conduct had been too high" (87).

In the end, Asa convinces Abigail to go to New York with him to settle some land for the divorce, and, having deceived her, leaves her there. Abigail makes her way back to New Hampshire by herself, with the aid of people along the way. As soon as she returns in June of 1792, she has Asa arrested as he tries to escape. Abigail chooses an informal settlement in the divorce, apparently to avoid the emotional trauma of a trial for her family, and having sacrificed a large property settlement by avoiding a trial, she has to give her children to homes where they can be cared for. Records suggest that Phebe went to live with an uncle and eventually joined the Shaker community at Enfield, New Hampshire, under an assumed name, Phebe Huntington.[5] By 1792, when it is believed that Abigail began composing her memoirs, members of the community had come to believe that Abigail had been too forgiving in welcoming Asa back several times, and they believed that she should leave town as well (Taves 11). The writing that began as a way to "bear her burdens" thus became a way for her to justify herself for what she had not done sooner. Her private writings were woven into a public document that blurs the too-easy distinctions between private/public, emotion/reason, sentimental/rational. Even in this early narrative, sexual and physical abuse erupt as neither one nor the other of these dichotomies, but all simultaneously, a merger of the intensely private/emotional/sentimental and the intensely public/reasoned/rational.

Although Abigail's memoirs are not written from Phebe's perspective, they are still arguably one of the earliest American narratives of domestic violence, particularly of incest. Abigail's account is startling to read, overflowing with her prayers and supplications, her grief, her anger. Like the colonial court records, *The Memoirs* is a public document and Abigail, as we have seen, calls on various "authorizing discourses" to understand and establish several truths about herself, her daughter, her husband, the act of incest, and God's mercy. In doing so, she adopts the rhetorical form of the captivity narrative as well as the traditions of conversion narratives and spiritual diaries that were a vital part of Puritan life (Taves 10; Kagle 29–30). One of her central struggles is to gather enough valid evidence to prosecute Asa, knowing that her own suspicions, observations, and information from her children are not enough to prove his crimes in the face of his reputation in town. We see Abigail trying to make sense of her husband's rages, deceptions, and repentances within legal discourses of what "incest" means as well as within her Congregational religious beliefs. This writing leads her to assert what power she has to keep her children and herself away from Asa's violence, but it also maintains the power structures imbedded in all the discourses she engages to "liberate" herself and her family.

As many historians and literary critics have argued, it was common during the eighteenth and nineteenth centuries for women to assert a degree of power through Christian ideology, maintaining their roles as "true women" even as they boldly transgressed them. Harriet Jacobs's *Incidents in the Life of a Slave Girl* is a fine example, a text in which, as Houston Baker argues, Harriet is also a victim of sexual violence (fatherhood under slavery connoted rape) (52). Unlike Abigail Abbot Bailey, however, Harriet critiques the power structure that enables such abuse to occur. Like Jacobs and Bailey, the young author of the letter that began this essay, "Grace," is trying to contextualize and argue for the choices she has made to leave her family and abdicate her role as caretaker and surrogate wife to her father. In writing to her caseworker, Grace situates herself within her Christian belief and adopts its arguments to justify her rebellion against her father.

In the twentieth century, Leigh Gilmore argues, Christian ideology has waned as a "self-authorizing discourse" and psychoanalysis has become a prevailing mode of understanding one's "self" and of structuring autobiography (108). Like any discourse, psychoanalysis and psychotherapy create certain truths about sexual violence, the people involved, and their consequent behaviors. As I have discovered, however, neither psychoanalysis nor psychotherapy dominate the ways of speaking about sexual abuse in student essays. While forms of pop psychology do emerge in some texts, the student essays I have studied employ a wide range of discourses, many of them from academic disciplines as well as popular culture. As I will argue later, psychotherapeutic discourses do populate ways of talking about sexual abuse, but, within composition studies, they seem to be the dominant modes teachers and critics use to interpret students and their textual representations, for disciplining what can be said, how, and by whom.

"By Speaking Out We Educate": Student Writing

> *Outlaw emotions stand in a dialectical relation to critical social theory; at least some are necessary to develop a critical perspective on the world, but they also presuppose at least the beginnings of such a perspective.*
> ALISON JAGGAR, *"Love and Knowledge"*

> *The pedagogical problem in the era of the post-modern is to place emotion, which has been severed from meaning, at the disposal of meaning once again and thereby to produce affective investments in forms of knowledge that will lead to empowerment and emancipation.*
> LYNN WORSHAM, *"Emotional and Pedagogic Violence"*

I began this essay by asking what it might mean for a student to contextualize his or her experience of being sexually abused within historical and social frameworks. In considering the court documents from 1660 and Abigail Abbott Bailey's *Memoirs* from 1815, I have explored some of the contexts, ideologies, and relations of power that shaped the ways these texts were written and then used. Because Christianity has lost much of its efficacy as an authorizing discourse in the twentieth century, it seems easy to note the differences between Abigail's interpretation of events and a contemporary reader's interpretation, and it is this jarring contrast that emphasizes the role of discourse in shaping reality and subjectivities. If a student were to read Abigail's text, then, she or he would encounter what the abusive experience has already taught, that reality and one's sense of self are figured by language and power. At the same time, the student would be confronted with the fact that such abuse has occurred for centuries, and that even in this unusual memoir the victim is silenced and almost effaced from the text, her subjugated knowledge part of what motivates her mother to write and to act, but not yet part of the critical dialogue that might intervene in this physical form of oppressive disciplinary power.

However, Abigail's position as both a sufferer of abuse and a witness to that of her daughter renders her both a disciplined subject and a subject with a degree of power to act on and for another. She locates these subjectivities within her Christian belief system, finding in its literacy practices a place to write her way into a discourse that allows her to act. In the process she constructs a self that enables her to suffer and yet still do what she can to protect herself and her children. Such a sense of wholeness, transient though it may be, is an identity that doesn't deny fragmentation and situatedness, but holds this in tension with discourses that construct a unified self free from the touch of culture and history. Although her text does reinforce a number of dominant ideologies about gender, race, religion, and class, it also figures moments of resistance. In reading her narrative, a student can become a witness of another kind, watching a woman find a language for her outlaw emotions that enables her both to reflect critically on them and to act critically in a social way.

Student essays about sexual abuse differ significantly from these historical texts, of course, but both adopt popular discursive traditions that not only structure how students understand their lives and their "selves," but determine whether they will be listened to and by whom. Students use their writing to sort through what has happened to them, to make sense of their suffering within the discourses available, to argue for the choices they have made and hope others will make upon reading their essays. Given all the venues in twentieth-century culture for discussing sexual abuse, some students choose to do so in writing classes, adopting the long and varied traditions of essay writing in the university along with prevailing discourses on sexual abuse, all of which guide what can be said, how, and for what purpose. But they do this, of course, within a college or university setting that carries with it expectations about textual production and the roles of students and teachers that influence how the subject of sexual violence can or should be written about. As I argued earlier, because sexual abuse has been "medicalized" in contemporary culture, constructed as an "illness" that can be "cured" with appropriate therapy, those who have been abused are assumed too emotionally unstable to write about the experience in an academic, dispassionate, and analytical way. It is thus acceptable to write *about* the experience as a phenomenon and the participants as "subjects," but less so to write *from* one's position of being subjected to such violence. I want to consider how students situate themselves in their college essays vis-à-vis these assumptions about the personal and the academic and examine the various cultural discourses they use to structure their texts. As I do so I will look at the ways "emotion" disrupts some of their appropriations of academic discourse.

In the course I was teaching on "Writing about Female Experience," one of my students, Emily,[6] handed in an essay about being abused by her uncle that, I realize now, appears to fulfill writing teachers' fears about this situation: I was the first person she had told about the incident, and the essay narrates the abuse with minimal detail and for the apparent purpose of "getting it out." With this line from her opening paragraph—"I could write about it and Michelle would understand"—she figures me as a potentially nonjudgmental listener who is willing to hear this secret, a move many of the instructors in my study read as the student's desire to have a therapeutic relationship with them.[7] The essay seems to be written only to me, not to a larger audience; in fact, not until the last paragraph of the essay does she move to shape the essay toward a purpose a writing teacher might expect. Yet it is important that she even makes this move (speculating on how society might deal with the consequences of this abuse for her and other victims) because it suggests her awareness that this draft must bear a likeness to "college writing," in this case an essay that poses a problem, analyzes it, and then offers solutions.

Even in an essay that seems to be a confession and evokes a therapeutic relationship, then, the student still tries to shape the draft for an ill-defined general audience, not just for me, the teacher, and expresses a concern for the social ramifications of this behavior. Her understanding of the discourse of "college essay writing" permeates this seemingly egocentric text. The structure of her paragraphs suggests that Emily is aware that an essay makes claims and then offers evidence. In the second paragraph, for example, the essay gives a one-sentence summary of the abuse—an assertion, "I was sexually abused by my stepuncle when I was four years old and again when I was eight"— and then offers support that provides context explaining why she ended up in such close proximity to this uncle and why she trusted him. The following paragraphs elaborate on the statements of the previous one, as well as on the responses of the adults she told at the time. In fact, the final paragraph of her essay speculates on possible solutions to the problems she now recognizes she has as a result of this experience, an explicit move toward a purpose that turns the personal, narrative details into support for a socially directed claim. While the general tenor of the essay is relatively dispassionate (again suggesting her sense of appropriate tone in a college essay), this tone is disrupted when she expresses anger at her brother for not believing her: "When he should have been big brotherly and beat the crap out of that skuzball he deserted me. My own flesh and blood turned his back on me and believed that disgusting waste of a human being. For that I don't think I will ever forgive him." This anger only seeps out again in a phrase or two later in the essay, and like the emotional descriptions in other students' essays, it seems to beg for a purpose in the text that hasn't yet been found.

This anger as well as her guilt for "los[ing her] virginity at fifteen" and feeling "like the biggest slut alive" are arguably the kind of "outlaw emotions" Jaggar describes, and they are more unconventional/unacceptable responses within the academic institution than within popular culture itself. As Emily says, she can watch "Oprah" and begin to feel connected to a larger group of people who feel these same emotions, but they strike a dissonant chord in this written text, and for many readers may overshadow the essay's move toward a problem-solving, socially oriented purpose. Emily, some may argue, is not in control of her emotions in this text, and this not only makes some writing teachers uncomfortable, it suggests she may not be able to fulfill the expectations of the course. Writers need to control their texts, particularly their emotions and personal investments. But who here is concerned about controlling Emily's emotions? I would argue that the issue is not that Emily cannot control her emotions, but that we as teachers cannot control them. In this sense, as Lutz would contend, Emily's text—the emotions it expresses—challenges the power differences of the student-teacher relationship.

Faigley and others would argue that Emily's essay celebrates a unique individuality and echoes a Western confessional tradition in which emotion leads to an "inner truth" about the self. By extension, the emotions expressed are perceived as part of the process of introspection. However, this argument assumes emotions are internal, biological responses, "least subject to control, least constructed or learned (hence most universal), least public, and therefore least amenable to socio-cultural analysis" (Lutz and Abu-Lughod 1). Yet the political struggle in composition studies over who gets to express what emotions in what contexts (if at all) suggests that emotions—discourses *on* or *about* emotions as well as discourses *from* them—are about power, discipline, and knowledge. So too, arguably, are the acts of sexual violation that these students are writing about. When interpreted as socially constructed, emotions become always already social, political, and subject to critique. If, as Lutz and others argue, "emotion discourses may be one of the most likely and powerful devices by which domination proceeds" (76), then it is imperative that we begin to read student texts like Emily's as a struggle over identity, discourse, and power, as well as a desire for what Jaggar calls a "critical social theory" (160): "Critical reflection on emotion is not a self-indulgent substitute for political analysis and political action. It is itself a kind of political theory and political practice, indispensable for an adequate social theory and social transformation" (164). Instead of seeing students like Emily as incapable of critical reflection because of their traumatic experiences, I propose that we respect their move to bring that experience into a public and disciplinary context and find ways to encourage the critical reflection already evidenced in their texts.

A recurring theme in the student essays I received for my study is the process of sorting through conflicting notions of "truth," a perspective on language and ideology that informs many critical and postmodern pedagogies. Students often merge the voices of others who disbelieve them, or believe them but don't act to protect the child, who seek to overlay family tales of deception and abuse with dominant constructions of the "normal" family. Who gets to decide what happened and why? Who decides whether an individual has "in fact" been abused, and on what terms? To begin to answer these questions, these student essays engage the authoritative discourses of various disciplines, from sociology, history, and the law, to feminist and various psychological theories. In doing so they not only begin to work toward some of the features valued in academic writing, but they begin to argue for a particular way of defining their experience and themselves.

Fanny, a nontraditional student and mother of high-school-age children, centers her essay around this permeable line between truth and lies. She chose to write about her abuse within the context of her family, and, like Emily, never steps into the academic research about her subject nor ventures to comment on the social conditions that may have allowed the abuse to occur. Written in a course explicitly focused on the tradition of the personal essay, Fanny's paper engages psychotherapeutic and feminist discourses as she structures her essay around themes of revision and the handing down of traditions and stories.

"My family is charming," she begins. "Through generations on both sides of my parents' family, the apocryphal tales and myths are all about dapper, witty men, and women who were warm, talented mothers. I collected these people and the stories about them with zeal; they gave me an identity, a persona, a tradition." What becomes clear is that this charm is a facade, a deception that enabled generations of women to be abused and to be oblivious when their own daughters were being abused: "Now, I am looking at all those charming people with new eyes. Now, I know I am part of a long line of abused women, and that I, too, was both abused and was unable to see when my daughter was, in turn, abused." Arguing and illustrating that revision leads to new knowledge, Fanny carefully chooses details to reveal both the charm and the violence of her male ancestors. Her grandfather, who had a mistress and was quite rich, was a Christian Scientist who refused his wife treatment for stomach cancer:

"I can hear my mother's voice as she told me this part—her father held her mother on the kitchen table, with my mother and uncle present as young children, while she died in extreme pain, screaming and weeping in front of her children. My charming grandfather did that."

The sarcasm in this last line becomes more explicit anger on the next two pages when she describes her father and her belief that he molested her. Again balancing details that describe a sinister and yet compelling charm, Fanny's apparent command over the artistic shaping of the essay gives way to language that seems inconsistent with the rest of the paper:

> I was the oldest, and the first to experience both his charm and his filth. He was rotten to the core; in fact, I don't think he had a core in the sense of having a character, some sort of moral sense. He stole my brothers' caddying money from their dressers, he lied and lied and lied. But, by god, he was charming . . . he fooled a lot of people. He even fooled us children into loving him.

This anger and sense of betrayal leads into a discussion about her mother, a woman who seemed loving and giving as well, but who "also coldly rejected my sister and me at times when we needed her most." After she describes the process of reconstructing the past with her siblings and discovering that her daughter had been sexually abused, Fanny focuses on the point she has been leading to, that she cannot simply stop with re-seeing her own family. She must also ask how her own behavior has been shaped by that. This self-reflection means she has to accept her own role in "not being there" for her daughter, in recreating the same neglect and "intolerance of fuzzy thinking and sloppy behavior." In the language of current discourse on sexual abuse, she no longer views herself as a victim, but as both a survivor and a participant in the abuse of another.

The purpose of this essay seems to be to describe her process of revision, arguing that when "I rebuild the past, I am beginning a process of inventing or maybe transforming my future." Fanny very clearly borrows from her therapist's discourse about family relations, physical, sexual, and verbal abuse: remembering one's past with one's family as a way of healing past wounds, accepting both the pain and the love of one's parents, understanding that when a survivor becomes a parent, she will need "to hold herself to such a high standard and to control both herself and her children in order to save us all from the abuse she [has] experienced." The very assumption implicit in her last line is consistent with most therapeutic approaches: "No amount of revision is going to influence that future if I cannot summon the courage to look behind that curtain."

Fanny's essay constructs a view of the family in which no one person is to blame for abusing the intimacies of familial relations, a view of the family consistent with family systems theory. As many feminists have argued, such a view posits a "dysfunctional" family against a "normal" one, reinscribing the unequal exercise of power that occurs in family structures (Bell 87). Yet much of the physical space of Fanny's essay is devoted to discussing her male relatives as abusive toward women, men who had economic and familial power that allowed them to sexually and physically exploit women in and outside the home. She calls her paternal grandfather's family a "charming patriarchy," evoking a set of feminist arguments about gender and violence that seem to stand in for a pre-existing set of social critiques. Given the popular currency of family systems therapy and some feminist arguments about sexual violence, it may be that Fanny is assuming her audience will bring this knowledge to her text. Nonetheless, there is an opportunity here to encourage her to reflect on the differences between these two discourses and to explore further what that might mean for her process of revision and reshaping her identity. Fanny is employing these discourses, as well as the expectations of personal essays discussed in her course, to reshape the "truths" handed down to her about her family and abuse. At the same time, she is establishing a few truths about these things herself, using the framework of these discourses to structure an argument, to give a context for naming and expressing emotions, and to illustrate the consequent changes to her understanding of her affective relationship and responsibility to others.

While Fanny may seem to be constructing a unified, individualized, humanist self through this writing, arriving at an "inner truth," I would argue that she is engaged in the very processes valued and encouraged by most epistemic approaches to composition. The controlling metaphor of the essay is revision, and its substance is the reconstructing of dominant familial epistemologies. She is using her own traumatic experiences and the authoritative, dominant discourses that define ways of speaking about families and abuse to critique those epistemologies, situating herself within a sociopolitical dialectic. The fact that she does not extend this critique to ideology and power is not a consequence of her analytic approach or her self-absorbed introspection. It is a place for teachers to begin talking about what such a critique might look like and what its consequences might be. Within a course informed by critical pedagogy, for example, a teacher might ask Fanny to further contextualize this experience historically. Within a postmodern pedagogy the teacher might point out the various discourses within which Fanny situates herself, asking her to pursue some of the conflicts between them and to consider what other discourses she might have chosen.

When the students in my study did draft essays that integrated academic research on sexual abuse, they too often used the arguments and purposes constructed in this material to shape their own, and they rarely questioned or critiqued what they were reading. This seems as well to be more a case of how the instructor might have guided or prompted them than of any inability to critically analyze an emotional and potentially destabilizing experience. A case in point is a rather extraordinary research essay written by a college freshman, Nicole. In it she weaves scenes and reflections on the memories she has of her uncle fondling her over a seven-year period with a broad range of outside texts and interviews, from the popular *The Courage to Heal* to psychological and sociological journal articles, to a government document and an interview with a perpetrator.

Nicole begins her essay in a rather unusual way for a research paper. Instead of opening with a general definition of sexual abuse or a statement about how horrible a crime it is, she describes a scene of the general sequence of events that usually occurred when "it" happened, when her uncle decided he "wanted some company." She speaks euphemistically about the abuse until the last third of the paragraph, when she describes his behavior as "fondling." [8] She sets up a scene with all the features now associated with sexual abuse: A young girl is alone with an older male, usually a relative she trusts, he entices her, abuses her, then threatens her if she tells anyone, calling her a "bad, dirty girl." From this introductory scene she then asserts that her "story is not uncommon," using this as a segue into the statistics of boys and girls who are abused by the time they are eighteen. Throughout her essay, Nicole uses either her own experience as an opening for a researched claim or uses the research to frame her own experience. Her specific details, opinions, and reflections primarily support and illustrate the research; rarely are they used to question or critique what she has read.

Nicole is explicit in the essay that her purpose in writing is to educate: "In order for this abuse to end our society needs to wake up. We have to work together, family, schools, and the legal system to stop this heinous abuse against children." In the final paragraph of the text she reiterates this sentiment and adds, "By speaking out we educate. As Ellen Bass [co-author of *The Courage to Heal*] stated: 'In truth itself, there is healing.'" This essay is not a conscious attempt to use writing to work through unresolved feelings, to ask for help from her readers, or to document in painful detail the emotional impact of the abuse. She presents the "truth" of her abuse as an event of the past, one that does affect her in the present, but one that does not interfere with her abilities as a research writer. Like the academic and psychologically based texts she has read, Nicole tells this "truth" about sexual abuse by addressing the who-what-where-when-and-how questions: why sexual abuse is underreported, what often happens if a child does tell someone, what the emotional effects are for the survivor, why some men molest children, what elements of popular culture contribute to this molestation, and what is being done legally to prosecute offenders. Given the sociological and legal rhetoric she assumes to educate her readers, Nicole really has no reason to mention her own experience at all—the research she quotes carries its own authority and offers "examples" that could illustrate her points.

Nicole integrates her personal experience in large part because her instructor introduces the research paper by having students write a personal essay, then an "argumentative" essay on the same subject without using research. After they draft an essay from the research they have done, she then asks them to combine all three drafts, resulting in a research paper that constructs an argument using personal experience and outside research. Thus Nicole's choices are prompted by the specific assignment,[9] and she rather skillfully composes a multiple-voiced, transactional piece of writing. What is striking about her use of experiential details, however, is the way they guide the shape of the essay and equally share actual "space" on the page.

After opening with a generalized scene of how her uncle usually touched her, Nicole moves from general statistics and her desire for change to a specific moment when her uncle is caught. A friend has come over to play and Uncle Karl grabs her, evidently attempting to fondle her, as well. Nicole's friend screams and brings "Grammie" into the room, arousing hope in Nicole that "Karl would stop touching me forever and Grammie would kick him out for being a bad man." When Grammie accepts Karl's pledge to never do it again, she tells Nicole not to tell anyone. This introduces the essay's next section, which is focused on why people do not report sexual abuse.

As in the previous student essays I've discussed, the issue of betrayal is a dominant theme in Nicole's essay, suggesting how much of an issue it is to determine a degree of "truth" about where to place responsibility. It is here that she expresses indirect anger at her grandmother for not taking the incident seriously enough. She describes a day that she overheard a conversation in a restaurant that "reminded me of what happened with my grandmother." In the lines that follow, notice the shifts in tone and discourse:

> The lady said: "I thought they were abusing their kids, but I wasn't sure so I didn't report it." I wanted to scream at her. It is much better to be overly cautious than to have an innocent child hurt. According to Gail Wyatt and Gloria Powell, in 1984 200,000 child sexual abuse cases were unreported in nineteen states. . . .

The juxtaposition here of several discourses is fairly clear. Nicole moves among her experience—as a sequence of events—her emotional responses to those experiences, and the ways in which the research echoes both the events and her responses. Her text is an extended example, I would argue, of a woman situating her outlaw emotions in relation to those of others, albeit conveyed through the voices of researchers, and then beginning the process of critically reflecting on those emotions, a process that opens the way to a critical social practice.

What is also significant about this section of Nicole's essay is the way she asserts her authority as a writer and researcher. Not only does she fairly equally interweave her experience and responses with outside research, she also comments on that research, positing herself as both the subject of this essay and a subject in control of it:

> These figures don't even take into account the countless children who, *like I did*, remain silent about their abuse. According to Elizabeth Stanko only about six percent of women sexually abused as children ever tell the authorities and one out of five had never told anyone (25). *To me,* this shows how prevalent sexual abuse is in our society and how hard it is for children and adult survivors to tell their experiences. . . . [emphasis added]

For the rest of this section, Nicole discusses the various reasons why children don't tell adults about their abuse, citing a campus sexual harassment and rape advocate as well as a 1952 study that argued sexual abuse had no lasting negative effects on children.

This study effectively opens up her next section, an examination of the effects of sexual abuse on children, and she returns to her grandmother's betrayal. She links this kind of silence to the conclusion many survivors draw that they are in fact the ones to blame for the abuse. She then describes in euphemistic detail the way Karl would approach her, and on this particular day, the way he forced her to perform fellatio.

> It made me feel so disgusting. I still don't remember everything that I felt that day, but I do remember running to the bathroom after and gagging. I brushed my teeth repeatedly as if that would change what he'd made me do. It was that day that I promised myself never to tell anyone because everyone would think that I was a dirty, terrible girl.

The scene Nicole describes here is one in which she has been socialized to name her emotional responses in a particular way, but in composing her researched essay, she is confronted with the arbitrariness of those names and freed to begin to address the issues of power that have mapped guilt and shame onto her body. Readers may wonder why Nicole feels the need to narrate this scene rather than simply telling them that she feels guilty and shameful. The words "guilt" and "shame" should carry her meaning here, one might argue, and she should avoid letting us peer into her vulnerabilities. Yet "guilt" and "shame" do not carry the emotional and imaginative impact of the scene, nor do they demand that the reader directly confront what it meant for this young girl to be forced to engage in oral sex. In fact, they serve to distance her from the reality of what she has experienced. If she has made readers uncomfortable, then she has affected the sites where dominant ideologies have conditioned "bodies" to respond to "distasteful" behaviors. Such an emotional response on the reader's part may feel "natural," but that naturalness obscures "the ways culture is present in the writer's very act of experiencing the composing process and in the reader's responses to the writer's texts" (Miller 272–73). By describing the scene, Nicole invites readers to confront their "natural" responses to her text, opening the way to an important process of critical reflection for them.

Nicole does not hesitate over this scene as I have, however, but instead moves into her own, equally "natural" self-doubting questions ("I wonder if I couldn't have done anything to stop Karl") and the explanations for that self-doubt given by the authors of the popular *The Courage to Heal*. She asserts that the child is never to blame, reiterating one of the dominant assumptions that operate in current theories about sexual abuse. Throughout the rest of the essay she calls on interviews, academic journal articles, incidents reported in the press, and specific laws being considered in other states to both create and advance her arguments. The essay is primarily informative, seeking to establish various assertions about sexual abuse with which the audience may be unfamiliar, but which people need to know if they are going to be motivated to change the conditions that produce such abuse.

As in other student essays I have read, Nicole chooses from a seemingly limited number of rhetorical purposes in writing her polyvocal essay: to render her experience and its significance in an essay form, to argue for social change through education and legal reform, and to criticize the media for its role in sexualizing children. These purposes are dictated by the discourses she and other student writers appropriate, just as Abigail Abbot Bailey's purposes were structured by the available narrative frames of the captivity narrative, spiritual diaries, and Congregationalist Christian doctrine. By engaging these discourses, writers—Abigail, other historical figures, and my students alike—restructure the meanings of their experiences, their identities, and the possibilities of socially oriented change. Seeing that this is so allows us to see ways in which discourse and discursive interplay have and continue to mediate and to bring about the dual possibilities of hurt and of healing on both personal and social levels. And as many students have said to me, they want as much to "heal"on a social level as on an individual one. This is not a healing that creates a unified, self-authorizing whole, but one that is continually in the process of accepting fragmentation, otherness, difference.

Undoing the Subject of Certainty

If the work of the student essays I've analyzed above can be considered a form of healing, however, it is one that occurs within a dialectical process, not only among the many discourses they employ, but between the teacher and student. While it may seem that I have begged the question of how teachers might respond to student essays about bodily violence, I have in fact been trying to rephrase the question: Our concerns about response, while important, still focus on teachers, not on students and what they may be doing in their texts. Instead, I have been asking what these students' texts might have to say about composition pedagogies and the assumptions that inform them. In analyzing the various discourses students adopt to situate their experiences and arguments about sexual abuse, I have illustrated some of the ways in which these texts are not simply representations of a stable identity or inner truth. Contrary to what critics like Faigley, Swartzlander, Pace and Stamler, and Pfeiffer contend, these essays blur the distinctions between emotion and reason, private and public, expressivist and social constructionist perspectives.

By analyzing historical texts produced as the result of sexual abuse, I have also been arguing that, as Jarratt and others posit, historically situating one's experience is part of the process of learning that one's identity is socially and politically constituted, and thus that language mediates one's experience of "reality." These students seem, in fact, arguably predisposed to developing a critical social theory: As Jaggar implies, their outlaw emotions are necessary for developing this critical perspective, and this is often apparent in the ways these outlaw emotions motivate their writing and their arguments.

Rather than focusing on the ways such essays reinforce romantic, humanist subjectivities and evince failures of expressivist pedagogies, we might better respond by considering the ways students choose to represent these experiences and their identities. Historicizing these essays is only one way to respond, but it presupposes that a teacher recognizes the discourses that inform his or her responses to sexual abuse, and that the teacher takes seriously the student's desire to write publicly about his or her abuse. Not to read a student essay is to read it in very specific ways.

If the trauma of sexual abuse is understood as the result of being "subjected to an experience for which [they have] not been socialized" (Davenport 79), then the survivors of that abuse have experienced a discursive trauma: Sexual violence disrupts one's confidence in a stable, knowable reality. Signifiers and signified constantly shift. Thus, reality and one's sense of identity are deconstructive texts. In this sense, then, the students in writing classes who have been sexually abused are always already postmodern subjects, always already decentered, their identities constructed from the violence of this trauma.

If postmodern pedagogies aim for a similar type of decentering—"unsettl[ing] the complacency and conceptual identities of the student" as Gregory Jay argues (790)—then what are the differences between these intended results and the results of sexual abuse? Are both processes of fragmenting the self doing so in equally violent ways? These student essays and the subjectivities they construct certainly point to one assumption of postmodern pedagogies like Jay's: the assumption of a subject/student who experiences himself or herself as centered, autonomous, existing in a knowable, stable reality. They also suggest the possible violence that may occur in decentering a subject. I am not arguing against postmodern pedagogy but considering the questions such student essays raise about it. Is there a place in a postmodern classroom for a student who is trying to appropriate an apparently stable and controllable discourse (in the form of academic writing and/or the cultural discourses that compete for meaning) as she or he struggles with what it means to have been violently decentered? What purposes does it serve to further decenter this student, or to encourage his or her belief that a stable identity might be found? Postmodern pedagogy educates a "wild subject," one who no longer has a self that can feel, creating "a kind of ultimate estrangement from or dissolution of the structures that traditionally have supported both self and world" (Worsham 133). Should not the subjectivities of the sexually abused then be welcome within a postmodern classroom?

Whether the emotions of these "wild subjects" are biologically based or not, these students have been taught to "name their affective lives" and to believe they have emotions to feel. Worsham argues that the prevailing Western belief that emotion is "a personal and private matter . . . conceals the fact that emotions are prevailing forms of social life, that personal life always takes shape in social and cultural terms" (126–27). Power relations determine "what can, cannot, or must be said about self and emotion, what is taken to be true or false about them, and what only some individuals can say about them" (Lutz 14). If, as Worsham argues, the primary work of ideological interpellation occurs by structuring the language of emotion, then "decolonization" needs to begin by recognizing the ways in which this occurs (126–67). The texts I have considered here, both historical and contemporary, are about the business of naming emotions within various contexts, "showing how emotion discourses establish, assert, challenge, or reinforce power or status differences" (Lutz 14). The process of renaming these emotions might begin with how the students are already in this process and how they might continue it by situating their texts and experiences within contemporary and historical discourses and reflecting on the various consequence of each. What does it mean to speak a particular emotion in an "inappropriate" context? What sources of power are challenged or reinforced, and why? Whose interests are being served?

Teachers, too, have been taught to name their affective lives within a Cartesian and Ramian context, and this seems all the more apparent in responses to student essays about abuse. The prevailing interpretations of sexual abuse—whether from "Oprah," psychotherapy, the law, or feminist-sociological theories—articulate ways that witnesses, listeners, or authority figures might respond to a story of sexual abuse, none of which feel appropriate for many writing teachers. Most compositionists have distanced themselves from associations between writing and therapy, and it feels "natural" to feel discomfort, disgust, horror, anger, sadness in the face of such an essay. Any intervention is suspect—the student naturally feels vulnerable and thus easily hurt and exploited; form needs to be separated from content, and yet doing so might further hurt the student (implying that the content is connected to the student's sense of self); the affective attachments that might occur between student and teacher might "drain" the teacher and further damage the student because the teacher is not appropriately skilled. What power relations are being maintained by talking about emotion and identities in these ways? Our resistances to such subjects may suggest some of the gaps and silences in postmodern pedagogies—particularly in terms of the role of emotion and power relations—to which we need to attend.

One of the challenges in reading student essays about sexual abuse, it seems to me, is attending to what our responses as teachers—whether described as intellectual, emotional, or physical—indicate about the way power is deployed in our classrooms and in discussions about the nature of academic work. Some students have been sexually violated, and they are in our classrooms whether we know it or not. If such violence is a form of oppression, and many agree that it is, then essays about such oppression are crucial to the projects of critiquing power and ideology. The students seem, indeed, to be part of the way there.

Notes

1. As one form of postmodern pedagogy, Jarratt's position is informed by a feminist theory which challenges postmodernism to have a "theory of

positive social value" (Faigley 20); thus it does not fully become what Lynn Worsham would call a "wild pedagogy," a type of postmodern pedagogy that dislocates a subject from all structures of meaning and emotion (133). The context of this wild pedagogy creates a different set of issues for students who write about sexual abuse; thus I will defer a fuller discussion until later in this essay.

2. Such "authorizing prefaces" were common in the published narratives of other eighteenth- and nineteenth-century marginalized writers like Harriet Jacobs, Frederick Douglass, and the Shakers.

3. According to some historians, this was common. If a man was convicted of sexual deviance, he was often reintegrated into the community within a year or two, regardless of his standing in the town. In a divorce case from the late eighteenth century, a woman accused her husband of incest with their fourteen-year-old daughter, but then dropped the charges and accepted him back into the family when he decided to reform (at his wife's request) (D'Emilio and Freedman 25).

4. See Linda Brodkey and Michelle Fine's article, "Presence of Mind in the Absence of Body," in which they analyze sexual harassment narratives. Although they were not asked to, most of the college women who responded went to great lengths to explain why the professor behaved as he did, rarely discussing the impact it had on the woman herself.

5. It may not be surprising that Phebe joined a religious group committed to celibacy and gender egalitarianism. Their founder, Ann Lee, was herself a survivor of abuse from her husband, as well as from townspeople who rejected her message.

6. Students' names have been changed, and where requested, some details have been altered to respect students' privacy.

7. In this particular course, Emily and I met a total of four times in conference, and this essay was her third of five. There was little time for us to meet individually and thus little opportunity for anything like a therapeutic relationship to even be sensed, let alone developed. During the conference when we discussed this essay, Emily was clear with me that she wanted to work on the draft as a piece of writing, that she did not want my compassion and concern to overshadow our talk about how she might shape the draft to become more effective.

8. Carol Barringer, in her article "The Survivor's Voice: Breaking Silence about Childhood Sexual Abuse" (NASA Journal 4.1 [1992]: 4–22) identifies several linguistic characteristics of sexual abuse narratives, one of them being the use of euphemism.

9. None of the students in my study were required to write about this abuse, as Swartzlander, Pace, and Stamler imply. A number of therapists I interviewed asserted that someone who has been abused will not speak or write about it until she or he feels psychically able to.

Works Cited

Baker, Houston A., Jr. *Blues, Ideology, and Afro-American Literature: A Vernacular Theory.* Chicago: U of Chicago P, 1984.

Barringer, Carol E. "The Survivor's Voice: Breaking Silence about Childhood Sexual Abuse." *National Women's Studies Association Journal* 4.1 (1992): 4–22.

Bass, Ellen, and Laura Davis. *The Courage to Heal: A Guide for Women Survivors of Child Sexual Abuse.* New York: Harper, 1988.

Bass, Ellen, and Louise Thornton, eds. *I Never Told Anyone: Writings by Women Survivors of Child Sexual Abuse.* New York: Harper-Collins, 1983.

Bell, Vikki. *Interrogating Incest: Feminism, Foucault, and the Law.* New York: Routledge, 1993.

Brodkey, Linda, and Michelle Fine. "Presence of Mind in the Absence of Body." *Disruptive Voices: The Possibilities of Feminist Research.* Ed. Michelle Fine. Ann Arbor: U of Michigan P, 1992. 77–95.

Coles, William E., Jr., and James Vopat. *What Makes Writing Good: A Multiperspective.* Lexington, MA: Heath, 1985.

Davenport, William H. "Adult-Child Sexual Relations in Cross-Cultural Perspective." *The Sexual Abuse of Children: Theory and Research.* Vol. I. Ed. William O'Donahue and James H. Geer. Hillsdale, NJ: Erlbaum, 1992: 73–80.

Deletiner, Carole. "Crossing Lines." *College English* 54.7 (1992): 809–17.

D'Emilio, John, and Estelle B. Freedman. "Family Life and the Regulation of Deviance." *Intimate Matters: A History of Sexuality in America.* New York: Harper, 1988. 15–38.

Faigley, Lester. *Fragments of Rationality: Postmodernity and the Subject of Composition.* Pittsburgh: U of Pittsburgh P, 1992.

Geertz, Clifford. "Religion as a Cultural System." *The Interpretation of Cultures.* New York: Basic, 1973: 87–125.

Gilmore, Leigh. *Autobiographics: A Feminist Theory of Women's Self-Representation.* Ithaca: Cornell UP, 1994.

Gordon, Linda. *Heroes in Their Own Lives: The Politics and History of Family Violence, Boston 1880–1960.* New York: Penguin, 1988.

Herman, Judith Lewis, and Lisa Hirschman. *Father-Daughter Incest.* Cambridge, MA: Harvard UP, 1981.

Jaggar, Alison. "Love and Knowledge: Emotion in Feminist Epistemology." *Gender/Body/Knowledge: Feminist Reconstructions of Being and Knowing.* Ed. Alison Jaggar and Susan R. Bordo. New Brunswick: Rutgers UP, 1989: 145–71.

Jacobs, Harriet [Linda Brent]. *Incidents in the Life of a Slave Girl, Written by Herself.* Ed. Lydia Maria Child, 1861. New ed. Walter Teller. New York: Harcourt, 1973.

Jarratt, Susan. "Feminism and Composition: The Case for Conflict." *Contending with Words: Composition in a Postmodern Era.* Ed. Patricia Harkin and John Schilb. New York: MLA, 1991. 105–25.

Jay, Gregory. "The Subject of Pedagogy." *College English* 49.7 (1987): 785–800.

Kagle, Steven E. *Early Nineteenth-Century American Diary Literature.* Boston: Twayne, 1986.

Lutz, Catherine A. "Engendered Emotion: Gender, Power, and the Rhetoric of Emotional Control in American Discourse." *Language and the Politics of Emotion.* Ed. Catherine A. Lutz and Lila Abu-Lughod. Cambridge: Cambridge UP, 1990. 69–91.

Lutz, Catherine A., and Lila Abu-Lughod. "Introduction: emotion, discourse, and the politics of everyday life." *Language and the Politics of Emotion.* Ed. Catherine A. Lutz and Lila Abu-Lughod. Cambridge: Cambridge UP, 1990. 1–23.

McLennan, Karen Jacobsen. *Nature's Ban: Women's Incest Literature.* Boston: Northeastern UP, 1996.

McNaron, Toni A. H., and Yarrow Morgan, eds. *Voices in the Night: Women Speaking about Incest.* Pittsburgh: Cleis Press, 1982.

Miller, Richard. "The Nervous System." *College English* 58.3 (1996): 265–286.

Pfeiffer, Kathleen. "Response." *College English* 55.6 (1993): 669–71.

Roiphe, Katie. "Making the Incest Scene: In Novel after Novel, Writers Grope for Dark Secrets." *Harper's* (November 1995): 65–71.

Swartzlander, Susan, Diana Pace, and Virginia Lee Stamler. "The Ethics of Requiring Students to Write about Their Personal Lives." *The Chronicle of Higher Education* (17 Feb. 1993): B1–2.

Tal, Kali. *Worlds of Hurt: Reading the Literatures of Trauma.* Cambridge: Cambridge UP, 1996.

Taves, Ann, ed. *Religion and Domestic Violence in Early New England: The Memoirs of Abigail Abbot Bailey.* Bloomington: Indiana UP, 1989.

Thompson, Roger. "Sexual Deviance and Abuse." *Sex in Middlesex: Popular Mores in a Massachusetts County, 1649–1699.* Amherst: U of Mass P, 1986. 71–82.

Ulrich, Laurel Thatcher. *Good Wives: Image and Reality in the Lives of Women in Northern New England, 1650–1750.* New York: Vintage, 1991.

Worsham, Lynn. "Emotional and Pedagogic Violence." *Discourse* 15.2 (1992/1993): 119–48.

Chapter Seven

From Trauma to Writing
A Theoretical Model for Practical Use

Marian M. MacCurdy
Ithaca College

As recent articles in *The Chronicle of Higher Education, The New York Times, College Composition and Communication,* and *College English,* among others, have demonstrated, a debate continues in the profession between writing professors who believe students are better served by writing courses that require strictly academic prose and those who argue that students, especially beginning writers, are more likely to find their own voices when asked to pursue autobiographical prose. David Bartholomae, for example, in an article in *College Composition and Communication,* called the personal essay "sentimental realism," and went on to label it a "corrupt, if extraordinarily tempting genre" (71). In some ways this discussion is moot: We have all seen the benefits of both academic and personal writing for our students, and indeed a course could offer students the opportunity to probe the same material from both perspectives. And, of course, some students will write these stories in our classes whether we ask them to or not, as many first-year writing instructors have discovered. I expect this debate will rage on, but while it does, some of us, in whatever circumspect or direct ways that seem appropriate to our situations, will continue to explore the benefits of the personal essay to our students and to our own pedagogy. Recent interdisciplinary studies in the fields of psychology, composition, trauma theory, and neuroscience have begun to produce important and practical models for use in the classroom and the writing workshop to help writers both produce good writing and experience positive psychological benefits from that writing. Indeed, what I have discovered from this study is that the methods which produce good writing are the very ones that facilitate healing: iconic image rather than voice-over narrative is the core of both processes.

My own odyssey with this subject began several years ago when I began teaching an elective upper-level course in the personal essay, which has become a popular one among students in our department. In a college of 5,600 students, we offer nine sections of this course each semester. In my early years with this course, I felt somewhat apologetic teaching it because so often students pick painful topics to write about. Indeed, I began to wonder why so many of my students' essays described very difficult, even painful, life events. I have occasionally received that extraordinary paper which looks with microscopic detail at a seemingly insignificant event and weaves that event into a metacomment about life. Most student writers, however, are more likely to choose the more obviously emotionally charged topics. In addition, once students get beyond the clichés that can undermine the power of the experience, I have found that those emotionally charged topics can generate sharp imagery, clear sensory detail, and thematic sophistication, a point we will investigate later.

Our students are the products of many years in our school systems, institutions which have historically maintained a division between the cognitive and the affective aspects of learning. Most college students, having also spent their first eighteen years living with their families, have internalized parental views on everything from politics to family taboos. Learning to combine the public and the private, the intellectual and the emotional in their writing can be a difficult task for young writers. Some writing instructors have extolled the virtues of "honest" or "authentic" writing, implying that autobiographical writing is superior because it is "honest." This argument, of course, begs a larger question: Who determines that personal writing, simply on the basis of its subject matter, is any more authentic than the argumentative or expository essay? Lester Faigley, in his book *Fragments of Rationality: Postmodernity and the Subject of*

Composition, makes this point: "Why is writing about potentially embarrassing and painful aspects of one's life considered more honest than, say, the efforts of [the] student . . . who tries to figure out what Thucydides was up to in writing about the Peloponnesian War?" (121). Of course, Faigley is right. Self-exposure and authenticity are not the same. However, this fact need not be construed as proof that personal or therapeutic writing has no place in the academy. The intellectual depth and honesty required of the effective academic essay are lauded by the academy while the emotional and intellectual truth of the personal essay in the context of the academy is not always equally valued. Since the academy has struggled with the place of the personal essay in the curriculum, autobiographical writing can feel dangerous to students. Presumably students do not willingly attempt this without some strong motivation. Many of our students have learned how to create a persona in their writing that is distanced from what they really believe, from the person they see themselves to be, in order to offer the teacher "what she wants," as they mistakenly believe. Maturity helps attenuate that distance, but the process may not be very far along when we encounter the student personal essay writer. Our students need to learn a new form of discourse in order to encounter the personal essay. Those of us who elect to teach this genre may also need new perspectives to help negotiate this difficult task.

In a recent article published in the *Journal of Advanced Composition*, Wendy Bishop follows up on Donald Murray's argument that all writing is autobiography: "If all writing is autobiography, a life in writing must of necessity consider writing as a process of self-discovery and the writing classroom as a site of such exploration" (505). She then offers a view on this issue from Lad Tobin: "We cannot create intensity and deny tension, celebrate the personal and deny the significance of the personalities involved" (Tobin qtd. in Bishop 505). Bishop goes on to argue that the distinction between therapy and writing instruction is clear but narrow: "The analogies between writing instruction and therapy have something to offer me and something I need to offer to the teachers I train" (514). What we have learned about the writing process requires that we engage with the psyches of those we are teaching. Therefore, Bishop argues, we need to learn more about the process of therapy and its intersection with writing instruction.

Writing professionals are, of course, acutely aware of the dangers of merging the processes of therapy and writing instruction. Writing instructors are not therapists. Even if we had the appropriate training, the purpose of the writing classroom is different from the purpose of therapy: Therapy's goal is mental health; our goal is to help our students become strong writers. However, the writing and therapy processes can inform each other. The common wisdom in working with the personal essay is to separate students' texts from their lives, and this distinction is indeed necessary, but as will be seen later, it is also at times more theoretical than real, at least in our students' minds. Research in trauma theory, neuroscience, and cognitive psychology can provide information to help writers move from the stories about their lives to the stories in their lives, that is, to move them from a narrative that skims the top of their experience to one that unearths it.

While many students choose to write about painful, even traumatic, experiences in their personal essays, they tend not to think of them as traumatic. "Trauma" to many connotes mental "unhealth" if not outright illness. Yet trauma does not only refer to catastrophic moments. Dictionaries define trauma as a bodily injury produced by some act of violence or some agency outside the body; the condition resulting from the injury; or a startling experience that has a lasting effect on mental life. Trauma can be a single incident or a series of incidents; it can be a broken finger received playing football or a psychic wound caused by the violent death of a close family member. In popular language we speak of one who has been "traumatized" by some terrible experience, but in point of fact no one can reach adulthood without some moments of trauma. However, we cannot judge how "traumatic" any particular experience may be for a given individual. What to one could be easily assimilated into life can for another become a defining life experience. Many of my students choose to write about these "traumatic" experiences—events as reality-shattering as a parent's death, to as seemingly trivial as a math tutoring session with a father. To the students these topics have great intensity, and I wondered why writers would lean in the direction of such emotionally charged topics. One possible explanation has come from research into trauma, its causes, results, and treatment.

Trauma and Memory

I discovered that trauma produces something called an iconic image, that is, a mental picture that is stored deep within the brain in the limbic system and is not easily available to the cerebral cortex. Traumatic memories are sensory, that is, the body reacts to them even when the conscious mind is not aware of the cause of such reactions. This is because these iconic memories are storied in the amygdala, a part of the limbic system which not only retains these images but gives them their emotional weight.

While these images are non-cognitive, they have deep emotional presence although they are not easily accesssible. They pop up sometimes unbidden when we smell, hear, see, or touch something that takes us back to the time the traumatic event occurred. It is these images that must be accessed if a story about the trauma is to be told. But these images are hard to verbalize because they are locked into a part of the brain that is pre-verbal. This is even a chemical process. Animal experiments show that when high levels of adrenaline and other stress hormones are circulating through the bloodstream, memory traces are deeply imprinted into the brain, as Judith Herman describes in her recent book *Trauma and Recovery*. She presents psychiatrist Bessel van der Kolk's concept that in "states of high sympathetic nervous system arousal, the linguistic encoding of memory is inactivated, and the central nervous system reverts to the sensory and iconic forms of memory that predominate in early life" (39).[1] In other words, we sense painful memories even if we cannot verbalize them, which is perhaps why we tend to be drawn to our emotionally difficult experiences. We seek a way to make the unknown known. This makes some psychological sense since happy times do not need to be processed. They can recede into the general soup of life to add to our sense of well-being whereas painful moments must be processed, adapted to, and ordered for the psyche—not to mention the body—to remain alive and healthy.

Pain is an exquisitely efficient teacher—short-term. (The long-term effects are, of course, something else. That is why negative reinforcement can work in child rearing to produce behavioral change. However, it has unacceptable side effects that are often not seen for years.)

In an article from a recent book edited by Daniel Schacter, researchers John H. Krystal, Steven M. Southwick, and Dennis S. Charney argue that traumatic events produce a shift away from verbal encoding of information toward encoding via "emotional, pictorial, auditory, and other sensory-based memory systems" (158). This shift helps to explain why a simple verbal statement of a painful event fails to convey accurately the horror of a traumatic experience. Indeed, they argue that "traumatic memories may not be encoded or retrieved linguistically" (163) unless that retrieval encourages the survivor to integrate the emotional memory with the description. In another article in the same collection, Larry Squire suggests that memory reconstruction is directly related to the visual mental system since they both appear to involve some of the same brain mechanisms (219). This means that traumatic memories are likely to be tied to sensory, iconic representations, not strictly linguistic, intellectual concepts about those memories.

The human brain is layered with three separate functioning systems that our evolutionary history built on top of each other: the cerebellum, which controls the autonomic nervous system; the limbic system, which drives our unconscious emotional responses; and the cerebrum, which allows cognitive functioning. We share the limbic system with other mammals, and as such it is a necessary component for survival. (See Alice G. Brand's article in this collection for a more complete description of brain biology.) Two important components of the limbic system are the hippocampus and the amygdala. The hippocampus provides a keen memory of context—for example, it registers where on a wooded path you saw a rattlesnake. However, it is the amygdala that registers the emotional reaction to that sighting. It produces the surge of adrenaline which signifies fight or flight. Neither of these responses goes first through the cortex, which of course saves much needed time in the event of danger. However, it also means that traumatic experiences are permanently encoded as

images and emotions together in the brain and cannot be retrieved independent of each other. Indeed, recent studies indicate
that this symbiosis is even more direct than we thought.

An important study reported by researchers Larry Cahill,
James McGaugh, and their colleagues in the journal *Nature* demonstrates that stress hormones released during an intense emotional experience actually enhance memory of that experience.
McGaugh and his associates designed a narrative with accompanying slides and offered that narrative to two groups: one which
received the beta blocker propranolol and one which received a
placebo. The subjects were exposed to two narratives, the first an
emotionally charged story about a little boy whose feet are severed in a terrible accident while going to visit his father at his
workplace. The father is a laboratory technician at Victory
Memorial Hospital. The boy is rushed to the hospital where doctors struggle to save the boy's life and successfully reattach the
boy's severed feet. The second version, an emotionally neutral
one, simply describes the boy leaving home, also with his mother,
to visit his father at the hospital where the father works. As the
researchers said, "Propranolol significantly impaired memory of
the emotionally arousing story but did not affect memory of the
emotionally neutral story. The impairing effect of propranolol
on memory of the emotional story was not due either to reduced
emotional responsiveness or to nonspecific sedative or attentional
effects. The results support the hypothesis that enhanced memory associated with emotional experiences involves activation of
the beta-adrenergic system" (702). The study demonstrates that
stress hormones released during traumatic experiences actually
imprint the images from those experiences into the brain. While
studies indicating this have been performed on animals, this is
the first such experiment I am aware of which studied the effects
of stress hormones on sensory memory in human subjects. The
study indicates that our hormones are activated not only for purposes of fight or flight, but also to imprint memory traces of difficult experiences deeply into the brain, probably for survival
value. Both *The New York Times* and National Public Radio reported the results of this study, indicating high public interest in
this material. One possible implication of this study is to offer
beta blockers to emergency medical personnel to inhibit retention

of painful memories. However, EMTs I have talked with have been horrified by this possibility. These professionals argue that their memories are a part of who they are and why they choose to do this difficult work. It makes more sense, they argue, to learn how these memories are encoded and how best to incorporate them into the rest of our psyches rather than to allow a kind of amnesia to reign. Sensory details from our lives are significant contributors to our humanity.

Re-experiencing sensory details encoded during extreme life moments is at the core of trauma recovery. Herman argues that traumatic memories can be distinguished from normal ones because "they are not encoded like the ordinary memories of adults in a verbal, linear narrative that is assimilated into an on-going life story" (37). Mental health professionals experienced in the treatment of post-traumatic stress disorder believe that essential traumatic memories lack verbal narrative and context; instead they are "imprinted in the brain in the form of vivid images and sensations," as Herman has said (38). When victims speak of the moments of their trauma, they do not produce clear narrative lines but instead describe pictures and sounds which remain permanently encoded in their minds. For example, I recently broke my finger by closing it in my car door. I do not remember even this relatively mild trauma as a consistent narrative. Instead I remember seeing the gray seat belt caught in the door, picture yanking on it with my right hand, remember seeing my left middle finger deeply grooved, bent, and blue. I do not remember opening the door and pulling my hand out of the door after I injured it. I remember not narrative but moments and images within that narrative.

However, verbalizing emotional experiences is actually quite difficult since the power of those experiences is encoded nonverbally. As Wilma Bucci, in her article "The Power of Narrative," explains: "To translate emotional experience into words, the massively parallel, analogic, subsymbolic contents of the nonverbal system must be connected to the single channel, symbolic format of the verbal code" (103). Most people find this hard to accomplish—evidenced by such statements as "I was struck dumb"; "I was speechless"; "My heart was in my mouth"; etc. Bucci argues that the best way to capture an emotional experience verbally is by the use of concrete, specific images "as poets know." She says: "Such concrete and specific images constitute the type of material for which the referential connections are most active, and which are likely to activate referential connections in the listener. Images and their concatenations in episodes constitute the essential symbolic contents of the emotion schemas. . . . In that sense, the telling of a story is precisely the expression of an emotion schema, or parts of a schema, in verbal form" (104).

Image and Detail

Robert Jay Lifton, who has studied survivors of Hiroshima, civilian disasters, and military combat, calls the traumatic memory an "indelible image" (Herman 38). Traumatic memories focus on fragments rather than narratives, "image without context" as Herman puts it (38). In their reliance on imagery and bodily sensations they resemble the memories of very young children. Research into trauma recovery indicates that healing is more likely to occur when survivors can describe not just the events of their trauma but the images their memories have encoded. Herman describes the therapeutic process which begins with reconstructing the story:

> Out of the fragmented components of frozen imagery and sensation, patient and therapist slowly reassemble an organized, detailed, verbal account. . . . As the narrative closes in on the most unbearable moments, the patient finds it more and more difficult to use words. At times the patient may spontaneously switch to non-verbal methods of communication. . . . Given the "iconic," visual nature of traumatic memories, creating pictures may represent the most effective initial approach to these "indelible images. The completed narrative must include a full and vivid description of the traumatic imagery. (177)

However, these images may not be immediately available. In order to cope with trauma and its aftermath, survivors often bury these images because they can get in the way of daily functioning. In those cases, the narratives of the experiences, when offered, often rely on clichés and the "story of the story," that is, the remembered tale which avoids the depth of feeling that clear images generate. The therapist's job is to help the survivor move beyond the story of the story in order to reach the level of direct experience.

Remembering details, specific images, and writing them down helps us to heal. The telling itself has efficacy, as Christina Miller reported in the May 1990 issue of *Longevity*. She described work done by researchers Pennebaker et al. at Southern Methodist University and the Ohio State University College of Medicine which shows that when college students were asked to write about past traumatic experiences for twenty minutes a day, four days in a row, while a control group wrote about trivial topics, those who had written about their emotional traumas showed a significant improvement in their bodies' immune functions. (For a more complete description of Pennebaker's work, see his book, *Opening Up*.) In another study (1994) by Pennebaker and Francis, subjects in the experimental group were asked to write about their thoughts and feelings about coming to college, for three consecutive days, while a control group wrote about neutral topics: "On average, the experimental subjects showed more positive effects, as indicated by fewer health center visits and improved grade point averages, compared with the control subjects" (cited in Miller 115).

The same thing that helps us recover from traumatic experiences—describing images in detail to another—produces writing which is alive with sensory description. Indeed, trauma theory can offer the writing instructor important insights into how to help writers reproduce the sensory images which aid in effective personal essay writing. Creating moments alive with sensory details requires, for the personal essayist, remembering those details, and this is not always so easy, especially when painful memories are being blocked. Writers may not move immediately into the defining images which have shaped their experiences. Most writing instructors can recall student essays which provide dispassionate accounts of deaths or accidents which seem devoid of vivid imagery. We have also read essays in which the writers label their emotions ("I felt angry, I felt sad, I felt excited," etc.) or lean on clichés and weak intensifiers which dull the emotional impact of the experience. However, once writers cease depending on these labels—often through classroom exercises including visualizations—images and the moments they convey can come forth.

In her article "The Power of Narrative," Wilma Bucci postulates what she terms "referential activity," a process for symbolizing emotional experience while retaining access to the "analogic components of the feeling state" (106). In other words, verbalizing an emotional state must convey a sense of the affect. These referential connections are most productive when direct, specific, and concrete images are being described verbally; they are less productive for abstract concepts: "Thus high RA [referential activity] is reflected in language that is concrete, specific and clear, that captures a quality of immediacy in the speaker's representations, and that is likely to evoke vivid and immediate experience in the listener as well" (109). Bucci offers the following example of low-RA prose:

> I love people and I like to be with people. And right now I feel very bad because I can't be with them and do the things I would like to do. But I'm looking forward to a happier and healthier future and—I don't know what else to say. What else can I talk about? (109)

As Bucci points out, this speaker is talking about emotions but is unable to connect her words to the emotions that underlie them. Bucci has developed systematic procedures for describing qualities of language style: "The methods of scoring RA include qualitative rating scales, and objective measures based on quantifiable linguistic features. These measures have been validated by . . . experimental and clinical work . . ."(110). The RA rating scales measure Concreteness, Imagery, Specificity, and Clarity of Speech. Bucci adds two more elements to the scale: ET (emotional tone) and AB (abstraction dictionary). The emotional tone word list consists of diction that demonstrates the emotional state of the speaker and is likely to produce an emotional reaction in the listener. AB words are abstract nouns that indicate intellectual concepts based on logical reflection and evaluation. Bucci has put together a computer dictionary (called CRA) to measure RA which reflects the style rather than the content of the speaker's words. The high-CRA list includes words people use when they describe images and events (such as prepositions) and other words representing spatial relations ("in, out, outside"). A low-CRA list includes words which generally represent logical relations and functions such as quantification. The referential cycle Bucci usually finds

> would begin with emotional arousal indicated by high ET [emotional tone], leading to a narrative of an incident, a memory, or a dream, which appears as an RA peak. This would then be followed by concomitant increases in ET and AB [abstract words]. The CRA peak is essential for the cycle. High ET and AB utterances without a CRA peak indicate activation of subsymbolic and verbal symbolic representations, without connections between them; thus the dissociation that is the focus of treatment is allowed to continue unchanged. (114)

In other words, Bucci argues that speech which does not integrate concrete images and the emotions those images convey into the concepts that they can produce will not provide a healing function for the individual. In the Pennebaker and Francis 1994 study of college students mentioned above, which studied the effects of writing about their thoughts and feelings about coming to college, the experimental subjects were classified into three subgroups, those showing health improvement, those who remained unchanged, and those who became worse. Bucci attempted to discover the factors that influenced these outcomes. She discovered that the initial writing session produced words high in emotional tone (ET) and CRA and low in the quality of abstraction (AB):

> . . . indicating the telling of narratives with considerable emotional content, and with little abstract language. . . . Subjects in this initial session were describing episodes representing emotion schemas, with both imagery and related emotional components. The second day is characterized by some decline in CRA and ET, and an increase in AB, as the subject begins to reflect on the stories and experiences he or she has reported. On the third day, these improved subjects show concomitant increases in all measure, indicating insights about emotional material expressed in concrete and specific form, not intellectual insight alone. . . . This pattern corresponds to the optimal pattern of a therapy session. . . . This pattern is not seen in the other groups. The unchanged group shows relatively low CRA and ET, while AB follows essentially the pattern of the health

improvement subjects. The subjects who became worse are clearly differentiated from the other two groups by high AB across all three writing sessions, and by ET consistently below the levels of the other students, as well as by CRA that never rises above the standard score mean. The measures indicate that this group begins by warding off emotional experience to a considerably greater extent than the other two, and consistently remains within the abstract verbal mode, rather than using language first to access emotional experience and then to represent it in symbolic form. . . . Emotion was aroused by the task, but they were unable to symbolize this adequately. (117)

I have offered here this material to demonstrate that researchers are finding ways to describe the process by which writers produce both effective prose and therapeutic benefits. When the writing connects the emotions with the images, healing occurs—and so also does good writing, as we will see. Particularly interesting in Bucci's system is the fact that AB begins to rise after ET and CRA peak, meaning that abstractions and intellectualizations of experiences follow when the emotions produced by the experiences have been expressed. In "Language, Power, and Consciousness: A Writing Experiment at the University of Toronto" (in Section III of this collection), Guy Allen argues that his students' academic writing improves once they learn to write effective personal essays. According to Allen, empowerment, confidence, and community can all be built up in the personal essay class and can positively affect writing ability; similarly, Bucci's work indicates that once writers can find the words to express their emotional lives, intellectual growth can follow. What David Bartholomae calls "a corrupt genre" can prove liberating to the intellect as well as to the emotions.

This process of liberation, however, is usually new to most writers, and therefore they need help to discover what techniques can work best. The personal essayist holds not a mirror up to nature but a motion picture camera. I suggest to my students that they imagine a film camera in their hands that is recording all that they saw, heard, and touched when the moment they are describing occurred. Such a camera will not record a voice-over or a narrator pasted on later; it will record the scene in the same way that a play conveys dialogue and details of setting—as they unfold. In fact, it helps writers to see narrative as a series of separate images linked by persistence of vision, the method that animators use, not as a series of abstract concepts about the event.

Re-Visioning Experience

The imagistic re-visioning of experience is not, initially, easy to accomplish. My first assignment in my personal essay class asks the students to write about a single incident from their childhood that had a helpful or a harmful effect on them during their youth. Most of the writers say they cannot recall anything particularly memorable from their childhoods. As they jiggle their memories through in-class freewriting, brainstorming, and visualization exercises, they begin to remember scenes, pictures usually, which pop into their minds, pictures which they had buried in order to do the hard work of coping with life. Such memories are often hidden by the labels which students give to their experiences: Summer camp was a time of growth, military school was a lesson in independence, the death of a grandparent taught them about the reality of human mortality, divorce taught them responsibility and provided them with double birthday presents. Yet labels are not actual experience but are often stereotypical categorizations of the experience.

For example, over one semester break I participated in a symphony performance of Haydn's *Missa Cellensis*. Just as I stepped up to sing my first solo, I looked out into the stone cathedral where we were performing, this huge open space big enough to land a small airplane in, stared up at the stained glass windows that framed us on three sides, their panes finely cut jewels with the late afternoon light burning through them, heard the symphony playing the introductory bars perfectly in tune, and realized that I was not paralyzed by pre-singing panic as had happened occasionally in the past. I understood why Middle English poets loved the image of light behind stained glass. I thought, "Music doesn't get any better than this." Instantly I was horrified. How could I have described one of the peak experiences of my musical life with such a cliché, a media cliché at that, one which conjures up Madison Avenue images of beer and male bonding? But of course I hadn't described this experience; I had labeled it. And this label separated me from my direct experience. As James Britton has pointed out, with respect to any experience we may either be participating in it or evaluating it out of a desire to understand it better. When language is used in the role of spectator, it strives to represent the world. The personal essayist cannot begin to encounter her subject until she can internally see the moments and participate in them once again. Only when that is accomplished can she step back to represent what she sees. From Peter Elbow and others we have learned how to help students find the moments they wish to focus on. However, we still need methods to help students reconstruct image, and trauma theory and new directions in cognitive psychology may be instructive here.

Trauma survivors rely on the mind's capacity to cope. However, we cannot both process an experience and cope at the same time. Therefore, survivors often have difficulty expressing the very images which can help them the most and can be aided in this process by techniques to reconstruct image. Jessica Wolfe describes her approach to the trauma narrative with combat veterans: "We have them reel off in great detail, as though they were watching a movie, and with all the senses included. We ask them what they are thinking" (Herman 177). Once the images are expressed, a full narrative can be constructed, but the story must begin with image. As Herman says, "A narrative that does not include the traumatic imagery and bodily sensations is barren and incomplete" (177).

In an article on survivor guilt in *Post-Traumatic Stress Disorders: A Handbook for Clinicians,* Tom Williams describes the therapeutic process involved in working with survivors of trauma: "For a therapeutic intervention to be successful, one must get the story of the trauma in precise detail. For example, it is helpful to know the details about environmental conditions, particularly smells, articles of clothing, and other situational cues. It is important for them to tell you about the trauma scene as clearly and vividly as possible. . . . The more they tell the story . . . the less intense the emotions become" (80). This technique may not at first be easy for the survivors to accomplish because it necessitates re-experiencing the emotions associated with the experience, something most survivors have carefully avoided just to cope with life. Once images start to come, so also do the feelings which have been suppressed, and Williams makes sure to tell his clients that "people do not die from crying, and that once they start crying they will stop" (80). This needs to be said because many survivors have spent years avoiding their feelings precisely because they feared being overwhelmed by them. Williams goes on to offer an excerpt from two interviews with a Vietnam War veteran. In the first interview, the veteran speaks utterly dispassionately about being shot and burned in a field, smoked out by the enemy in an ambush. The vet demonstrates no connection to the horrors described. It is as if these events happened to someone else. In the later description he begins to allow some emotional material to enter his speech. Williams's point is that only after connecting emotions to the events can healing occur, and in his opinion one of the best ways to facilitate this connection is to encourage the survivor to describe the setting and the events in as much imagistic detail as possible. In an article on sexual assault victims in the same volume, Carolyn Agosta and Mary McHugh describe a similar technique: "You encourage her to talk about what happened in detail. As she experiences a safe place to discuss her rape, she begins to feel the emotions of that violent encounter, then she may begin to recover her memory. . . . As this occurs, her fear level will heighten, she will become more in touch with her pain, and she will experience relief" (244).

Granted, the traumatic experiences these therapists deal with are severe. I include this material to demonstrate two things. First, the process for connecting with images and emotions is recursive and holistic. Seeing the images draws out the emotions and vice versa. Second, healing can occur when this process is undergone. Whether a student is describing a family's experience with divorce, getting lost in a Turkish bazaar at the age of ten, or a car accident, the goal is to avoid the generalizations, the dispassionate accounts often replete with clichés but lacking concrete images which can plague student papers. Helping our students to connect with their emotions by finding the images, the pictures that lie inside their memories, can move them beyond the clichés and into the uniqueness of their moments, beyond the comments about an experience to the experience itself. This technique can be used in many contexts. One young woman, Tina, was trying to write an essay about her grandmother's house and was drawing a blank. The piece was vague and unfocused because she could not locate herself in the setting for the paper. We tried a visualization exercise in which she listed as many pictures as she could remember from that house and discovered to her surprise that even though her grandmother had died when she was ten, she could remember whole rooms, even down to running her finger-nail along the grooves in the couch, playing with the doilies that covered each tabletop, and noting the half-empty bottle of Canadian Club on the counter. Her final essay was grounded in both an emotional and a physical reality that she had thought was unknown to her.

The following is a list of images that popped into my student's mind as she completed the in-class visualization exercise of her grandmother and her home: "tall, thin, beautiful, soft velvet hands, smoke, tin-foil flowers and spoons, cheek bones, elegance, manners, polyester pants, wrinkled face, floral aprons, china figures, little horses, garden in the field, tomatoes, pumpkins, doilies, pledge, fried chicken, hockey, gray outside, cold, pin with white stone and lady's face on it, designer imposters—giorgio—wobbled voice, scratched from smoke, red cigarette box with young queen Elizabeth on cover, spoon collection on wall above chair, hand-crocheted pot holders, sand-dune fencing against the snow, tea bags without strings, sugar cubes, special phone that buzzed, rhubarb jelly, shuffleboard outside, Mirium, peephole making the hallway look long, oil of olay, stained pillowcase, skin sliding on her arms, sewing needles and pin cushions, lace over her bedspread, Canadian Club with coke."

My student then wrote the following first draft of her paper, based on the images she recalled:

I used to love going to grandma's apartment. I really don't know why. Her apartment building was filled with senior citizens and it smelled like a hospital. The smell would hit me as soon as the buzzing door opened. I'd walk up the stairs with my mother, and it would smell like old people, sickness, and mothballs. But it reminded me of grandma. Grandma's door would always be opened. I think after she buzzed us in she'd open the door and then sit on her green chair with doilies on the arms, looking as though she'd been waiting for hours. There was no desperation in her face, just impatience that we had kept her waiting.

Sometimes mommy would leave me there while she ran errands for grandma. Grandma would teach me how to make tinfoil spoons out of the her cigarette wrappers. I'd place my tiny thumb at the top of the foil and twist a stem with my other hand. When grandma knew I was coming she'd save the wrappers in a kitchen drawer next to the crocheted pot holders and poached-egg holders. Sometimes I would make twenty at a time, depending on how many packs of cigarettes grandma had smoked the week before my arrival.

Grandma's apartment was fun because there were so many knick-knacks to play with. Ceramic mommies, babies, ponies, stuffed animals, dolls, snowing shake-up domes, mugs with faces on them, . . . bibles with four leaf clovers pressed in the pages and old, yellow pictures of mommy when she was my age. There were show-off trips down the hall to Mirium's, or to the lounge downstairs which had sliding doors leading to shuffle board courts. In the fall, we would go outside to the garden where we could pick pumpkins & tomatoes. When it was cold I would watch her cook. She made apple pie and rhubarb jelly, and pemiel bacon and fried chicken. Sometimes we would sit and my grandmother, the true Canadian she was, would watch hockey and sip her cc & coke while I cheated at solitaire.

When grandma visited us daddy would get mad because the house smelled like smoke. Sometimes he would say something and she would get annoyed. She would never give him excuses, she just got angry. She always began sentences with people's names, and she would say, "Now Carl" as she tilted her head and looked sternly at him.

She would always tell me to help my mother and get mad at me when I played with the boys next door. Sometimes she would just hug me and I would feel the bones in her back and smell her shirt, a mixture of designer impostors giorgio and cigarette smoke. She would hold my hand and I would stroke her arm because her skin would slide around on her arm and it was soft like velvet. I would touch her face and feel her high cheekbones. She was so elegant and so beautiful. Now she was wrinkled and had short tight, white curls on her head.

The phone rang one night the day after I got an extension in my room. It was about twelve-thirty in the morning. I answered late, and before I picked up the phone I knew it had to do with grandma. I heard Mirium on the phone with mom. "Helen," she kept saying, "Helen."

My mother left the next morning to see grandma in the hospital. Mommy told me that grandma was very sick, that she was probably going to die. Grandma kept talking about grandpa, who had died when I was one or two. She was stubborn about being in bed; mom said it took three people to hold her down.

I didn't cry at the wake. I was laughing at one point, and then I was mad at myself for it. I was scared but bent down at her casket. Grandma's cheeks were too puffy. She had too much make-up on. When no one was looking, I touched her arm. Her skin didn't slide on her arm anymore and she was cold. It wasn't my grandma, just her body. Before the funeral, our family sat in front of grandma's casket. I watched two strangers close my grandma's box. They dropped the lid, I started to cry. Grandma was dead. Tears rolled out of my eyes, I couldn't see. My cousin Richard held me as I shook and sobbed. I didn't stop crying until after the car ride, after the prayers, after we left the cemetery. On the ride home the funeral procession left the cemetery. As we drove down the street, all other cars followed the Canadian tradition of pulling over and stopping to pay respect. It was then I realized no one had let me say goodbye.

And of course this is why Tina's first attempt to write had produced a blank—because no one had let her say goodbye, and her emotional responses were therefore hidden within her. She had to connect with how she really felt about her grandmother's death before she could connect with her life. I asked Tina after she wrote this first draft to describe her writing process, and the following is an excerpt from her response:

When you asked me to close my eyes in class on Wednesday, I faced very strong images of my grandmother and her apartment. Grandma died when I was in sixth grade, and I found it remarkable that I remembered some of the items on this list. When I went home after class I called my mother to share the images with her and she was amazed. She couldn't believe some of the details I remembered, and to quote, she got "goose pimples"!

Upon closing my eyes, my grandmother's apartment was in front of me. Piece by piece the furniture in her apartment "appeared." I could remember the entire room. Once the settings of the rooms were established, I swear I could almost smell her apartment. The rest of the images were almost like a dream sequence. I remembered running my fingernail along the grooves in her couch. Playing with the doilies that covered each tabletop. The fence outside her window. Bottles in her bathroom. Even the bottle of Canadian Club that was on the counter half-empty. (This image was the spookiest to my mom because I told her that I remembered that bottle and grandma mixing it with coke, something that my mother never would have mentioned in conversation.) I don't know why this was so vivid to me. I surprised myself in how much I remembered! Writing my essay later that night was so easy because everything just spilled out.

Seeking the Commonality of Experience

When writers connect with the images behind their narratives and the emotional weight of those images, their stories can spill out. Holding a mental camera up to nature can bring to consciousness those detailed images and lead to a kind of epiphany, a revelation of the commonality of experience. Trauma victims of course feel isolated by their experiences. They believe that no one can possibly comprehend what has happened to them. And in some ways they are right. They have been irrevocably changed by their experiences. However, as they tell their stories they discover that others have been touched by pain as well, perhaps a different pain, but pain nonetheless. This commonality helps to ameliorate the excruciating isolation that is a by-product of trauma.

The same discovery occurs in the personal essay classroom when students begin to discover that while experiences may be distinct, a painful awareness of being utterly different from others can be shared. Differences can even bring people together and give them permission to speak. In one of my classes, a tall, handsome, but mute young man sat with his arms crossed in my classroom for weeks without saying a word—to me or to anyone else. He appeared either terminally shy or disenfranchised, perhaps even angry with the class. In office hours, he finally told me what was troubling him. At the beginning of the semester his brother had been murdered by a gang of thugs in Boston—and he couldn't write, think, be. He felt completely alone—who could possibly understand his pain? As he stared at me with brittle eyes, I looked at him for a minute and then told him that such a murder must be just the worst horror he could imagine, and while I couldn't pretend to understand that, I had lost my husband not too long ago, so I understand grief. Perhaps others would too. His eyes

melted, and he began to weep for the first time since his brother
was murdered. After that moment he began to write—just a little.
He went to Boston, sat down by the Charles River where he and
his brother had often gone, and talked to his brother—and himself. He knew then that his brother would not want him to be
silent, frozen in unexpressed rage and grief. He knew then that
he must come back to Ithaca and attempt to communicate his
story to others. The day he read his essay in class, he did not weep,
he did not show anger in his voice, but his face was red and his
hands shook. I studied the other students' faces. Would they
speak, would they respond to him, or would they retreat from
such a story? One by one they spoke: "Thank you for daring to
tell us; thank you for trusting us enough." And then the other
stories began to be shared—the hidden traumas that too many
know and too few express. My student's bravery changed the
class and made us all a little more honest.

Most of us who teach writing have encountered situations
such as these, moments when our students reach to us (rather
than to instructors in huge lecture courses) for understanding.
Of course, some of these students need a kind of help which a
writing class cannot offer, and at that point we need to nudge
these students in crisis to the appropriate support service, as I did
in this student's case. However, this class offered him his first opportunity to speak of his experience to anyone, and both his
writing and his psyche improved as a result.

In another course, "Women and Writing," a class that happened to be composed of all women, one young woman kept
writing stories about a goddess figure that was beautiful, blond,
and omnipotent, but this character had no humanity and the stories lacked depth. The goddess was a stereotype, a composite
cross between Wonder Woman and Madonna. I asked her what
drew her to these stories. I also told her that they seemed removed from her, like an overlay rather than something that came
from her core. She stared at me, nodded her head, and said she
would rethink the assignment. She came back the next day with
a powerful poem about a rape, her rape, and said, "This is what
this goddess protected me from." After first discussing her option of taking this issue to our campus counseling center, I asked

her how she felt about sharing her writing with the class in our usual workshop. She said she didn't know if she could, that she would have to see how she felt in class. When the time came, she chose to read it. In a faint, wispy voice, this young woman, her head down, her legs twisting into each other, read her poem to her fellow writers. Again, bravery changed the class. Of the eighteen women in that class, nine had been the victims of sexual abuse, but we did not realize our commonality until this one student dared to tell her story. She risked public embarrassment as well as the possibility of being overwhelmed by what she had suppressed. However, unearthing her story provided both a therapeutic advantage and a literary one. This student's first stories were flat, with stereotyped characters and bland description. She had not yet been able to reach her creative core because she had blocked her experience and with it, the pictures and emotions which motivated her as a writer. Psychic blocking isn't selective; when we block, we lose our connection with our deepest selves. (This is why some trauma survivors can have flat affects.) This student's new material included the kinds of details that characterize effective writing, and she was much more fully in control of her material than even she had expected. In addition, her entire classroom demeanor changed. She looked up and out to the other students, not down to her feet.

In another student example, a young man wrote a charming essay about wandering off from home one day at the age of six. The paper recounted the child discovering neighborhoods, meeting strange new playmates, and finally placing a phone call home which alerted his frantic parents to his whereabouts. While the paper offered some interesting moments, it rambled, led nowhere, had no clear focus. In a conference I asked why he chose that topic, what emotional weight it had for him. In other words, why was he drawn back to that day? We tried some exercises in which he could return to that time in his life, and he suddenly remembered that his parents were in the process of getting divorced during this period, and he often ran away to escape their fights. He had blocked those arguments and remembered only their result—he wandered away. By returning to the scene of his motivation, he was able to write a more coherent piece with a focus that was not only more truthful to his emotional state at the time, but turned the writing from an episode in autobiography into a personal essay.

I have further evidence of the relationship between trauma recovery and image from my own life and teaching. I was giving my students their next essay assignment—to write a paper about their bodies or some aspect of their bodies that they liked or didn't like or some time when they felt their bodies worked well or let them down. They could also write about an accident, a time when they realized they were not immortal, that their bodies were vulnerable. They asked for an example. I told them of a time when I was six and was hit by a car as I was sledding down the sidewalk. The car was turning into a driveway just as I was passing the driveway on my sled. I slid under the car, receiving only a sprained wrist. My students wanted details. What part of the car did I pass under—between the wheels or behind them? I hadn't thought about this before. I was silent for a moment, and then said, "I remember smelling a muffler, remember looking up and seeing a muffler, so it must have been behind the four wheels." All of a sudden I felt claustrophobic; I re-experienced what it felt like to be flying under that car, and I realized that the reason I never could hide under beds like other kids could was because of that car. This realization could not have come without the memory of the smell of that muffler above me being recalled. So sensory image is the precursor to making the kinds of conscious connections that can free us from the past. It is also the core of writing that engages the reader.

The technique that therapists often use—to encourage clients to re-experience specific moments from the past—is the very one that helps writers unlock their memories. I do not ask students to begin writing whole essays. We begin with visualization exercises that allow them to make lists of the pictures they see in the mind's eye. In one exercise, they visit their childhood bedroom and make a list of all the objects they see there. In another, they imagine being in a grandparent's home and make lists of what they see, smell, hear, touch, taste. Only after they have a firm grasp of the pictures in front of them, do they begin to write a full essay. Once a writer decides on a topic that has energy and power for her, we use the same technique to flesh out the memory details and enable the writer to re-experience the moments. Vivid details are, of course, essential for clear, compelling writing. Nor is this awareness limited to the personal essay. All writing can benefit from this approach, academic as well as personal, joyous as well as traumatic. I am arguing here for a technique which has, I believe, universal efficacy; however, the personal essay presents distinct problems for writers since so often they do not have clear access to the images which drive their experiences and may therefore drive their narratives.

Brain Hemisphericity and Image

Medical science is beginning to investigate the connection between memory and image. One such study completed by Michael Gazzaniga, at the Cornell University Medical School in New York, looked at the results of severing the two sides of the brain, done occasionally with epileptics whose seizures cannot be controlled with medication. One subject was shown a computer screen. On the left side was the word "orange," while on the right was the drawing of a bird. The man was asked to look at the left side of the screen and describe what he saw. The man drew an orange, then quickly changed it into a bird. When asked why the change, he said that he first saw an orange but then realized that it was really a bird. When asked how to account for this shift, he said he didn't know, that perhaps he was thinking of the Baltimore Orioles. The right side of the brain—which saw the word "orange"—could not decode it verbally, and the left side—which saw the bird—could not relate it to "orange." The subject created a narrative to make sense of images which his brain could not process, given his condition. Narrative jumped in to make sense of a reality that made no sense, but image was the precursor to that narrative. In another experiment described in *Left Brain, Right Brain*, written by Springer and Deutsch, Gazzaniga and LeDoux tested the subject with pairs of visual stimuli presented simultaneously to each side of a point located on a screen:

When a snow scene was presented to the right hemisphere and a chicken claw was presented to the left, (he) quickly . . . responded correctly by choosing a picture of a chicken (with) his right hand and a picture of a shovel (with) his left. The subject was then asked, "What did you see?" "I saw a claw and I picked the chicken, and you have to clean out the chicken shed with a shovel." In trial after trial, we saw this kind of response. The left hemisphere could easily and accurately identify why it had picked the answer, and . . . without batting an eye, it would incorporate the right hemisphere's response into the framework. While we knew exactly why the right hemisphere had made its choice, the left . . . could merely guess. Yet, the left did not offer its suggestion in a guessing vein but rather a statement of fact as to why that card had been picked. (263–64)

Gazzaniga and LeDoux interpret these results to mean that the primary task of the verbal self is to construct a reality based on behavior. They believe that our verbal selves are not always aware of the origin of our actions and therefore cannot be depended upon to interpret those actions correctly. As quoted in Springer and Deutsch: "It is as if the verbal self looks out and sees what the person is doing and from that knowledge it interprets a reality" (264). In this context the verbal self assumes information it cannot actually have, producing an inaccurate narrative.

Work with split-brain patients may indeed offer insights into clinical psychology as well. David Galin believes that split brain research can validate Freud's theory of an unconscious. Galin argues that normally the right and left hemispheres function together, but under certain conditions they can be opaque to each other. As a result, a situation resembling split brain can occur: "Imagine the effect on a child when his mother presents one message verbally, but quite another with her facial expression and body language; 'I am doing it because I love you, dear' say the words, but 'I hate you and will destroy you,' says the face" (Springer and Deutsch 261). If this occurs, the two hemispheres may be in conflict, in which case the left may try to prevent communication from the right side. During these moments, the left dominates completely, while the right goes underground, functioning as a Freudian unconscious, "an independent reservoir of inaccessible cognition" (262) which can create emotional turmoil. Both the Gazzaniga and LeDoux and the Galin studies indicate that necessary information may not always be accessible to the conscious mind, research findings which may have consequences for writers, particularly those investigating emotionally charged images and topics.

Another area of research interest involves the interrelationship of brain hemispheres, image, and emotion. Nonverbal sounds which produce a left ear advantage (right hemisphere) are crying and laughing. Indeed all these sounds processed by the right hemisphere are highly emotional. As Segalowitz argues in *Two Sides of the Brain,* "Recognition of them automatically involves dealing with feelings as much as with auditory perception" (101). Emotional questions compared with non-emotional ones produce left eye movements indicating right brain involvement. In another experiment, subjects were presented with a list of words which had either positive, negative, or neutral connotations (e.g., kiss, mother, pleasure, loyalty; snake, morgue, greed, cancer; cottage, ink, apparent, bland). The words were also either high or low in imagery. The emotionally charged words induced right hemisphere responses as did high-imagery words (Segalowitz 102). Some clinical researchers argue that positive emotions are more usually linked to left hemisphere activity and negative emotions to the right, but this is a controversial area at present. In any event it appears that the right hemisphere is more able to identify emotional stimuli. Since it also processes visual, sensory stimuli, this can account for the emotional wave that can hit writers when they begin to access long-buried experiences, especially those that have imagistic power. This recursive process can flush out the emotional truth and imagistic clarity of a given moment. When we are back in time to a specific experience, we can be flooded with images and emotions at the same time. Even smells long forgotten can assert themselves. One student told me as she was visualizing her grandmother's bedroom, she suddenly smelled her perfume. Another—just from looking at her grandmother's old wooden-handled fork—smelled pirogies cooking. Tina, in the essay about her grandmother referred to above, wrote that she could "almost smell her apartment."

Ornstein and Thompson, in *The Amazing Brain,* describe a study in which the brain activity of subjects was monitored while they read two types of written material: technical writing and folk tales. The left hemisphere registered no changes, but the right was more activated while the subject was reading stories than while reading the technical passages. Stories evoke images and feelings which appear to be right brain activities (162). In another experiment recounted in the same volume, subjects were asked to relive intensely emotional experiences. Here the left hemisphere seemed to process the happy experiences, while the right handled the negative ones. The authors speculate that the "left hemisphere may be involved in fine motor control, the right hemisphere in the control of large motor movements such as running and throwing. It might be that it was useful in our evolutionary history to have the control of large movements placed closely in the brain to the focus of negative feelings, so that if something had to be done, such as running or hitting, it could be done quite soon" (162). These studies indicate that we process pain and pleasure quite differently. Discovering exactly what these differences are can help us to access those moments more efficiently both in our writing and in our lives. As Hildy Miller argues in her essay "Sites of Inspiration," some composition specialists encourage writers to access the site of inspiration that relates to emotion and image by "having them intentionally regress into concrete and experiential ways of thinking. Such a process is necessary because in both our individual and cultural development, a split between concrete experience and abstract thought widens over time" (114). The more we learn about brain biology, the more we will be able to develop techniques that can help us access those parts of ourselves and our experiences which can provide the emotional and imagistic weight to our writing.

Image into Narrative

Writers have known for a while that the process of writing, of ordering our images into a coherent narrative, seems to give some measure of control over that which we cannot control—the past. The first step—recalling image—is followed by creating moments that are a string of images, just as film is a series of still pictures combined and perceived as a moving narrative line by our persistence of vision. While recalling our images helps us to re-experience the past, which can lead to insights about it, creating narrative from those images locates our stories outside of us, which enables us to feel that we have begun to form order from chaos. The relationship between thought and language is a close but mysterious one. As Orwell wrote in "Politics and the English Language," as thought corrupts language so does language corrupt thought. Perhaps the same feedback loop exists with image and narrative. First, we must access image, then connect with the experience that generated the image, then incorporate that image into a narrative that informs our lives, which then affects the way we process images in the future. As we do this, we have changed the organism so that we have become more conscious of image as a powerful factor in our lives. As we saw earlier, telling our images to another helps us to recover from trauma. Such tellings allow us to put our experience outside of ourselves. The images become stories which can be told, retold, studied, and compared with others' stories. A cultural context becomes possible. Individual barriers of isolation have been broken.

Another student, Meg, a young actress and a fine writer, was struggling with her first essay—a single moment that affected her as a child. She chose to write about an argument between her mother and her aunt. While the paper was inventive and well written, it lacked a core of truth that makes personal essays speak to others. It offered no details that create immediacy and verisimilitude. I wasn't sure why the paper was written, how the topic touched the author. As Meg and I talked about the paper I told her that I felt she had told her mother's story, not her story. She thought for a moment then said, "I know what I really want to write about. You gave us a class exercise to write about two moments in our lives, a happy one and a sad one. I'd like to write about the sad one. It's about my dad helping me with math, but I'm afraid to write about it because it will be depressing. He was awful when he helped me learn math." I told her, "No, Meg, now this is depressing. After you write about it, it will just be sad." She smiled, nodded her head and turned in the following paper, a universe away from the first attempt:

I take small steps out of my room of fish tank mural and Apple computer and clothes hamper and paint pens and green almanac and blue globe and *Little Women* and rainbow stationery and corduroys and turtlenecks and acrylic sweaters and size 10 Carter's and Pine Bros. cherry cough drops. I'm new to this school and this state and thirteen years old and school newspaper founder and editor, and too short hair, and thick glasses and school lunch and principal's favorite and bussers and walkers and morning announcements and gym and was there recess? and Space Shuttle memorial and *Romeo and Juliet* and David Bowie and writing short stories with heroines named Audrey and Kate Wing and Stephanie Lerner who were my only two friends and no bra and no breasts and no hips and no period and no boyfriend and needing to be out of Owen Brown Middle School before I had begun and Suzi Lobbin, Sun-In streaky hair and popular whose sole purpose on this earth was to torture, ridicule, and berate me, yet I was mature and well-adjusted and highest reading group and gifted and talented and high potential and intelligent and task commitment and works well with others and a pleasure to have in class.

And failing Algebra One.

There is acid swishing about in my stomach as I walk out of my bedroom onto the brassy orange carpet that lines the hall. Angry red algebra book open to the homework, notebook open too. My tall girl's body in a nightgown, flannel with puffy sleeves, lavender floral pattern that my mother can't touch because it tears at the dry skin of her fingertips in winter. Book and notebook against chest, breathing strained, I keep swallowing and composing sentences in my head. I make my way through yellow linoleum kitchen and orange dining room. . . .

I am headed to the den, where my father sits, with the *Wall Street Journal* and a TV sitcom blaring.

"Dad, kenyou help me with this?" indicating the book, I ask in a voice softer and higher than my own.

"Aaaheee," he replies exasperatedly. "Jesus Christ, Meg, you might want to think about this before the last minute." Acidic sarcasm raises the inflection and with it his dense, wiry eyebrows.

"It's not the last minute, Dad. I've been doing it in my room, there's just so much stuff I don't get. Couldja help me?"

"Yeah," he says, brows furrowed. He crumples the newspaper down on his lap. I walk to the couch to sit next to him. "What is it? Gimme," reaching for the red book. My handwriting is precise. My numbers are well formed and the problem headings lettered beautifully. "Meg, how many times do I have to tell you? You HAVE TO WRITE DOWN EVERY STEP."

And I wonder, is this a rhetorical question? If forced to answer I fear the number would be quite large.

"Dad, I don't know what that means, write down every step. What do you mean?"

"YOU'VE GOT TO WRITE EVERYTHING DOWN! YOU CAN'T LEAVE ANY STEPS OUT! YOU HAVE TO WRITE DOWN EVERY STEP, GODAMMIT."

This is spoken fortissimo. Dad and I have an understanding that the more decibels he employs, the more clear these mathematical concepts will become. This system, thus far, has been somewhat unsuccessful, but neither of us has given up yet.

The lesson continues with Dad doing an example problem, muttering about "new math" and procrastination, then instructing me to do the next problem while he turns back to the regularly scheduled programming. I start to work the equation, hunched over my flannel lap, stingy tears forming in my eyes, heat crawling up my back, my breath caught. I get stuck, don't understand, how did he get from here to there? Why do I have to be in smart math? Why do I always leave the den crying, nose running, my algebra understanding still minuscule?

My father is a chemical engineer for a steel manufacturer. He earned two degrees in college, one in chemical engineering, the other in metallurgy. He's a member of MENSA. He reads a lot of science fiction books, the kind that feature scantily clad, buxom women on the covers. He knows the scientific name of nearly every growing thing. He hybridizes day lilies and fashions ornate walking sticks from branches of trees in the neighborhood. He has a neon-colored Super-Soaker water gun which he purchased at KIDS 'R US so he can terrorize the neighborhood kids. Monsters, as he calls them. He snacks on uncooked spaghetti. He drinks a lot of wine and would smoke cigars in the house if my mother would let him. I don't know much else about him except that he yells, he's impatient, he says the wrong things, he's got an explosive temper, he makes broad judgments and character assassinations not based in truth, he's got a fairly closed mind, he's a horrible algebra tutor, he's cynical, thinks everything's a fraud, and he gets a lot of speeding tickets.

I did indeed fail algebra one that year. It was probably the best thing. I took it again my freshman year with the "average" kids and did fine. Suzi Lobbin was in my class. I think it was the next year that she got pregnant and stopped attending school.

I never asked my dad for help with math again. I never much asked for anything from him after my thirteenth year.

I have included this essay to demonstrate the depth of detail possible when writers are fully connected to their subjects. Meg's mind was full of pictures from her childhood; she just needed the "permission" and the opportunity to access them. While this incident might not be classified as "traumatic" by most, Meg still blocked writing about this scene, which demonstrated a side of her father she found difficult to accept. She wanted to protect him—and herself—from her truth, her responses to his behavior. But in doing so she blocked the source of her energy and creativity by telling someone else's story. Only by recovering her images, her memories, and then her voice could she become an effective writer.

Another student wanted to write about her grandmother, whom she loved very much. She turned in a first draft, but it was almost totally lacking in details. In conference I asked her to close her eyes and try to visualize her grandmother, her grandmother's house, and the things they did together. She could only remember playing Scrabble® and hearing the clock ticking on the mantle—tick, tick, moment after moment, the clock on the mantle next to the photograph of her grandfather, who died when he was fifty-four, and a photo of her grandmother's brother, who also died relatively young. Neither man was ever mentioned by her grandmother. Of her grandmother she remembered almost nothing. She finally realized the reason her essay had no details was that she had no substantial experiences with her grandmother to remember. What began as a tribute to a woman she loved became an expression of sorrow for a relationship that she never had.

These realizations do not come easily. Meg tried so hard to censor the girl who was angry at her father for his math "brutality" that while she remembered those moments, she buried their import for her. She simply took them as a part of her history, without letting herself feel how hard it was for her to accept those experiences. Another student, Brian, had a step-grandmother he loved. She was a strong, determined woman who could work longer and harder than most men. But the inevitable happened: She got old and senile. One day when the phone rang and Brian asked his grandmother to answer it, she agreed, shuffled over to a bowl of ripe bananas and picked up one, holding it to her ear.

"Hello, hello," she said. He ended the paper with that scene, which left both him and us hanging. In a conference the student expressed some dissatisfaction with his ending. I asked him if he had told all the story. No, he said, but what follows was hard for him to remember. She had gone into a nursing home, and he didn't want to remember that part. But he did remember it—and so well. His last memory of her is her smile:

> Zola was in room 205. I hesitated in front of the door, waiting for what I thought would be the perfect time to make my entrance. I took a deep breath, grabbed the handle and slowly turned the door knob. Zola lay in a bed that rested in the center of a dimly lit chamber that felt like a hospital room. It was apparent she didn't recognize me because when I came into her room she gave me a wide-eyed gaze that looked right through me, past the door, and to the other side of the hall. I took a chair, pulled up alongside her bed, and sat gazing out the window. The evening sky was coming across the land and the sun was quietly surrendering to the dark night. I reached over and grabbed Zola's hand in mine. . . . What once were strong hands full of muscle now lay floating in my palm. Zola's hand didn't move the slightest. These tiny wrinkled fingers had surpassed their working use long ago.
>
> It was getting late and suddenly I realized I had been there a good hour and a half. Zola looked tired. I got up, kissed her lightly on the cheek, and walked towards the door. Just as I was approaching the entrance, I turned around towards Zola for my last look. Zola returned my glance by craning her neck in my direction. She looked directly into my eyes, and suddenly she smiled that same yellow-toothed grin that I had seen so many years ago.

That smile is the real story; it's what she really was to him. He had abandoned his memory of that smile because remembering her smile meant he also had to remember saying goodbye in that nursing home, something that caused him much pain. But in blocking that memory he had also blocked out her greatest gifts to him as well—her strength and her sweetness. In reconstructing the image of her smile he reconstructed his conscious memory of her, and both he and his essay grew in the process. His last memories of her are no longer of the senile old woman holding a banana and believing it was the telephone, but of the strong, loving woman who helped anchor him to the planet, and now he has shown that to us as well. He was able to integrate his traumatic images of her into his happier ones, creating a more holistic memory of her—and of their relationship.

Narrative is the chain that links our moments together. But image is what we see in the dark of night, what we wake up with from dreams, what we remember when we recall those we love. It is image that burns itself into our minds whether we want it to or not, and it is image which can free us from a past that will always have a hold on us until we look straight at the images that live behind our eyes. Image is also the lifeblood of the personal essay. It grabs us and forces us to see through the writer's eyes. It sutures reader and writer into a living unit.

Personal Essays in the Academy

Our students have few academic opportunities to probe the images I have been talking about. Some in our discipline are understandably uncomfortable with autobiographical writing. The 1993 debate in the *Chronicle* about the ethics of requiring students to produce personal writing reflects a genuine concern many teachers have regarding this genre (see Swartzlander, Pace, and Stamler). But, as outlined earlier, if the personal essay course is an elective, students can choose to open themselves up to this genre; they will not be coerced into it by an enthusiastic first-year composition instructor, and they can pick their own topics, which offers them the control. The intensity of the experience is theirs.

The personal essay has at times been denigrated as simply a therapeutic genre, an exercise in catharsis, or even a moment of voyeurism on the part of the reader. This vision of the genre creates problems with assessment. Rolf Norgaard, in a letter published in the *College English* "Comment and Response" section, expressed discomfort with this issue, believing that we cannot separate the content from its execution:

> How are we to assess such writing? Can we tell a student that her experiences or family life weren't terribly original or

striking? . . . Perhaps personal, autobiographical writing can promote a more graceful style . . . but to what end? If we use writing to teach students to understand their psyches, not a shared world of issues and ideas, we leave ourselves little room for anything but tangles about assessment. (100)

This comment blurs together two major issues: First, the personal essay is an art form, and as such it can be held accountable to the rules of that art form. Students can be taught how to write a personal essay in the same way that they can be taught to write any other genre. Meg's experiences with her father and math are not uncommon in our culture. But she created the moment so clearly and with such honest detail that we can identify with her. The details are unique, the theme universal. In fact, it is not the uniqueness of her theme which draws us but the underlying truth it conveys, one we all share. It is the *craft* that conveys this truth, and that can be taught—and, therefore, evaluated. However, teachers of the personal essay need to feel comfortable with the principles of the art form, just as teachers of academic writing must understand the rules of that genre. Once that is accomplished, grading the personal essay is no different from grading a research paper. Most students welcome the distinction between their lives and the craft of telling the stories about their lives. It provides them with a safe distance that helps them see their work as malleable, dynamic. Most of my students choose to rewrite their essays, sometimes many times, and take great pride in doing so. At this point the grade often becomes irrelevant. The writers simply wish to produce the best possible story they can. The process offers them the opportunity to transform the past into art.

The second important issue here is Norgaard's concern that the personal essay lacks a shared world of issues and ideas. We need to remember the long tradition of autobiography, memoir, and personal commentary, which is a part of the Western rhetorical tradition. Montaigne, White, Orwell, and contemporary writers such as Alice Walker clearly have contributed to our collective awareness of what it means to be human. The personal essay carries us into a universe of shared experience and shared humanity. And when the essay moves into sensitive areas, we are reminded that trauma is an integral part of human experience. We cannot proclaim our humanity without acknowledging our capacity for suffering and the results of that suffering. The successful personal essay does not wallow in itself; it promotes identification. Personal essay writers learn how to communicate their experiences without alienating their readers with narcissistic sufferings. And paradoxically enough, the very technique which works in therapy—to describe specific scenes with as much detail as possible—is the same one that creates reader identification and thereby prevents the uncomfortable sensation of being a voyeur inside someone else's life. In addition, the practice and time spent with the genre and the distance which comes from writing enable students to recognize where their experiences fit into the greater life of the culture as a whole. They then begin to see themselves as part of a larger environment.

An article in *USA Today* (11 January 1994), reported a poll which demonstrated that almost one-half of young adults had witnessed an act of violence in the last year, and nearly a fourth were crime victims. Even if our students are lucky enough to escape the violence of our cities, many have endured the familial anguish of parental divorce, abuse, neglect, or death. These are the students who appear before us in our classrooms. Most of us who have spent time in the classroom understand that students who are currently caught by difficult experiences have a hard time putting those aside to learn. Indeed, those moments can define what and how we learn. Giving students an opportunity to integrate past and present can be an aid to learning.

I am not suggesting that we require autobiographical writing of all students, only that we offer the opportunity for those students who seek it. Although some of my students tell me that they expect the personal essay class to be easy, they discover that it is one of the hardest classes they will take since it demands so much of them. They must probe, question, peer into their deepest most significant moments to write a good personal essay. They must tell the truth, their truth, something not easily done in our culture.

Most of us blank out in order to cope. We can't do two things at once—both process an event and deal with new ones—and survival depends on coping with what is currently in front of us.

Research into brain functioning can help to explain this phenomenon. In a report from *Scientific American* written by Mortimer Mishkin and Tim Appenzeller (the former is chief of the laboratory of neuropsychology at the National Institute of Mental Health), the authors state that the same organ which processes sensory memories, the amygdala, also allows them to acquire their emotional weight. The authors suggest that the amygdala not only "enables sensory events to develop emotional associations but also enables emotions to shape perception and the storage of memories"(10). In other words, we cannot recall a difficult memory without also re-experiencing the emotional charge it produces. This can certainly account for writer's block in some cases. We tend to avoid unpleasant memories, and writing about them revisits them and the emotions attached to them. Yet we are drawn to writing about them when the time is right because without encountering them at some point, we will remain their prisoner. A typical example of this phenomenon was the plight of a quiet, sweet-faced young female student who could not find a topic for her final paper assignment—to write about a conflict in her life or within herself and how it was resolved. My student said she had written about everything important earlier in the course. I asked other students in the class to share their topics with the class in the hopes of offering possible inspiration for others. One student's subject was her father's explosive temper. After class, the quiet young woman came up to me and said, "I can't believe I didn't think of this until class today. It's so obvious. My father was alcoholic most of my childhood. We never talk about it, especially now that he is sober." She turned in a powerful essay which greatly pleased her—both because the writing was excellent and because she started making connections between her father's past alcoholism and her passive stance in life.

Separating the Text from the Life of the Writer

It is important to stress that I am not suggesting that writing teachers assume the role of amateur therapists. The purpose of any writing class is to foster good writing and the concomitant thinking skills that accompany such an activity. But the original meaning of the word "amateur" is instructive here. Our love for our students, for their truths, for their potential clarity of vision and writing talent can motivate excellence more than anything else. Our profession has, for a number of years now, adopted the process model in writing instruction; that model necessitates a clear understanding that writing is a recursive act. Conscious and unconscious processes engage in a dialogue in which each is informed by the other, and the writing teacher is the facilitator for that dialogue. Yet our profession is understandably uncomfortable articulating any link between writing and therapy. The most effective and ethical approach to this issue, as I have already suggested, is for writing teachers to deal with the author's text, not his life, recognizing, however, that this distinction does not take into account the recursive nature of the writing process. And indeed, we must be aware that our students do not always make this distinction, since to write about a moment often means we must re-vision it, and to re-vision a moment often means to open our lives to its consequences.

I encountered a striking example of this dilemma in my personal essay class. A student's first essay described an experience he had at the age of eight. His parents were engaged in a loud argument which became violent. My student was in his bedroom, unable to avoid hearing every word, every pounding of a fist on a table, every slap. He also desperately had to use the bathroom, but to do that meant crossing into the room where his parents were fighting. He waited until he thought he would burst and finally ran into the room. While the essay was both funny and tragic, it clearly described a young boy frozen into himself by fear. The rest of the semester he wrote essays in which he functioned, in his life as well as in his essays, only as observer. The essays were emotionally and stylistically flat. Clearly, he was not an engaged participant but the protected observer. Certainly, I could demonstrate from the texts themselves that his writing needed engagement, but this student was intuitive and would go beyond my discussion of his text to discover the source of his blockage once his essays' limitations were pointed out. I knew that if I had this conversation with my student, the door would be opened to a subject he might or might not wish to handle—and one which went beyond the confines of the writing class. I decided to have this conversation with my student. He, of course, did make the connection, which began a long period of self-discovery and soul-searching. He discovered that many of his interactions with others were flat too, a result of his childhood experiences. In a moment of ironic humor he asked me what my qualifications were for my job—and no, I do not have an MSW; however, this student understood that his writing—he was a film/screenwriting major—would always be limited until he looked hard at that night so many years ago.

I learned from this experience that even adhering to the dictum that we deal with texts, not lives, can engage us in broader more personal discussions than our profession generally sanctions. As Phillip Lopate argues on page xliv of his introduction to *The Art of the Personal Essay,* "The self-consciousness and self-reflection that essay writing demands cannot help but have an influence on the personal essayist's life." Montaigne himself described the convergence of life and text in the following way: "I have no more made my book than my book has made me" (Montaigne qtd. in Lopate). Students quickly recognize that the separation of text and life is artificial; therefore, conversations with our students regarding their work can become problematic. To allow such conversations with our students is to risk overwhelming them with psychic material of which they are unaware. To avoid such conversations is to limit their growth as writers and as people. I have no easy answers for this dilemma. I will say, however, that no one should teach the personal essay without recognizing with brutal awareness that she may well encounter student papers which grapple with extremely difficult topics. This is not a course for everyone—not for all teachers, nor for all students. This is why I do not advocate a first-year personal essay course, nor do I mandate paper topics. Students need the safety of writing about what draws them. They should not be forced to write on topics they do not wish to pursue, even if the instructor believes certain topics to be necessary to their growth as writers. We can provide our students with the opportunity to pursue topics via classroom exercises, visualizations, and suggestions for further writing, but the rest is up to them. If and when they come to their chosen moments with complete free will, they are ready to write, to look at their pasts in new and perhaps surprising ways. In *Technologies of the Self*, Michel Foucault argues: "What would be the value of the passion for knowledge if it resulted only in a certain amount of knowledgeableness and not, in one way or another and to the extent possible, in the knower's straying afield of himself? There are times in life when the question of knowing if one can think differently than one thinks, and perceive differently than one sees, is absolutely necessary if one is to go on looking or reflecting at all." My student needed to go beyond his usual way of seeing himself and his world. Perhaps those of us who are called to teach writing also need to re-vision our roles with students and the historical distinctions between text and author, therapy and writing, and public and private discourse.

One of the reasons why David Bartholomae finds little to recommend the personal essay in the academic curriculum is his concern that such a course maintains "the figure of the author at a time when the figure of the author is under attack in all other departments of the academy" (70). Of course, I am not so sure that every other department in the academy will so readily give up personal authorship of conference papers, individual ownership of patents, literary awards, and perhaps even Nobel prizes (or for that matter, articles in *College Composition and Communication*), but be that as it may. My concern here is with this concept of "the author," of "the self" even. Our students come to us with selves just beginning to become aware of the forces that have pressed on them for eighteen to twenty years. Recognition of "intertextuality" can only come with an awareness of the texts we all write from the moments of our lives, and those that are written upon us by experiences over which we have little or no control. Those of us who work with writers just beginning to recognize how their experiences have affected them witness time and again the empowerment that can come from expressing the inexpressible; we watch as writers gain a measure of control over their pasts by constructing voices that can order experience and witness the sense of community that can be built from communicating those experiences to others.

As Pennebaker and others have shown, most people are helped by speaking or writing to another of their experience, even if the "other" is not a trained therapist (Christina Miller 75). Felman and Laub argue in their book *Testimony* that personal and cultural recovery from trauma requires a conversation between the victim and a witness, that indeed the witness is an utter necessity to complete the cycle of truth telling. If we shy away from offering our students the opportunity to tell their truths, we may be preventing them from learning what control they can have over their own lives. The more violent and threatening our culture becomes, the more we need to acknowledge the effects of trauma on our students. Those of us whose professional lives are defined by the classroom need to be aware that every pair of eyes facing us has probably borne witness to some difficult moments that can affect learning. At the 1996 National Association for Poetry Therapy Conference, poet Lucille Clifton said to a room full of educators and clinicians about the children they work with: "Every pair of eyes facing you may have endured something you could not bear."

Some may argue that the mission of higher education does not include attention to personal healing; however, as James Moffett argues in a response to "The Spiritual Sites of Composing," an "Interchange" in the May 1994 *College Composition and Communication,*

> We get good at doing something as a part of getting well and realizing our deepest being. I know, the university feels it shouldn't play doctor or priest, dirty its hands with therapy and its mind with religion. But if it has real live students on its hands, its hands are already dirty. . . . Unhealed wounds and undeveloped souls will thwart the smartest curriculum. (261)

Many students move toward wholeness in a course such as personal essay, and we certainly hope that this occurs. As writers move from their narratives to the personal essay itself, they become both owners of their moments and witnesses for others. The particular becomes contextualized for both writers and readers. Personal essays begin with the individual but end with the universal, a process which itself creates connections that can heal. However, for our purposes as writing instructors, we seek academic benefits for our students which can be demonstrated, and certainly nothing will encourage a student to discover her "voice" faster and more directly than probing her history to seek her truth of it. Writing someone else's history, or something else's, can be fascinating and enlightening, but students cannot form the connections between worlds without unearthing their own values, ethics, and underlying assumptions produced by their past experiences and how they have encountered them. The personal essay asks students to begin a journey into themselves, but the journey will take them ultimately out of themselves and back to a community which can reestablish our common humanity.

Notes

1. For a full discussion of the neurobiology of trauma, see Bessel A. van der Kolk, et al., *Traumatic Stress,* New York: Guilford Press, 1996.

Works Cited

Agosta, Carolyn, and Mary McHugh. "Sexual Assault Victims: The Trauma and the Healing." *Post-Traumatic Stress Disorders: A Handbook for Clinicians.* Ed. Tom Williams. Cincinnati: Disabled American Veterans, 1987. 239–51.

Bartholomae, David. "Writing with Teachers: A Conversation with Peter Elbow." *College Composition and Communication* 46.1 (1995): 62–71.

Bishop, Wendy. "Writing Is/and Therapy?: Raising Questions about Writing Classrooms and Writing Program Administration." *Journal of Advanced Composition* 13.2 (1993): 503–16.

Britton, James, et al. *The Development of Writing Abilities (11–18).* London: Macmillan Education, 1975.

Bucci, Wilma. "The Power of the Narrative: A Multiple Code Account." *Emotion, Disclosure, and Health.* Ed. James W. Pennebaker. Washington, DC: American Psychological Association, 1995. 93–122.

Cahill, Larry, James McGaugh, et al. "Beta-adrenergic activation and memory for emotional events." *Nature* 371 (1994): 702–4.

Clifton, Lucille. Keynote Address. Association for Poetry Therapy National Conference. Columbia, Maryland, 1996.

Faigley, Lester. *Fragments of Rationality: Postmodernity and the Subject of Composition.* Pittsburgh: U of Pittsburgh P, 1992.

Felman, Shoshana, and Dori Laub. *Testimony: Crises of Witnessing in Literature, Psychoanalysis, and History.* New York: Routledge, 1992.

Fincke, Ronald A. *Principles of Mental Imagery.* Cambridge: MIT P, 1989.

Foucault, Michel. *Technologies of the Self: A Seminar with Michel Foucault.* Ed. L. Martin, H. Gutman, and P. Hutton. Amherst: U of Massachusetts P, 1988.

Herman, Judith Lewis. *Trauma and Recovery.* New York: Basic, 1992.

Krystal, John H., Steven M. Southwick, and Dennis S. Charney. "Post-Traumatic Stress Disorder: Psychobiological Mechanisms of Traumatic Remembrance." *Memory Distortion: How Minds, Brains, and Societies Reconstruct the Past.* Ed. Daniel Schacter. Cambridge: Harvard UP, 1995. 150–72.

Lopate, Phillip. *The Art of the Personal Essay.* New York: Anchor/Doubleday, 1994.

Miller, Christina. "Mental Powers." *Longevity* 2 (1990): 74–75.

Miller, Hildy. "Sites of Inspiration: Where Writing is Embodied in Image and Emotion." *Presence of Mind: Writing and the Domain Beyond the Cognitive.* Ed. Alice G. Brand and Richard L. Graves. Portsmouth, NH: Boynton/Cook, 1994. 113–24.

Mills, Joshua. "In Your-Faceism vs. Light." *The New York Times Educational Supplement* (8 Jan. 1994): 19–20.

Mishkin, Mortimer, and Tim Appenzeller. "The Anatomy of Memory." *Scientific American* 256 (1987): 80–89.

Moffett, James. "Interchanges: Spiritual Sites of Composing." *College Composition and Communication* 45 (1994): 258-61.

Norgaard, Rolf. Letter. "Comment and Response." *College English* 56 (1994): 98–100.

Ornstein, Robert, and Richard Thompson. *The Amazing Brain*. Boston: Houghton, 1991.

Pennebaker, James W. *Opening Up: The Healing Power of Confiding in Others*. New York: Avon, 1992, 1997.

Segalowitz, Sid. *Two Sides of the Brain*. Englewood Cliffs, NJ: Prentice, 1983.

Springer, Sally, and Georg Deutsch. *Left Brain, Right Brain*. New York: W. H. Freeman, 1985.

Squire, Larry. "Biological Foundations of Accuracy and Inaccuracy in Memory." *Memory Distortion: How Minds, Brains, and Societies Reconstruct the Past*. Ed. Daniel Schacter. Cambridge: Harvard UP, 1995. 197–225.

Swartzlander, Susan, Diana Pace, and Virginia Lee Stamler. "The Ethics of Requiring Students to Write about Their Personal Lives." *The Chronicle of Higher Education* (17 Feb. 1993): B1–2.

Williams, Tom. "Diagnosis and Treatment of Survivor Guilt—The Bad Penny." *Post-Traumatic Stress Disorders: A Handbook for Clinicians*. Ed. Tom Williams. Cincinnati: Disabled American Veterans, 1987. 75–91.

CHAPTER EIGHT

Healing and the Brain

ALICE G. BRAND

State University of New York College at Brockport

On August 15, 1989, *The New York Times* (Goleman) reported that neuroscientist Joseph LeDoux, experimenting with animals, discovered nerve pathways that led *directly* to a small structure buried in the brain called the amygdala. According to LeDoux, when, for example, you think you see something that looks like a snake, the amygdala gets the message forty milliseconds before the intellectual part of your brain does. You jump because your emotions react first, not because you reasoned through the danger of the snake. William James hypothesized this for basic emotions like fear and anger about one hundred years ago.

I was first drawn to this biology because I was trying to find a way to talk about emotion and language besides in opposition to cognition. I was angry with cognitive scientists for insisting that intellectual enterprises have sovereignty over emotion, for insisting that with the human intellect comes an objective reality, an ineluctable truth. We now acknowledge through such terms as social construction, cultural indeterminacy, and interpretation that this is phenomenologically a lie. But cognitivists in general are slow to come to terms with the evolutionary given that affective processes determine the "life and death selection" of behavior (Brown 408). When LeDoux confirmed what philosopher Bain, psychologist Bartlett, social scientist Zajonc, and others (Brand, *Psychology*; "Defining") claimed of emotional primacy, I found it in brain biology. I found new evidence for committing our energies to the entire affective continuum from arousal to human values. And I found much to celebrate about our cognitive biology.

Our profession has passed through this territory before: Emig, Shook, and Rico and Claggett—bait for articles on language and rhetoric, but rarely for articles on the biology of writing and never on healing.[1] Indeed, language, cognition, and emotion come together in the brain. That is why we should study it.

But how could I talk about the brain to colleagues, so that it would be interesting, understandable, and relevant? How could I tell colleagues I was no longer afraid to be confused by its convoluted processes or its technical terms? I was no longer afraid to mispronounce a term, and I wished to pass this courage on. I was learning how the mind arises from the brain as a physical entity in evolutionary history; how such a discussion tells us who and how we are; the rightness of knowing how we know; how brain science helps explain learning; how the properties of language that the brain empowers us with make for change—the very basis of healing.

Components of the Brain

Ontogeny recapitulates phylogeny. Brain development of the species parallels the mental development brought about by biological maturation (see Figure 8-1). The *hindbrain* is part of the brain stem and spinal column and, as such, is the oldest part of the brain. It houses the cerebellum, pons, medulla oblongata, the center of which contains much of the reticular formation, charged with our nonspecific states of alertness, arousal, and gross adaptive behaviors.

The hindbrain controls the involuntary[2] (respiratory, circulatory, digestive) systems and arousal behaviors and converts general decisions into basic muscle or motor commands. The next and smallest section of the brain stem is the *midbrain* (sometimes considered part of the upper brain stem). It is made up of the remaining reticular formation and primitive sensory centers developed to perceive from a distance (Heath 5; Penrose 380–2). Both hindbrain and midbrain control the automatic or unconscious aspects of behavior.

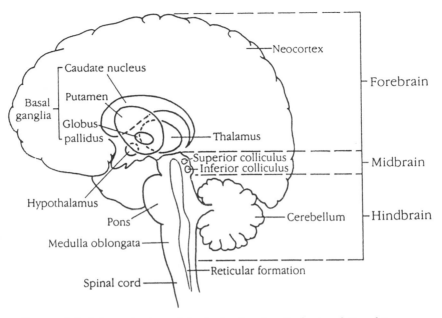

FIGURE 8-1 *Schematic view of the brain showing the basic relationships of deep nuclear groups and brain-stem structures. From M. S. Gazzaniga, D. Steen, and B. Volpe,* Functional Neuroscience, *Fig. 3.13, p. 61. Copyright © 1979 by Harper & Row Publishers, Inc. Used with permission of Michael S. Gazzaniga.*

The newest and largest section, the *forebrain* or *cerebrum,* is divided into four lobes (occipital, parietal, temporal, and frontal) or two cerebral hemispheres that are linked by the neural fibers of the corpus callosum. Covering the surface of the cerebral hemispheres is the outer layer of gray matter, 60 percent of which makes up the neocortex or associative cortex and 40 percent, specific motor and sensory regions. All in all, an estimated 100 billion cells[3] reside in the brain—not to mention their 10^{15} synaptic connections.

In the deepest recesses of the forebrain sit the thalamus, hypothalamus, hippocampus, and amygdala, part of the relatively hard-wired structure of the proto or reptilian brain called the limbic lobe.[4] The tradition regarding the growth of the central nervous system is that from bulb-like projections at the upper end of the spinal column developed the limbic lobe, the proto brain or transitional cortex, and the forebrain. The limbic lobe had initially such rudimentary but crucial emotional responses as approach and withdrawal and gustatory and reproductive functions, which are in many respects as affective as they are organic. In fact, some neuroscientists (MacLean; Papez) have called the limbic lobe the visceral brain—suggesting how closely it is allied to these organic functions.

For many years the conventional thinking was that our reticular system aroused, our limbic system "felt," and our neocortex, the thinking part of our brain, controlled. This last is particularly true in contemporary therapy. Since the higher brain emerged after the proto brain, it makes sense that the prevailing view of how therapy works is that the cortex exerts top down or executive control or inhibition (of the emotional excesses) of the subcortex within the limbic area.

Cognitive Therapy

The standard cognitive position is that to evaluate stimuli, the brain analyzes the situation *before* producing the emotional response and/or emotional experience (Lazarus; Mandler). At the risk of oversimplifying, mental "analyses" may in principle be considered of two kinds: One is purely informational; the other relates stimuli to the self and thus carries emotion (usually negative) with it. The former occurs in the absence of feeling. Linked to emotion, the latter would require more elaborate mental processing of the stimulus and its meaning.

Assessing the affective significance of experience is considered a cognitive process under several circumstances.

Most obvious, as feelings ascend the biochemical pathways and arrive in consciousness, one way to express and/or communicate them is by naming them. We make language, a complex cognitive act. In other instances, affective arousal is ambiguous until the cortex does a meaning analysis of the situation. Also cognitive. In still other situations, when feelings are complicated like shame, pride, frustration, and anxiety[5] (Brand, *Psychology*; LeDoux, "Emotional" 70), sensory signals also pass to the neocortex for analysis of meaning and integration. To break the thought is to break the anxiety.

Early psychological theories debated these processes. The James-Lange theory postulated that emotional experiences resulted *from* biological/behavioral changes. Cannon hypothesized the opposite. He maintained that emotional experiences were generated *centrally* by way of thalamic activation of the cerebral cortex, with the muscles or senses only providing feedback (Goleman C9). Fifty years ago Papez postulated the hypothalamus as the organizing unit of the emotional/cognitive circuit. Finally, holding sway during the last forty years in determining the significance of experience has been the limbic system (MacLean; LeDoux).

Research indicates that the limbic system of the paleocortex is responsible for the "*uncognized* universal *psychobiological* experiences*" (Kleinman 173), similar to those of lower mammals. The capacity of lower animals for *learning* and *remembering* the significance of internal and external events is built into the brain. It is organic and adaptive, but it is limited. However, the neocortex of humans has evolved a quantitatively greater and profoundly more elaborate capacity for determining the significance of stimuli. Uncognized responses, along with their electrical and chemical signals, evolve into emotions influenced by cognition as well as by social and cultural specifics, something lower animals are only incipiently capable of.

The hippocampus, the small sea horse–shaped structure and principal part of the limbic lobe, is considered central to healing—but for reasons other than what would be assumed by its neurological and anatomical proximity to other limbic structures (LeDoux, "Cognitive" 269; O'Keefe and Nadel). Given its location, the hippocampus would be expected to regulate affective experience. Oddly enough, the hippocampus participates in healing to the extent that psychotherapy occurs on the cognitive level.

This is what it does. The hippocampus is responsible for processing spatial, configural, contextual, and relational information when nonemotional or cognitive aspects of a task require it (LeDoux, "Emotional" 70). This is called cognitive mapping, in which it is theorized that we build psychological maps of meaning and space. The left hippocampus regulates semantic maps.

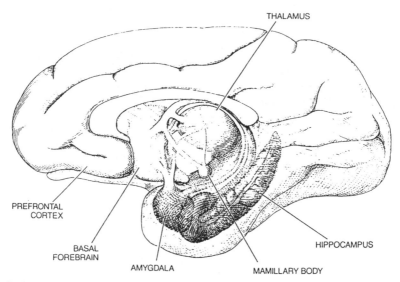

FIGURE 8-2 *Mishkin, Mortimer, and Tim Appenzeller. "The Anatomy of Memory."* Scientific American *256.6 (June 1987): 80–89. Used with permission of Carol Donner.*

The right hippocampus is responsible for physical or spatial maps—including the visual forms of words (O'Keefe and Nadel; Wheeler A10). Together they form long-term context-specific memory for episodes and narratives (O'Keefe and Nadel 410).

This leads me to what the hippocampus has become best known for: its participation in the conscious, declarative, explicit recollection of events—the key to intellectual functioning. Put another way, although memories per se are not stored in it, the hippocampus is essential for laying them down permanently (Neimark 46; O'Keefe and Nadel).

One important aspect of hippocampal activity is accounting for autobiographical memory, emotional or not. However, as we may realize from our own experience, autobiographical memory starts at about age three or four because the hippocampus is not fully mature at birth. But, relative to the hippocampus, the amygdala is (LeDoux, "Cognitive" 281) (see Figure 8-2).

Emotional Biology

Therefore, if the limbic area survives as a contributor to human mental experience, the newest literature indicates that it is due not only to the cognitive work of the hippocampus, but also to a tiny almond-shaped structure called the *amygdala*. Exquisitely sensitive, the amygdala gives affective significance to events. Considering its size, the amygdala is so densely differentiated as to demonstrate "how rich the human neural substrate" is for emotions.

Moreover, because of its early maturation and the intimate relationship between memory and emotion (Aggleton and Mishkin 296; Heath 32; LeDoux, "Cognitive"), it is responsible for the first nondeclarative, implicit, or unconscious memories that are lost to the hippocampus. The results of those autobiographical memories may be experienced, but their reasons can only be inferred. At the anatomical crossroads of the cortex and limbic system, it is thus a major player in healing.

But that is not all it does. Particularly labile among the neural circuits (LeDoux, "Emotional"), the amygdala and other parts of the brain are reciprocally active:

1. The amygdala receives input from the hypothalamus, the seat of the biological impulses of aggression, sex, pleasure, rage, fear, and hunger (Aggleton and Mishkin 296; Fonberg 320).

2. With the hypothalamus, the amygdala is involved in base motivational states (Fonberg 303), an essential form of emotion (Brand, "Defining"). So that "a hungry [person] may be less fearful than a satiated one" (LeDoux, "Emotional" 76)—hunger being more rudimentary than fear.

3. Concurrent activation of the amygdala and hippocampus results in deep memory. This means that memory comes to exist "independently" of the hippocampus[6] but still influences experience (Neimark). It is as if memory is burned into the brain.

4. The amygdala receives data from the hippocampus about the *context* of stimuli (LeDoux, "Emotional" 73) when ambiguity in the internal or external environment requires conscious consideration (71).

5. The amygdala-thalamus circuit is responsible for infant memory not available to the hippocampus (LeDoux, "Cognitive" 275, 281).

6. The amygdala receives sensory information directly from the thalamus, the major relay station. For example, the eyes transmit signals to the thalamus which, with the amygdala, transmits them to the visual cortex where they are integrated. We recognize them and determine what they mean, that is, perceive them (Aggleton and Mishkin 295–96; LeDoux, "Cognitive" 282–83; Goleman C9).

7. The amygdala-hippocampus circuit facilitates sensory integration, converting *specific* sensory input (olfactory, auditory) into feelings and behavior according to their emotional value, for example, fear that is learned through hearing (LeDoux, "Emotional" 76).

However, what deserves notice is that the amygdala also *bypasses* the cortex or "cognitive" brain. Not elaborate but basic emotions from their initial sensory or internal phases yield information *directly* to the muscles and viscera for behavioral, autonomic, or humoral response, *unmediated* by the intellectual apparatus. The amygdala also converts sensory input *directly* into feelings (LeDoux, "Cognitive" 272; Zajonc). For example, LeDoux's studies on fear found a *direct* path between the thalamus and amygdala bypassing the hippocampus, which "allows the amygdala to respond faster" than the hippocampus to a stimulus, the hippocampus "being separated from the thalamus by several [more] synapses" (Murphy and Zajonc 57–58). The amygdala can register "memory before it even reaches our senses" (Neimark 46). As a result, "emotional responses can be rapidly initiated on the basis of crude stimulus properties prior to and independent of" the intellect (LeDoux, "Cognitive" 272)—just like when seeing the snake.

Activity that operates through the amygdala, though less complete than that involving complex transformations, allows us to like something without knowing exactly what it is, to feel good or bad without knowing precisely why (Nisbett and Wilson). The existence of multiple connections returning to various sensory areas from the amygdala may also explain why one stimulus event can trigger several memories (Mishkin and Appenzeller 88).

Events passing through the amygdala are rapidly learned and long-lasting. What's more, once our emotional system learns something, we may never let it completely go. This means that in any given situation, fundamental feelings may be more immediate than the intellect, however crucial both are for learning and remembering.

Conscious Healing

In fact, if we did not believe in learning and remembering, we could not believe in healing. But we also cannot believe in learning and memory without also believing in emotion (Bartlett). The amygdala influences *what* gets stored and the *strength* with which it gets stored because it reads emotions. And "[e]motion is the determinant in the learning experience from which consciousness evolves" (Heath 6).

While it is clear that much learning is spontaneous and incidental and some of the best learning cannot be articulated, the ability to undertake therapy, in our case, through language, is in no small matter due to our consciousness. While learning and memory are not necessarily based in language, when they intersect in consciousness, healing is enabled.

I will discuss two matters in this regard: (1) consciousness, because making things conscious is one way to approach healing, and (2) the language centers, because learned language engages the consciousness. And language is one medium for sharing it.

Primary Consciousness

Whether we agree on cognitive primacy, affective primacy, or some combination of the two, according to Popper and Eccles (251), the old cortex accounts for the experience of "primary" consciousness elaborated with its emotional overtones. It is now conventional wisdom that cognitive processing and the emotional significance of events are initiated outside of conscious awareness, with only the products entering awareness (LeDoux, "Cognitive" 272; Nisbett and Wilson; Zajonc).

Enter language. True language evolved from what neuroscientist Gerald Edelman calls a primary consciousness, an awareness of ongoing experience. Among the key mental events marking primary consciousness are (1) perceptual categorization, (2) memory, (3) learning, and (4) the self-nonself distinction (*Remembered* 93). It is easy to see why. These mental events are an outgrowth of the proto brain: the limbic lobe (with its value-laden hedonic centers), the perceptual apparatus (of the early cortices), and the hippocampus (an early cognitive structure) (151–53). I will focus on the first item because, as the basis for the other three, perceptual categorization may be explained in terms of brain biology.

Perceptual Categorization

What Francis Crick considered the most daunting of mental phenomena is precisely what Edelman attempts to unravel with his construct of perceptual categorization. Perception may be considered the *nonmediated* impact of external stimuli on the brain (Vygotsky 38–39). In keeping with evolutionary biology, Edelman takes a more specialized but not contradictory position on perception when he refers to it as the "*adaptive* discrimination of an object or event" from its background or other phenomena (Edelman, *Remembered* 49; *Bright* 87). He further defines perception as the *selective* sampling of external stimuli by sensory circuits—what I call biology + interpretation (Brand, "Defining").

The story starts with genetic instruction which provides general guidelines for each neuron's eventual location and function. While developing brain cells become progressively limited in what they can do, neurons are not "carved in stone." Repeated encounters with a stimulus allow neural patterns to be activated preferentially. Facilitated pathways mean the selective strengthening of these cells. Such differentiation leads to a means "for assigning salience to some events over others" (Edelman, *Remembered* 94). This competitive selection process makes minuscule changes in our brain cells. It alters synapses by increasing their branching. It captures cells and forms groups that change their shapes and that adhere to each other in different strengths

(*Neural* 45–46). The brain network is thus "created by cellular movement during development and by the extension and connection" to each other and to experience (*Bright* 25). Neural systems are similar in shape, number, size, and connectivity from person to person but are not identical—even in identical twins (25).

As cells cluster together, they form neural groups, then networks, then systems, and finally "functioning circuits in maps" (Edelman, *Remembered* 41). Just as various parts of the body are mapped onto the sensory and motor cortex, so too do neural groups eventually create and consolidate maps. For Edelman these maps are, first, unique motor and sensory structures. Second, they are dynamic. They contain multiple recursive paths that change in endless layer and loop fashion. With each microinstance of sensory or internal perception, neural circuits form and re-form themselves ever so slightly (Edelman, *Bright* 25). At the cellular level, these processes cause us to categorize things differently. Their intricate genetic map or morphology alters form without our even knowing it. Put simply, on its own, each neuron makes an insignificant change. Together, neuronal groups alter behavior in subtle or even glaring ways (48).

Insofar as categorizing, Scribner and Cole claim that virtually "[a]ll psychological theories" about what characterizes the human intellect "rest heavily on [our] ability to classify things and events" (117). So too in theoretical brain biology.

The cellular movement outlined above prepares us for concept formation by making us capable of connecting perceptual categories to each other (Edelman, *Bright* 108). As most cognitivists agree, the earliest forms of intellectual activity include the ability (1) to single out specific attributes of objects from several features, (2) to create optional arrangements by manipulating attributes, (3) to name or label them, and (4) to explain the grounds for class inclusion or exclusion (Scribner and Cole 118). Piagetian in tradition, Edelman's concepts are formed first from the concrete and sensory interaction of individuals and experience. They are by definition relational and require memory. They are, however, *not* dependent on a speech community or language, and therefore precede lexical meaning (Edelman, *Bright* 108).

Because perceptual categorization is neurologically ongoing, Edelman explains that it is based on real time. This means actually living through events, so that our befores, durings, and afters

are automatically but fully experienced as such. Perceptual categorization also means using our senses and muscles to explore
and establish spatial relationships: our nearness, farness, high-
ness, low-ness, and so on.[7] In so doing, we develop the ability to
distinguish objects from actions (Edelman, *Remembered* 93+,
112+), a subject-predicate relationship.[8]

In order to prepare for semantic activity and language, some
form of mental ordering is also necessary. Building on the ability
to carry out perceptual sequences and ordered behaviors (e.g.,
see, then reach for) is the mental chaining of events in time and
patterning of objects and actions in space (Edelman, *Remembered* 112–14, 147). "Remembering" them roughly corresponds
to what Vygotsky recognized as the natural memory of perception (38–39). Edelman hypothesized a "presyntax" to account
for the special sort of memory that places objects and actions in
ordered relations. Unlike grammatical syntax, presyntax occurs
without symbols. But because such perceptual chaining eventually extends to the ability to string syllables and words together,
it provides a cognitive analogue for linguistic thought (147–48).
The world ultimately becomes "labeled" and manipulated as a
consequence of these particular neural adaptations (41).

The Self-Nonself Distinction

Primary consciousness also requires a fundamental self-nonself
distinction. This has its analogue at the cellular level. At birth,
for example, our bodies already discriminate between the anti-
bodies of the immune system (the self) and bacterial invaders
(the nonself) (Edelman, *Bright* 75). Our experience of self is
linked to the salience of perception. This is derived from evolutionary givens described as values—of which self-preservation is
the quintessential. One of the earliest perceptual distinctions in-
fants make is between their physical selves and objects. Sensory
interactions with the world are palpable. When babies pinch a
rubber duck, they do not hurt. Primary consciousness is based
on the difference not merely between the self and the rubber duck,
but between *categories* related to the self and to rubber ducks in
general and gradually to the category of toys.

From biological individuality evolved "personhood," the social experience, the capacity to see mental images from the "vantage of a socially constructed self" (Edelman, *Bright* 124). This also refers to our reportable subjective life (*Remembered* 24). We are conscious of being conscious (*Bright* 131). With primary consciousness begins speech, semantic capabilities, and higher-order consciousness (Edelman, *Remembered* 103; *Bright* 149).

Language and Higher-Order Consciousness

For all intents and purposes, we have no mind without consciousness. "Consciousness arises from a special set of relationships between external signals or precepts, internal categories or concepts, and memory" (Edelman, *Bright* 149). The gradual specialization and connection of phonemic and symbolic memory provide the neural seedbed for legitimate language.

It is clear that we did not need language to survive. As a matter of fact, the primitive brain is protected by the skull and the neocortex—for good reason: We could not survive without the old cortex, but we could survive without the cognitive functions built into the new cortex. And in fact have. Lower animals like chimpanzees imitate, participate in means-end reasoning, exhibit a rudimentary self-concept, and are capable of simple semantics. In short, they think in very limited ways (Edelman, *Bright* 125; Gazzaniga 104–5). But "since language and cognition probably represent the most salient and the most novel biological traits of our species . . . it is . . . important to show that they may well have arisen from extra-adaptive mechanisms" (Piatelli-Palmarini in Gazzaniga 9), those unnecessary for survival.

Like the mind, phylogenetically, consciousness as we know it did not always exist. Similarly, "language is too complex" to have arisen out of nowhere (Gazzaniga 22). True language evolved in much the same way as consciousness did (Edelman, *Bright* 149). It emerged epigenetically, that is, key language events occurred only after certain other events have taken place.

Early language, so-called meaningless primitive utterances in the speech community, prepared us for making meaning with language, for understanding it, and for producing a grammar.

With the evolution and biological maturation of the vocal tract, the speech-sound system became linked first to meaning (Edelman, *Remembered* 175; *Bright* 126+). The brain related sound and semantic sequences recursively. As sound became differentiated, meaningless sounds became meaningful words. Vocabulary grew. Words and sentences became symbols for things, categories of things, concepts, categories of concepts, and so on. The semantics of speech arose from connecting preexisting concepts to a lexicon (*Bright* 129).

In neural terms, meaning arises from the interaction of the affective memory of the amygdala, and the conceptual and speech centers of the "frontal, temporal, and parietal lobes . . . [which] do not mediate semantics [and syntax]" but are needed (along with Broca's and Wernicke's areas) for developing them (*Remembered* 174). As for syntax, the mind generates syntactic correspondences by manipulating the order of sounds until they "make sense." True language means putting together individual words with established meanings in order to make new meanings. Stringing them together and remembering their arrangements produces a true syntax (*Bright* 129–30).

As for higher-order consciousness, if primary consciousness means being aware of the world in the present, then higher-order consciousness means being aware of the self in the past and future (Edelman, *Bright* 112). And language stands at its threshold (*Remembered* 140). While Edelman notes that true language is probably unnecessary for higher-order consciousness except its "later elaborations," it is clearly enriched by language (187, 267). The gradual addition of symbolic memory to existing conceptual centers results in the ability to create, refine, and remember concepts, to communicate (*Bright* 103), to express emotions and modify them—all the states of consciousness that we associate with higher-order thinking: recording, recognizing, manipulating and transforming ideas, and imagining.

In sum, language (not to mention the language of healing) is inconceivable without the ability to produce a primary consciousness and a conceptual memory and to act on them (Edelman, *Bright* 126). Important as this is, it cannot happen without parallel growth in brain size and specialization.

Language Centers

Uniquely specialized in humans is the cerebral organization for language and visual/spatial brain activities. With the development of the speech tract, cortical regions dedicated to linguistic functions settled in relatively restricted areas on the left side of the brain—ergo, hemispheric lateralization of language, having been identified by Broca and Wernicke more than a hundred years ago, wherein language abilities were organized into two subsystems.

The labor of language was divided up between comprehending language and producing language. Wernicke's area in the temporal and parietal lobe areas of the forebrain understands language in speech, reading, and writing, which produces meaning and stores sounds of words diffusely represented in the associative cortex. Broca's region in the lower rear of the frontal lobe translates language formulated in the brain into syntactic production or movements of the mouth and throat—and so is concerned with the ability to speak fluently. A nerve bundle connects the two.

According to Edelman, the Broca and Wernicke centers do not "contain" concepts. Nor are they themselves sufficient for realizing "meaningful speech." They connect the acoustic, motor, and conceptual cortices, and they coordinate the understanding, production, and categorizing of speech (*Bright* 127). An interesting by-product of this localization is that it frees the uncommitted associative cortex for higher-order thought. More of the brain's capacities may thus be allocated for memories, dreams, values, the imagination, open-ended creativity, spirituality, and healing.

In the end, the paths between the proto brain and the neocortex are bi-directional. Our self-conscious mind exercises a superior interpretive role on neural events. The neocortex governs and corrects emotional expression on the basis of rational thought. At the polar opposite, our emotional apparatus keeps us alive. It makes sure we breathe, eat, and stay warm. The important idea here is that the higher-order consciousness linked to healing is a developmental and socially constituted process—bottom-up, from childhood into adulthood, from biology to rationality (a biology of a vastly different sort) (Brand, "Defining").

But I must highlight one point. Emotions do not exist merely to be harnessed or to ensure reproduction of the species. As the frontal lobe of the forebrain emerged, it incorporated the old brain into itself for higher-order mental activity. "Without the activation and arousal systems of the proto reptilian brain stem, we could not achieve the attentional control required for tenacious reasoning or for an expansive imagination" (Tucker, Vannatta, and Rothlind 163–64).

Given our phylogenetic and ontogenetic history, there appears to be more neuronal flexibility, more plasticity in the brain than we would have believed. It therefore matters greatly what we do with our students in the habitat called the mind, the counselor's office, or the classroom. Composition studies bears a deep ignorance about what makes our students tick. As a field, we have studied language from virtually every vantage point except from that of its potential for healing. Except for the work of Brand in 1980 and that of Kelley a decade later, little has been done to make visible and acceptable the salutary effects of writing in writing education. The study reported in *Therapy in Writing* about a deliberate attempt to help young persons in their personal becoming was published at a time when such direct discussions were simply out of the question. Until professor Patrick Healey at UC-Irvine introduced it, emotion did not exist in the biocurriculum. It hasn't existed in the language curriculum either.

Yet, when things are stalled in a classroom it is because of emotion. When things go well, it is also because of emotion.

I have tried to show anatomically why: The circuitry of the amygdala that sends projections into several cortical regions makes a crucial affective contribution to the parts of the brain involved in cognition (the neocortex and hippocampus). It increases cognitive efficiency and is in fact needed to perform certain tasks. But the amygdala also bypasses those regions. Simply stated, research suggests that the brain can perform some tasks without the cortical regions but not without the amygdala (LeDoux, "Brain"; Mishkin and Appenzeller).

Because the amygdala can circumvent the cortex, the emotional tone of a stimulus may be dissociated from the conscious content of the stimulus. Studies show that although persons may not consciously know what the stimuli are, they are able to access how they feel about them (LeDoux, "Brain" 205):

> "[K]nowing what we feel," joining the body and mind . . . is [particularly] the business of writers. . . . Interpreting what our bodies tell us . . . [f]iguring out what we mean, then what we really want to mean. . . . [p]aying attention . . . to the road signs of the senses. Mapping ourselves. And then "composing ourselves," arranging and rearranging the notes we've made into [texts] that will truly represent . . . whatever it is we think we feel. (Goedicke 17)

Among educational goals, psychological health cannot be incidental. As H. G. Wells said, human history becomes more and more a race between catastrophe and education. Whether we like it or not, the mind-body relationship is so powerful that it is humanly impossible to dissociate the two without grave consequences. We make a serious mistake by not helping students to address their psychological lives, to continually humanize themselves. Some adaptation for education of the learning process that takes place in psychotherapy seems like a promising possibility. Students make peace with themselves by writing about their experiences; they understand what is happening around them.

If learning and memory are defined by the capacity to make changes and remember them, then healing through language has evolved from the ability of the brain to modify thoughts, feelings, and behavior. It is nothing short of astonishing that in some way my words alter the neurons in my brain, the impulses of my motor cortex, the contractions of my muscles, and the design of my activities. In a word, thoughts change behavior. If we did not believe in change, we could not believe in therapy. Learning and memory may recruit cognitive processes as the negotiated symbol system, but healing almost always begins and ends in emotion. As central as cognition is, without emotion memory and learning could not occur. And what is healing if not learning.

Notes

1. Healing through language, however, is hardly new. For its brief history in Western civilization, see my book, *Therapy in Writing*.

2. The autonomic nervous system controls involuntary actions, smooths muscles and glands, and includes the sympathetic and parasympathetic systems: Although more complex than that, the sympathetic division is concerned with arousing the recuperative, restorative, and nutritive functions; the parasympathetic is concerned with inhibiting them.

3. This figure is derived by multiplying twelve billion distinctive neurons by nine glial cells for each neuron.

4. There is some dispute over which structures belong in which parts of the brain (LeDoux, "Emotional" 70). Penrose, for example, places the thalamus and limbic lobe in the midbrain (5). Edelman calls the hippocampus a cortical appendage (*Remembered* 127).

5. Anxiety, the hallmark of neurotic dysfunction, has been shown to be a complex "cognitive emotion," having both negative and positive components (Brand, *Psychology*).

6. This is called long-term potentiation.

7. Haptic perception combines touch and kinesthetic senses. Kinesthesis is the ability to know where in space the parts of our body are without having to look at them. We "feel" where they are in a proprioceptive way. We receive feedback from muscles, joints, tendons, etc.

8. Edelman sees this as a neural precursor to the syntax associated with true language.

Works Cited

Aggleton, John P., and Mortimer Mishkin. "The Amygdala: Sensory Gateway to the Emotions." *Emotion: Theory, Research, and Experience: Volume 3. Biological Foundations of Emotion*. Ed. Robert Plutchik and Henry Kellerman. Orlando, FL: Academic Press, 1986. 281–99.

Bain, A. *The Emotions and the Will*. 3rd ed. London: Longmans, Green, 1875.

Bartlett, Frederic C. *Remembering: A Study in Experimental and Social Psychology.* Cambridge, England: Cambridge UP, 1932.

Berthoff, Ann E. *The Making of Meaning: Metaphors, Models, and Maxims for Writing Teachers.* Upper Montclair, NJ: Boynton/Cook, 1981.

Brand, Alice G. "Defining Our Emotional Life." *Presence of Mind: Writing and the Domain Beyond the Cognitive.* Ed. Alice G. Brand and Richard L. Graves. Portsmouth, NH: Boynton/Cook, 1994. 155–78.

―――. *The Psychology of Writing: The Affective Experience.* Westport, CT: Greenwood, 1989.

―――. *Therapy in Writing: A Psycho-Educational Enterprise.* Lexington, MA: Heath, 1980.

Brown, Terrance. "The Biological Significance of Affectivity." *Psychological and Biological Approaches to Emotion.* Ed. Nancy L. Stein, Bennett Leventhal, and Tom Trabasso. Hillsdale, NJ: Erlbaum, 1990. 405–34.

Edelman, Gerald M. *Bright Air, Brilliant Fire: On the Matter of the Mind.* New York: Basic, 1992.

―――. *Neural Darwinism.* New York: Basic, 1987.

―――. *The Remembered Present: a Biological Theory of Consciousness.* New York: Basic, 1989.

Emig, Janet. "The Biology of Writing: Another View of the Process." Report 1 of the Annual Conference on Language Arts. *The Writing Process of Students.* Ed. Walter T. Petty and Patrick J. Finn. Buffalo: SUNY, 1975.

Fonberg, Elzbieta. "Amygdala, Emotions, Motivation, and Depressive States." *Emotion: Theory, Research, and Experience: Volume 3. Biological Foundations of Emotion.* Ed. Robert Plutchik and Henry Kellerman. Orlando, FL: Academic Press, 1986. 301–31.

Gazzaniga, Michael S. *Nature's Mind: The Biological Roots of Thinking, Emotions, Sexuality, Language, and Intelligence.* New York: Basic, 1992.

Goedicke, Patricia. "Singing & (Listening) for the Record." *AWP Chronicle* May/Summer (1995): 15–20.

Goleman, Daniel. "Brain's Design Emerges as a Key to Emotions." *The New York Times* (15 August 1989): C1, C9.

Heath, Robert G. "The Neural Substrate for Emotion." *Emotion: Theory, Research, and Experience. Volume 3. Biological Foundations of Emotion.* Ed. Robert Plutchik and Henry Kellerman. Orlando, FL: Academic Press, 1986. 3–35.

James, William. *Principles of Psychology.* New York: Dover, [1890] 1950.

Kelley, Patricia, ed. *The Uses of Writing in Psychotherapy.* New York: Haworth Press, 1990.

Kleinman, Arthur. *Patients and Healers in the Context of Culture: An Exploration of the Borderland Between Anthropology, Medicine, and Psychiatry.* Berkeley: U of California P, 1980.

Lazarus, Richard S. "On the Primacy of Cognition." *American Psychologist* 39 (1984): 124–29.

LeDoux, Joseph E. "Brain, Mind and Language." *Brain and Mind.* Ed. David A. Oakley. London: Methuen, 1985. 197–216.

———. "Cognitive-Emotional Interactions in the Brain." *Cognition and Emotion* 3.4 (1989): 267–89.

———. "Emotional Memory Systems in the Brain." *Behavioral Brain Research* 58 (1993): 69–79.

MacLean, P. D. "The Limbic System ("Visceral Brain") and Emotional Behavior." *Archives of Neurological Psychiatry* 73 (1955): 130–34.

Mandler, George. *Mind and Body: the Psychology of Emotion and Stress.* New York: Norton, 1984.

Mishkin, Mortimer, and Tim Appenzeller. "The Anatomy of Memory." *Scientific American* 256.6 (1987): 80–89.

Murphy, Sheila T., and Robert B. Zajonc. *Affect, Cognition, and Awareness: Priming with Optimal and Suboptimal Stimulus Exposures.* Unpublished manuscript, 1993.

Neimark, Jill. "It's Magical! It's Malleable! It's Memory." *Psychology Today* 28 (1995): 44–49, 80, 85.

Nisbett, R. E., and T. D. Wilson. "Telling More Than We Can Know: Verbal Reports on Mental Processes." *Psychological Review* 84 (1977): 231–59.

O'Keefe, John, and Lynn Nadel. *The Hippocampus as a Cognitive Map.* Oxford: Clarendon, 1978.

Papez, J. W. "A Proposed Mechanism of Emotion." *Archives of Neurology and Psychiatry* 38 (1937): 725–43.

Penrose, Roger. *The Emperor's New Mind.* New York: Oxford UP, 1989.

Popper, Karl, and John C. Eccles. *The Self and Its Brain.* New York: Springer International, 1977.

Rico, Gabriele, and Mary Frances Claggett. *Balancing the Hemispheres: Brain Research and the Teaching of Writing.* Berkeley, CA: Bay Area Writing Project, 1980.

Scribner, Sylvia, and Michael Cole. *The Psychology of Literacy.* Cambridge: Harvard UP, 1981.

Shook, Ronald. "The Two Brains and the Education Process." ED 218 360. ERIC, 1981.

Tucker, Don M., Kathryn Vannatta, and Johannes Rothlind. "Arousal and Activation Systems and Primitive Adaptive Controls on Cognitive Priming." *Psychological and Biological Approaches to Emotion.* Ed. Nancy L. Stein, Bennett Leventhal, and Tom Trabasso. Hillsdale, NJ: Erlbaum, 1990. 145–66.

Vygotsky, Lev S. *Mind in Society: The Development of Higher Psychological Processes.* Ed. Michael Cole et al. Cambridge: Harvard UP, 1978.

Wheeler, David L. "Research Notes: Brain's Right Hemisphere Shown to Be Used in Language Tasks." *The Chronicle of Higher Education* (20 November 1991): A10.

Zajonc, Robert B. "On the Primacy of Affect." *American Psychologist* 39 (1984): 117–23.

CHAPTER NINE

Pathography and Enabling Myths

The Process of Healing

ANNE HUNSAKER HAWKINS
Pennsylvania State University

My intent in this essay is to discuss the writing of pathography—autobiographies and biographies about illness—as a reconstruction of experience that promotes healing.[1] What it is like to have AIDS, or cancer, or multiple sclerosis, or manic-depressive illness, and what is entailed in seeking treatment for such illnesses—these are the typical themes of pathography. Such books are remarkably popular today. Gilda Radner's pathography about her experience with ovarian cancer stayed on *The New York Times Book Review* best-seller list for months; Norman Cousin's *Anatomy of an Illness*, an account of his recovery from a rare collagen disease using unorthodox therapeutic measures, can frequently be found on a hospital patient's bedside table. Within the past few years there has been a surge of pathographies about various forms of mental illness, especially books written by such prominent literary or medical figures as William Styron (*Darkness Visible*), Susanna Kaysen (*Girl Interrupted*), and Kay Jamison (*An Unquiet Mind*).[2]

Pathography as the Voice of the Patient

Perhaps what is most striking about this genre is that it seems a contemporary phenomenon. In previous eras, autobiographical accounts of sickness are woven into a journal or diary; almost never does illness constitute the sole focus of the work.[3] It is only in our own era that the illness narrative constitutes a genre all its own. One explanation for this is that in earlier times, illness seems to have been considered an integral and inseparable part of living (and dying)—illness thus takes its place in autobiographical writings along with other factors of a life. It is only in the twentieth century that serious illness has become a phenomenon that can be isolated from an individual's life—perhaps because such illness is set apart from normal life by hospitalization or perhaps because we now tend to consider health as normative and illness as a condition to be corrected, rarely to be simply accepted.

Yet another way to look at the popularity of pathography today is to see it as a reaction to our contemporary medical model, one so dominated by a biophysical understanding of illness that its experiential aspects are virtually ignored. As Richard Baron observes, the patient is in a sense "subtracted out" of the medical paradigm: "The disease manifests itself through the patient, and the patient comes to function as a kind of translucent screen on which the disease is projected" (Baron 7). Modern scientific medicine tends to focus on the disease process and on ways in which this process can be interrupted and reversed; only peripherally, or secondarily, is the focus on the person with the disease. But the person with the disease also needs attention. Disease can be treated and in some cases even cured; people, though, require healing. Pathography shows us the ways in which this process of healing is accomplished—a process sometimes facilitated by healthcare givers but other times obstructed by a frequently depersonalizing medical system.

Pathography restores the person ignored or canceled out in the medical enterprise, and it places that person at the very center. Moreover, it gives that ill person a voice. Reynolds Price, writing in *A Whole New Life* about his treatment for cancer of the spinal cord and subsequent paralysis, laments the way in which the technological sophistication of modern physicians is often acquired at the cost of "the skills of human sympathy" (Price 145). Norman Cousins in *Anatomy of an Illness* describes how he disregards conventional medical advice and recovers from a severe illness by generous doses of laughter and vitamin C. Physician-author Anthony Sattilaro, in *Recalled by Life*, recounts how he deals successfully with advanced metastatic prostate cancer by following a rigid macrobiotic diet.

The pathography written by the ill person can be seen as the counterpart to the medical history written by the physician or by the medical staff assigned to a particular patient. The true subject of case history is a particular disease process and its treatments, whereas the subject of pathography is illness and treatment as experienced and understood by the ill person. The multi-authored medical report is usually composed of brief factual statements about present symptoms and body chemistry, whereas a pathography is an extended narrative situating the illness experience within the author's life and the meaning of that life. In their focus on documenting biochemical processes, medical histories tend to reflect (and to help perpetuate) the pervasive habit in contemporary medicine of focusing narrowly on the disease while disregarding the fact of the experiencing patient. Pathography, then, can be seen as offering what is missing in the case report: the rich, subjective experience of the patient, "thickly" described.[4]

Perhaps most important, the very act of writing about one's illness experience seems to be an integral part of an individual's healing process. Pathography stems from the need to communicate a painful, disorienting, and isolating experience. Indeed, the need to come to terms with a traumatic experience often involves the need to project it outwards—to talk or write about it. As Max Lerner observes of his own motive for writing a pathography: "I passed through a searing experience that tested and changed me in ways I never foresaw. And like the Ancient Mariner I want to tell my story, to whatever listeners it finds" (Lerner 20). Pathographies are cautionary parables of what it would be like if our ordinary life-in-the-world suddenly collapsed: They show us the drastic interruption of a life of meaning and purpose by an illness that often seems arbitrary, cruel, and senseless; and by treatment procedures that too often can appear equally arbitrary, cruel, and senseless—especially to the person undergoing them.

There is a quality to the experience of illness today that seems to set the ill person radically apart from others. Such persons are special, different—to themselves and to others. Pathographer Kenneth Shapiro observes of himself, "I exist in the world as most people see it, but I live in the world of the person with terminal cancer" (Shapiro 130). Robert Murphy writes about the social milieu created by his spinal cord disease: "Through [illness and disability] I have sojourned in a social world no less strange to me at first than those of the Amazon forests" (Murphy ix). Pathographies concern the attempts of individuals to orient themselves in the world of sickness—the world Susan Sontag calls "the kingdom of the sick"—and to achieve a new balance between self and reality (Sontag 3). The task of the author is not only to describe this disordering process, but also to restore to reality its lost coherence and to discover, or create, a meaning that can bind it together again. In this, pathographies answer the need for what Sam Banks has called "meaningful, satisfying closures in a slippery world always threatening to open at the seams" (Banks 24).

The Personal Story as Construct

If pathography restores to the therapeutic paradigm the missing voice of the patient—the phenomenological, experiential dimension of illness—then one may be tempted to assert that the patient narrative gives us the "true" or "real" story of what the experience was actually like. Pathographies may indeed be read as "true stories," but the emphasis must be as much on the word "stories" as the word "true." Pathography cannot be seen as simply a chronicle, or record, of experience—for narrative form alters experience, as autobiographical theorists have demonstrated. As in all forms of autobiography, the narrative description of illness is both less and more than the actual experience. It is less, in that remembering and writing are selective processes—certain facts are omitted either because they are forgotten or because they do not fit the author's narrative design; and it is more, in that the act of committing experience to narrative form inevitably confers upon it a particular sequence of events and endows it with a significance that was probably only latent in the original experience. Writing about an experience—any experience—inevitably changes it.

The assertion that there is a significant difference between the original "real" experience and the retrospective autobiographical narrative is now a commonplace among critics and theorists of autobiography. Most critics see this difference as caused by the author's creative imposition of order and meaning on what is remembered of one's life. Back in 1960, the literary critic Roy Pascal discussed autobiography as a narrative that interpreted rather than documented a life. The past, he observed, is not simply recorded in the autobiographical act but given a structure, a coherence, and a meaning (Pascal). Thus the process of autobiographical recollection is part self-discovery and part self-creation.

Pascal's careful qualifications about the factual authenticity of autobiography were followed by a fierce critical skepticism about the ontological status of the autobiographical self and its past. Borrowing heavily from revisionist psychoanalytic theory, autobiographical critics emphasized the similarity between the task of psychoanalytic reconstruction and that of autobiographical reconstruction. In essence, the "self" in autobiography came to be understood to be a fiction of language. As James Cox observes of this kind of theory, "Language is thus the signifier presumptively making the self it signifies increasingly so absent that it can only be traced like a ghost between the long sequence of lines and text that make up a convention or a tradition" (Cox 3). More recently, this issue of the reality of the self is bypassed by focusing on the primacy of social and cultural realities. So Albert Stone, arguing against the recent tendency to treat autobiography solely as a fictive enterprise, cites as equally important the "complex processes of historical re-creation, ideological argument, and psychological expression." Considered as "social document," autobiography "affords a special kind of information about a culture and the individuals embedded in it" (Stone 19, 7, 6). Burton Pike uses the term "extrospective" to characterize contemporary autobiographies that take the author's experiences and attitudes as representative of particular cultural forces (Pike 342).

Pathography offers an important perspective on the various claims and emphases of autobiographical theory. First, pathography challenges the skepticism of critics and theorists about the self, making that skepticism seem artificial, mandarin, and contrived. In narratives describing illness and possible death, the reader is repeatedly confronted with the pragmatic reality and experiential unity of the autobiographical self. The self of pathographical writing is the self-in-crisis: When confronted with serious and life-threatening illness, that fictive "ghost" of the self is contracted into a defensive ontological reality—primed for action, readied for response to the threat of the body, alternatively resisting and inviting the eventual disintegration of the self that is death. Perhaps it is true, as Freud maintains, that the ego is first and foremost a bodily ego and that "self" is bound up with the biological integrity of the body.

Moreover, in many pathographies the reality of selfhood is asserted through its capacity for transformation. It is common in pathographies for authors to describe dramatic psychological changes that accompany and follow upon a life-threatening illness. Some assert that illness forces them to stop and examine their values and their true needs; some report that illness becomes an insighting experience; some observe that they feel as though they had been "reborn." Arthur Frank observes three ways in which pathographers claim their lives have changed. In some narratives the author discovers the self to be "what I have always been"; in other narratives, the self discovered is "who I might become"; and in still other narratives, "authors reflect on living with an illness throughout most of their lives and conclude that whatever they have become has been formed in and through this illness."[5] In pathography, then, the reality of the self is never called into question: Rather, the idea of self is concretized in its capacity for change. Indeed, it may be that the impetus towards self-transformation provided by writing a pathography is a part of its healing function.

Second, pathography validates a critical stance that emphasizes the importance of sociocultural elements in writings about the self. Many contemporary literary critics see a text not as a creation by an author but as a product of a society, with the authorial role diminished to that of a facilitator or producer. Pathographies support this emphasis on society and culture, though they do so in a way that does not diminish or efface the self. A great many AIDS pathographies by homosexual men use the military myth as the figure for all aspects of the author's experience of illness and treatment: This surely reflects social experience as much, if not more, than medical experience.[6] Fran Peavey, in *A Shallow Pool of Time*, perceives AIDS as a cultural disease, the product of a toxic environment: In this society "we all have AIDS," she writes, and those who actually contract the disease are like the canaries that used to be carried down into mines to test the toxicity of the air (Peavey 72). Her pathography is an example of what Thomas Couser calls "prophetic autobiography"—a personal narrative that situates the author in a position of serving the larger culture by his or her unique ability to comprehend a particular societal crisis.

The fact is that illness is always experienced in relation to a particular configuration of cultural ideologies, practices, and attitudes, and these shape the various components of our healthcare system: professional personnel, particular diagnostic tests and therapies, and institutions such as the hospital and the clinic. All pathographies, even those that eventually discard traditional medical approaches, are situated within the social praxis of modern medicine; therefore, they all can serve as commentaries on it. The fact that so many recent pathographies record the author's experimentation with alternative therapies is surely a commentary on unsolved—perhaps unrecognized—problems with orthodox medical theory and practice.

And finally, if pathography challenges recent critical skepticism about the self and confirms the recent emphasis on cultural context, it significantly advances the critical position about maintaining autobiography to be a re-creation of the past. As most autobiographical theorists now assert, the past in any autobiography is not simply recorded but is changed, reordered, even re-created in the act of writing about it. The study of pathography is important because it discloses the particular ways in which authors discover pattern and impose meaning upon the experiences they claim to be faithfully documenting. This transition from experience to narrative is one that, in achieving a formulation of experience that the author finds "satisfying," exposes certain metaphoric and mythic constructs about illness.

Mythic Thinking in Pathography

It is the constructive aspect of pathographical writing that is an essential aspect of the healing process. Anatole Broyard's remarks in his pathography about prostate cancer are instructive: "My initial experience of illness was as a series of disconnected shocks, and my first instinct was to try to bring it under control by turning it into a narrative" (Broyard, "Doctor" 19). To render illness experience into narrative is one way to come to terms with it, or as Broyard says, to "bring it under control": The process is one of discovering patterns, imposing order and structure, and creating meaning. Such pattern and meaning often take on a metaphoric dimension, and this is surely true of Broyard's pathographical essays with their layered multiple metaphors: for example,

> My ideal doctor would be my Virgil, leading me through my purgatory or inferno, pointing out the sights as we go. He would resemble Oliver Sacks. . . . I can imagine Dr. Sacks entering my condition, looking around at it from the inside like a benevolent landlord with a tenant, trying to see how he could make the premises more livable for me. He would see the genius of my illness. He would mingle his daemon with mine: we would wrestle with my fate together. (Broyard, *Intoxicated* 36)

Pathographies, then, serve a healing function because they interpret experience rather than record it, and, as I shall show, because they do so in a way that discloses underlying cultural and cross-cultural mythic attitudes about illness and treatment. Mythic thinking of all kinds becomes apparent in that delicate autobiographical transition from "actual" experience to written narrative, since this transition is one that constructs necessary fictions out of the building blocks of metaphor, image, archetype, and myth.

The word "myth" can mean different things to different people. For some, a myth is an illusion or a fiction, a primitive mode of thought that we indulge in when we do not know or try to deny the truth. So seen, "mythic thinking" is simply delusory or wishful thinking. But scholars who study myth emphasize its other meaning—that of a deeper or more profound truth. Philip Wheelwright, for example, argues that the mythic offers a unique perspective on experience, "a set of depth-meanings of perduring significance" that transcend "the limits of what can be known through ordinary thinking" (Wheelwright 159). The myths that one finds in pathography can be seen both as fictive and as profoundly true. Illness myths are fictions in the sense that when people write about their "journey" into the realm of illness, they may have traveled no further than their local hospital. But such myths must also be seen as profound truth in that they describe the inner configuration of the ill person's experience. For some people, the myth of the journey is the way they actually experience their illness: It suggests the various progressive stages in an illness, it means leaving the familiar and the known to embark on an unpredictable experience involving risk, danger, and fear, and it has a goal, which can be simply returning to health or learning from their illness in such a way as to redefine the priorities and values in their lives.

In addition to seeing myths about illness as both fictive and profoundly true, we must recognize the dynamic nature of myth—its potential impact on every dimension of an illness experience. Susan Sontag sees metaphoric thinking about illness as harmful and destructive. Thus she prefaces *Illness as Metaphor* with the observation that "illness is not a metaphor, and that the most truthful way of regarding illness—and the healthiest way of being ill—is the one most purified of, most resistant to, metaphoric thinking" (Sontag 3). But ironically, her book participates in the very mythic thinking it criticizes. Though not literally a pathography, *Illness as Metaphor* is inspired by her personal experience of cancer. And like conventional pathographies, her book is organized around a mythic formulation; in this case, what might be called the myth of "metaphorlessness." This is the notion that illness can and should be experienced without recourse to metaphoric thinking—a functional myth that appears to help Sontag endure and recover from her illness.

This discrepancy between precept and practice is instructive. For even if we agree with Sontag that illness should be stripped of metaphor, myth, and symbol, it is an expectation that few could live up to. Metaphoric thinking is built into our mental faculties. As Robert Jay Lifton so aptly remarks, "We live on images. As human beings we know our bodies and our minds only through what we can imagine. To grasp our humanity we need to structure these images into metaphors and models" (Lifton, *Broken* 3).

The myths and metaphors that one finds in pathography function not just as heuristic devices that give meaning to the illness, organizing and interpreting it, but also as dynamic constructs that actually shape and "in form" the experience. Just to consider the titles of pathographies gives some indication of the mythic thinking that lies behind them: *Coming Back, Signs of*

Spring, A Private Battle, Cancer Winner, Embracing the Wolf, A Whole New Life. Not only, then, does pathography restore the phenomenological and the experiential to the medical encounter, but it also restores the mythic dimension that our scientific, technological culture ignores or disallows.

Myth as Formulation

Though all autobiography "constructs" experience in such a way as to confer meaning on it, it would appear that pathography, more than other forms of autobiography, tends toward constructions of experience that involve myth, metaphor, and image—most likely because of the frequently traumatic nature of the experience that is the author's subject. Indeed, myths of various kinds tend to proliferate around those life experiences that hold for us a good deal of uncertainty, and thus it is not surprising that the attempt to deal with a serious illness should prove fertile ground for the mythicizing imagination.

The subject of pathographies is generally something that is so destructive and disorienting to the experiencing self that it stimulates a counter impulse toward creation and order. This counter impulse is what Robert Jay Lifton, in his celebrated study of the survivors of Hiroshima, calls "formulation," a reparative process that deals with trauma by imagination and interpretation (*Death in Life*). Formulation, Lifton remarks, is a kind of "psychic rebuilding," the construction of certain inner forms or configurations that function "as a bridge between self and world"—a psychological process whereby the individual suffering from trauma "returns" to the world of the living (*Death* 525–26). The illness myths that one finds in pathographies resemble these inner forms or configurations: Both "reconstruct" the experience in such a way as to facilitate healing. Formulation, Lifton observes, involves the effort to reestablish three elements essential to psychic function: the sense of connection (between self and other), the sense of symbolic integrity (seeing one's life as meaningful), and the sense of movement (the capacity for change). Lifton further describes the formulative process as "intimately bound up with mastery"; successful formulation "not only enhances mastery but, in an important sense, contains the mental representation of mastery" (*Death* 367, 536, 567). The act of formulation, then, involves the discovery of patterns in experience, the imposition of order, and the creation of meaning—all with the purpose of mastering a traumatic experience and thereby reestablishing a sense of connectedness with objective reality and with other people. It is these things that enable human beings not only to live through severe illness or the death of a loved one but also to live beyond them.

Lifton's discussion of successful formulation is very similar to Roy Pascal's description of successful autobiography: Such autobiographies, Pascal observes, "seem to suggest a certain power of the personality over circumstance . . . in the sense that the individual can extract nurture out of disparate incidents and ultimately bind them together in his own way" (Pascal 10–11). The psychological process of formulation as articulated by Lifton and the narrative act of reformulation embodied in pathography are in some sense parallel: Both involve an individual's mastery of a set of circumstances; both suggest the act of construction or piecing together a set of disparate events into a coherent whole; both concern the aesthetic act of finding or imposing patterned design and its epistemological analogue—the imposition of meaning.

Lifton finds that survivors whose formulative process is impaired often carry with them an "indelible image" of the experience—an image that prevents the individual from ever moving beyond the traumatic experience (*Death* 528). In pathography, instead of the "indelible image" that impairs formulation for Lifton's Hiroshima survivors, one often finds a "mythic image" that enhances formulation. Many pathographers will use a particular metaphor or mythic construct to describe and explain their experience. Quite often this central image functions as an organizational principle encompassing all aspects of an illness—disease, treatment, medical institutions, and personnel.

Some organizing myths are highly idiosyncratic. Thus Joanna Baumer Permut's pathography about lupus—the disease that takes its name from the Latin word for "wolf"—is shaped around her thoughts about the wolf. Each chapter is preceded by an epigram or quotation about wolves; each chapter title bears some reference to the wolf. The use of the name of the disease as an organizing metaphor seems successful in helping her come to terms with her condition. The pathography moves from an initial sense of victimization (the first chapter is entitled "The Wolf Stalks His Prey") to a final accommodation (the last chapter is called "Wolf and Patient Negotiate Peace"). For Permut, the wolf is an enabling metaphor: As she observes, "the wolf image works for me. The metaphor serves the disease, and therefore my self positively" (Permut 163).

But idiosyncratic images such as Permut's wolf are atypical. In contrast, the mythic paradigms that one commonly finds in pathography seem at once more conventional and more "archetypal." It is striking that so many of these very personal accounts of illness, though highly individualized, tend to be confined to certain repeated themes—themes of an archetypal, mythic nature. Over and over again, the same mythic or metaphorical paradigms are repeated in pathographies: the myth of the journey into a distant country, the idea of illness as a battle, the paradigm of death and rebirth, and "healthy-mindedness," the idea that positive attitude or right behavior can affect the cause and the course of an illness.[7] Of course, division between these myths is to some extent arbitrary. Quite often, various myths will overlap: The person who experiences illness as a form of death and rebirth may also see it as a quest for a new and more meaningful life. Or the individual who pursues alternative therapy or adopts radical changes in lifestyle may do so out of the conviction that these are ways to "fight" one's illness: Here, the healthy-minded mythos shades into the military myth. And sometimes these myths will generate similar though discrete mythic patterns: The notion of illness as an athletic contest, for example, can be seen as an extension of the battle myth. Both paradigms celebrate courage and self-reliance, both disallow dependency, passivity, and self-pity, and both share the sense that recovering from an illness is like winning a battle or an athletic contest—"beating" an adversary, or the odds, or both.

Of course, in any discussion of mythic formulations it is well to remember that such deep-lying patterns emerge in forms that are culturally inflected, shaped by a particular time and place and informed by the ideological constructs and social institutions that are particular to a given culture. If pathography is an imaginative reformulation of experience that reconnects the isolated individual sufferer with his or her world, the connecting "formula" needs to be both culture-specific and transcultural, for the patient's world includes both a particular society at a certain moment in history and the larger and more timeless human community that underlies it. For example, in Audre Lorde's *The Cancer Journals,* the battle myth finds expression in her frequent allusions to herself—post-mastectomy—as an "amazon warrior." This image is one that is appropriate to the specific needs of this African American lesbian feminist who decries breast prostheses as "a way of avoiding having women come to terms with their own pain and loss, and thereby, with their own strength" (Lorde 49). Illness formulations serve a healing function because they integrate different aspects of the self: For Lorde, in her pathography, the battle myth serves to link her disease and its disfiguring treatment to a narrative myth about female strength.

Examples

It may be helpful at this point to examine how myths about illness are deployed in several pathographies, observing the different ways in which myth can be rendered as personal formulation.

The idea of illness as warfare is one that occurs over and over in pathographies of all kinds. The battle myth is an ancient one, readily found in the legends of a great many cultures. In our own culture, this myth is widespread: It undergirds not only our actual military practices, but also our way of conceiving reality. Military metaphors are pervasive in contemporary medicine. The habit of associating battle imagery with disease and therapy is one that is reinforced by our medical epistemology, whereby certain medical conditions are reified as disease entities, perceived as separate from the life and body of the patient, and further objectified by a therapeutic modality aimed at attacking the disease, not treating the individual whose body is affected by the disease. Yet another factor contributing to the association between military metaphor and illness—or perhaps one deriving from it—is the recent claim that passive, compliant patients fare less well in surviving a serious illness than their aggressive and noncompliant counterparts. So Kenneth Shapiro declares in his pathography: "It is a well-documented fact that those people who have the mental tenacity to fight do better than those who just quit" (Shapiro 9). Another pathographer alludes to "scientific evidence" demonstrating "that cancer patients who have a fighting spirit and who don't accept a negative verdict are far more likely to improve than those who stoically accept feelings of helplessness and hopelessness" (Mitchell 203). A stance such as this is pervasive in pathography, as patients with various illnesses concentrate their energies on fighting their disease, or the effects of their therapies, or their own attitudes.

The military myth seems particularly appropriate to cancer, since cancer is so often characterized as an alien intruder or an invading enemy, and its various therapies considered as weapons with which to attack or destroy the disease. The protagonist in one pathography, hospitalized for terminal leukemia, sums up this attitude: "It's like going to war only the battlefield is inside my body. I have to fight a battle with the enemy and destroy it. This damn disease is my enemy—it is trying to kill me" (Panger 160). Another author similarly observes about her "war" with ovarian cancer: "Now here I was, deeply embroiled in the battle of my life—a war against cancer taking place in my own body" (Radner 125). As these examples demonstrate, military imagery seems readily accessible to ill persons as they describe their experiences. Significantly, too, it is a metaphoric construct often shared by the physicians who treat them: Unlike some illness myths, that of the battle is syntonic with much of medical theory and practice.

In many instances, the battle myth seems to enhance the ill person's sense of dignity, self-esteem, and active participation in treatment. Cornelius and Kathryn Ryan's *A Private Battle* turns occasional imagery of warfare into a sustained allegorical figure. The fact that Ryan, a military historian, is writing about his cancer experience at the same time that he writes his final book about World War II, *A Bridge Too Far*, makes it clear that his comparison of the worlds of illness and of war is a conscious one. The likeness between illness and war for Ryan is both descriptive and functional; not only does he see an analogy between his private battle with cancer and the historical battle, but he is able to exploit those analogies to help him live with cancer and die from it with the courage and dignity that he so values.

A Private Battle is permeated with references to war. Ryan's cancer is, of course, the enemy, the therapies function as weapons, his many helpful friends recall the courageous civilians of the Resistance, and his physicians are like the various generals of World War II about whom he writes in his histories. The initial surgical procedure is referred to as an attack, the possibility of further metastases as a "counterattack," and his physician's later recourse to estrogen therapy as a "second line of defense" against "the enemy." Remission means a temporary success for the forces of treatment; relapse a victory for the foe. Ryan himself in this private allegory becomes a commander in chief, who, in consultation with his generals, plans the military strategy that best promises success. And in the end, Ryan sees himself as a brave and courageous soldier who dies fighting, and thus does not ever really "give up."

The change from seeing himself as commander in chief to seeing himself as an ordinary soldier demonstrates how Ryan makes the analogy with war into an enabling myth, for each role embodies what he needs at specific stages in the development of his illness. The image of commander in chief suggests an aggressive, decisive stance; that of soldier suggests a more passive, less controlling image: the one is appropriate to early stages of the disease process, when Ryan aggressively pursues state-of-the-art treatment protocols; the other to the latter stages in the progression of his cancer, when fighting the battle seems almost more important than winning. The success of the military myth, for Ryan, results from his ability to adapt it to his needs—needs that change during the course of the illness. After all the many battles fought in the long campaign between those two enemies—cancer and its treatments—the war finally ends with the triumph of the disease. But at the same time, the value he places on winning the battle undergoes a transformation in which survival becomes subordinate to something else. For when Ryan learns that his efforts to reverse his illness have not succeeded, he transposes the entire war to another level, where what matters is not winning or losing but such qualities as courage, compassion, pride, and heroism. Healing can come about in the absence of reversal of the disease process; healing can even come about when a patient dies. Cornelius Ryan dies from cancer; but in a real sense, he is also healed.

Some authors recognize and then deliberately reject the association between the military myth and illness and its treatment. Terry Tempest Williams's pathography, *Refuge*, offers an example of this kind of thinking. Accompanying her mother for her first chemotherapy treatment, the author muses on the way "medical language is loaded . . . with military metaphors: the fight, the battle, enemy infiltration, and defense strategies." She wonders whether "this kind of aggression waged against our own bodies is counterproductive to healing" and asks, "How can we rethink cancer" (Williams 43)? Her response to this question is grounded in her recognition that the cancer process is similar to the creative process. Though cancer is often viewed as an external, foreign, reified entity, in fact it originates within one's own body, slowly and invisibly growing, just as ideas are born and develop within the recesses of the unconscious mind. Overtly rejecting the association between cancer and military thinking, Williams uses nature metaphors as the organizing construct of her pathography: She finds a striking analogy between her mother's fatal illness and the gradual devastation of a local bird sanctuary by the rising waters of Utah's Great Salt Lake. The author's realization of the continuity between her mother's body and the land, and her perception of the embeddedness of human life within the cycles of nature, are consistent with her identity as a woman, as a naturalist, and as a Mormon with deep ties to the historical land of her people.

But Williams's book is also social commentary, as she chronicles the ominous relationship between the high incidence of cancer among the women in her family and the series of above-ground atomic tests conducted by the U.S. Department of Defense over some ten years. Unlike the story of her mother's illness and death, these encounters with cancer are not accepted as part of the cycles of nature but are directly attributed to radiation released by nuclear testing. It is only at this point that the reader fully understands the book's complete title: *Refuge: An Unnatural History of Family and Place*. It is ironic that the military way of thinking, which she repudiates as a metaphor early on in her pathography, should return at the end as a literal and destructive reality. This author's healing formulation thus includes the ratification of one metaphor (nature) and the repudiation of another (the military mythos). Moreover, it is a formulation that involves coming to terms with her own and her family's experience in such a way as to lead to social action.

A third example of the healing dimension of pathography is Oliver Sacks's *A Leg to Stand On*. Sacks likens himself as a physician to an explorer of "the furthest Arctics and Tropics of neurological disorder." But when he himself experiences a neurological complaint that he does not understand and that his physicians do not even acknowledge to be real, he faces "a chartless land," feeling as though he "had fallen off the map, the world, of the knowable" (Sacks 110–11). The journey myth is the organizing metaphor of Sacks's pathography. The time he spends as a patient recovering from surgical treatment for a leg injury turns out to be very much like a pilgrimage, a journey into a mental landscape that he initially experiences as "limbo." Linking his experience to the spiritual pilgrimages in the writings of Saint John of the Cross and in Dante's *Divine Comedy*, Sacks finds the process of injury, treatment, and recovery a kind of Dantean "journey of the soul" in which he "journey(s) to despair and back" (Sacks 113).

Sacks's description of his experience in his pathography closely parallels what anthropologists call "rites of passage," rituals that signify the transition from one state or condition of life to another (examples being the initiation rites accompanying the transition from childhood to puberty, marriage rituals, or funeral ceremonies). In Sacks's case, the rite of passage marks a journey from the world of health into and then back out of the world of sickness. The classic rite of passage is marked by three phases: The first is that of separation, whereby the individual is detached from his or her position and relationships in the world; the second is one of transition or marginality—a liminal state in which the individual traverses a world that has none or few of the attributes of ordinary reality; the third is one of aggregation or incorporation, in which individuals return to the world they have left, reassuming prior status, rights, and relationships.[8]

Sacks describes in great detail the process of becoming a hospital patient, a ritual in which a person is systematically transformed into a patient as his clothes are replaced with an anonymous hospital shift and the obligatory identification bracelet substitutes a number for his name. What would ordinarily be a negative experience for most individuals becomes positive for Sacks, since it is perceived as part of a mythic paradigm. Sacks comes to see all these rites of patienthood as necessary, though the necessity is a ritual one: Being in the hospital, he observes, reduces an individual to a kind of "moral infancy" appropriate to "the biological and spiritual needs of the hurt creature" (Sacks 165). Such a ritual regression enables the patient to then move forward toward recovery.

Being a patient, for Sacks, is analogous to the second phase of "liminality," a state characterized by passivity, humility, and near-nakedness. "Liminal entities," observes anthropologist Victor Turner, are expected to be passive, humble, obedient, and ready to accept punishment without complaint (Turner 95). For many, this is an apt description of patienthood. Sacks experiences being a patient as "limbo"—a metaphysical emptiness where, imprisoned in a "roomless room" and confused by a sense of his body that his doctor refuses to acknowledge, he feels alone, disoriented, and alienated. His description of the need to relinquish his active self and assume a stance of passivity is an eloquent description of liminality: "I found this humiliating, at first, a mortification of my self—the active, masculine, ordering self, which I had equated with my science, my self-respect, my mind." It is with his acceptance of this condition, which he characterizes as "an intense and absolute and essential passivity," that his sense of regeneration begins. And when this happens, he is able to perceive the whole experience as a "dark night of the soul," a journey of the soul to despair and back (Sacks 111–14).

The third phase, the return to the world, is ritually structured as "a 'pilgrimage,' a journey, in which one moved, if one moved, stage by stage, or by stations" (Sacks 160–61). Sacks describes his recovery in spatial imagery consistent with the journey metaphor dominating the pathography: Each literal move to a new room or place is accompanied by an existential movement out of the contracted world of illness and into a new and wide dimension. This spatial dimension is marked by a gradual sense of expansion and freedom. So Sacks observes that "the essence of getting better" is in "emerging from self-absorption, sickness, patienthood, and confinement, to the spaciousness of health, of full being, of the real world" (Sacks 156). The fact that he spends several more weeks in a convalescent home reinforces the ritual aspects of his return to the world of the well. He sees this space and time as bridging the gap between sickness and health, as an "in-between" place that serves existential as well as medical needs.

Sacks's pathography is characterized by a great many literary quotations and allusions—the Old Testament Psalmist, John Donne, T. S. Eliot, Dante, Saint John of the Cross, and Nietzsche all find their way into his pathography. These allusions are not fanciful or arbitrary; rather, they are instrumental to his successful undertaking of the journey back to health. Perceiving himself as abandoned by his doctor, he turns to literature to provide a "guide" to negotiate this pilgrimage. The mythic pattern of the journey is refracted in a range of literary sources, all of which interact to interpret and direct his experience. These writings become for him the guide that he lacks, and his own book can be seen as offering to serve this same function for others.

Much that is negative or confusing in the experience of being a patient makes sense in the metaphoric perspective that Sacks provides. For him, the painful ordeals of illness and patienthood take on meaning and purpose because they are perceived as a rite of passage, initiating patients into the world of sickness and ushering them back out of it again. By the end of the pathography, Sacks has "returned" from his ordeal, healed both physically and psychologically.

The pathographies by Ryan, Williams, and Sacks demonstrate the way in which a particular mythic formulation helps turn an experience in which one is primarily acted upon into an experience in which one can be a participant—precisely by giving it meaning. Such mythic formulations of illness are empowering: The ill person understands the way sickness is like a war or a journey into a distant country or a natural (or unnatural) process; but at the same time he or she is *choosing* to give that meaning to it, and this is an act of creative choice in an area of life where choice and creativity are almost wholly denied.

Conclusion

The reinterpretation of experience that goes on in pathography is not entirely retrospective and ex post facto: Rather, as the above examples make plain, it is continuous with processes that arise in the experience itself and inform it even as it is going on. There is not the usual sequential division between the life and writing about the life: The writing completes and formulates an imaginative process that is intrinsic to the experience it re-creates. For the patient with a life-threatening illness, the need to understand what is happening to him or her and determine how to respond to it is not the same as the autobiographer's wish to give some aesthetic or meaningful form to a remembered past. Serious illness threatens not just the existence of the body but also the integrity of the self. The writing of pathography can be an integral part of the drive toward reintegration and recovery. The process of selective remembering, ordering and re-ordering, interpretation, and mythic formulation helps heal the trauma of illness, enabling ill persons not just to get through their experience but also to go beyond it.

That individuals in these situations have recourse to myth, and find its symbols a source of help and strength, attests to the resourcefulness of the imagination in healing. Pathographers resort to mythic thinking because it serves a healing function. Indeed, the mythic constructs that have emerged over decades to help human beings deal with the unknown are a part of our cultural legacy. The capacity to engage in mythic thinking offers the sick person a way of integrating a deeply traumatic experience into his or her life: It also offers a means to transcend it.

The pathography itself can be seen as a reformulation of the experience of illness, as the artistic product and continuation of the instinctive psychological act of formulation: It gathers together the separate meanings, the moments of illumination and understanding, the cycles of hope and despair, and weaves them into a whole fabric, one wherein a temporal sequence of events takes on narrative form. Pathography can also be seen as the final stage in the process of formulation, completing the bridge between the suffering self and the outside world by an overt act of communication. Moreover, in pathography, the need to tell others so often becomes the wish to help others: Perhaps the movement from catharsis to altruism is a signal of the success of the formulation. The very existence of pathography demonstrates that healing the self often involves the act of reaching out to heal others. As Bernice Kavinoky remarks of her pathography in a letter accompanying the manuscript:

> This was a book that had to be written. I wrote it originally for myself, because it clarified my thinking and emotions. Then I began to ponder over it and felt perhaps it was for everybody—not only those who had my operation but everyone who had been through an experience of shock and loss, and who had eventually—after the flying of flags and lifting of the chin—to face it, in his own waiting room, alone. (Kavinoky 71–72)

Notes

1. Portions of this essay were included in my book-length study of pathographies, *Reconstructing Illness: Studies in Pathography* (West Lafayette, IN: Purdue UP, 1993).

2. Gilda Radner, *It's Always Something* (New York: Avon, 1989); Norman Cousins, *Anatomy of an Illness as Perceived by the Patient* (New York: Norton, 1979); William Styron, *Darkness Visible: A Memoir of Madness* (New York: Random, 1990); Susanna Kaysen, *Girl Interrupted* (New York: Random, 1993); Kay Redfield Jamison, *An Unquiet Mind* (New York: Knopf, 1995).

3. A notable exception to this generalization is John Donne's *Devotions Upon Emergent Occasions,* a narrative account of his experience with typhus.

4. I am alluding, of course, to ethnographer Clifford Geertz's idea of "thick description," discussed in Chapter 1 of *The Interpretation of Cultures: Selected Essays* (New York: Basic, 1973).

5. Arthur Frank, "The Rhetoric of Self-Change: Illness Experience as Narrative," *The Sociological Quarterly* 34.1 (1993): 45–56. See also Frank, "What Kind of Phoenix? Illness and Self-Knowledge," *Second Opinion* 18.2 (1992): 31–41.

6. For example, Paul Monette's *Borrowed Time: An AIDS Memoir* (San Diego: Harcourt, 1988) and Emmanuel Dreuilhe's *Mortal Embrace: Living with AIDS*, trans. Linda Coverdale (New York: Farrar, 1988).

7. I use the term "healthy-mindedness," which I have borrowed from William James's *Varieties of Religious Experience*, to refer to a congeries of attitudes, assumptions, and practices that challenge the corresponding assumptions and practices of orthodox medicine. A healthy-minded mythos is most often expressed in the use of alternative medical therapies. For a full discussion of this mythos, see Chapter 5 in my book, *Reconstructing Illness*.

8. Victor W. Turner, *The Ritual Process* (Chicago: Aldine, 1969). See also ethnographer Arnold van Gennep, *The Rites of Passage*, trans. Monika B. Vizedom and Gabrielle L. Caffee (Chicago: U of Chicago P, 1960) and mythographers Mircea Eliade, especially *Rites and Symbols of Initiation: The Mysteries of Birth and Rebirth*, trans. Willard R. Trask (New York: Harper, 1958), and Joseph Campbell, *The Hero with a Thousand Faces* (New York: Meridian Books, 1956).

Works Cited

Banks, Sam A. "Once Upon a Time: Interpretation in Literature and Medicine." *Literature and Medicine* 1 (1981): 5–23.

Baron, Richard. "Bridging Clinical Distance: An Empathic Rediscovery of the Known." *Journal of Medicine and Philosophy* 6.1 (1980): 7–8.

Broyard, Anatole. "Doctor Talk to Me." *The New York Times Magazine* (26 August 1990): 36.

———. *Intoxicated by My Illness and Other Writings on Life and Death*. Ed. Alexandra Broyard. New York: Clarkson Potter, 1992.

Campbell, Joseph. *The Hero with a Thousand Faces*. New York: Meridian Books, 1956.

Cousins, Norman. *Anatomy of an Illness as Perceived by the Patient*. New York: Norton, 1979.

Couser, Thomas. *American Autobiography: The Prophetic Mode*. Amherst: U of Massachusetts P, 1979.

Cox, James M. *Recovering Literature's Lost Ground: Essays in American Autobiography*. Baton Rouge: Louisiana State UP, 1989.

Donne, John. *Devotions Upon Emergent Occasions*. Ed. Anthony Raspa. New York: Oxford UP, 1987.

Dreuilhe, Emmanuel. *Mortal Embrace: Living with AIDS*. Trans. Linda Coverdale. New York: Farrar, 1988.

Eliade, Mircea. *Rites and Symbols of Initiation: The Mysteries of Birth and Rebirth*. Trans. Willard R. Trask. New York: Harper, 1958.

Frank, Arthur. "The Rhetoric of Self-Change: Illness Experience as Narrative." *The Sociological Quarterly* 32.1 (1993): 45–56.

———. "What Kind of Phoenix? Illness and Self-Knowledge." *Second Opinion* 18.2 (1992): 31–41.

Geertz, Clifford. *The Interpretation of Cultures: Selected Essays*. New York: Basic, 1973.

Hawkins, Anne Hunsaker. *Reconstructing Illness: Studies in Pathography*. West Lafayette, IN: Purdue UP, 1993.

James, William. *The Varieties of Religious Experience*. New York: Mentor/New American Library, 1958.

Jamison, Kay Redfield. *An Unquiet Mind*. New York: Knopf, 1995.

Kavinoky, Bernice. *Voyage and Return*. New York: Norton, 1966.

Kaysen, Susanna. *Girl Interrupted*. New York: Random, 1993.

Lerner, Max. *Wrestling with the Angel: A Memoir of My Triumph Over Illness*. New York: Norton, 1990.

Lifton, Robert Jay. *The Broken Connection*. New York: Simon, 1979.

———. *Death in Life: Survivors of Hiroshima*. New York: Random, 1967.

Lorde, Audre. *The Cancer Journals*. Argyle, NY: Spinsters/Aunt Lute, 1990.

Mitchell, Joyce Slayton. *Winning the Chemo Battle*. New York: Norton, 1988.

Monette, Paul. *Borrowed Time: An AIDS Memoir*. San Diego: Harcourt, 1988.

Murphy, Robert. *The Body Silent*. New York: Henry Holt, 1987.

Panger, Daniel. *The Dance of the Wild Mouse*. Glen Ellen, CA: Entwhistle Books, 1979.

Pascal, Roy. *Design and Truth in Autobiography*. Cambridge: Harvard UP, 1960.

Peavey, Fran. *A Shallow Pool of Time: An HIV+ Woman Grapples with the AIDS Epidemic*. Philadelphia: New Society Publishers, 1990.

Permut, Joanna Baumer. *Embracing the Wolf: A Lupus Victim and Her Family Learn to Live with Chronic Disease*. Atlanta: Cherokee Publishing, 1989.

Pike, Burton. "Time in Autobiography." *Comparative Literature* 28 (1976): 326–42.

Price, Reynolds. *A Whole New Life: An Illness and a Healing*. New York: Atheneum, 1994.

Radner, Gilda, *It's Always Something*. New York: Avon, 1989.

Ryan, Cornelius, and Kathryn Morgan Ryan. *A Private Battle*. New York: Fawcett, 1979.

Sacks, Oliver. *A Leg to Stand On*. New York: Summit, 1984.

Sattilaro, Anthony, and Tom Monte. *Recalled by Life: The Story of My Recovery from Cancer*. Boston: Houghton, 1982.

Shapiro, Kenneth A. *Dying and Living: One Man's Life with Cancer*. Austin: U of Texas P, 1985.

Sontag, Susan. *Illness as Metaphor*. New York: Vintage, 1979.

Stone, Albert E. *Autobiographical Occasions and Original Acts: Versions of American Identity from Henry Adams to Nate Shaw*. Philadelphia: U of Pennsylvania P, 1982.

Styron, William. *Darkness Visible: A Memoir of Madness*. New York: Random, 1990.

Turner, Victor W. *The Ritual Process*. Chicago: Aldine, 1969.

van Gennep, Arnold. *The Rites of Passage*. Trans. Monika B. Vizedom and Gabrielle L. Caffee. Chicago: U of Chicago P, 1960.

Wheelwright, Philip. *The Burning Fountain: A Study in the Language of Symbolism*. Bloomington: Indiana UP, 1954.

Williams, Terry Tempest. *Refuge: An Unnatural History of Family and Place*. New York: Pantheon, 1991.

Writing and Healing in the Classroom

Every pair of eyes facing you may have endured something you could not bear.

Lucille Clifton, *Keynote Address, Association for Poetry Therapy National Conference (1996)*

CHAPTER TEN

Language, Power, and Consciousness

A Writing Experiment at the University of Toronto

GUY ALLEN

University of Toronto

In 1979, the dean of humanities at the western campus of the University of Toronto asked me if I would take over from him a half-course (one semester) he had been teaching called "Effective Writing." The college calendar listed the course in a catch-all non-department called Interdisciplinary Studies: The University's English Department wanted nothing to do with teaching writing skills because, it was felt, serious scholars did not teach writing and worthy students should know how to write by the time they get to university. The dean, himself a member of the English Department and a respected English Renaissance drama scholar, did not share the view that teaching writing fell beneath the concerns of a serious language department. He had decided to teach this course himself and had done so for several years.

The dean came to me because I believed writing belonged in the university curriculum and because he felt discouraged by his own efforts in the course. "I haven't been able to do much with this," he told me. "One or two students produce some interesting work, but I don't think many students improve much. It's a hard course for me to teach because there isn't a subject matter in the usual sense. Do what you can with it," the dean said. "There's nothing to lose."

I didn't know how to teach writing, so I adopted the dean's syllabus and book list: a grammar workbook and the *Norton Reader*, a collection of classic nonfiction essays by Plato, Jonathan

Swift, George Orwell, Joan Didion, Martin Luther King Jr., and Art Buchwald, among others. These procedures reflected North American writing and rhetoric course orthodoxy: have students read and discuss model prose, teach them about the errors that afflict student writing, and assign essays on topics based on the readings: "Respond to Jean-Paul Sartre's claim that we invent God to evade responsibility for our lives."

I used the dean's procedures. I taught grammar, structure, and style. I assigned topics based on the readings. I graded the students' papers and returned them with comments.

I suffered icy silences as I coaxed class discussion about the readings. George Orwell's "Politics and the English Language" intimidated most students. They didn't know what to say. They wanted me to tell them what to say, and I found myself cooking something up before class so that I would not stand as mute as they did before these splendid essays. It was my job to know what to say.

The essays in the *Norton Reader* were real writing, the students thought, unlike the writing they did for me. The students were right. Their work lacked authenticity. They had no idea how to engage meaning around the kinds of topics they found in the *Norton Reader*.

They did know how to project engagement, how to playact it. Their writing was all make-believe. The teacher wants engagement; show the teacher engagement. Unlike the masterpiece writers, the students had no sense of a style that expressed their personalities and experience. They focused on "not making mistakes." Writing brought them into a dangerous, uncharted swamp. Even if they didn't die there, they knew they would feel lost and scared, and they knew the passage would be tough and unpleasant.

After two years and four sections of teaching this way, I felt sure that this course did not teach students how to write. In fact, the course, for all my positive intentions, confirmed the students' belief that they could not write. I felt shame as I walked into and out of those classrooms: This charade wasted public money, squandered the students' time, and insulted my image of myself as someone doing useful work.

Much of what the students wrote was acceptable in a university—that is, their writing was correct and in required form—but outside of the academic setting, the writing they did would have interested no one. Their writing fulfilled requirements, but it did not do what good writing should do. It did not engage a reader's interest—no one who was not being well paid to do so would read it—and, worst of all, it made no original meaning. Essay after essay repeated the tedium. The students had no idea that writing could be part of life. Life for them resumed *after* they got their essays in. I felt ashamed of my job. I didn't know what to do. The students gave this sad enterprise positive ratings—they didn't know any better.

I used the dean's procedures. I got the dean's results.

Luck; Or, the Students Teach the Teacher

I wanted change, but I had no idea what I wanted to change or how to bring it about. Then something happened in one of my classes. A new wave (this was 1982) orange-and-purple-haired, high-spirited student broke rank. Catherine Johnson ignored, or improvised upon, the topic I had assigned: "With reference to John Kenneth Galbraith's essay on inflation and government intervention in the economy, write an essay in which you defend or question the role of government in regulating the workplace."

Johnson handed in a piece about her job in a mice-infested bakery. The bakery failed to pass a health inspection. The incompetent owners blamed her and her co-workers for the mice that skittered over cakes and breads and into the flour sacks. This writing expressed meaning. I read Johnson's piece to the class, not to teach anything but to escape the embarrassing emptiness of my *Norton Reader* teaching.

The following week, another student handed in a well-written (and now published in one of my collections of peer models) piece about teenage shoplifting, about "the ultimate heist," "stealing the little silver bells that hung on the back of the heavy wooden doors of Mr. Bong's Variety . . . , the very small store behind our house where I went . . . after school [and] . . . spent the thirty-five cents my mother gave me for milk on a licorice twist and six pieces of Mr. Chuckle's Bubble Gum":

> Four of us swarmed into Bong's Variety wearing dirty red and white uniforms with Burlington Midget Bears stenciled across the front. The four silver bells tinkled, and Mr. Bong assumed his usual position. His eyes darted back and forth from one intruder to the next.
>
> I watched Mike Fass, the skinny center fielder, reach in the refrigerator for a Coke. Mr. Bong's eyes took in Mike's reaching hand, and I grabbed the four silver bells. Within minutes, the outfielders had their drinks, and the heavy wooden doors closed silently behind us.
>
> The next day, Mrs. Ellis caught me taking two packs of Smarties from the candy counter at Zellers.[1]

I read "Mr. Bong's Variety" to the class. Someone said, "That's brave to write about something like that." Someone else said, "This really tells me something because it's so honest, but I didn't know we could write like this."

Why did this writing make meaning that we cared about? How did it do it? We talked about the simple, direct style and the detailing. One student said, "I like 'licorice twist and Mr. Chuckle's Bubble Gum' because that's what we all used to buy and I can really picture it and it sticks in my mind. I can remember it."

"So," I asked, "if the writer just said 'candy' instead of 'licorice twist and Mr. Chuckle's Bubble Gum,' the piece wouldn't mean as much to you?" People agreed that the writer's detail animated the piece.

"I don't like the conclusion," someone said. The conclusion, not the conclusion in the excerpt above, moralized. "The conclusion's a cop-out. If you're going to write about stealing then write about stealing. Don't tell me it's bad."

Another student said, "Yeah. Don't tell us what to think. You've trusted us so far with your honesty. Don't blow it at the end."

Someone else said, "A lot of writing ends with a moral." "But because a lot of writing does that, doesn't mean it's good to do that." The students talked for fifteen minutes about how to end the piece.

"So, what do I do?" the writer asked me about the conclusion after class. "Should I change it?"

"I don't know," I said. "There's no right-and-wrong answer on writing issues like this. You've heard what people have to say. I guess you'll have to make up your mind. Think about what you've heard and decide what meaning you want to make."

A week later, Glen Ricketts, the writer, came with a revised version of "Mr. Bong's Variety." I asked him to read it to the class. He had produced a new conclusion, the one in the excerpt I have reproduced here. This conclusion refuses to moralize but still shows how the world meets the shoplifter's hubris. The class approved.

Students felt engaged by this piece and its writer because its subject and its setting came out of a world they knew about and felt qualified to comment on. Ricketts used language that was right for the experience he described. The students activated. They became a board of editors. The writer acted like a real writer, and the students acted like real editors. This was the real world of writers and editors come into the classroom.

Their discussion of the piece reminded me of the way I talked with other writers and artists in the performance art work I was doing after my academic workday. In the following weeks I received more assignments that expressed something and that had fine writing qualities. But, like the bakery piece and like "Mr. Bong's Variety," the best writing stepped outside usual expectations of what students in an academic setting should write.

Innovations: Getting Students to Work like Writers

The next time I taught the course, I maintained the orthodox frame the dean had passed on to me, with some changes. I set up assignments designed to encourage the students to work and think like writers rather than like students—assignments that I hoped would lead to more of the kind of work Ricketts and others had done.

"Write about a job you have held," one assignment read. "Choose one incident or a series of incidents to present details that will show the reader what your job was like. Don't tell your reader what the job was like. Show it. Use detail that will allow readers to come to their own conclusions about the job. Make your readers participants in your piece." Another assignment read: "Present a short, detailed account of an experience you had as a child. Use details of setting, dialogue, and incident to show what happened. Present scenes and events. Do not tell us how to interpret the events you present." Along with these assignments, I read and passed out photocopied examples of what others at the same experience level had done with these topics. These peer models demonstrated originality, craft, a range of different voices and experiences, and freedom. These models made it clear to my students that they were, as *real* writers are, "condemned to be free." [2]

I parked these innovations—they felt naughty at the time—into one corner of my course. The orthodox paradigm remained predominant. Even so, I felt like I was breaking rules and doing something that I shouldn't tell anybody about. The students loved the innovative assignments, and I liked reading the vibrant personal essays that I was beginning to see. I edited these essays and returned them to the students for revising. Sometimes we revised the same piece as many as ten times. This exchange between writer and editor resembled writing as I had come to know it outside of the academic setting. Students were acting like writers, and I like an editor, more ally than judge.

The more I put good models of personal essays in front of my classes, the more quality writing I received. After about three years I had shifted the balance of work in my courses to about 50 percent traditional expository essays and 50 percent personal essays. In the personal essay assignments students used their own experience as subject matter.

I realized as I was doing this that all writing roots somehow in experience and observation. The research essay, for example, documents the controlled experience the writer creates with the research object. The lab report documents a precisely defined experience designed to yield specific information. My students' personal essays, I realized, were not really so different from the other writing they were expected to do in university. Yet in this form and working with their own experience, the students seemed so much better able to take on the issues of craft that every writer faces. The personal essays solved a problem that dogs university writing courses: the absence of real content. Under the new format students became directly responsible for content. Students reflected on themselves and their experience. Students came to recognize that their lives and the lives of their families contained meaning that could be the subject of writing.

The work I received during the personal essay segment of the course stood out in technical quality, honesty, vividness, and originality from the work they did in the traditional expository essay format. In the one form, students seemed engaged, ready to learn and take on the writer's craft. In the other, they seemed frozen, detached, fixated on not making mistakes (and therefore prone to mistakes), indifferent to meaning.

The expository essays improved slowly, I observed, but seemingly as a result of their work in the personal essays. I did not know what to make of it. I thought each class was a fluke that defied reasonable expectations. Then something else, something very mysterious, happened. Students reported again and again that the personal essay work they did in these classes improved their performance in other courses. Even more mysterious, students credited their writing work for better performance in courses like math and science. The more I deviated from orthodox procedure, the keener the results seemed. I felt baffled, confused, and suspicious. How did I know that the writing quality was really that good? Perhaps I saw what I wanted to see. How could I trust what the students were telling me? What do students know?

One more odd event occurred. Two professors, both academically conservative and notoriously tough on writing issues, referred many of their students to my course because, so they told the students, they had realized by observing the work of previous students that my course was the surest way for the students to bring their writing up to standard. This was strange: If these faculty members had known about the procedures I used in my course they would not have approved. Yet they endorsed the result, a result they observed in the writing they received in their courses, philosophy and survey law.

I felt excited. I felt afraid. Somebody, I thought, is going to call me a charlatan. I also thought that perhaps I had stumbled onto something important. I felt isolated; it didn't feel safe to talk about things I saw happening in my course. On the one hand, I was getting results that committed teachers dream about. On the other hand, I used procedures that many academics would dismiss as bogus and unprofessional. I needed evidence to deal with my own doubts and to confront the skepticism of colleagues.

Collecting Evidence: Do I See What I Think I See?

My teaching became research. I set out to devise qualitative and quantitative measures that might yield some rational perspective on what felt to me like almost mystical events. Here is what I came up with:

1. I interviewed students before their first exposure to my personal essay system. I recorded their answers to these questions:

   a. What do you think about yourself as a writer?

   b. What have teachers told you about your writing?

   c. Why are you taking a course in writing?

2. I surveyed students at the end of my course and asked for written answers to these questions:

   a. What do you think about yourself as a writer?

   b. What have others told you about your writing and any changes in it since you have been in this course?

   c. What, if anything, did you get out of this course? [Students provided this information on anonymous forms collected by a student volunteer who gave me the forms after I had assigned grades.]

3. I tracked grades and comments received by students on their written work in other courses in the university before, during, and after their writing course with me.

Finally, I needed some way of validating writing quality, some way to confirm that much of the writing I saw in my classes was as good as I thought it was. One standard measure is publication. I made submitting work for publication a regular part of my teaching. I encouraged and helped students to submit their best assignments to the same places where new writers publish their short prose work: magazines, newspapers, prose collections.

I introduced one innovation at a time and maintained other aspects of the course as constants. This way I could isolate and identify the effect, if any, of the innovation. For example, I set out to determine optimal assignment frequency. I taught two sections with an essay to be handed in every two weeks, and I taught two sections with one essay to be handed in every week. Here there was a clear result: Frequency improves learning in a writing course. However, another set of experiments showed that two essays per week, when students are taking a full load of other courses, reduces learning.

I have conducted a wide variety of experiments, and some of what I have learned has violated not only widely held beliefs about teaching writing, but even my own common sense. One such experiment, which I have repeated several times, has shown that direct attention to the expository essay does not improve students' performance on the expository essay. I will say more about this later. Another experiment has shown an unexpected way to help students whose first language is not English or else is some dialect of English that is considered unacceptable in the Western university. My experiments show that these students master the English usage demanded by the academy far more quickly and effectively when they are encouraged in various writing assignments to mix their home languages with the academy's "standard English."[3] I would have felt skeptical about this relationship if someone had told me about it, but repeated tests show that this procedure produces positive results whether the student's home language is a foreign tongue or working-class English. Why and how this procedure works, I do not know. It deserves investigation; many students and faculty members report frustration around the work of students who struggle with academy English.

The point is that unexpected results have shown me how important it is to examine and test what we do, especially in a field like the teaching of writing where most practitioners adopt conventional procedures passed down from predecessors. Practices and truisms that we take for granted as common sense sometimes prove invalid when we examine them systematically. The best knowledge often comes out of the collapse of cherished ritual practices.

Over a period of ten or fifteen years, a careful process of innovation, observation, and measurement has produced grounded knowledge about what enhances learning and what does not. The course I have experimented with is a half-course that I taught as many as five times a year on two different campuses of the university. Frequent repetition of the same course created optimal conditions for controlled experiments.

How Students See Writing before the Course

Here is a summary of student responses to my surveys about their sense of writing before they have any experience with the course I teach:

1. More than 95 percent of students entering my course have a negative view of their abilities as writers and a negative view of the experience of writing in a school setting. This astonishing statistic has varied almost not at all from year to year for fifteen years. The one in twenty who report a positive view of themselves as writers always trace that view back to a parent or a teacher who taught them that they have something important to say. This statistic becomes more dramatic when we consider that the sample is limited to students in a university with high standards. These are successful students.

2. More than 70 percent of incoming students report that they take the writing course to reduce the number of "mistakes" they make in their writing. The focus on mistakes comes from their previous experience with teachers. Most students expect teachers to criticize their work and to focus on formal errors. Even those with positive images of themselves as writers almost never say anything about the content of their work. They often say, "I don't make many errors" or "My teachers told me my grammar was basically okay." The students think of good writing as mistake-free writing. Almost none show any awareness of an editing process.

3. More than 85 percent report their dread of writing in an academic setting. They expect to perform poorly and to be criticized for violations of rules that they experience as a mysterious labyrinth of half-visible tripwires.

4. More than 70 percent of entering students believe they must adopt an artificial voice to write in an academic setting. This voice, they feel, must project sophistication through reliance on unfamiliar vocabulary, bloated phrasing, long sentences, and complicated syntax. When I teach them to simplify, they often tell me that they had not realized that simplicity is acceptable. Some object. "But that's how I got my A's," they say when I cut verbiage. Few have experience producing simple prose.

5. More than 65 percent of entering students feel that they must keep themselves out of their writing. When asked about writers who write about themselves and their lives, about 85 percent feel that this kind of writing can be done only by writers who are "gifted" with extraordinary talent. About 50 percent of students feel that they should avoid the first person in serious writing. More than 70 percent of entering students feel that the passive voice sounds more sophisticated and authoritative than the subjective "I." Most feel that writing should sound "objective."

6. Even with the cluster of negativity surrounding writing and the dread of stern judgments, the students feel writing will be important to them academically, professionally, and personally. Despite previous bad experiences, they want to try again. The students who come to my course are a select sample: These are students who have gone out of their way to choose a writing course. There must be many who have given up, who go through life avoiding situations where they might have to write. There must be those who believe that because they "don't make many mistakes," they have nothing more to learn.

How Students Regard Writing after the Course: Attitudes and Results

The course requires students to produce one original piece of writing each week for ten weeks as well as continuous revisions of their original work. Alongside the writing of these assignments, students attend weekly lectures and workshops on prose basics, a prose boot camp that I will outline later. They also attend three one-on-one sessions with the course instructor, in which the instructor, working as an editor, recommends edits and revisions for their original work. Here is what students have reported after exposure to one course of three-and-a-half months with at least two months of intensive work in personal essays:

1. Most students who have courses where written work is required report improved grade results that they trace directly to their experience in the writing course. Seventy-two percent of these students report improved grade results in written work in other university courses. Thirty-one percent of the students reporting improved results report an average one letter-grade (i.e., C to B, or B− to A−) rise in evaluated written work such as essays and lab reports; 69 percent of these report a fractional letter-grade rise (for example, B− to B+, or C+ to B−, or B to A−). Of those reporting improved results, 21 percent reported that other instructors commented explicitly on the improvement in their writing. Students attribute their improved results mainly to three circumstances: increased confidence, knowledge of editing principles, and simplified style.

2. Some students have reported improvement in courses which require no writing, courses where, for example, they have only multiple-choice or short-answer tests. They attribute the change to increased personal confidence and sharpened awareness of language.

3. Most students report relief from the tension and trauma associated with writing. They attribute the change to intensive experience with writing, increased confidence and better knowledge about writing process, especially editing. A typical observation: "Writing used to be a torment; now it is a strength for me. My friends always ask me to edit their work."

4. Seventy-four percent of the students report feeling more positive about themselves as a result of writing personal history. Many report positive life effects that reach beyond the academy. Increased confidence, self-awareness, and assertiveness are the commonest. Some report breakthroughs with issues they feel have interfered with their ability to realize their potential. Some comment on the redemptive power of writing. For example, a number report that their engagement with personal essays has helped them achieve perspective on personal shame resulting from racism, family breakup, physical and psychological abuse, relationship failures, cultural alienation, academic and job failures, and sickness: "After I wrote about that, it didn't bother me anymore" or "I used to try to hide that from people, but now I feel I can talk about it as part of who I am." Many report simply that they had never before thought of their lives as

containing subject matter of interest. "I never thought there was anything in my life worth writing about" is a typical comment. "I have learned that being myself is good enough—and interesting" is another. Some come to a new appreciation of family members: "I never realized what an amazing thing my father had done until I interviewed him about his escape from Uganda."

5. Some students have reported that their engagement with personal essays has shown them how to bring aspects of their own lives into their academic work. One student, the daughter of a woman who immigrated from China in 1950, interviewed her mother, a peasant farmer from an isolated area in southern China, for several of her essays in my course. Later, in a Chinese history course, she again interviewed her mother about how her mother survived the Japanese invasion of China in the Second World War and used the things her mother told her as evidence in the essay (her professor, noting the freshness of her primary research, gave the essay an A+). Many students could supplement library research with material from their lives or the lives of people they know, but few realize this is possible or desirable. They see the academic universe as not welcoming original material found outside of the library.

6. Of the 451 students who have contributed responses to my surveys, more than 100 have published or read in public readings personal essays they wrote as assignments for my beginning prose course. In exceptional cases, they have published independently of any help from me in newspapers, magazines, and campus publications. In most cases, they achieve public exposure in venues I have helped them to contact. I have myself published much student work, and I use collections of personal essays by students as my course texts. Students who publish or read for the public report that public exposure and acceptance have provided validation and confidence-building recognition. For many, forms of public acceptance confirm that their experience in the writing course amounts to more than "just one professor's opinion." Well-written personal essays can attract readers. The purpose of writing is to communicate; public interest suggests success.

7. More than 90 percent of the students who took part in classes where I offered instruction in both the personal essay and in the expository essay felt that the work with personal essays accounted for their positive experience in the course. In almost all cases, it is the work with personal essays that students remember most about the course. Students also identify the personal essay work as the part of the course that helped them improve results in their other academic writing.

8. A few students, less than 3 percent, have found the course and the personal essay instruction unhelpful and frustrating. All of these have been students who came to the course looking for an anything-goes creative writing course. These students have found my prose boot camp "uncreative and formulaic." The instructor's insistence on nonfiction prose essays, coupled with assurance that students are free to select their own subject matter, seems to them "narrow-minded." Some wanted to write poetry or science fiction.

I have one observation to add. The student surveys have suggested that the personal essay work teaches them more than work with expository prose. I tested this notion. I taught sections of the course with 30 percent of the course devoted expressly to expository essays. I taught other sections purely on the personal essay with no attention to expository prose. What I found surprised me. Direct attention to the expository essay did not enhance students' ability to produce good expository essays. The students have it right: They learn most about writing through instruction and work on personal essays. And what they learned in their work with personal essays transferred to other genres, such as the expository essay, the lab report, and the book review. This result surprised and puzzled me. Teaching X enhances the ability to handle Y. Teaching Y does not much improve the ability to handle Y. This result suggests irrational processes and connections. We have mystery here.

The Prose Boot Camp

Colleagues who feel threatened by my questions about orthodoxy have often insulted my procedures as a soft, anything-is-okay-here anarchy that does not belong in a formal academic enterprise. Anarchy does not yield writing people want to read, at least not often. I teach students to write prose that makes meaning and attracts readers. That is not a soft enterprise.

I do teach about the value of unstructured free association in the "Twenty-Minute Journal" exercise:

Sit down every day and write about anything as fast as you can for twenty minutes. Write as much as you can. Don't worry about quality. Do not think. Just write. Write as many words as you can in twenty minutes. I want to see that you do this, but I am, of course, not going to read your twenty-minute journals. This is a standard writer's warmup. You may get ideas doing this, but this is not real writing. This warms the writing engine. Almost all writers keep journals. Unless the writers become objects of public curiosity, these journals never see the light of day. Still, the unselfconscious journals help their writing.

But unstructured free association is only a first step in producing a crafted piece of writing. As Richard Rhodes puts it,

> Writing is a craft. Its primary function is communication. I mean "craft" strictly: like carpentry or pottery, writing is handmade. Like other crafts as well, writing can sometimes be organized to the special depth and resonance people call art (Rhodes 15).

Students learn the craft of writing by learning editing. Students must learn to be editors of their own and other people's writing. Through editing, writing attains clarity, shape, precision—the power to communicate the message the writer intends. Teaching editing requires what I call *boot camp*, tough basic training in prose essentials.

In a thirteen-week course, students must hand in one original assignment per week for ten weeks. Here is a sample assignment schedule.

Assignment 1: Write a short, detailed narrative about something that you experienced or observed as a child.

Assignment 2: Write a short, detailed narrative about something that you experienced or observed in school.

Assignment 3: Write a narrative designed to show us a place you know. Do not describe the place. Depict the place by showing what happens in it. Your place may be a room, a town, a store, someone's living room, anywhere.

Assignment 4: Write about a person. Use dialogue, setting, action, and other details to show this person to your reader.

Assignment 5: Write about a job you have held. Detail one incident, a series of incidents, or a period of time to present your experience of the job.

Assignment 6: Write about something you have observed or experienced about relations between women and men. Do not generalize. Detail particular incidents to make your points.

Assignment 7: Present a picture of life in a family. Detail an event or chain of events you have experienced or observed.

Assignment 8: Write an evaluation of some event or of some person such as a teacher in a position of responsibility. Do not tell your reader what to think. Guide your reader's response through your selection of details.

Assignment 9: Interview someone about something that interests you. Write a piece based on the material you collect in your interview.

Assignment 10: Write an argument, a piece designed to change someone's mind about something. Address a specific difference you have with someone in your life right now. Your objective is to get your addressee to see an old issue in a new way. Use details to show the issue as you see it.

Students may edit and revise assignments as many times as they like. During the course I review their work as editor, not judge. Most produce three or four versions of some assignments. Some revise one or two of their pieces as many as ten times. Revision is not a process of correction. I encourage students to edit their finest pieces and to forget about their duds. The best five pieces of writing in their file at the end of the course determine their grades. Because they have the opportunity to revise and because only their best work counts, I set high standards for final submissions.

Alongside the stream of assignments and revisions, I assign exercises, sometimes as many as four a week. Basic training exercises include collecting and revising examples of wordiness and clichés, replacing passives and forms of "to be" with active, specific verbs, replacing vagueness with detail, building parallel phrases, sentences and paragraphs, and transforming weak writing into strong writing. At the end of thirteen weeks, students' files are four or five inches thick with writings, revisions, and exercises. One faculty member who read my syllabus said, "Well, anybody could learn to write under a system like that." That's my philosophy: Writers are made, not born. To make writers, we must stimulate students to do what good writers do — to sharpen their language skills, to write and write and edit and edit, and to use these skills to explore themselves and their world.

Repeatability: What Happens in Different Settings?

My experiments have shown me that the more I abandoned orthodox practice for new procedures which my experiments validated, the better the outcomes. Doubts persisted, however. The results I observed made a travesty of common wisdom about teaching writing in universities and colleges — that students' skills are so weak that they cannot be expected to behave like writers, that they need to be taught what they should have been taught a long time ago, mainly grammar and form.

I felt insecure about whether or not the results I was seeing could be repeated by other instructors. Were these procedures tied somehow to my personality? I enlisted teachers of writing at several universities and colleges to try these procedures and to report results. Five reported, with pleasure and amazement, results like those I have seen. One reported disappointment and said, "This system scared me, and I felt I was losing control."

One feature of personal essay work is its adaptability to individual cases. Writers use personal essays to explore aspects of self and life that arise as they sit alone before the blank page. Most often the writers at this stage do not see themselves as exploring themselves or as approaching significant issues. Their concerns are practical and immediate: They have a deadline to meet, and they need a topic. New writers often apologize for their topic choices: "I couldn't think of what to write, and I don't think this is very good, but I couldn't think of anything else." Yet, the first few essays, where students may experience their topics as desperation choices, contain the kernel of issues that lie at the heart of their lives. Later, as they come to recognize the importance of these subjects, they direct their writing with more confidence.

Survey results tell only so much about this process. Individual cases will tell us more. I will put before you a detailed case, Martha Kofie, that includes two of her essays and describes her experience with personal essay work. I highlight this case because it shows with particular clarity the healing potential of personal essay work (the focus of this collection). I will follow the long case with two brief case summaries to show how students adapt this process to their individual situations.

The Long Case: Martha Kofie

Martha Kofie took my course in the fall of 1990 when she was twenty-one. She came upon the course "just looking through the calendar":

> I had given up on English. I never did well in English, and I tried really hard. I got C's and low B's. I wasn't sure what the teachers wanted. I tried to follow the rules, I would put everything I had into a piece, and in the end usually got a nonresponse from teachers. I took this course at the university because it sounded like I could try again. Writing had always been a part of my life. It was something that interested me. But I needed someone to say it was okay before I could do it on my own. I was shocked when I found a course like yours at the University of Toronto. I remember an instant feeling of relief. Halfway through the first class, I felt I was going to get another chance. I felt a lot of freedom. You said to the class, "Nothing you write will surprise me." I had suspicions about that. I took it as a dare. I thought, "Let's get clear exactly what I can write about in here."

Kofie sat in the back of the room and spoke so softly that I strained to understand what she said. She radiated fragility. I avoided calling on her in class. I came to know her through her writing.

The daughter of middle-class professional parents, an African father and a white Canadian mother, Kofie wrote about growing up amid the racism in a nearly all-white Ontario city. She wrote about the child's terror in the house of angry, warring parents. Her first story documents both the racism she experienced in her community and the combat she experienced at home. "Kwame," the title of the story, is her brother's name.

Kwame

© 1993 Martha Kofie

An imaginary but enforced line drawn through the yard of St. Berna-
dette Elementary School divides the big kids' side for Grades Four to
Eight from the little kids' side for Junior Kindergarten to Grade Three.
The swing set on the side for older students is the most popular attrac-
tion on the playground. Every lunch hour, Nicole and I wolf down
peanut butter sandwiches so we can be the first ones on the swings.

Nicole digs the toe of her blue sneaker into the sand under her swing.
"It doesn't matter if your Dad had him," she says. "Kwame can't be
your real brother if your Mom adopted him."

I lean back and straighten my legs as I swing past Nicole.

"Kwame *is* my real brother," I say.

"He can't be. You two aren't even the same colour. He's dark like
your Dad, but you're light brown, in between them and your Mom."

"So?" I see Sister Joanne walk out the rusted back doors for playground duty.

"So my Dad says your Mom is a nigger-lover, and he says Kwame
is only your half-brother."

I drag my feet through the sand and jump off the swing. "Kwame's
my brother. Okay? Kwame's my brother."

∞

"Thirteen-zip," says Kwame. "Ready?"

The green ping-pong table spreads through half of the brown-
panelled basement. Behind Kwame is a TV and a brown plaid chester-
field with grey stuffing sticking out the side where Tipper sharpens his
claws. The staircase to my side of the table leads out to the back door,
then up into the dining room and kitchen. Brown and yellow circles
pattern the wallpapered wall that borders the left side of the staircase.
On the right side, a beige wall rises half the height of the left wall to
meet the dining room floor.

Kwame smacks the ping-pong ball with his red, rubber-lined
paddle. The white ball top-spins low over the net and slips past my
paddle as I swing.

"I can't get those ones, Kwame. Don't serve like that. It's not fair
because you're way older."

"A game's a game, Martha," Kwame chuckles.

"Why can't we pretend I'm winning sometimes?"

"Fourteen-zip. Ready?" Kwame lifts his paddle.

The crash on the staircase wall shakes me to the floor. I peek over my end of the ping-pong table. Kwame looks at me, frozen in the serving position.

"What was that?" Kwame asks.

"Well, I don't care either!" Mommy yells from upstairs.

I look up the stairs and see the next dish before it hits the wall.

Kwame drops his ball and paddle. He runs over to me in time to see two halves of a dinner plate thump and tumble down the carpeted stairs.

"What are Mommy and Papa fighting about now, Kwame?"

"Beats me, but they must be throwing the dishes right from the kitchen cupboards. Mommy's got a good arm."

Two more dinner plates smash the wall. A pie-shaped chunk of one plate ricochets off the wall and clanks against the metal banister before it thuds to the floor.

Kwame drops his paddle on the table. "I can't stand to hear them fight anymore. Come on, let's try and get outside without them seeing us."

We make it to the fifth step. Plates, two at a time, fly over our heads, slam into the wall and pelt our backs as we duck. Kwame quickly leads me around the plate fragments on two more steps. Two coffee cups and saucers split and shatter against the wall. I scream and curl onto the stairs.

"Come on," Kwame yells. He leaps up the last three steps. "Hurry!" Kwame runs out the back door.

I try to stand. A soup bowl hits the wall and throws splinters against my back. I scream again.

"Did a dish hit you?" Papa calls from the kitchen.

"No, but it . . ."

Four more coffee cups smash the wall and spray my back. I cover my head with my hands and cry into my skirt.

∽

Kwame shakes my shoulder. "Are you all right? Don't move. I've got shoes on. I'll go get some for you too."

Kwame and I go back down into the basement. He sits beside me on the couch and picks splinters out of my afro. "Why didn't you come outside with me?"

"I was too scared."

"I didn't mean to leave you like that. I stuck my head in the back door to see if I could make it down to you. I almost got a dish in the face."

I play with the loose thread on the hem of my skirt.

"What if I had to explain that one to my basketball coach, Martha? What would I say? 'Hey, Coach, I can't play in the city finals this weekend. Got hit by a flying saucer.' He'd lock me up."

I don't smile.

"It's over now, Martha. It's okay."

"But Kwame, what are we supposed to eat lunch on?"

Kwame leans toward me when he sees my tears. "Don't worry," he whispers. He looks down at the splinters of glass in his palm. "I'll fix us something good. Something real good."

Kofie's second story tells about pre-adolescent shenanigans and the horrific parental response. Like "Kwame," this story takes us between school and home. Here the writer probably suggests more than she knows: Her story emphasizes both the disconnection and the connection between school and home. What happens at home clearly sets the tone of the inner life of the child who goes to school, and yet the classroom on test day goes through its prescribed motions as the teacher tells the narrator to "stop talking." School requires silence; the narrator needs talk. The split between the inner and outer life of the child is one the personal essay can address. Here is "Testing, Testing":

Testing, Testing

© 1993 MARTHA KOFIE

"No. No. No. If it *sticks* it's done, if it *falls down* it needs to cook some more." Mandy whips a spaghetti noodle at the kitchen wall. The noodle slaps, peels and falls, curling with the others on the floor, just in front of the orange-and-blue flowered wall. Mandy and I stand behind strings of spaghetti marking the throw line on the beige linoleum. Pots of spaghetti and sauce sit on pot holders on the counter. Math books lie open on the kitchen table. Mandy and I celebrate the first PD (Professional Development) day of Grade Six at my house. On PD days, teachers work and students get the day off.

Mandy takes the bowl of drained spaghetti from me.

"Are you sure, Mandy?" I ask. I pick the last noodle out of the bowl and throw. "I thought it was the other way around." My noodle joins the heap of white swirls on the floor.

"No, it's not. Lisa told me and she's Italian."

"I know that. Lisa taught me how to swear in Italian in Grade Two."

"And besides," Mandy says, "these walls don't work. You're not supposed to test spaghetti on wallpaper. Lisa told me that too. Let's try it in your room."

"Okay."

Mandy holds the strainer while I pour more spaghetti out of the pot. Inside the door of my bedroom, I place the bowl of spaghetti on the purple-speckled carpet between us. I throw the first noodle over my pink-flowered bedspread at the mauve wall. The noodle sticks.

"See?" Mandy says. "I told you it doesn't work on wallpaper. My turn." Mandy throws a noodle. Her white squiggle clings to the wall above mine. "I wonder if it will stick to the ceiling," Mandy says. She bends her knees and like a cheerleader tossing a pom-pom throws a noodle at the ceiling. "Hey," Mandy says, hands on hips and looking up, "this spaghetti is really ready."

"Maybe it sticks to glass," I say. I whip a noodle at my mirror.

"That's a great idea. We can try it on your window too."

The bowl of noodles empties as strings of white slap and stick to the ceiling, mirror, window and walls.

"Hey, let's see if the meatballs are ready." Mandy runs to the kitchen.

"What?" The noodle I was about to throw falls to the rug. I run after Mandy.

"You gotta be . . ." I flatten myself against the kitchen wall, afraid Mandy might spill the jiggling pot of spaghetti sauce she carries as she runs back past me.

Mandy puts the pot on the carpet and dips her hand into the sauce. "Ow. I forgot this was still hot." Mandy scoops out a meatball and throws it at the wall. The meatball flattens to a semi-circle and slides to the carpet. "Nope," says Mandy. "This stuff ain't ready yet."

"You didn't throw hard enough. Here, I'll show you how to throw a meatball." I sweep my hand through the sauce and pull out another meatball. Winding up, I swing my arm behind my head. The meatball slips out of my hand and splatters against the wall behind us.

Mandy and I turn to look at the bits of hamburger forming a dripping red circle on the wall. "That is one ready meatball," I say.

Mandy doesn't laugh. "When are your parents coming back?" she asks.

I look at Mandy. Her eyes widen. Two car doors shut outside.

"Oh, my God. Oh, my God." Mandy dances on the spot, shaking her arms. She runs out ahead of me toward the kitchen window. "What are we going to do? I mean, we only got about ten seconds to pick up the spaghetti, wash the walls and the ceiling and the mirror and the window and the light—did you know I got a noodle to stick to your light?—and then we gotta put all the food away and make like we're studying for our test tomorrow."

I reach the window. Mandy grabs both my arms. She jerks me toward her. "It's just the Keshleys coming home next door, Marth."

Mandy collapses laughing. She smacks the kitchen floor. I laugh too, leaning against a kitchen wall and holding my stomach.

"Got ya that time," Mandy says, one hand on the floor, the other pointing at me.

I kneel and reach over to tickle Mandy's waist.

"I'm not ticklish," she says. She hugs me and laughs over my shoulder. Our bodies jiggle against each other. The shaking slows to a quiver and an occasional spasm. Mandy sniffs hard.

I flatten my palms against the sides of my face. "My cheeks hurt."

"Mine too," Mandy says. "Seriously now, we better clean up. I'll get the bleach and you get the rags. My mom says bleach will clean anything."

∞

I lie on the edge of my double bed farthest from the bedroom door. I stare at patches of yellow paint showing through my mauve wall.

I hear Papa's steps coming toward my room. He pushes open my door. The door bangs against the wall. I shut my eyes and squeeze. The weight of his knee on my bed makes me slide toward him as he reaches across. With a finger, he pokes my bum. "Get up."

He stands beside my bed. I fake a slow stretch.

"I said 'Get up.'"

I sit on the edge of my bed, facing away from him.

"I want to see you in the kitchen."

"Okay."

"Look at me when I speak to you."

I stand slowly and turn. "Okay," I say. "I'm coming to the kitchen."

Before he leaves, Papa looks through my nightshirt at my breasts.

I walk to the kitchen. Papa pulls out a chair from the table. "Sit down."

I grasp the edge of the table and ease into the chair.

"Maybe Martha shouldn't go to school today." Mommy walks toward the table, tying the belt of her blue, terry-cloth housecoat.

"She's okay. Now stand up and sit down properly."

I stand, close my eyes and sit down quickly.

"That's better. Get ready to go to school."

In my room, I bend and look behind me at the mirror. Pink and puffy, the long, horizontal welts are still there. I touch one gently. The sting sucks air in through my closed teeth. I reach for my red-and-blue dotted underwear and pull them up.

Mandy watches me sit in my desk behind hers. "You got in shit, didn't you."

I force a smile.

"I'm sorry, Marth. I mean, I was the one who . . ."

"We both did it, Mandy. So forget it. We had fun."

Mr. O'Donnell hands out our math tests. "Stop talking and put your books away. You have until recess to finish the test."

Addressing the Split: Kofie's Experience with Personal Essays

Plain words and terse understatement lend Kofie's stories power and grace: low-key language portrays high-key events. Ominous multiple meanings of "testing" suggest more than is said. The indirect revelation of the parental violence that precedes the breakfast table scene shocks. Restraint sets cruelty in relief. Style, ironically cool and controlled, leaves horror to the reader. With dignified reserve, the writer reports; the reader feels. This, I saw, was a writer doing what writers do—very well.

Events have confirmed my sense of Kofie as writer. She went on to publish most of the work she wrote in the two courses she took from me, including "Kwame" and "Testing, Testing."[4] Kofie read some of her work on a Toronto radio program. Listeners phoned and wrote to say that her stories had helped them understand their own experiences of racism and family violence. Writing became central in Kofie's life. After she graduated, a publisher dedicated to women's writing hired Kofie as managing editor. Kofie attended international conferences where, despite shyness, she made speeches to publishers and prodded them to search out writing about people and lives that rarely make it into print. Kofie knew about the healing power of writing and urged publishers to make this available to as many different kinds of voices as possible. While she worked as managing editor, Kofie earned a master's degree in philosophy.

Kofie is a talented student, and her exposure to the writing process can claim limited credit for her academic successes. However, this case offers good evidence for the power of the writing process to release latent capacity. In Kofie's case, her writing appears to have catalyzed the healing of wounds that, unhealed, impeded performance. According to Kofie, the first writing course provided a pivot point for her. She had been in therapy since a suicide attempt six years before, when she was fifteen. Here is her account of her experience in that course:

> When I worked on my stories for the course, I started crying and I cried every day for two years after that. I delayed taking your second course for a year. I cried every day, and it was all about my dad. I remember feeling really driven to put to paper the scenes that were the most painful. I saw those scenes in my head. They never left me. Those were the scenes I wrote in my stories. Those were the scenes I had to put down.

What was my role during Kofie's confrontation with her trauma? I did not know about the crying. I did not discuss any of the psychological implications of Kofie's writing with her. That is not my role. As editor and teacher, my role is to guide students in issues of writing and language. Kofie wrote personal essays to confront and redeem damage suffered at the hands of heedless caregivers. That was her project. Mine was helping her to find her way to a clear, original, expressive language that would allow her to communicate clearly to herself and others. The process is self-regulating. Students take on what they are ready to take on. I have never seen writing students use their writing to wander into issues they could not manage.

Four years after her last course with me, I asked Kofie what made this writing process work for her.

> I'm not sure I totally understand. It's something about having a witness. But for years, I had had witnesses—counselors and therapists. Something about putting it on paper took the witnessing to another level. I became my own witness. Emotional damage is so hard to articulate in a story. It takes so much work to show in a story that something had the impact it had. Through all that labor, I relived those scenes. It was the first time I realized I had really been harmed—even though I already had the labels: I had heard of physical abuse; I had even heard of emotional abuse.

For me, writing those stories stopped all the circling that goes on in the head. Yet, before I wrote them, that's what these thoughts did. They circled around and around in my head. Now, they're out of my head, and I can always go pick up the book and read those stories if want to.

Before I wrote those stories, I needed to think about those scenes to remember them—even though I don't know why I would want to remember them. Now I have forgotten them. Just recently I read the stories in the book where they're published. I was shocked. I had forgotten.

I asked Kofie how the technical training around language, the prose boot camp, had contributed to her changes:

The technical direction was like an anchor. There's such potential to drown in emotional stuff. The writing technology meant I was *en route* to something else. There was more than pain. I remember especially the lessons about sound patterns. I liked the softer vowels and the hard consonants—very different effects. For some reason, work with these sounds gave me a way to contact really sad places in me.

Kofie has not always enjoyed success. After her first year, when she received one A−, failed two courses, dropped another and received a D− in another, the university put Kofie on academic probation. By her fourth year, when she took the first of two writing courses with me, she had brought herself to a B− average. The year she took the writing course she received one A+, five A's (one for writing) and one B+. In her fifth and final year, she received six A's, one A+, one A−, and graduated with a major in philosophy. Kofie found herself as a student during her university years, and the personal essays played a role. "Formal essays became a lot easier for me," Kofie reports. "And learning about editing helped. I started to pretend I was the editor of the books and articles I was reading for my courses. This way, I could get quickly to the meaning of the piece."

Kofie's writing experience enabled her to take her life experience into her academic work. Before she wrote her stories, she says, "academic" and "life" were artificially split, and yet one intruded on the other. Her writing led to integration:

Before my experience in your writing course, I didn't take chances with my courses. I did what was expected. After, I learned to see my experience as having meaning that could be used in analyzing ideas, I took chances. I brought my experiences into essays in my philosophy courses. As a graduate student I included a journal entry in an essay. I always got good responses.

When I heard generalizations about people, I tested them by asking: "Does my experience fit here?"

In one presentation to students and faculty in the Philosophy Department, I talked about my father. I talked about how I suffered abuse from him if I did not do well in school. Race was such an important factor. I inherited my father's fears about what would happen if I weren't a superior performer. "You have to listen to the teacher," my father said. But what about teaching that denies the place of my and my father's race in the history of thought? Racial bias in the curriculum puts me in a contradiction between listening to the teacher and accepting myself as a black woman. I explained this to [philosophy faculty members] to help them understand my reactivity to the subtlest hints of racism in the philosophy curriculum. My ability to connect my life to the theories I study has amounted to breakthrough for me. Theories and assumptions can be measured against experience.

Kofie, the writer, has put the abuse stories behind her. Still a fine stylist and still an acute observer of people in family settings, Kofie is now writing a series about unconventional human relationships that work well. Compassion, humor, and understanding distinguish Kofie's stories. Kofie reports that she is now in her fourth year of a new course of psychotherapy. She has applied to medical school, where, if accepted, she wants to qualify herself as a psychiatrist. Her writing forms an important part of the evidence she has presented to the medical school admissions committee.

Kofie's testimony suggests the catalytic potential of students developing writers' voices and using those voices to discover and develop themselves. Students choose the issues and incidents they want to explore, and as they write they learn how to use language that makes meaning. Students select the truth they want to tell and by telling come to know. They work to set their truth in language that expresses their personalities and experiences and that has the power to earn credibility with a reader.

A Short Case: Addressing a Cultural Split

June Irwin immigrated to Canada from Trinidad when she was eighteen, with her mother and sisters. In Trinidad, Irwin's mother, extremely poor, washed clothes by hand to support five children in a tiny rural village. In Canada, Irwin worked in a factory for ten years and took educational upgrading. In her late twenties, she gained entrance to the University of Toronto through a special access program. In her first year, Irwin dropped three courses, failed one, and passed one that her English professor told her was "a gift."

Irwin spoke tentatively in a beautiful Trinidadian accent. Professors, she told me, complained about her grammar and her writing. She had been told she "did not belong" in university. She had been told, "You live in Canada now and must leave your past behind." Irwin came to my course in distress.

Irwin's first essay told about an accident she witnessed as a six-year-old: A truck passing through her village hit and decapitated one of her playmates. The first version of this piece reported the incident in bare outline form and contained sentence fragments, run-ons, and faulty verb agreements. Irwin had not set the scene. The village, its people, and the way they speak were all absent. Irwin had tried to write about her past while leaving her past behind. I interrogated Irwin through another four versions of this piece: "What would we see if we could see the village? What did the people say? What did your mother do? Show me the place and the people, and show me what happened. I've never seen that village or anything like it. I want to see and hear it in your essay."

After three weeks and several drafts, Irwin produced details of setting and dialogue in the local tongue to produce a fine journalistic piece with a fascinating portrait of life in her town. Formal sentence problems disappeared. "You can write," I told her. Irwin eventually produced twenty essays for me in two courses. She set nineteen of these in the village of her childhood and mixed dialogue in the local tongue with the "standard English" of the narrator's voice. Her work presented a precise, unsentimental picture of the poverty her mother faced as she raised five children. Irwin's classmates felt educated by her picture of poverty and village life. Irwin had been determined at the beginning to keep the poverty of her childhood secret; she told me she felt ashamed of it.

Irwin went on to publish and receive extensive recognition for her work. She showed her stories to her professors. Her past, including her mother tongue, became a source of esteem rather than shame. And her problems in producing academy English withered. The year Irwin took the writing courses she received two A's and two B's and came off probation. She became an excellent student and has now applied to law school. Irwin claims that the work on personal essays enabled her academic transformation. She feels more confident, more decisive, and happier. Irwin used the personal essay to integrate her two lives, her life in university in Canada and her life in the village in Trinidad. Her mother tongue has helped her to produce rich literature and, it turns out, is an asset, not a liability. Irwin used her personal essay work to address and mend a cultural split that alienated her from a part of herself, her origins.

A Short Case: Addressing the Split between the Self and the Writing Self

Mike Demarco, a twenty-one-year-old commerce major, is the son of Italian immigrant parents. His father worked the assembly line at a Ford plant. Demarco, the first in his family to attend university, announced that he would never read his work aloud in the class editing sessions. His fear was phobic. "Flunk me if you have to," he said, "but I'll never read"—this from a student preoccupied with grades. Demarco wrote his first assignments in a stiff, this-is-how-you-write-for-a-professor style: turgid, bureaucratic, formally correct, dead. Yet Mike Demarco the person radiated informality, honesty, and self-mocking humor. When he sat down to write, Demarco encountered a split that divided him from the confidence that informed his actions on other occasions. Writing required a contrived self—a dry, dull, self that denied his origins.

Relations between us remained tense until he turned up with an essay about his family, whom, he had told me earlier, he could not write about because "there's really nothing interesting about them—and they're not educated." This essay presented an anarchic, funny, touching family dinner scene. The piece used dialogue, including the mixture of Italian and English spoken in his house, sharp detail, and a spare, informal style. "This is it," I said. "You are doing it." Demarco had fused his writing life with the rest of his life. Even in essays that had nothing to do with family, Demarco's family now made cameo appearances. The family was indeed "something special," he realized, and made a good subject. One day Demarco came in with an essay, "The Calculus Test," that presented a scene after a test where many students realized they would have to give up dreams and plans because they could not pass calculus, a prerequisite for many programs. "The Calculus Test," as good literature often does, evokes an ambivalent response; the scene is both comic and terrifying. I praised the piece. "This may seem funny to you, sir," he said, "but, if you want me to, I'll read it in class." He read not only in class but later before an audience of 200 university faculty members at a conference where I spoke about personal essays. The Math Department requested a copy of "The Calculus Test" to post on its bulletin board. Demarco has since given a public reading of one of his essays. Demarco reported other developments. His grades in written work for commerce assignments rose by 25 percent. He also reported that he became "chief editor" of his friends' writing, and, as Demarco put it, "I must be doing okay because they keep coming back." Demarco used his personal essay work to address the split between the person he is and the person he thought he had to be to succeed in the academy. Because of this split, he had left some of the most compelling aspects of himself out of his academy life. The fusion strengthened the person and his academic work.

Explaining Change: How Does the Personal Essay Work?

The evidence I have seen shows that work with personal essays produces better outcomes in expository writing than work directly on expository writing does. There is substantial qualitative

evidence that work with expressive narrative enhances performance in courses where there is no writing, in courses where, for
example, performance is measured only in multiple-choice tests.
Academic results offer one kind of evidence of personal growth,
of the person's ability to operate effectively in a setting the person has chosen as a kind of test. What do these results mean?
Probably that something about the writing process releases or
catalyzes potential otherwise trapped in the psyche. In other
words, the expression of the self and its experience through language somehow develops the whole person, so that the evidence
of development appears in the various things people do with
their lives. Most students report not only improved academic results but improved confidence—better mental health.

How do we account for the capacity of this engagement with
language and the self to catalyze positive change?

Bill Buford has written recently in *The New Yorker* about the
revival of interest in storytelling. Stories, Buford writes, "protect
us from chaos, and maybe that's what we, unblinkered at the end
of the twentieth century, find ourselves craving." Buford goes on:
"Implicit in the extraordinary revival of storytelling is the possibility that we need stories—that they are a fundamental unit of
knowledge, the foundation of memory, essential to the way we
make sense of our lives. . . . We have returned to narratives—in
many fields of knowledge—because it is impossible to live without them" (Buford 11–12). For Alamatea Usuelli, "Story-telling
creates the illusion that subject and object, the inner and the
outer world, correspond, and that the subject's experience has
meaning and is preserved from chaos." This view sees storytelling as a defense against the loss of the illusion of "a completed
universe . . . in which we may stroll in relative safety." For
the reader, according to Usuelli, the narrative may arouse "a
play of identifications which enable [a person] to overcome the
usual limits of . . . ego" (Usuelli 183–84). The illusion of "protection from chaos" creates an artificially safe place for development just as the illusion of safety created by caring parents does.
The world is not a safe place, but the temporary illusion of security offers a time-out, an opportunity to gather real strength in
preparation for the unsafe world.[5]

Beyond the possibility of this illusion, how does the making of stories in this blend of the academic and the personal stimulate development? The answer cannot be easy because the elements— self, expression, development—are complex and elusive. I suggest that the results I report here arise from three kinds of relatedness encouraged, or permitted, by the process I have described: the relation of the self to meaning, the relation of the self to the self, and the relation of the self to language.

Meaning

"I see," William Kerrigan writes about life in North America today, "careerism gone totally out of control, generating new jargons that seem to exist only to supply a place of dignity (lucrative dignity) for a priesthood able to manipulate them" (Kerrigan 23). Knowledge of the priestly codes signifies belonging. Students want to belong; that's why most come to university. For many, success means learning to reproduce mechanistic imitations of the specialized dialects of the academic disciplines (Saul 38–71). These dialects simulate seriousness and authority. They often substitute for and prevent genuine communication. They serve as membership cards, a way of telling who belongs and who does not belong in the narrow corridors of expertise our university departments stake out and defend. The empowering capacity of language to make meaning is lost. Writing becomes an act of subservience.

The "writing problem" we hear so much about in the university is really the "meaning problem." Students learn to fake meaning. Competent students, even when they have not read assigned material, know how to reproduce the dialect that will earn them the right to stay in the corridor. Students, who honor this survival strategy with terms like "bullshitting," do not confuse it with making meaning. They feel sure it has no meaning.

Complainers about the "writing problem" commonly see this problem as a deficiency of learned form: grammar, sentence structure, paragraphing, and so on. These are symptoms only, I believe. The real problem lies in the students' habit of generating language that fakes a relationship to meaning.

Writing in the academic setting easily becomes a negation of meaning, correct form filled with very nearly nothing. This writing expresses, clearly and unintentionally, the students' alienation from meaning. Most students feel the academic setting does not offer a safe place to make meaning that they can take responsibility for. Their alienated discourse derives from and reinforces not humility, but self-loathing. Most of the students I meet—and these include some of "the best" in our system—do not consider themselves worthy or capable of making a meaning that could matter to anyone, including themselves. Most think they have no meaning to make.

The personal essay system I have outlined confronts writers with responsibility for making meaning. Form follows substance. Jean-Paul Sartre's understanding of reflective consciousness has influenced my understanding of the writer's relationship to meaning. According to Sartre, we are "condemned to be free" (Sartre 707). We face a void, and we alone must fill it. We choose meaning and are responsible for the meaning we make, or decide upon.

The act of filling the page with the meaning the writer chooses to put into the world alters the writer's relationship to self and world: The writer becomes conscious of consciousness and at once defines and transcends a situation. The writer acts upon the world, and in so doing produces a changed world and a changed self in the world, a self that takes responsibility for deciding what meaning is. As R. D. Laing writes, "In so far as I put myself 'into' what I do, I become myself through this doing." The converse, Laing says, is to "go round in a circle, in a whirl, going everywhere and getting nowhere" (Laing 109). Laing's circle describes the world of the faker of meaning.

Personal essays confront students with the void because they encourage the putting of the self *into* their writing, into the academy, into the world. They must search themselves and their experience for meaning. Most resist. "What do you want me to write?" they ask. "What do you want to write?" I reply. Peer models, collections of writing by other writers at their level, make clear that they are indeed free *and* responsible for what they produce. This is tough practice, but when students learn to take responsibility for meaning, they become better writers of standard-form writing, like research reports, business letters, or the academic expository essay. Many move decisively in the direction of the free and responsible citizens that we talk about so much in Western universities. The responsible maker of meaning becomes a more responsible receiver of meaning.

Their confrontation with meaning yields a product: writing that contributes original meaning to the writer's world. The world desires and honors fresh meanings. Martha Kofie's stories are now taught in university courses. The self moves into the world and changes it. The self becomes partly responsible for the world it inhabits.

Self

Personal essays provoke reflections: Who am I? What is my experience? And, finally, what is its meaning? The writer creates a reality, "some vision of the subject in the world" (Schafer 361). Most new writers make a story or a series of stories that represents a decision about who they are and how they got that way.

Martha Kofie represented herself as the child of a father who suffered racist scorn and who poured his own scorn onto his imperfect daughter. She, isolated by the father's anger, fought her own race battles on the playground. Before she wrote her stories, Kofie told me, she had never thought about the problems her African father had living in a white Canadian town. They had more in common than she had realized.

Freud articulated a "talking cure," a system that creates a safe place to piece together a narrative, to find and make meaning from seemingly scattered pieces. Freud and his theoretical descendants, even those who challenge his system, agree that expression, and its opposite, repression, operate as powerful invisible agents in human health. A new wave of psychologists and researchers such as James Pennebaker now study the relationship between writing and healing.[6]

Jeremy Holmes, a British National Health Service psychotherapist, describes successful psychotherapy in these terms: The patient makes a story, "a model of the world as it was, transmuted into a form which can be stored, used, and, when necessary, updated." The desired outcome to psychotherapy, according to Holmes, is "autobiographical competence"—"to become a person is to know one's own story." There is a connection between the ability to build a coherent story, "and the sense of self-esteem and effectiveness which underlie a strong sense of identity. In order to know who you are, you need to know where you have come from, to be able to *own* your origins" (Holmes 13–17). Another psychiatrist, Rex Kay, puts the point succinctly: "When we are being creative, we are bringing order to chaos," "forming islands of consistency," "giving birth to the self." Partly this happens through allowing "disorganization to emerge" (Kay).

The successful writer of personal narrative must brainstorm, must free associate, must court the whirl of unassociated particulars to produce the patterns of detail that make a narrative thrive. Writers report that they had not realized just how much they have stored in their memories, that the search for detail and the shaping of that detail in a narrative changes the way they see themselves.

Psychoanalytic theorists point to the "therapeutic frame," a place where ordinary rules of "logic, common sense and taste" are temporarily suspended so that the analysand may go through "disorganization and reorganization" (Skura 376). A writing course that includes personal essays facilitates a similar process. The classroom, the course, the assignment—these are frames that set up a time and a space where the work of free exploration can happen. Controls are set aside so that the writer may discover the pieces that make up the story. The final product is shaped and organized, but the process requires a suspension of the usual controls. The writing derives urgency from the risks the writer has taken. The writer's care becomes the reader's care. The writer's risk draws the reader's attention and respect. The self in transition is an arresting subject.

In this way of looking at personal essays, the process operates in what Donald Winnicott calls a "transitional space," an area of creative and spontaneous "play" and discovery, and the writing becomes a "transitional object," an object that mediates between the writer's inner self and the world the self inhabits. This is the process Kofie seems to describe when she says that her personal essay writing linked her inner and outer worlds, and that the link facilitated healing and much more creative, productive, and effective work in the other world of the academy. When, according to Winnicott, the inner self is neglected because of demands of the external world, as I believe occurs when students feel restricted to writing that ignores the presence of the self, there develops "a high degree of split between the True [inner] Self and the False Self [attuned to outer demands]" and "there is found a poor capacity for using symbols, and a poverty of cultural living." In place of cultural pursuits, Winnicott observes, we see in such people poor concentration, anxiety, and a need to court external distractions to avoid the threatening claims of the inner self (Winnicott 150).

The teacher is not, and must not be, a therapist. However, the teacher sets the frame, a "facilitating environment" (Winnicott's term), which becomes a safe place for students to carry on their work, a work of play. Students decide how to use the space and time within this frame. I have found it remarkable that so many use this space, as Kofie did, to explore and develop the links between their inner and outer worlds. Where the opportunity is provided, a substantial percentage will use it to grow themselves academically and personally.

Language

The act of choosing or making genuine and revealing meaning brings the writer to both the obstinacy and the creativity of language because the writer must make words "say something they have never said" (Merleau-Ponty 91). The language resists new meanings, and the writer must always push the language beyond itself and into the service of the inevitably new meanings to be made by the self. Here the writer becomes an acting subject rather than an acted-upon object.

Writers are people who have learned to give conscientious and expert attention to language. When we teach writers we teach the tough discipline and openness and creativity that close attention to language involves. Too often, though, students get only a sense of restriction and hazard from language instruction in schools. Our educational system too often fails to communicate that language is a living system of endless creation. Rather many students experience language as a system of menacing, mysterious, and fixed rules.

Grammar is not a dress code. Grammar, as Chomsky and other linguists have pointed out, is the internal system that allows us to generate and understand infinite new meanings from finite vocabulary. "The normal use of language is . . . free and undetermined but yet appropriate to situations, and it is recognized as appropriate by other participants in the discourse situation" (Chomsky 56–59). The academic addiction to rigid, formal discourse situations is like putting on a tuxedo every time we step out of the house. Language is amazingly flexible and able to address varying degrees of formality. Students learn how to use language by confronting its creativity and its flexibility, its capacity to meet and express a range of life situations.

Merleau-Ponty asserts that language *is* meaning, that our thoughts are not really thoughts until we express them in words. Language, endlessly creative, "like a wave, gathers and poises itself to hurtle beyond its own limits" (Merleau-Ponty 197). When we speak, when we write, we inevitably re-make, re-create the language. Language changes through usage, despite the efforts of many educators to pin the language down to something right or wrong. Within the past twenty years in North America, creative and influential changes in the English language have come from people who have opted out of education, kids in the streets of the poorest neighborhoods of the United States' big cities. Street-based rap culture has added much to the vocabulary and syntax of our language as we use it today, perhaps as much as the stream of new words and phrases from science and technology.

The personal essay, with its requirement that students find styles appropriate to the situations presented by their content, forces students to confront their potential to shape language. The meaning-making capacity of language becomes primary. Students must ask: Does this language express the meaning I intend? I know my teaching goes well when I hear my students echo the traditional writer's complaint: I can't get the language to say what I want it to say. That shows me that the students are working to stretch the language, to make it do more than it wants to do, as writers everywhere do.

Jacques Lacan was surely right when he sharpened the psychoanalytic focus on language. Lacan distinguished *"parole vide"*—Empty Speech from *"parole pleine"*—Full Speech (Lacan

61). The psychoanalytic interchange has as its goal, according to Lacan, the movement from Empty Speech to Full Speech. Full Speech makes meaning. Empty Speech evades meaning. "What determines whether or not [speech] is called 'empty' or 'full'? Precisely the extent to which it impedes or facilitates the realization of the truth of the subject [the speaker, or, in this case, the writer]" (Muller and Richardson 70). For Lacan, the successful analytic process leads to Full Speech. The same is true of the writing process. Full Speech means "'the birth of truth in speech'" (Lacan qtd. in Muller and Richardson 71). This leads to a full engagement of language that "renders the past *present*" (Muller and Richardson 72). Empty Speech avoids change because, as James DiCenso puts it, Empty Speech "confirms antecedently given perspectives and opinions; it is narcissistic in the sense that one always finds one's ego intact and unchanged." Full speech, on the other hand, "may be described as 'performative' because it acts on and effects changes in the ego's orientation . . . [by opening] the ego to repressed and unseen dimensions of meaning" (DiCenso 49).

For Lacan, the laws of language govern human interchange. Thus full and unrestricted engagement with language facilitates the student's ability to make original meaning and to incorporate the past within the present (represented in the act of writing). The instructor enables this process by guiding the student on language issues. The instructor points the student away from degenerate language, Empty Speech, alienated discourse, and toward the difficult process of finding language suitable to the meaning to be expressed. The instructor does not guide with regard to *meaning* and *self* but does guide with language. Here the instructor guides students toward precise, original, concrete, economical, and direct language. My linguistic boot camp jolts students who have become accustomed to filling out their essays with Empty Speech—and who have become accustomed to being rewarded for it. Many resist, at first, but persistent, supportive editing roots out concealing clichés and hollow phrases. As students move toward Full Speech, their language sharpens and their writing engages, rather than evades, life issues.

The work with language leads inevitably to work with the self and its life among other selves. The self uses sharpened language skills in a free and undetermined way to speak to itself and to speak to others. Stephen Marcus points out that once a "narrative account has been rendered in language, in conscious speech," it "no longer exists in the deformed language of symptoms. At the end, at the successful end, one has come into possession of one's own story. It is the final act of self-appropriation, the appropriation by oneself of one's own history. This is in part so because one's own story is in so large a measure a phenomenon of language" (Marcus 56). I add: For most university students, this process includes their appropriation of the language that will express *their* situations. This often means moving out of academy dialect, if only to return to it with more confidence, skill, and a heightened awareness of its strengths and weaknesses.

The Humanities Problem

The "writing problem" in our universities is really a humanism problem. We teach humanism and dodge its practice. We ask our students to study and understand meaning at the same time that we offer little opportunity for them to make original meaning. Only the person who has attempted to make original meaning can understand how difficult that is. We tell our students through the messages of Greek philosophy, of Aquinas and Augustine, of Freud and Jung, that "Know thyself" represents the most important knowledge, the necessary base for other knowledge. Yet we offer scant occasion for them to include this kind of knowledge in their education, except by accident.

We report to our students about the release of creativity and knowledge that accompanied the use of vernacular by Boccaccio, Chaucer, and Dante and other writers as part of the European Renaissance. We make little provision for vital new language in our institutions of higher learning, where self-perpetuating, archaic, and stifling dialects prevail. We make artificial distinctions between academic and creative writing, and we press these distinctions on our students. The personal essay process I have outlined in this chapter allows a parallel discourse, one that traverses the artificial chasm between the creative and the academic, between the subject and the object, between the self and the society.

The "writing problem" roots in our students' alienated discourse. My experiments with writing point to people's natural drive to make original meaning, to get beyond the idiot's tale that signifies nothing more than belonging. People want to make meaning even though it involves risk and makes intense demands of the maker. My experiments show that, given opportunity and knowledgeable support, writing students move toward using language, the language appropriate to their situation, to make meaning that appears to catalyze positive change in their relationships with themselves and with the world around them. As John Ralston Saul has put it, "the best hope for a regeneration of language lies not in academic analysis but in citizen participation" (Saul 173). Language is the tool of the human mind, whatever the mind's enterprise. Language can help us to live unconsciously, or it can help us to live consciously. Students who live consciously in language inform themselves and their fellow students and the society in which they seek a role. They become citizen participants in learning, citizens who come not only to learn, but to teach us and change us.

Notes

1. G. F. Ricketts, "Mr. Bong's Variety," in Allen 22–23.

2. For a published collection of peer models, see Guy Allen et al., *No More Masterpieces: Short Prose by New Writers* (Toronto: Canadian Scholars' Press, 1989).

3. I have learned to encourage students to use their home languages in appropriate situations—for example, in narratives where they quote the speech of someone who uses their language or where they use expressions from their home languages that do not translate well. Sometimes phrases from their home language will contribute to the understanding or atmosphere of the piece they are writing. I first tried this procedure when I came across awkward passages in essays where it was obvious that the student had tried to translate expressions that have no equivalency in academy English. When students use dialects or other languages, they provide translations in parentheses or footnotes.

4. Twelve of Kofie's stories are published in Nancy Chong, Martha Kofie, and Kwanza Msingwana, *Only Mountains Never Meet: A Collection of Stories by Three New Writers* (Toronto: Well Versed Publications, 1993), 57–116.

5. The illusion of security may be what Charles Anderson, in his essay earlier in this collection, means by "sense of self." Certainly, it functions in the same way.

6. Marian MacCurdy offers a fuller discussion of writing and healing in this collection.

Works Cited

Allen, Guy, et al., eds., *No More Masterpieces: Short Prose by New Writers*. Toronto: Canadian Scholars' Press, 1989.

Buford, Bill. "The Seductions of Storytelling." *The New Yorker* (24 June 1996): 11–12.

Chomsky, Noam. *Aspects of a Theory of Syntax*. Cambridge: MIT P, 1965.

Chong, Nancy, Martha Kofie, and Kwanza Msingwana. *Only Mountains Never Meet: A Collection of Stories by Three New Writers*. Toronto: Well Versed Publications, 1993.

DiCenso, James. "Symbolism and Subjectivity: A Lacanian Approach to Religion." *The Journal of Religion* 74 (1994): 45–64.

Holmes, Jeremy. *Between Art and Science: Essays in Psychotherapy and Psychiatry*. London: Routledge, 1993.

Kay, Rex. "The Meaning of Creativity in Psychoanalytic Process." Mt. Sinai Hospital, Toronto, Ontario, Canada: unpublished, 1996.

Kerrigan, William. "*Macbeth* and the History of Ambition." *Freud and the Passions*. Ed. John O'Neill. University Park, PA: Pennsylvania State UP, 1996. 13–24.

Lacan, Jacques. *Le Séminaire: Livre I: Les Écrits techniques de Freud, 1953–1954*. Paris: Éditions de Seuil, 1953–54.

Laing, R. D. *Self and Others*. 2nd ed. New York: Pantheon, 1969.

Marcus, Steven. "Freud and Dora: Story, History, Case History." *Essential Papers on Literature and Psychoanalysis*. Ed. Emanuel Berman. New York: New York UP, 1993. 36–80.

Merleau-Ponty, Maurice. "On the Phenomenology of Language." *Signs*. Trans. Richard C. McCleary. Evanston: Northwestern UP, 1964.

Muller, John P., and William J. Richardson. *Lacan and Language: A Reader's Guide to Écrits.* Madison, CT: International Universities P, 1982.

Rhodes, Richard. *How to Write: Advice and Reflections.* New York: Morrow, 1995.

Sartre, Jean-Paul. *Being and Nothingness.* Trans. Hazel E. Barnes. New York: Washington Square, 1956.

Saul, John Ralston. *The Unconscious Civilization.* Concord, Ontario: House of Anansi Press, 1995.

Schafer, Roy. "Narration in the Psychoanalytic Dialogue." *Essential Papers on Literature and Psychoanalysis.* Ed. Emanuel Berman. New York: New York UP, 1993. 341–68.

Skura, Meredith Ann. "Literature as Psychoanalytic Process: Surprise and Self-Consciousness." *Essential Papers on Literature and Psychoanalysis.* Ed. Emanuel Berman. New York: New York UP, 1993. 374–402.

Usuelli, Alamatea Kluzer. "The Significance of Illusion in the Work of Freud and Winnicott: A Controversial Issue." *International Review of Psycho-Analysis* 19 (1992): 179–87.

Winnicott, Donald W. *The Maturational Processes and the Facilitating Environment: Studies in the Theory of Emotional Development.* 1965. Rpt. Madison, CT: International Universities P, 1988.

CHAPTER ELEVEN

Writing about Suicide

JEFFREY BERMAN AND JONATHAN SCHIFF
University of Albany

*Reaching for the key was like reaching for a means to un-
lock my family's secret, the mystery of my father's death.*

JON

Though poets and novelists have long known about the healing power of writing, believing, as D. H. Lawrence did, that
"one sheds one['s] sicknesses in books—repeats and presents
again one['s] emotions, to be master of them" (2:90), teachers
have been reluctant to encourage their students to write about
personal conflicts. Teachers fear, first, that students may be
harmed by unleashing powerful forces beyond their understanding or control, and second, that they themselves will not know
how to respond appropriately to a student's admission of being
depressed or even suicidal. These fears, which are probably held
by a majority of teachers, are understandable and, in some cases,
warranted. Teachers are seldom trained to recognize and respond
to a student's verbal cry for help, despite the fact that it is not uncommon for them to receive an essay or diary indicating a personal crisis. And yet it is possible to create the pedagogical
conditions in which students write about traumatic subjects and
achieve important insights into their lives—and it is the story of
one such teaching experience that we want to share with you here.

The story began in the spring of 1994, when Jeffrey Berman
taught a graduate course on "Literary Suicide" at the University
at Albany. The course focused on major twentieth-century writers who committed suicide and whose novels and poems reflect

a lifelong preoccupation with self-inflicted death. Jeff opened the semester with a discussion of the various theories of suicide, including those of Sigmund Freud, Emile Durkheim, Karl Menninger, and Edwin Shneidman. After spending two weeks on theory, the class read a novel written by an author who was not suicidal, Kate Chopin's *The Awakening,* and then turned to selected poems and novels by four well-known writers who did commit suicide: Virginia Woolf, Ernest Hemingway, Sylvia Plath, and Anne Sexton. The semester ended with William Styron's *Darkness Visible,* an autobiographical account of the novelist's suicidal depression and recovery.

Jeff believed that the course could be helpful not only in sensitizing students to the problem of suicide but also in encouraging suicide prevention. Suicide remains a major problem for high school and college students. According to the national school-based Youth Risk Behavior study, sponsored by the United States Centers for Disease Control, 27 percent of all high school students thought seriously about attempting suicide in 1990; 8 percent of all high school students actually attempted suicide; and 2 percent of all students sustained injuries in the course of a suicide attempt serious enough to warrant medical attention. The study, which surveyed 11,631 high school students from every state in the country, estimated that over a quarter of a million high school students made at least one suicide attempt requiring hospitalization in the preceding twelve months.

As disturbing as these figures are, Jeff was not entirely surprised by them. For close to twenty years, students in his undergraduate "Literature and Psychoanalysis" courses had been writing a weekly diary in which they explored many of the conflicts they found most bedeviling to them: parental divorce, eating disorders, sexual abuse, and suicide. Introspective and ungraded, the diaries encouraged students to apply insights acquired from readings and class discussions to their own lives. Jeff found that, year after year, about one-third of the students in each class wrote about another person's suicide or suicide attempt or their own battle against self-destruction. By writing weekly diaries and hearing a few of these entries read anonymously to the class, students were often able to experience breakthroughs in aspects of their lives which they rarely discussed.

In the mid 1980s Jeff began asking his undergraduates for permission to use their diaries in a book exploring the relationship between writing and healing. He was convinced that, with the proper safeguards, and contrary to the fears expressed by a number of educators, the classroom could be an appropriate site for personal as well as intellectual growth and self-discovery. Jeff's book, *Diaries to an English Professor,* was published in late 1994. He had given the students in his Literary Suicide class a manuscript copy of the chapter on suicide survivors so that they could understand how the problem touches so many lives in both expected and unexpected ways.

Before asking students in "Literary Suicide" to write a weekly diary, Jeff sought permission from the University Human Subjects Research Review Board. Fearing that some students might be put at risk by writing on such a sensitive subject, the review board suggested that, unlike the diaries which students signed in Jeff's "Literature and Psychoanalysis" courses, the diaries in the "Literary Suicide" course should not be signed, thus guaranteeing complete confidentiality. The review board also recommended that the diaries be made entirely voluntary rather than a requirement of the course. After receiving approval from the review board, Jeff distributed to each student a copy of the guidelines for the diary:

> Each week you will be requested to turn in to me a diary entry (one or two pages, typed, double-spaced); you will receive the entry back, with my comments, the following week. Before I hand the diaries back to you, I will read about five of them aloud to the class. I will always read the diaries anonymously, and there will be no class discussion of the diaries afterwards. Each person in the class will thus draw his or her own conclusions about the diaries read aloud: the diarists' identities will never be revealed. If you give me permission to read your diary to the class, please indicate so at the bottom of the diary with the word *yes.*

As it turned out, the graduate students' diaries on suicide resembled those written by Jeff's undergraduate students. Nearly all of the students took diary writing seriously, turning in an entry either every week or every other week. They almost always gave Jeff permission to read their diaries to the class, and when he did so, the other students were deeply moved. A dialogic relationship soon developed in which students commented on their classmates' diaries without knowing each other's identities. This "distanced intimacy," as Jeff called it, created an extraordinary bond of trust among the students. They wrote about past suicide attempts, reactions to friends' and relatives' self-inflicted deaths (including Kurt Cobain's recent suicide), and—to use a term coined by one of them—their own "suicideophobia." Many wrote about the contradictory tendency to romanticize suicide in fiction while deploring it in real life. They were astonished by the degree of self-disclosure of their own and classmates' diaries. For many, the diaries turned out to be the most important part of the course, allowing them to explore feelings about which they had never previously written.

At the end of the semester, sixteen of the eighteen students gave Jeff permission to use their diaries for the book he was planning to write on literary suicide. Many had revealed their diary identities to him at some point in the semester. They felt comfortable with Jeff knowing who they were, though it was important for them to preserve their anonymity to fellow students. Other diarists, such as "Number Nine," maintained anonymity throughout the semester.

Jeff was particularly interested in Number Nine's diaries because they revealed an ongoing effort to understand the impact of early parental loss. Number Nine had given Jeff permission to use his diaries, and, a few months after the course ended, when Jeff was invited to contribute to *Writing and Healing: Toward an Informed Practice,* he sought to determine the identity of the unknown diarist to see whether he would be willing to co-author an essay on the experience of writing about suicide. Jeff eventually guessed Number Nine's identity, and the latter enthusiastically welcomed the opportunity to revisit his diaries. He also decided to use his real name: Jonathan Schiff.

Jon's Diaries

In what follows, six of Jon's nine diaries appear, without any changes. The diaries indicate his attitude toward "Literary Suicide," beginning with his early feelings toward the course, and ending with his final evaluation. The middle diaries reveal a journey of self-discovery that continued, as we shall see, after the course ended:

(1)

When I mention to people that I am in this course, I usually receive responses from them which everyone else in this course has no doubt heard too. "Sounds cheery," people say. Or, "Sounds like a lot of fun." Then silence.

Sometimes when you tell people that you are in this class, you become afraid that they will think that *you* are suicidal. I guess if you are suicidal, you should not be afraid to admit it, but there is such a stigma attached to suicide that you wouldn't want to admit it. And if you are not suicidal, you still don't want to be suspected of it. After you mention that you are taking this course, an invisible barrier seems to go up between you and the person you are speaking to.

A similar barrier seems to appear when we have gotten half an hour or an hour into one of our classes. I begin to have this feeling, and I cannot stop having this feeling, that we in this classroom are the only people on the planet at this moment discussing the subject of suicide. There is one person in one pocket of the country and another person in another pocket privately considering committing suicide, but we in this class are the only ones engaged in discussing it aloud. That's the feeling I begin to have, and when we leave the classroom at the end of class, it seems like we have returned from the dead. Everything seems quiet in the hallways and in the outdoors, and no one seems to notice us. While I recognize the risk of comparing our experiences to the terrible struggle of someone considering suicide, I can't avoid thinking how similar our worlds are. We both feel to some extent cut off from the world.

By the same token, the people who are not in this course seem themselves to have something in common with suicidal people. People want to cut us out of their lives, as it were, when they find out we are taking this course. I have heard some people say about this course, "I don't think I could take the feeling of being in that course." Similarly, you hear about suicides who can't "take it" anymore.

I guess this diary is trying to show me that all people like to cut themselves off from others. While we are intuitively aware of this fact, this course is making it more vivid.

(2)

When I was about two years old, my father died of something called endocarditis. Endocarditis is not something a two year old can understand, so it must have been impossible for my mother to explain to me how he died. I do not remember how she did try to explain my father's death to me, but whatever she said, I apparently did not understand.

Frequently in my childhood I attempted to figure out the reason for my father's death. Once when I was about three or four I saw a bottle of insecticide in the tool closet in our garage. The bottle had a picture of a skull and crossbones on the label, so I knew it was poison. Making one of those random associations that children make, I wondered whether my father had died from drinking this bottle. Some time after, I was in the garage with my mother, helping her to carry groceries into the house. My mother was feeling tired at this time. She was always feeling tired nowadays, working full time and raising three kids. As we passed by the tool shed, I asked her if Daddy had died from drinking from the bottle of poison. I guess my mother didn't know what she should say. She said, "Yes."

I felt relieved, for I finally understood why my father had died. But I also felt confused. How could my father be so stupid to drink something I knew to stay away from? I didn't know what suicide was at the time, but it certainly seemed to me at the time that there was something self-destructive about his drinking poison.

Either because I felt embarrassed by my father's mistake of drinking the poison, or because I began to suspect that my father had not died in this way, I began to look for other possibilities for why my father died. In kindergarten, I told stories to my classmates about how my father had died. These stories often involved some dramatic plot, such as one in which my father died in a plane crash after giving his parachute to me as we fell through mid-air, so that I might survive. In another version of this story, *I* had attempted to save *him*.

It seems little wonder to me, then, that I later became an English major. Creative writers, of course, also make up stories in order to understand death. I in turn attempt to understand these stories, just as I attempted as a child to understand my father's death. If I felt as a child that my father was self-destructive, how might this thought have poisoned my own mind? That is something I am continuing to consider.

(3)

Last week I wrote about how as a child I felt for a time that my father had died drinking from the bottle of poison that lay atop the tool closet in our garage, next to the key that was used to unlock our garage door and enter our house. Though I am not sure for how long I believed in this story of my father's death, the story continued to hang with me, so that even today, it seems full of resonance.

We had to leave a key atop the tool shed because my mother had to take a full-time job after my father's death, and thus my brother, sister, and I had to let ourselves into our house. As a youngster, in order to reach this key, I had to stand on my tippy-toes, stretch my arm as high as it would go, and then feel around with my fingertips for the exact spot where the key lay. The tool closet was about as tall as an adult. Sometimes while standing in this precarious position I lost my grip on the key after momentarily gaining hold of it, and then usually the key tumbled down into the tool closet, in which was a mess of sharp gardening tools, old flower pots, and loose soil. Then with self-reproach, I would have to dig around in this mess, which was half-hidden in the darkness of the garage, so that I could find the key and enter my family's house, and all the while, I was afraid of getting my hands cut by the sharp tools.

Though I knocked the key into the tool closet many times, I always avoided knocking over the poison that also lay atop the closet. Perhaps the poison scared me so much, I was especially careful to keep my straining arm away from it as I searched around for the key.

This whole business of the tool shed, the key, and the poison seems an uncanny real-life example of family skeletons in the closet. Reaching for the key was like reaching for a means to unlock my family's secret, the mystery of my father's death. My older brother and sister could remember my father and how he died, and similarly, they had an easier time reaching the key. But I could not remember my father, and had to strain in order to reach the key and enter the house.

It seems little wonder to me that thoughts of these images from my childhood stick with me so persistently, even painfully. My mother still lives in my childhood house, and every time I reach for the key in the garage, I wonder if the bottle of poison is still there, though it has not been for years. Because these images have always seemed so meaningful to me, it also seems little wonder that they are so confusing. I often tried to understand how the bottle of poison led to my infantile theory of my father's death, but my only conclusion was that as a child I felt my father had made a very silly mistake by drinking the poison.

But only last week while writing about this matter and thinking about the topic of this course, did I realize that even if I had not felt as a child that my father's action was suicidal, I had thought it was such a silly mistake that it was self-destructive. Before this course, I had not considered how closely linked suicide and self-destructiveness were, and how our reactions to both are similar. I saw last week how as a child I had a romantic view of self-destructiveness, since I often fantasized other stories in which my father had also died self-destructively. Though I have never felt suicidal, I see to a greater extent now how so many of my thoughts and actions have been particularly self-destructive, almost as if I have been struggling to mimic behavior I incorrectly associated with my father. As I continue to strain for acceptance from my family, I have to be careful not to knock over the poison.

(4)

This course is helping me to grasp thoughts which, before the course, were just on the edge of my consciousness. I look forward to writing them. Just this morning, I thought of something to write.

I mentioned in previous weeks that as a child I held this theory that my father poisoned himself, though in fact he died of natural causes. Every time I look at the place in my mother's garage where years ago the bottle of poison used to lay, I still expect it to be there. This morning I experienced another visual association which I repeatedly make, and which I only now realize has something to do with suicide. I was looking into my medicine cabinet this morning (which, I might note, also contains substances that can be harmful to drink in large doses), when I spotted the slot in the back where you are supposed to dispose of old razors.

When I was about eleven or twelve, approximately ten years after I came up with that theory about my father poisoning himself, I spotted a similar spot in one of the medicine cabinets in my mother's house. I had never noticed this slot before, and as I looked at it, I thought of my father, when he had been alive, carefully taking his razor blades and putting them into the slot, so as not to cut himself. Even though I understood what the slot was, I went to my mother to ask her its purpose. Just as she once answered "yes" when I asked her if Daddy drank the poison in the garage, she now confirmed that the slot was for disposing of old blades. In both cases, I felt somehow comforted, as if I had figured out something important. Now every time I see in a medicine cabinet a slot for the disposing of blades, I think of my father trying very hard not to slice himself. When I first experienced this association, I did know at the time that people commit suicide by slitting their wrists with razor blades.

Although I know that you will not feel that I am constructing this whole episode in order to make my childhood more dramatic, I guess that I am skeptical of what I have just written. But in order to answer my lingering self-doubt about what I have written, I think I should ask myself: why else would I think about my father trying to avoid cutting himself every single time I see the disposal slot in a medicine chest, if this image did not somehow recall my childhood fears that my father was self-destructive, even suicidal?

(5)

Sometimes I get the feeling that biographers of suicidal writers feel that their subjects were doomed, that they were fated to commit suicide. I got that feeling after reading some of the biographical writings on Hemingway, Woolf, and Plath. A newspaper reporter writing about that rock star who recently committed suicide said it outright: "Cobain was doomed from the start." I guess we're supposed to feel better if we say that someone was doomed. Maybe that will allow us as a society to feel that we are not responsible.

But when you read Diane Middlebrook's biography of Sexton, you do not get that feeling. Sexton was not doomed, for she had someone who helped keep her alive. Her psychiatrist encouraged her to write poetry and made her life more livable. It was only when she began seeing another psychiatrist who forbade her from seeing the first psychiatrist that she completely lost her hold on life. So she wasn't doomed. She was treatable.

I noticed something similar when I worked at a walk-in clinic for suicidal people about ten years ago. A regular visitor was this old man, a playwright. He was in extreme pain from a chronic illness, and because he was bed-ridden, he had to be driven to the clinic. He had a loving son who came to see him in his apartment, but for the most part he was very lonely. He recognized that his son had his own life, but it was so difficult for him to be alone that he felt suicidal. He came to our clinic several times a week, and I felt that as long as he could be with his son or with us, he would never in fact commit suicide.

I think he was in too much pain to write or type for extended periods of time, and maybe his artistic powers were diminished in his old age, but he now channeled much of his anguish into his conversations with his son and us. You could see that he had been a good playwright, because he could describe his situation so vividly.

If I ever read his obituary in the newspaper and it says that he committed suicide, I will wonder what freak circumstances prevented him from seeing his son or going to the clinic. I will not conclude that he was doomed.

(6)

The question of which diaries were the most memorable of the ones you read aloud is an easy one to answer. The most memorable ones to hear in class were the ones I had written myself. It was a valuable experience for me to hear other people's diaries, but it was even more valuable to hear my own read aloud. To see other people listening to my words and looking as if they understood was a truly moving experience. Like many other people, I assume that my problems are just strange little problems that no one could understand, but when I looked around the room as my diaries were read, I could see that my words made sense to people. I wasn't sure that my childhood theory that my father had poisoned himself would make any sense to anyone, but it did. I can now continue to think about the implications of that theory without constantly doubting whether or not this is something I should be concerned about. . . .

The diaries changed the course in that it gave us a better understanding of the nature of suicide, but what surprised me a little was the extent to which they changed my reading of literature. The fiction we read seemed so much more real when read in the context of this course. I liked Woolf a lot before the course, but I now feel even closer to her than I had before.

Jon's Analysis of His Diaries

Although Jon spoke about an "invisible barrier" going up whenever he told his friends he was taking a course on "Literary Suicide," the diary component allowed him to explore a part of his life that remained enshrouded in mystery and fear. Introspective writing thus allowed him to break down the barriers to self-discovery. He felt secure enough to begin analyzing in detail and depth his childhood theory that his father had swallowed poison; and in writing about the key which he associated with his father's death, Jon realized that he was unlocking his family's secret.

In revisiting his diaries six months after the course ended, Jon offered the following impressions of each entry, in the process reaching new insights into the relationship between writing and healing:

First Diary

I mentioned in the first diary that people reacted to me strangely when I told them I was taking the course, and though this was true, part of what I took as their reaction was probably my own projection; I felt strange for taking it. My desire to confront the issue of suicide in literature and in society did not seem perfectly "normal" to me. You had told me the semester before about the diary component of Literary Suicide, and before the course began, I wondered if there was something voyeuristic and exhibitionistic in my desire to hear others' diaries and my own read to the class. I did not know why I had a lifelong fascination with suicide, and throughout the semester I attempted to find an answer to this question.

Second Diary

There was only one fear I had that made this diary difficult to write: that no one would believe the story. I felt that people would think I was deliberately misinterpreting childhood experiences in order to make them dramatically fit into the concerns of the course, and I now see, at the moment I write, that this fear too can be traced back to my youth.

As a child, I must have wondered whether it really was a fact that my father had drunk poison. The only time I ever mentioned to anyone my belief that my father had drunk poison was when I was eight years old. I think that at that time I was beginning to realize he had not done so. A friend of the family, whom I will call Ms. X, interviewed me about my father's death as part of her research for her psychology dissertation. When she asked me how my father died, I mumbled to her that he drank poison. Because I spoke so softly that my words would not have come out onto her tape recorder, she asked me to repeat my answer again in a louder voice. I remember not wanting to tell the story again. After several years of believing this story, I was now beginning to suspect that it was untrue, and that it would be a painful thing for an eight year old to realize he had been lying to himself about his father's death. I did not want to tell the story to Ms. X because I irrationally feared that I had made it up in order to be dramatic, not, as was the truth, to make sense of my life.

Thus, I was beginning to realize as an eight year old that my lie to friends about my father jumping from airplanes was only a twice-told tale. I now suspected that it postdated an earlier fiction—that my father had drunk poison. Because I felt anxious as a child that my friends would not believe the second tale, and since I realized around the age of eight that the first tale was also untrue, I feared when this diary was read that no one would believe it, that people would think I was deliberately misinterpreting events in order to create a dramatic story.

When you read aloud this diary as if you believed its author were telling the truth, I remember thinking that I could not have read it aloud to myself with half as much conviction in my voice. Then I looked around the room and saw people listening as if they believed me, and I no longer feared that people would think I was making up everything in the diary. Since I feel a strong aversion to the way the day-time talk shows sensationalize and exploit people's lives, I think I would immediately recognize a similar false intimacy in this class, but I never did feel uneasy in the class. I will admit that people did chuckle a little when you read the part of the diary in which I say that I lied as a child about my father jumping from an airplane, but it was gentle, delayed laughter, as if people were making sure that it was okay to laugh when they did so. Though I was surprised for a moment to see people laugh, because I could tell that they had been listening sympathetically to the diary (as

I felt when other diaries of mine were read aloud), I realized for the first time that there was something humorous about this part of the story. I was not at all upset by their reaction.

Your written response to the diary (as with your other comments) reinforced my feelings that my diary was believable. You mentioned that you were deeply moved by the writing and expressed appreciation that I shared it with the class. I think that this week of class made me feel a lot less ambivalent about showing up for future classes.

Though as a teacher I have not run my classes in the same way that you do, I see from being a student in your class that silence can be productive. I often become worried when my own students read each other's personal essays in small group workshops and do not comment on them, but I now recognize how important it can be for students to see others reading their work and comprehending it. When I oversee workshops in the future, I will be less insistent that students constantly talk at each other.

Third Diary

Whereas the previous diary contained many thoughts that had taken me years to arrive at, this diary was the product of only a few days' thought. I had frequently made the "razor blade association" before, but I had never interpreted its meaning. Six months after writing the diary, I still feel that my construction of childhood thoughts and emotions here is extremely accurate. I think that if I had not been taking a course about suicide, and if I had not experienced my classmates' sympathetic reactions to my previous diary, I would not have felt an impetus to develop this construction.

This is perhaps the worst written diary I handed in, and though we are not attempting in these diaries to create finely polished pieces of writing, I do wish that I had not ended it with the cliff-hanging last sentence. In truth, I am not any more self-destructive than the average person. I think that my childhood anxiety that I would knock over the poison has affected me in a very general, abstract way, and that it would not be wise for me to attempt to link it to any particular actions. It is much more helpful for me to take from this diary a basic awareness of how my mind works.

In writing these diaries, I was engaging in a process of free association. I have found, in my experience of teaching, that students often meet with success when they employ a similar method of generating ideas for personal essays on their childhood. When I have encouraged my students to free associate, they frequently see after some reflection that layers of meaning underlie the events that they randomly recall.

Fourth Diary

At the moment, I do not know what to make of this diary. When I read this diary now, I cannot arrive at the same feeling I possessed when I wrote it. On the one hand, the screen memory may not contain actual childhood thoughts. If so, I would be reluctant to admit to myself that I was putting trust in a fiction when I presented it as truth six months ago—a similar problem to the one I experienced around the age of eight. On the other hand, I may have trouble thinking about this screen memory because I do not want to think about it, because I have come too close to the truth. In any event, I still feel, as I did when I wrote this diary, that I would not remember seemingly trivial incidents from my life if they were not in fact of importance to me, if they did not contain meanings that affected the workings of my unconscious mind.

One might see my confusion here as evidence that people do not have the ability to analyze themselves critically. But since it was a positive experience for me to hear my previous diaries read aloud, I feel less defensive about my diaries, less worried that I am deliberately misinterpreting them. Thus, I now feel more able to question my assertions in them.

Fifth Diary

This diary gets to the heart of my feelings about diary writing. I cannot say for certain, but I think that these diaries can provide me with a reason why I decided to take the course in the first place.

I would like to add to this diary a brief discussion about the experience of hearing other people's diaries. In listening to my classmates' diaries, I sometimes felt as if I *were* them. I did not feel like a voyeur. Unlike the day-time talk shows, in which you watch people for one hour and then forget about them, in this class there were people I see every day. When I now run into people who were in the course, even though I do not know if they were the authors of any of the diaries I heard in class, I feel a certain concern for them.

In addition, listening to people analyze themselves gave me much more confidence in my ability to analyze myself. I think a reason why I waited a few weeks before writing about the bottle of poison was that I was not sure if I could sensibly write about it. Similarly, before I began work on this article, I read Marian MacCurdy's unpublished manuscript *Anatomy of Grief*, which contains page after page of lucid observations of very personal material, and I felt more certain that I could discuss my own diaries in a way that would make sense to others.

Although now that the course is over I can see that I wrote nothing in these diaries that I would not personally say face to face with a concerned listener or listeners, I am glad that you did not know during the semester that I was the writer of these diaries. Since I did feel anxiety while writing the diaries that no one would believe them, it would have caused me more anxiety if I had signed my real name to them. Because in your comments you did not question my sincerity, when you asked me after the course if I was the writer of them, I had no difficulty in telling you that I was.

My pseudonym "Number Nine" was an ironic name. I was thinking of the Beatles's song "Revolution Number Nine" in which a man intermittently repeats the words "Number Nine" in spoken voice with a proper British accent. In the background, a tumult of various noises—human and nonhuman, organized and disorganized—is heard. The man seems to be repeating these words in an attempt to block out the chaos around him. Ultimately, however, he is overwhelmed by it; a few minutes into the song, his words can no longer be heard above the din. I attempted in my diaries to use words that might address the noise, not block it out.

Jeff's Responses to Jon's Diaries

As he makes clear, Jon was able to write about suicide because (1) he felt increasingly confident that his teacher and classmates would believe him, (2) he knew that he would not be criticized for anything he wrote in his diary, (3) he was emboldened by his classmates' introspective writings, (4) he realized that his anonymity would be preserved, and (5) he appreciated the positive comments that his teacher wrote on his diaries.

In reading Jon's diaries, Jeff generally limited his comments to praising Jon's honesty, empathizing with his feelings, and raising questions for him to pursue in later diaries. Jeff did not analyze or interpret Jon's diaries, thus avoiding the role of the therapist. Here is what Jeff actually wrote on each diary:

First Diary

To your comment, "Sometimes when you tell people that you are in this class, you become afraid that they will think that *you* are suicidal," I wrote in the margin: "I guess I hadn't realized this before; a number of people wrote diaries about this." When you speculated that "we in this classroom are the only people on the planet at this moment discussing the subject of suicide," I responded: "We may well be the only English course in the country that is doing this—particularly with the diary writing component. That does indeed make us unique." At the end of your entry I wrote: "An intriguing diary, one that I bet lots of people in the class would identify with. Thanks for writing this."

Second Diary

To your comment, "I didn't know what suicide was at the time, but it certainly seemed to me at the time that there was something self-destructive about his drinking poison," I wrote: "yes, I can see how you would reach that conclusion." When you concluded the diary by asking, "how might this thought have poisoned my own mind?" I responded: "good word choice." On the bottom of the entry I wrote: "This is an intriguing diary, one that I doubt anyone could invent unless it actually were true. I'm fascinated by the implications of this: growing up with the idea that one's father committed suicide when, in fact, he did not. Perhaps in a future diary you can describe when you learned the truth about your father's death—and how you reacted to this truth. This is an absolutely fascinating diary—thank you for letting me share it with the class."

Third Diary

I was struck by your observation that "every time I reach for the key in the garage, I wonder if the bottle of poison is still there," and I responded by saying: "this testifies to the power of childhood experience." To your statement, "Before this course, I had not considered how closely linked suicide and self-destructiveness were," I replied: "yes: I usually equate the two words." My comment at the end of your entry was: "Another terrific diary. I think that this course, particularly diary writing, is heightening your self-awareness. I suspect that for you, the course would not nearly have been so helpful without the diary component. Isn't it extraordinary how one childhood misunderstanding—your mother answering 'yes' to your question of whether your father drank poison—has had such long-lasting repercussions? Would it be fair to say that this course is serving, in some small degree, as an antidote to that poison? Please let me know—"

Fourth Diary

Although you expressed lingering doubts in the concluding paragraph about your childhood theory of your father swallowing poison, I felt it necessary to reassure you that I believed what you were saying. And so I wrote: "This sounds like a very plausible interpretation. Incidentally, not for a moment do I feel that you or anyone else are constructing diaries in order to dramatize your lives. This diary reveals your efforts to understand your life and to come to terms with particular conflicts."

Fifth Diary

I wrote several affirming comments throughout your entry, including agreeing with your statement that Sexton "wasn't doomed" to commit suicide. At the bottom of your diary I wrote (along with scrawling a happy face): "This is a *great* diary; I believe that you are absolutely right here in your observations and conclusions [about the treatable nature of suicidal depression]. This diary reveals your insight and compassion and commitment. Thanks again for allowing me to read this."

Students' Evaluation of Diary Writing

How did the class as a whole evaluate the diary component of the course? Were Jon's classmates also able to write about suicide in a safe and meaningful way? The results of an anonymous questionnaire at the end of the semester indicated that, without exception, all seventeen students in the course found the experience of diary writing valuable. (One student was absent from the final class.) Asked to grade the experience of diary writing, twelve rated it an "A" and five a "B." Hearing the diaries proved to be almost as beneficial. When asked to indicate whether they were honest in their diaries, sixteen said "yes" and one indicated "not sure." Fifteen stated that there were adequate safeguards to preserve confidentiality; two were not sure. All seventeen rated Jeff's comments as empathetic. No one believed that he or she was being coerced into making self-disclosures.

Perhaps most significant, when asked whether they found diary writing therapeutic—"Did writing about conflicts encourage you to understand those conflicts better and find constructive ways of dealing with them?"—fourteen students indicated yes while the remaining two were not sure (one person did not answer the question.) No one believed that writing about suicide increased his or her vulnerability to suicide; four students believed that writing about suicide decreased their vulnerability to suicide. All seventeen students recommended that Jeff continue to ask future students to write a weekly diary, though when asked whether other teachers in the university should consider using diaries in the same way that Jeff did in "Literary Suicide," seven indicated they were not sure.

No serious problems arose during the semester, but Jeff was concerned about two students who acknowledged that the course was emotionally difficult for them. One found herself experiencing intense anxiety when writing about an experience of sexual abuse that had occurred many years ago. Unable, as she wrote in her diary, to repress the experience, which she had never written about before, she felt that she was not yet ready to talk about it. Although he did not know her identity, Jeff wrote on her diary that if she wanted to speak to him about her feelings, he would be available to her. He also recommended therapy. A couple of weeks later she visited him in his office and spoke about her diaries. A few months after the course ended she entered therapy, which she has found helpful.

Another student said that contrary to the hopeful ending of *Darkness Visible*, he found himself "slipping into a depression the likes of which I have not experienced for years. Styron's descriptions of what his depression felt like disturbingly matched my own experiences with depression. In fact, his accuracy was uncanny." Shortly after the course ended, he wrote Jeff a letter reassuring him that his depression had passed and offering the following explanation for what had happened:

In a sense I now consider reading *Darkness Visible* as a kind of inoculation against depression. You know the way inoculations work: you get injected with a little bit of the virus and your body develops a resistance to it that protects you from it in the future. In doing so, however, you may come down with some symptoms of the disease you're being immunized against. So I suppose in this analogy, my evanescent depression was simply a side-effect of the inoculation.

Teachers who encourage their students to write about personal conflicts need to be sensitive to those who may be at risk, and they must be prepared to make appropriate referrals when necessary. Signs of suicide include statements like "I won't be around here much longer," prolonged depression, dramatic changes of behavior or personality, giving away prized possessions, withdrawal from family and friends, abuse of alcohol or drugs, and making arrangements for one's death. Although confidentiality is essential for introspective diary writing, in certain situations the need for confidentiality is outweighed by moral and legal considerations. If a student writes a diary or personal essay revealing the possibility of an impending suicide attempt or the intention to hurt another person, it is incumbent upon a teacher to notify the university's counseling or health service. Jeff has never been in this situation, but there have been several times when he has suggested to students that they might find it helpful to speak to a therapist.

The Writing Cure

Despite the obvious differences between psychotherapy and expressive writing, both the "talking cure" and the "writing cure" encourage people to express their problems, find constructive solutions to them, and thus achieve control over their lives. Talking and writing are therapeutic regardless of the explanatory system that is used and regardless of whether anyone hears or reads one's words. As James Pennebaker has demonstrated, while writing about traumatic experiences is often painful, writing leads to short-term and long-term improvements in both physical and psychological health. Whether one believes that writing leads to the discovery of truths by which to live or the construction of these truths, what is most important is that by writing about our life stories, we are able to compare them with others' and broaden our point of view. If knowledge is power, then there is no better way to empower ourselves than through reading and writing.

Heightening Literature

Apart from its therapeutic implications, writing about suicide heightened students' understanding and appreciation of the literature in the course. Jeff had taught "Literary Suicide" once before, in 1992, without the personal writing component, and he was struck by the differences between the two courses. Without the opportunity to write expressively, the 1992 students remained more detached from the literature, reluctant to connect the novels and poems they were reading to their own lives. They approached "Literary Suicide" as simply another academic course. The 1994 students, by contrast, viewed Woolf, Hemingway, Plath, and Sexton not simply as distant authors writing about a theoretical problem, but as fellow human beings who were struggling bravely to transmute personal conflicts into art. Without simplistically reducing novels and poems to an artist's autobiography, the 1994 students sought connections between the writer's art and life, and they were more attuned to reader-response issues, such as the extent to which they identified or counteridentified with a suicidal character.

Deromanticizing Fictional Suicide

One of the most striking differences between the two courses is that when the 1994 students wrote expressively, they were less inclined to romanticize suicide at the end of the semester than the 1992 students, for whom suicide remained more of an abstraction. One 1994 student was struck by her tendency to idealize Edna Pontellier's drowning at the end of *The Awakening* despite the fact that the student was still angry at her sister for attempting to kill herself a few years earlier. She wrote several diaries trying to reconcile the contradiction between suicide in literature and suicide in life. Although the reasons for fictional and real suicide may be similar, the consequences are far different:

> Suicide (in life and literature) can be so perceived because of its links with pain, love, yearning, disappointment, tragedy, separation, desire, and unfulfillment. To witness someone's pain and suicidal resolution of that pain *on paper* is a mental experience. I appreciate the separation of my own life from that aching fictional person's hellish experience. When someone *in life* has all that pain, it's not romantic—witness my sister's suicide attempt and my anything-but-sentimental reaction to it.

At the end of the course she vowed not to romanticize literary suicide and to empathize with those real-life people whose suffering drives them to desperate acts. Other students reached similar conclusions, recognizing the dangers of glorifying a subject in literature that wreaks so much devastation in real life. (For a fuller description of the course, see Berman, *Surviving Literary Suicide*.)

Intertextuality

All the students believed that the personal writing component had profoundly changed the course, creating a unique educational experience that was at times almost maddeningly complicated:

> This is the strangest class I have ever taken. There were so many things going on simultaneously: the literature, the class discussions, the in-class response paragraphs, my own personal diaries, the diaries of others that were read aloud. All these divergent paths did not make for a simple experience, but that's OK. Talk about intertextuality! A person could go crazy trying to follow all the threads presented.

This intertextuality, which they had never encountered before, made literature seem more real and alive to them. Most of the students would agree with Jon's observation in his sixth diary:

> The diaries changed the course in that it gave us a better understanding of the nature of suicide, but what surprised me a little was the extent to which they changed my reading of literature. The fiction we read seemed so much more real when read in the

context of this course. I liked Woolf a lot before the course, but I now feel even closer to her than I had before.

Conclusion

So, too, will teachers feel close to their students, a closeness that intensifies the learning experience for teacher and students alike without compromising boundaries. Jeff felt connected to his students despite not knowing their diary identities, and there was never a problem in responding nonjudgmentally to their diaries and grading their two fifteen-page formal essays. In their anonymous questionnaires, none of the students believed that he or she was graded unfairly in the course. Nor did the personal writing component make the course less rigorous. Quite the opposite: Students wrote far more than they anticipated, and their personal writing was often insightful and eloquent.

Finally, teachers who encourage their students to write on subjects like suicide need not have unusual empathy or clinical training: only the desire to facilitate their students' self-discovery and to put into place necessary safeguards. (For an expanded discussion of the importance of anonymity, see Berman and Luna.) Once teachers realize what poets and novelists have long known—that writing promotes healing—students like Jon will be able to find the key to unlock their own family secrets.

Works Cited

Berman, Jeffrey. *Diaries to an English Professor: Pain and Growth in the Classroom*. Amherst: U of Massachusetts P, 1994.

———. *Surviving Literary Suicide*. Amherst: U of Massachusetts P, 1999.

Berman, Jeffrey, and Alina M. Luna. "Suicide Diaries and the Therapeutics of Anonymous Self-Disclosure." *JPCS: Journal for the Psychoanalysis of Culture and Society* 1.2 (1996): 63–75.

Centers for Disease Control. "Attempted Suicide among High School Students—United States, 1990." *Morbidity and Mortality Weekly Report* 40.37 (20 September 1991): 633–35.

Chopin, Kate. *The Awakening.* New York: Simon, 1996.

Lawrence, D. H. *The Letters of D. H. Lawrence.* Ed. James T. Bolton, George Zytaruk, and Andrew Robertson. 3 vols. Cambridge: Cambridge UP, 1979–84.

Middlebrook, Diane Wood. *Anne Sexton: A Biography.* Boston: Houghton, 1991.

Pennebaker, James. *Opening Up: The Healing Power of Confiding to Others.* New York: Morrow, 1990.

Styron, William. *Darkness Visible: A Memoir of Madness.* New York: Random, 1990.

Chapter Twelve

Teaching Emotional Literacy

Jerome Bump
University of Texas at Austin

On September 3, 1985, at 4 a.m., my wife and I were awakened by the doorbell and the phone ringing at the same time. On the phone was a policeman telling us that my wife's car had crashed into a guardrail and was abandoned. At the door was an ambulance driver looking for our fifteen-year-old daughter and her friend who had hitchhiked home and then called EMS. All this came to us as a complete surprise and shock; we thought our daughter had been sleeping in her room all evening! The next day we had to admit that she had a problem with drinking and drugs.

The outpatient treatment center insisted that each client's family be involved in the therapy. I soon became very conscious of alcohol and drug abuse in our society, especially among teenagers and young adults. As one whose job was to educate that population, I wondered what I could do in the classroom to help prevent the kind of substance abuse that had devastated my family and many others.

I began to encourage class discussion of alcohol and drug abuse in literature. For example, when I taught nineteenth-century English poetry, I included not only Coleridge's "Kubla Khan," which glorifies opium use for some students, but also poems such as Keats's "Ode to a Nightingale" (in which opium is associated with the death wish and alcohol with escape from life) and Tennyson's "Lotus Eaters," in which opium is subtly associated with dreams and death.

Though poetry is more popular in bibliotherapy, fiction seemed the more obvious genre for such a discussion; certainly alcoholism and drug addiction are represented much more extensively in the fiction rather than the poetry of the Victorian era

(McCormick; Bump, "Innovative" 356). However, college students usually do not like to be reminded of the disadvantages of substance abuse, for it is widespread in colleges. In any class of thirty or more students there are probably some who have already crossed the line from abuse to addiction and their denial is so great that they strongly resist any direct attack on their drug of choice. When we expanded the context to other ways fictional characters deny their feelings, such as by vicariously living other people's lives rather than their own, there were drawbacks as well as advantages. Those who had simply blamed substance abusers had a chance to look at their own modes of denial and repression and perhaps even their own codependence, and thus gained some insight into the nature of addiction. However, some of those who had most resisted criticism of substance abuse seemed to feel liberated because they felt less shame about their own chemical dependency. Some rationalized that because everybody seems to deny feelings on occasion, or because everybody seems to have been addicted to something at some time, they were entitled to their own addiction. Of course, the basic arguments against chemical dependency and other modes of denial of feelings still applied, but a purely cognitive approach, trying to "educate" people about the dangers of substance abuse, worked no better for me than it has in the public schools or in clinical practice.

Seeking a more effective approach to these problems, I remembered the first question asked of us in family treatment for our daughter's alcoholism: "How do you feel?" We answered with the usual vague generalities—"fine," "OK," and so on—but to our surprise we were told that would not do. Like our daughter's, our feelings had been shut down, though by more socially approved means than substance abuse. For our sake as well as our daughter's, for the first time in our lives we had to become fully conscious of what we were feeling and then had to put those feelings into words. We soon discovered that in this language, that of our own emotions, we were illiterate. We soon became aware that without true emotional literacy, not merely psychotherapy but all kinds of intimate relationships were jeopardized.

Unfortunately, I discovered that precisely because I was an educator I had more difficulty than most people accessing my emotions. It seemed the more education I received, the deeper became my lobotomy, cutting the left side of my brain off from the right, splitting reason from emotion, language from feeling, my head from my heart. Nine years of college and fifteen years of ostensibly objective "research" in an institution that the student newspaper once labeled "the church of reason" had not only anesthetized me, but endowed me with an amazing ability to spin complex webs of words to defend myself from emotion. Somehow I had to undo all that intellectual defensiveness just to get on a par with the other parents in the quest for emotional literacy. That mission was crucial because we were told we had to model what we wanted for our teenagers: If we wanted them to feel and express their emotions instead of trying to drown them in alcohol and drugs, we had to become able to articulate precisely what was happening in our own emotional lives.

Roots of the Movement for Emotional Literacy in Schools

So began the longest journey I have ever made, from my head to my heart. As I began to come out of my anesthesia and rebuild the connections between the two sides of my brain, I became part of a movement that began with teacher education experts in the 1930s (although I did not know it at the time). They were "convinced that education and mental hygiene were one and the same thing," supported by humanistic psychologists who believed that "therapy could take place not only behind closed doors but . . . in school and community settings as well" (Brand, *Therapy* 31–32). In the 1950s, Jersild, who

> anticipated the criticism that teachers "playing amateur psychologist" in the classroom could be harmful . . . asserted that teachers were in no way assuming the role of professionally trained psychologists nor taking on psychiatric functions. . . . "[W]hether they will it nor not, whether they know it or not, teachers are already practicing psychology in their dealings with children. All the teacher's relationships with his pupils are charged with psychological meaning." (cited in Brand, *Therapy* 34).

In the next decade Moustakas was but one of many who emphasized that "'Intellectual accomplishments represent only one small aspect of human experience. To emphasize facts and information [exclusively is] to contribute excessively to alienation, desensitization, and personal fragmentation'" (Moustakas, *Personal Growth*; Brand, *Therapy* 35). Brand documents the growth of this movement into the 1970s (*Therapy* 41–43).

A key tenet of this movement is emotional literacy, a requirement of personal growth, healthy relationships, and effective teaching so basic that it cannot be relegated to psychotherapy. Redl and Wattenberg pointed out in 1951 "'that the teacher can and must assume some share of responsibility for the emotional as well as the intellectual development of his students'" (Redl and Wattenberg, *Mental Health in Teaching*; Brand, *Therapy* 36). Carl Rogers was particularly persuasive on the need for teachers' emotional literacy: "in the school context, the first essential was that teachers reveal themselves in honest ways and exhibit the range of feelings that differentiate living persons from 'automatons'" (Rogers, *On Becoming a Person*; Brand, *Therapy* 33). Hence, "At the joint frontier of psychology and education in the 1960s, a movement that assigned to the emotional factor in education a role as important as—or perhaps, more important than—traditional academics emerged with profound implications for teachers. The idea of affective education, otherwise called 'psychological' or 'confluent' education, mobilized teacher interest in the realm of emotion and feelings. . . . The Ford Foundation sponsored several efforts to renew education for the 'whole' person" (Brand, *Therapy* 39–40).

In 1995, the best-seller, *Emotional Intelligence* by Daniel Goleman, publicized the flowering of the emotional literacy movement in the 1990s and demonstrated that it is even more crucial as we move into the twenty-first century. Goleman adopts the definition of emotional intelligence developed by the Yale psychologist, Peter Salovey: [1] knowing one's emotions, [2] managing emotions, [3] motivating oneself, [4] recognizing emotions in others, [5] handling relationships. Salovey subsumes in these categories Howard Gardner's earlier theory of multiple intelligences, including the interpersonal, intrapsychic, spatial, kinesthetic, and musical.

Goleman's extensive documentation of studies of the difference between normal academic intelligence and emotional intelligence and the importance of the latter for mental health, education, social competence, business success, intimate relationships, and physical health brought this movement into the mainstream of American life.

He cites successful emotional intelligence programs developed to combat rising rates of aggression and depression in the schools, such as the Social Competence Program at Troup Middle School in Connecticut, the Resolving Conflict Creatively Program in the New York City public school system, the Child Development Project in Oakland, the PATHS curriculum in Seattle, and the Self Science class at the Nueva Learning Center in Hillsborough, California. Goleman concludes that "the next step is to take the lessons learned from such highly focused programs and generalize them as a preventive measure for the entire school population, taught by ordinary teachers" (263).

Goleman does not spell out what responsibilities colleges have in this movement, but the goals are obviously relevant to college courses: "an emerging strategy in emotional education is not to create a new class, but to blend lessons on feelings and relationships with other topics already taught. Emotional lessons can merge naturally into reading and writing," for example, and most classes can include "basic study skills such as how to put aside distractions, motivate yourself to study, and manage your impulses so you can attend to learning" (271–72). Goleman in fact focuses on the usual subjects of English courses: "the emotional mind's special symbolic modes: metaphor and simile, along with poetry, song, and fable, are all cast in the language of the heart. So too are dreams and myths, in which loose associations determine the flow of narrative, abiding by the logic of the emotional mind" (54).

Others in the nineties introduced the movement to the college campus. In 1994, for example, in his pioneering *Diaries to an English Professor*, Jeffrey Berman concluded that though "few literary critics, apart from feminists, reader–response critics, and composition theorists, have recognized the affective components of knowledge . . . effective teaching is . . . affective teaching. . . . Classroom discussions of literature awaken intense emotions within teachers and students alike—love, hate, passion, jealousy, fear—and these emotions cannot be relegated to 'guidance counseling'" (226). As we see in the chapter on his teaching in this anthology, "for many, the diaries turned out to be the most important part of the course, allowing them to explore feelings about which they had never previously written."

Course Design: Evolution of an Effective Approach to a Difficult Subject

Expression and denial of feelings became one of the subjects of my courses in the 1980s, especially in the context of family and gender interactions. In my honors freshman "Composition and Reading in World Literature" course (E603), for 1987–88, for example, I focused on developing "writing skills to communicate our emotions as well as our thoughts to others and to ourselves." In the description for the 1990–91 course I stated that

> The primary goal of the course will be to identify and articulate our emotions, especially those which drive our habits, in our responses to family dynamics, including sex roles, as represented in literature. We will try to develop a sense of literary works as potential calisthenics of emotions which we can enjoy and profit from for the rest of our lives. . . . Students will keep journals of their emotional and other responses to the works we read and at times bring these to class to help initiate discussion.

Partly as a result of this change in my teaching, I was selected by the administration for a teaching fellowship and by students as a Mortor Board Preferred Professor.

I began to focus on literary works as storehouses of emotion that could serve as models of how to communicate emotions to self and others. To that end, I changed the texts in my Victorian novels course (Bump, "Innovative" 357). To help students identify and articulate what they felt as they read the novels, I asked them to record their emotions in a journal divided with quotes on one side of the page and reactions on the other. Our first goal was to identify a range of feelings, but I asked for other responses to be recorded as well: self-esteem issues in the text and in themselves; personal associations, especially family memories; awareness of family dynamics in the text and of functional and dysfunctional interactions as defined by family systems theory (the primary approach in alcoholism treatment; see Bradshaw *Bradshaw;* Bump "Family"); and the characters' emotions and their ability to express them. The students coded their journals for each of the features, counted the number of entries in each category when a novel was completed, and charted their progress.

While the family systems theory entries called for cognitive responses, I gave the following journal instructions for emotional literacy:

> I will be looking, first of all, for your awareness of and ability to articulate your emotional reactions to the book. This is not to be confused with your awareness of emotions in the characters in the book, and is not quite the same as speculation about how you would feel if you were one of the characters.... Use the following format: "I felt" followed by an emotion, like those listed in the "Vocabulary of Feelings" which follows [in the photocopied anthology]. Focus on how you felt when you read the passage or feel now rereading it, not what you think about it. "I felt that" or "I felt like" can lead you away from feelings and into thoughts. Try to get into deep emotions, such as fear, sadness, and love, rather than merely intellectual surprise, confusion, amusement, curiosity, etc. Be as specific as possible. It is good to note, "I felt moved," or "I felt touched," but better to specify exactly . . . what emotion was touched or moved within you. Try to give some sense of "why" you have these reactions (some personal relevance) at least once in a while.

The students in one of my E603 courses suggested substituting words and characters while reading. For example, while reading Medea's speech to Jason, one student saw the possibility of working

> out some of my own anger. Reading along, I substituted some of my own words so that I could say, "How dare you abandon me!" to my father, or "How dare you beat my mother and steal my childhood!" to my stepfather, or "How dare you use me and treat me like an object!" to various boyfriends. Through Medea I was able to confront people I may never see again; she

let me vent my anger through her. When I read *Medea* I felt anger that I have suppressed for years come up and make itself known; even if it is not dissolved, at least I am more aware of its presence and its impact on my life.

The student allowed me to include these instructions in my anthology.

As a result of my teaching along these lines, I was awarded another teaching fellowship; was asked by the campus counseling center to make presentations on literature as therapy in its outreach programs; and was invited by the campus Center for Teaching Effectiveness to speak on "Teaching and Psychotherapy" at their annual Conference for Experienced Faculty and on "Exploring Alternative Teaching Methods: Left Brain, Right Brain" at their New Faculty Teaching Orientation.

The course continued to evolve. When I wrote the description for my Victorian novel class for the summer of 1990, I set emotional literacy in the context of brain hemisphericity research and was more explicit about family systems theory:

> Unless one is familiar with psychological, reader-centered literary theory and criticism, this course will probably be very different from any English course you have had in the past. For most students all or almost all of the forty or more courses taken in college focus on the left brain rather than the right, on thought rather than emotion, the mind rather than the heart. This is one attempt to redress the imbalance. . . . We will focus on learning to feel, identify, and articulate our emotions. . . . We will also explore the interface between Victorian fiction and family systems theory, which developed as a way to explain and assist families with individuals suffering from chemical dependence or psychosomatic illness such as anorexia nervosa, though today therapists know that many other compulsions contribute to dysfunction in families. Designed for students interested in self-exploration, this course may be especially valuable for students who have experience with or interest in counseling, psychotherapy, experiential learning, or twelve-step groups. . . . In addition, students may be given surveys and self-report psychological measures at the beginning and end of the course to measure shifts in expressiveness, individuation, relationship skills, etc. . . .

To the Victorian novels I added Bradshaw's *The Family* and a collection of photocopies that included "Group Participation Guidelines" (two pages), a "Vocabulary of Feelings" (four pages), videotape information about the Bradshaw and related series, counseling center information, and selections from F. Walsh, *Major Models of Family Therapy;* the Myers-Briggs Scale information from *Please Understand Me;* Jerry M. Lewis, *Optimal Families; Competent but Pained Families;* Anthony Wohl, *The Victorian Family;* Patricia Parker, "Charlotte and Branwell Brontë: A Family Systems Approach"; Maria McCormick, "First Representations of the Gamma Alcoholic in the English Novel"; Ghinger and Grant, "Alcohol and the Family in Literature"; Paula Cohen, "The Heroine as Anorectic: Scapegoating and Guilt in the Nineteenth-Century Domestic Novel"; Christy Moore, "Mate selection in *Jane Eyre*"; Michael E. Kerr, "Chronic Anxiety and Defining a Self"; Gloria Steinem, "Looking for a Family of Equals"; and my list of contemporary novels with similar themes.

It was primarily on the basis of this course that I received one of the most prestigious teaching awards on campus, the Holloway Award, the only major award chosen by students rather than administrators. More important, I knew from my own experiences that students were being affected. For example, at one point I had Dr. Cindy Carlson, a professional counselor and professor of family systems theory at the university, answer questions at a session of the Victorian novel course. After the class, a student handed her a note revealing that she had tried to kill herself. As there was no name on it, Cindy passed the note on to me. At the time I was grading student journals and was able to match the handwriting. I contacted the campus counseling center, and they kindly provided me with a packet of information on how to deal with such situations. Following their advice I put some of their information and a note from me in her journal. My heart dropped when she did not appear at the following class meeting. However, she did come to the next one and spent the whole time during class reading the material I had put in her journal. After class she came up to me and thanked me, saying that she had not been able to talk about this with anyone at the university. I took her immediately to the counseling center, where she made an appointment.

I recalled my own daughter's struggles with depression and suicide and wondered how many students had been sitting in my classes throughout the years with similar problems, and how many there were at that moment attending classes throughout the university. I felt like my eyes had been opened and that I had made a breakthrough in my teaching and in my capacity for being fully human. I recalled what Leo Buscaglia, a professor of education at USC, had written:

> In the winter of 1969, an intelligent, sensitive female student of mine committed suicide. She was from a seemingly fine upper middle class family. Her grades were excellent. She was popular and sought after. . . . I have never been able to forget her eyes; alert, alive, responsive, full of promise. I can even recall her papers and examinations which I always read with interest. . . . I often wonder what I would read in her eyes or her papers if I could see them now. . . . I was not blaming myself for her death. I simply wondered what I might have done; if I could have, even momentarily, helped. (9–10)

Eventually I shifted the student journal more and more in the direction of autobiography. Although I did not know it at the time, again I was participating in a movement in teacher education: "Inspired to some extent by the ideas advanced by Rogers, psychologists Arthur Jersild and Clark Moustakas elevated the study of self above any subject matter or external skill that could be studied in school" (Brand, *Therapy* 34). I was also becoming part of an old tradition in the teaching of writing. I remembered that the best course I had ever taken in college, freshman English at Amherst College, was devoted solely to self-exploration— there were no books at all. My sense of the value of that approach was confirmed twenty years later when forty-eight nationally famous writing teachers were asked to contribute an example of the best student writing and an explanation of its excellence "at least thirty of the examples in the collection are personal experience essays—twenty of them autobiographical narratives—and several of the remaining eighteen include writing about the writer" (Coles; Faigley 120). In my courses, journals, brief writing exercises, and computer-assisted writing began to culminate in essay-length writing and finally in embryonic autobiographies. I also added to the photocopied anthology selections from *Writing the Natural Way: Using Right-Brain Techniques To Release Your Expressive Powers*; "Support Urged for Gay Teens"; *Drawing on the Right Side of the Brain*; *Using the Right Brain in the Language Arts*; *Wild Mind*; "Where Emotions Come From"; and our counseling center pamphlets on perfectionism and depression.

An Administrator's Critique

Not long thereafter, I encountered opposition to my course. I suppose I should not have been surprised. When, inspired by the suicide of his student, Professor Buscaglia started to teach a non-credit course on love, he began receiving odd looks "from some colleagues. One professor, in discussing my plans over lunch in the Faculty Center, called love—and anyone who purported to teach it—'irrelevant!' Others asked mockingly and with a wild leer, if the class had a lab requirement and was I going to be the primary investigator" (11). I was not teaching or even facilitating a class in "love"—just beginning to try to include both sides of the brain in my teaching—but I too began to perceive that some males thought that all there was in their "right brains" was the equation "love = sex." They seemed to be completely unaware of the Christian and Platonic meanings of the word and thus of the possibility that it could mean simply a very basic feeling of oneness and connection with other human beings.

Although I had shifted more and more to teaching autobiography in the separate Division of Rhetoric and Composition, in the Spring of 1992 the undergraduate advisor in the English Department wanted me to do a nineteenth-century literature course. So I came up with a course on "Nineteenth-Century Autobiographical Writing" for the fall. I changed my assignments from journal writing about nineteenth-century fiction to autobiographical writing to be inspired by and compared with nineteenth-century autobiographies. The goal was what is variously called "active," "discovery," "experiential," or "inquiry-based" learning. Ever since Charles Eliot introduced laboratory approaches to studying science at Harvard more than a century ago, this has been the ideal learning method. With rate of change and quantity of knowledge accelerating exponentially, John Dewey's argument in 1909 for teaching "method" as well as "content" has become even more important. Recent research in education has demonstrated that students do not retain "content" very well. However, in discovery learning, they can learn how to think, learn, and create. What they learn is retained because discovery learning makes use of personal associations and episodic memories, and is thus much more likely to be remembered by the student. Hence in science courses there has been a shift away from mere content, much of which is now obsolete by the time the student graduates, to how to think like a scientist. What is comparable in the humanities? Langbaum, Holloway, and others have shown that the equivalent in the humanities of the empirical approach is the laboratory of "personal experience." In other words, a student tries out, say, the world view of the writer of an autobiography, and then analyzes its effects on his or her experience of life and decides whether or not to incorporate any elements of that world view in his or her own philosophy of life. I knew that this kind of assignment would be much more effective for student retention of various autobiographies than the usual memorize-and-regurgitate test system.

As students were registering for the course I was shocked to discover that an administrator pulled the course out of the registration system at the last minute. I received a letter informing me that this course proposal had been returned "without approval" because he and his curriculum committee had concerns about the subject matter of the course and my qualifications to teach such a course. I was told that a course in literature should be a course in literature, not one in which students are asked to explore their feelings, are evaluated on how much they write, and are given referrals to various counseling groups. In their view, my goal was not to read literature "from a psychological point of view" but "to perform therapy on" students. The administrator concluded that he could not give course credit for "conducting therapy" even if I were a psychologist or psychotherapist. "To do so would be to put students in a potentially exploitative relationship, one where the teacher is both therapist and evaluator."

"Then too, the committee questioned the appropriateness of grading students on the basis of journals recording their 'emotional and other responses'." They feared that students "would have access to these journals or essays in which their fellow students are encouraged to explore psychological states." He emphasized that "for reasons of both professional training and of ethics, the course itself cannot be a forum for psychological testing or therapy." "Such 'experiments in the classroom' might prove injurious to students."

Though I was dismayed and offended by the wording, I thought that these were legitimate concerns. I made concessions, and it seemed that we were going to be able to come up with an amicable compromise, but apparently one member of the committee resisted. Eventually, neither the course proposal nor my actual teaching record were the subject of the committee's final accusations. They focused on an article, "Innovative Bibliotherapy Approaches to Substance Abuse Education," that I had published in *The Arts and Psychotherapy,* in which I explore how teachers and clinicians can learn from each other ways to combat substance abuse. In treatment programs "I noticed the emphases on learning to identify and articulate the feelings that had been shut down by substance abuse, on awareness of family dynamics (especially as explained by family systems theory), and on participation in group psychotherapy and Twelve-Step groups" (357).

To prove that the goal of my course was "to engage students in counseling and psychotherapy," the administrator cited the phrase "on principles more like those of Twelve-Step groups" from the description of one version of my course in the article. I was surprised that anyone would confuse twelve-step peer-support groups with counseling or psychotherapy. I had received nothing but praise and encouragement for teaching in this way for years and thus was totally unprepared for this unexpected blow.

First of all, I wrote in my reply,

> I wish to make as clear as I possibly can that [psychotherapy] is NOT the goal of the course. . . . I would be pleased if students

found aspects of my course healing or therapeutic, but I do not want to engage in any kind of clinical counseling or psychotherapy that presumes to give advice, tell students how to live their lives, etc. I do not feel qualified to tell others how to behave and, for my own sake, I certainly don't want even to give the impression that I am taking on that kind of responsibility.

Before this course came under attack, in the freshman composition course I was teaching at the time, to make sure students knew that the course was not clinical counseling or psychotherapy I referred them to page 64 of John Bradshaw's *Homecoming*:

> These exercises are not intended to replace any therapy or therapy group that you might be involved in. They are not intended to replace any 12 Step group that you belong to. In fact, they should enhance your therapy or 12 Step work. If you are an adult victim of sexual abuse or severe emotional battering, or if you have been diagnosed as mentally ill or have a history of mental illness in your family, professional help is essential for you. If, as you experience these exercises, you start to experience strange or overwhelming emotions, *stop immediately.* Obtain the help of a qualified counselor before you proceed. While this work can be extremely powerful and has been highly therapeutic for many people, it is not intended as a magical kind of "how-to potion." Another caution: if you are in an active addiction . . . the work I am presenting here requires that you have at least one year of sobriety under your belt.

In my response to the administrator I added, "In fact I do not make that much use of Bradshaw's exercises, but, to see if my current students noticed this caveat, at the end of the semester I administered a questionnaire that asked, among other things, 'Do you recall reading the following passage in Bradshaw's book?' and then the passage was presented. Sixteen out of seventeen students checked 'Yes, I recall reading this passage and I took it seriously' and one checked the answer, 'Yes, I recall reading this passage, but I did not take it seriously.'"

I also supplied the committee with a set of my course materials that included "Group Participation Guidelines" that "clarify the operating principles in my classroom," principles quite different from counseling, including the following guidelines, among others:

1. Our aim is to work on ourselves, to give mutual support and to practice non-judgmental listening and sharing.

2. We recognize that each person's process is important, not our judgment of it. Being accepted where we are makes it easier to accept rather than judge others.

3. We share what works for us . . . rather than giving advice. We let other people find their own answers. . . .

4. We respect each other as unique; we recognize that each knows himself better than anyone else. If we listen to the voice within, we will find our own best answer.

5. We are here to support each other's inner guidance and assist one another to focus on what is meaningful to each of us rather than to confront or preach.

6. The roles of student and teacher are interchangeable; they fluctuate from one to the other regardless of age or experience.

The next set of guidelines included the instructions, "Speak with the first person 'I'. Instead of 'people feel' or 'you get to feeling . . .', etc., say: 'I think, I feel . . .' such and such"; "Don't speak for others. Such as '. . . most men think . . .', 'a man always feels . . .', etc. Speak for yourself or ask the person—or all men present—what they are feeling or thinking."

Concerning twelve-step groups, I pointed out that they "are neither counseling nor psychotherapy. In fact I compare my classroom practices to the operation of such groups to demonstrate how they are different from rather than similar to counseling and psychotherapy." The section of the article from which the quotation was taken reads: "A unique feature of this classroom was the way it facilitated operating the groups on principles more like those of Twelve-Step groups. For instance, one of the most striking features of Twelve-Step groups is the absence of hierarchy, of permanent leaders" (360). I had earlier indicated in the article how such techniques might "threaten both the usual patriarchal classroom structure, especially that of a teacher addicted to control, and the usual therapy group directed by a psychologist" for they result in "a much more student-centered approach than most teachers, administrators, or perhaps even students, can accept, and apparently a more client-centered approach than most clients and psychotherapists want" (358).

I could see how upsetting this could be, but I suspected that the basic problem was fear of emotion. In the administrator's initial letter he complained that the phrases using the word "emotional" in my course proposal were not "sufficiently defined." I replied by citing the definition in the *Arts and Psychotherapy* article: my "primary goal became emotional literacy: helping students identify and articulate the feelings they felt as they read" (355). I also pointed out that "in the course materials I submitted to the Committee I included quite a few materials which explain what is meant by 'emotion,' including 'Educators Combat Emotional Illiteracy'; 'Where Emotions Come From'; 'Vocabulary of Feelings'; and selections from *Drawing on the Right Side of the Brain, Using the Right Brain in the Language Arts,* and *Writing the Natural Way."* Finally, I asked the obvious question, "Are you afraid that students will become too 'emotional'? That they will 'break down', blame the university, and sue the university?" I received no answer to this question.

Surprisingly, in his next letter the administrator stated that "the committee members have no problem with drawing upon literary theory to teach about the emotional responses to literature." The many contradictions between this and his other sentences disturbed me. The original course description that the committee found so objectionable stated explicitly that that was indeed my approach: "The chief approach will be reader-centered criticism as in David Bleich's *Readings and Feelings."* I pointed out that Bleich's book was published by the National Council of Teachers of English and listed the table of contents, with entries such as "Thoughts and Feelings" (including "Guidelines for Obtaining Emotional Response"); "Feelings about Literature"; and "Using the Book: Pragmatic Suggestions and Elaborations." I then asked, "Which, if any, of these topics am I to be prohibited from exploring in the classroom? If the Committee is opposed to this text, will not the committee member[s] then have to start censoring the supporting works listed in the bibliographical guide at the end of the book as well? And will they not have to start with Aristotle? Bleich points out that [Aristotle] defined tragedy in terms of the emotional response to it: pity and fear" (110).

I wondered if the problem was "that I take Bleich's last section seriously, 'pragmatic suggestions and elaboration'? Am I to be restricted merely to discussing theory in a vacuum, ignoring its pedagogical implications in our own classroom? Is the objection of the Committee to 'the idea of studying the actual responses of actual readers' as Bleich puts it (110–11)?" I asked, "Would not then the committee's censorship have to begin with I. A. Richards' *Practical Criticism* (1929) and be extended to Norman Holland's *Poems in Persons* and *Five Readers Reading* and the many related works of literary theory and criticism published along those lines in the last sixty years or so?" Bleich's last paragraph begins: "The reader is invited to carry the conclusions of response-criticism in whatever directions he finds most compelling. It is obvious that a great deal more needs to be understood about how people function when they confront manifestations of language." I asked, "Has not the Committee prohibited me from carrying the conclusions of response-criticism in the directions I find most compelling?"

Then I focused directly on the committee's reaction to the phrase "corrective emotional experience" in my article. The original sentence was "Like Yalom, my goal was primarily 'the corrective emotional experience' (pp. 25–29), or 'catharsis' as it is called in the more psychoanalytic model of Schrodes and others." I wondered if the committee was "disturbed by the 'psychoanalytic' or 'psychotherapeutic' overtone of the phrase 'corrective emotional experience'? It does seem to have a Freudian sound to it. However, that is because 'Freud adopted Aristotle's view of literature," as Bleich points out (110). It was Aristotle who 'conceived literature as cathartic for the audience—literature as a stimulus for emotional purgation'" (110).

I went on to argue that "exploration of emotional and other forms of right-brain knowledge and the politics of the family are common in feminist" literary criticism and theory as well, and I supplied six other kinds of books to the committee: Alice Brand's *Therapy in Writing* and her *The Psychology of Writing: The Affective Experience*; Harvey F. Clarizo's *Contemporary Issues in Educational Psychology* (which has a section on "Classroom Dynamics and Mental Health"); Weinstein and Fantini's *Toward Humanistic Education: A Curriculum of Affect* (which focuses on the needs of "poor, minority-group children"); Clark Moustakas's *The Authentic Teacher: Sensitivity and Awareness in the*

Classroom (including a discussion of "emotions in the class-room" and related issues); and *Mental Hygiene in the Classroom* by the NEA and the AMA's Joint Committee on Health Problems in Education.

Moving from theory back to practice, I then addressed the fear conveyed in the administrator's sentence, "That other students would then have access to these journals or essays in which their fellow students are encouraged to explore psychological states also raised concerns." I stated that "I too am concerned to assure as much privacy as possible, and now allow students to mark essays, pages, or portions of pages as private, to be read only by the teacher, or by no one. Nor should any student's writing be made available to future students or any other readers without the writer's permission."

Searching for what else might have prompted rejection of the course, I also noticed the preceding sentence in the original letter of rejection: "Then too, the committee questioned the appropriateness of grading students on the basis of journals recording their 'emotional and other responses'." I replied, "I want to do everything possible to avoid putting students 'in a potentially exploitative relationship, one where the teacher is both therapist and evaluator.' My system of grading journals is described in the article in detail: the students are graded in terms of the quantity of the entries in the categories, not my subjective evaluation of how 'therapeutic' any of this might be for them. I believe that students should have the option of not writing about their emotions, if they wish. A grade should not be determined by whether or not someone is willing to be [self-disclosing]. Basically, students are graded on how much work they put into the course, not what personal changes, if any, result. This grading system is not ideal and I would welcome any constructive suggestions the Committee has to offer."

What was the result of my letter? I received no reply, was removed from the list of teachers eligible to teach the Plan II Freshman English honors course ("Composition and Reading World Literature"), and was assigned a large lecture course where my emotional literacy approach is less practical. I still get to teach "Personal, Expressive Writing" and "Autobiography" at times in the Division of Rhetoric and Composition. When I do so I take some of the committee's objections into account. For example, I rarely use the metaphor of the inner child and have dropped Bradshaw's self-help books as required texts, substituting Denis Ledoux's *From Memories to Memoirs* and Robert Atkinson's *The Gift of Stories*. However, the committee's intervention has had its intended chilling effect. My courses in autobiography and personal, expressive writing have given way to courses on nature writing and computers where any discussion of feelings tends to be brief and superficial.

Conclusion

Personal writing courses obviously raise many questions, such as what is the best format for student writing—reading journal, personal essay, family vignette, weekly diary, full-length autobiography, or . . . ? How can such highly personal writing be "corrected" and graded without seeming to correct and grade the person who wrote it? What preparation should the teacher have? To what extent should the teacher make his or her own autobiographical writing available? To what extent, if any, should students be encouraged to write about dramatic, traumatic, or difficult personal experiences and/or to tell difficult truths or half-truths about themselves? If they do, how should the teacher and other students respond?

I do not know how to deal with the problem of grading students on their autobiographical writing. I know I have to be sure they do not get the impression that they, rather than their writing, are being graded. I remembered how personally I took the grades I received in the best course I have ever taken, freshman English at Amherst College, in which the students themselves were the texts. To avoid what I saw as the pitfalls of that course, I graded the autobiographies not on their content but only on the basis of how much work was put into them and whether or not they met certain basic formal requirements. Some of these issues are addressed by Professor Berman. Since 1976 he has assigned personal diaries in his "Literature and Psychoanalysis" courses. Emotional literacy is not his primary concern, but he has important and useful answers for related questions. For example, he assigns weekly diaries, which are not graded, in addition to his regular assignments. Grades depend solely on the latter.

What about student confidentiality? Both of us allowed students the option of marking any of their writing for our eyes only. With the permission of the students, he read five of the diaries aloud to the class each week, allowing no response from the class. With networked computers at my disposal, my approach was quite different. Every third or fourth class, in groups of four or five, students communicated to each other on the computers whatever they wanted to share about their experiences. At the end of the class period a transcript was generated of all the exchanges in all the groups and made available to the whole class. Although the students knew this would be the case, to their surprise they ended up sharing more than they would have face to face (Bump, "Radical"). In addition, they were required to write two formal essays. They knew that the first drafts of each essay would be made available to the class via an electronic mail program which allowed one-on-one student response. Students were asked to avoid any kind of criticism or judgment of the content of other students' essays, making suggestions for revision only to help the authors communicate their feelings as well as their thoughts more effectively. The final drafts of the essays were read only by me. At the end of the semester students gathered together these and any other related materials they wished in an embryonic autobiography, again read and evaluated only by me.

In any case, I hope more college teachers will learn from my mistakes and be the focus of the next article with a title like "Educators Combat Emotional Illiteracy" (Goleman). The lives of our students will benefit in more ways than we can know.

Works Cited

Atkinson, Robert. *The Gift of Stories*. New York: Greenwood, 1995.

Berman, Jeffrey. *Diaries to an English Professor: Pain and Growth in the Classroom*. Amherst: U of Massachusetts P, 1994.

Bleich, David. *Readings and Feelings: An Introduction to Subjective Criticism*. Urbana: NCTE, 1975.

Bradshaw, John. *Bradshaw On: The Family, a Revolutionary Way of Self-Discovery.* Pampano Beach, CA: Health Communications, 1988.

———. *Homecoming: Reclaiming and Championing Your Inner Child.* New York: Bantam, 1990.

Brand, Alice G. *The Psychology of Writing: The Affective Experience.* New York: Greenwood, 1989.

———. *Therapy in Writing: A Psycho-Educational Enterprise.* Lexington, MA: Heath, 1980.

Bump, Jerome. "The Family Dynamics of the Reception of Art." *Style* 31.2 (1997): 106–28.

———. "Innovative Bibliotherapy: Approaches to Substance Abuse Education," *The Arts in Psychotherapy* 17.4 (1990): 355–62.

———. "Radical Changes in Class Discussion Using Networked Computers." *Computers and the Humanities* 24.1 (1990): 49–65.

Buscaglia, Leo. *Love.* New York: Fawcett, 1978.

Clarizo, Harvey F. *Contemporary Issues in Educational Psychology.* Boston: Allyn, 1970.

Cohen, Paula. *The Daughter's Dilemma: Family Process and the Nineteenth-Century Domestic Novel.* Ann Arbor: U of Michigan P, 1991.

Coles, William E., Jr., and James Vopat. *What Makes Writing Good.* Lexington, MA: Heath, 1985.

Edwards, Betty. *Drawing on the Right Side of the Brain: A Course in Enhancing Creativity.* Rev. ed. Los Angeles: Tarcher, 1989.

Faigley, Lester. *Fragments of Rationality: Postmodernity and the Subject of Composition.* Pittsburgh: U of Pittsburgh P, 1992.

Ghinger, Carole, and Marcus Grant. "Alcohol and the Family in Literature." *Alcohol and the Family.* Ed. Jim Orford and Judith Harwin. London: Croom Helm, 1982. 25–53.

Goldberg, Natalie. *Wild Mind: Living the Writer's Life.* New York: Bantam, 1990.

Goleman, Daniel. "Educators Combat Emotional Illiteracy." *Austin American-Statesman* (30 March 1992).

————. *Emotional Intelligence.* New York: Bantam, 1995.

Goode, Erica E. *U.S. News and World Report* (24 June 1991): 54–61.

Holland, Norman. *Five Readers Reading.* New Haven: Yale UP, 1975.

————. *Poems in Persons: An Introduction to the Psychoanalysis of Literature.* New York: Norton, 1973.

Holloway, John. *The Victorian Sage: Studies in Argument.* London: Macmillan, 1953.

Kerr, Michael E. "Chronic Anxiety and Defining a Self." *Atlantic Monthly* (September 1988): 35–58.

Kiersey, D., and M. Bates. *Please Understand Me: Character and Temperament Types.* Del Mar, CA: Prometheus, 1984.

Langbaum, Robert. *The Poetry of Experience.* 1957; rpt. New York: Norton, 1963.

Ledoux, Denis. *From Memories to Memoirs: A Handbook for Writing Lifestories.* Lisbon Falls, ME: Soleil, 1993.

Lewis, Jerry M., and John G. Looney. *The Long Struggle: Well-Functioning Working-Class Black Families.* New York: Brunner, 1983.

McCormick, Maria. "First Representations of the Gamma Alcoholic in the English Novel." *Quarterly Journal of Studies on Alcohol* 30 (1969): 957–80.

Moore, O. Christene. "Family Patterns in *Jane Eyre* and *Wide Sargasso Sea.*" Unpub. M.A. Thesis, University of Texas at Austin, 1990.

Moustakas, Clark. *The Authentic Teacher: Sensitivity and Awareness in the Classroom.* Cambridge: H. A. Doyle, 1966.

————. *Personal Growth: The Struggle for Identity and Human Values.* Cambridge: H. A. Doyle, 1969.

National Education Association and the American Medical Association, Joint Committee on Health Problems in Education. *Mental Hygiene in the Classroom.* Chicago: American Medical Association, 1955.

Parker, Patricia. "Charlotte and Branwell Brontë: A Family Systems Approach," Unpub. seminar paper.

Redl, Fritz, and William Wattenberg. *Mental Hygiene in Teaching.* 2nd ed. New York: Harcourt, 1959.

Richards, I. A. *Practical Criticism: A Study of Literary Judgment.* New York: Harcourt, 1956.

Rico, Gabriele. *Writing the Natural Way: Using Right-Brain Techniques to Release Your Expressive Powers.* Los Angeles: Tarcher, 1983.

Rogers, Carl. *On Becoming a Person: A Therapist's View of Psychotherapy.* Boston: Houghton, 1961.

Schrodes, C. *Bibliotherapy: A Theoretical and Clinical-Experimental Study.* Unpub. Doctoral Dissertation, University of California at Berkeley, 1949.

Sinatra, Richard, and Josephine Stahl-Gamble. *Using the Right Brain in the Language Arts.* Springfield, IL: Thomas, 1983.

Steinem, Gloria. "Looking for a Family of Equals." *Christian Science Monitor* (17 June 1980).

Walsh, F. "Conceptualizations of Normal Family Functioning," *Normal Family Processes.* Ed. F. Walsh. New York: Guilford Press, 1982.

Weinstein, Gerald, and Mario D. Fantini, eds. *Toward Humanistic Education: A Curriculum of Affect.* New York: Praeger, 1970.

Wohl, Anthony, ed. *The Victorian Family: Structure and Stresses.* London: Croom Helm, 1978.

Yalom, I. D. *The Theory and Practice of Group Psychotherapy,* 3rd. ed. New York: Basic, 1985.

CHAPTER THIRTEEN

Writing through the Fear to Reframe Experience and Discover Values

REGINA PAXTON FOEHR
Illinois State University

Those of us who have been teaching for a while rarely think of teaching as intimidating, but for those just entering the profession, teaching can be a frightening proposition. Even experienced teachers and professors can encounter fear-producing episodes related to one's subject matter or to professional relationships with students, parents, administrators, or other faculty members. Fears are exacerbated, however, for student teachers, graduate assistants, and new, nontenured professionals whose reputations have not been established. Their future employability, they fear, hangs upon their ability to uphold professional standards in their teaching, in the atmosphere of their classrooms, and in their professional productivity. Their deep-seated concerns about job security and survival become intensified in areas where enrollments are declining. They get clear messages that new teachers and student teachers "are to be seen, not heard" (Hamilton 70), and many experience brief identity crises (Graves 71). Among new teachers especially, the strain created by such situations can lead quickly to shattered self-esteem, burnout, and the decision to leave the profession. The stresses of the profession are so great for newly trained teachers, in fact, that one-third to one-half of all new teachers leave the profession within their first five years of teaching (Darling-Hammond 5).

This study investigates two main questions:

◆ Can writing about teaching fears reduce teaching apprehension, insecurity, and anxiety?

◆ Can reframing one's fears through the lens of their opposites, one's values, affect teachers' images of themselves and their sense of power over their professional lives?

Emotional Responses to Fear

Emotional responses to fear can contribute to an individual's inability to cope with personal and professional stress. In fact, according to Daniel Goleman in *Emotional Intelligence,* a lack of emotional intelligence can sabotage the intellect and ruin careers. Emotional intelligence includes the ability to manage emotions, motivate oneself, recognize emotions in others, and handle relationships by, in part, managing emotions in others. Whereas failure to monitor emotions leaves us at their mercy, Goleman discusses the keystone of emotional intelligence as recognizing feelings as each one happens (43). "Emotions matter for rationality," guiding decisions, enabling or disenabling thought (28). They have the power to disrupt thinking altogether, but when we can harmonize thought and emotions, we can think clearly and make rational decisions (27). Carl Jung says that individuals are so unconscious that they fail to see their own potentiality for decision making, looking instead for external rules to guide them in their perplexity. Moreover, he asserts, "a good deal of the blame for this rests with education, which promulgates the old generalizations and says nothing about the secrets of private experience" (172).

The fears/values approach discussed later in this study allows participants within academe to harmonize thought and emotion by reframing the experience of fear in a new context— one that acknowledges and integrates emotion and re-cognition. This process breaks old response patterns to fear, thereby reducing it and its power over the individual. The process increases intellectual and emotional intelligence. It is based on the concept that "Beyond all our daily reacting lies a self that knows the way home" (Campbell and McMahon 85). Reframing allows us to unveil the pathway home.

The Shadow, Teaching as
Heroic, and the Need to Reframe

Carl Jung characterizes the personal shadow as one of the major archetypes in the personal unconscious. Archetypes are molds or frames of experience within the unconscious that are shared universally at a profound level of experience. Because fear is universally shared and understood, it is an archetype; it can protect us from dangerous realities. Fear can also exemplify the archetypal shadow. The shadow contains aspects of an individual or a system hidden from self-awareness and often from the awareness of others. As long as the shadow remains hidden, it is activated and exerts negative power over our lives. At the personal level, fear affects our state of mind, our ego, and our self-perception. It can create negative attitudes, emotional and physical health problems, and reduced productivity. Professionally and institutionally, we may see it in cut-throat politics, professional sabotage, and irrational hiring practices. Whether dealing with the fear shadow at a personal, institutional, or global level, its effects upon function when it remains unconscious are the same—all negative.

In teaching and in life, some realities we construct are fearful, and the heroic need to reframe them is crucial if we are to have control over them. Viewing fear as an archetype allows us to modify our behavior on a larger screen than just the immediate experience—it allows us to make meaning out of fear. Even though most of what we fear never happens, we may avoid addressing our fears out of the fear of making matters worse; subconsciously, we fear that addressing our fears will not only exacerbate them but intensify the problem. We fear that *fear* has a shadow, worse than the fear itself. Deena Metzger says, "As we move toward the shadow, we are overwhelmed by the fear of being engulfed" (299). But fear *is* the shadow. "If we do not move toward the shadow, we run the risk that the shadow will come to us in a meeting that will be furtive and violent" (299).

Although addressing the shadow takes *heroic* courage, it can be transformative: we experience enlightenment when we make the darkness conscious (Jung; Levinson; Metzger). This is the case when dealing with fears, whether legitimate or irrational. When we discover that our fears are ill-founded, we feel transformed— by relief. Paradoxically, even when our worst fears are confirmed, at some level we usually experience transforming relief in *knowing*; we are no longer immobilized, but heroically empowered to make the quest. As Dan Levinson maintains, the nobility and the defect are two sides of the same heroic coin. Because genuine tragedy is heroic, it does not end simply in defeat even when the hero does not attain initial aspirations. By confronting profound inner faults, accepting them as part of the self and of humanity, the hero is to some degree transformed into a noble person. The personal transformation outweighs the worldly defeat and suffering; thus, the hero is ultimately victorious (264).

Writing and Healing

Numerous clinical studies, featuring alternative medical therapies, have shown a positive correlation between meditation, visualization, writing, and healing. Larry Dossey, M.D., director of the Panel for Alternative Medicine, National Institutes of Health, has documented a broad range of these studies in his book *Healing Words*. The Wellness Center, San Francisco, uses journal writing, including letter writing to one's own disease to reduce fear and help AIDS patients integrate the disease with "Who I am" (Colt 47). Writing to illumine the shadow can be a powerful consciousness-altering experience. Dossey and psychologists Thomas Moore and John Bradshaw all identify writing as the single most effective therapeutic tool for healing (Foehr 64–66). Comparing writing instruction with therapy, Wendy Bishop describes both activities as pedagogical, clarifying that writing is not therapy but that the writing process is therapeutic (503–4). Chuck Anderson says narrative writing invites us "to act by creating the conditions within which healing may take place" (11). In *Pain and Possibility*, Gabriele Rico chronicles the power of writing to heal through serious illness or other personal crises, and Beverly and Wallace Kahn write about the therapeutic value of student-authored books based on personal experience (157). Countless examples from composition studies illustrate the healing effects of writing upon self-esteem (Nancie Atwell, Peter Elbow, Gabriele Rico, and Mike Rose).

James W. Pennebaker and others have conducted and replicated extensive research on the relationship of writing to health. Pennebaker and Beall found significant drops in health center visits among students asked to write about traumatic experience for six months after writing occurred when compared to those who wrote about non-emotional topics. In a replicated study, Pennebaker, Kiecold-Glaser and Glaser found enhanced immune function after the last day of writing as compared with the control students. Pennebaker found that even though confronting psychologically upsetting experience through writing may be painful and psychologically arousing in the short run, in the long run doing so can be associated with improved physical and psychological health (546). Even technical writing, considered by many as a "cognitive" activity, can be a source of healing. John Stibravy and John Muller argue for using technical writing in a therapy program to improve self-confidence (382). Psychiatrist James A. Bourgeois agrees with this use of technical writing, considering it "therapeutic" (381). Nonetheless, though the literature suggests a strong connection between writing and the healing of emotional wounds, in academe we rarely ask students to write about their emotions. Emotions, after all, call forth the shadow: "Transference and counter-transference emotions are threatening because they are so powerful. But they are most destructive and inhibiting in the writing class when we fail to acknowledge and deal with them" (Lad Tobin qtd. in Bishop 509).

Fear/Values Theory

To determine their deepest values, psychologist John Florell[1] asks workshop participants to consider the question: "What do you value most in life?" Florell says, "What you *think* you value and what you *really value* may not be the same. If you want to determine what you *really value*," he says, "you need only to answer the question, 'What am I most afraid of?' Behind our deepest fear," he argues, "is our greatest value." In teaching, for example, if we are afraid of looking foolish or incompetent, what we value is the respect and admiration of others. If we are afraid of not being liked, what we value most is human relationships. If we are afraid of losing control, what we value is personal power and being in control of our personal lives. Florell, like other psychologists, also argues that our fears are the greatest driving force behind our behavior, whether we are aware of them or not. Refusing to face them can lead to symptoms of insecurity, anxiety, depression, ill health, and additional, irrational fears. But when we understand our fears by reframing them in terms of their opposites—our values—we can make informed choices and modify our behavior and expectations personally and professionally in appropriate and reasoned ways.

Research Study

To determine if writing about fears can reduce fear and stress in teaching and lead to new self-awareness, I conducted a study which involved thirty-one senior English education majors during the semester before they were to begin student teaching. I asked them to complete several tasks in the following stages: (1) to list and then discuss their greatest fears of student teaching; (2) to write a worst-case scenario of themselves in the situations they feared most; (3) to analyze each fear they had listed for its opposite to discover, and then write down, the underlying value behind the fear; and (4) to write the effect of having confronted and analyzed their fears in these stages.

This approach is not simply an expressivist writing activity. It is based upon Paul L. Wachtel's theory of paradoxing, that is, *suggesting the opposite of the expected experience by having participants imagine the experience in all its negativity.* Participants immerse themselves in their greatest fears, leaving no stone unturned, no fear unaddressed. Even though participants may previously have experienced stages of fear avoidance, this approach forces them to face the shadow, the unknown, the unconscious, and in so doing to make it conscious. Wachtel claims that participants exercise at least some measure of control over an experience in their efforts to increase their anxiety about it (200). Pennebaker found that such processes can lead to better health

(539). As students gain control of the experience—the fears—
through facing them, they gain further control by paradoxing
and reframing them as values.

In this paradoxing of fears and reframing them as values—
Florell's theory—they can change not just how they *view* the experience, but how they *experience* it. For example, students who
fear not having enough knowledge to teach are afraid of looking
foolish, ignorant, and unprepared; this fear can have a gnawing
effect upon their subconscious, their self-confidence, and their
mental and physical health. Yet, by paradoxing this fear, seeing
themselves as the foolish object of students' laughter and ridicule
because of their ignorance, for example, they bring the shadow
into the light of consciousness, and it loses its subconscious
power over them. They may experience the circumstance in a
new way—as less frightening or perhaps as humorous and no
longer frightening at all. When they recognize their value—
knowledge, preparation, and the respect of others—they see the
positive side of their fear and of themselves and know that they
are likely to work hard to maintain their values. This new insight
awareness gives them confidence. The process requires a focus on
the negative (fear) and the positive (values) in ways that lead to
new insights. Pennebaker found that subjects making a higher
use of negative and positive words in writing about their traumatic events experienced improved health (539) and, when using
such words together with insight, causal, and associated cognitive words over several days, they also experienced health improvement (539).

Translating events through writing affects the way we organize and encode the experience in the mind, changing the memory
of it and allowing us to more readily assimilate the experience
and set it aside (Berry and Pennebaker 18). This process precludes
the need to suppress thoughts and emotions about the experience
and reduces reliance on medical facilities (18). Though some may
fear that writing about their fears might reinforce or intensify
them, in fact, to paradox them in writing can further transform
them, changing them from something negative to something positive. Both Halberstadt and Pennebaker found that subjects who
wrote essays over four days about traumatic events experienced
greater health benefits long-term than did those who simply
vented emotions related to the event (Berry and Pennebaker 18).

Findings

Using response frequency as an indicator, I have divided students' fears into twenty main categories. Their fears and the values they identified as underlying their fears can be found in Tables 13-1 and 13-2.

Table 13-1. Most Frequently Identified Student Teaching Fears and Their Correlating Values for Thirty-One College Seniors

Stage I: Categories of Fear Identified	Number of Students Naming Each Fear Category	Stage II: Correlating Values Identified (No. of Times Listed If More Than Once)
Lack of knowledge	15	Knowledge (6), education (3), preparation (2), intelligence (3), freedom of expression, wisdom, success, respect, being educated in a way that will benefit my students, my students' success, ability to retain information, acceptance, belonging, security, competence, doing a job well, and preparedness
Lack of respect and acceptance by students	15	Acceptance (3), integrity (2), honor (2), love, control, order, respect for my age and my position, being liked, respect, attention, learning from mistakes, being an individual who gains respect and admiration from peers, co-workers, and students
Lack of confidence (in own abilities and abilities to reach students, looking foolish)	12	Confidence (2), security (2), respect (2), braveness, calm, trust, concern for students, integrity, being interesting to others, being liked, success, self-confidence, others' opinions of me, strong work ethic, competence, organization, self-control
Opinion of cooperating teacher	11	Experience, good manners, cooperation, professionalism, cohesiveness (being a team player), respect (2), human relationships
Unmotivated, bored students	8	Being interesting and excited, how my actions affect others
Insufficient time, preparation, affecting teaching and family	7	Organization, avoiding embarrassment, love, my children and not neglecting them
Violence in the schools, safety	7	Peace (3), respect, non-hostile environment, safety for myself and others

Table 13-2. Less Frequently Identified Student Teaching Fears and Their Correlating Values for Thirty-One College Seniors

Stage I: Categories of Fear Identified	Number of Students	Stage II: Correlating Values Identified (No. of Times)
Incompetence, ineffective communicator, dull, boring, looking stupid	5	Success (2), effective communication, trust in abilities to teach, realizing my own limitations, confidence, charismatic, exciting people, desire to be seen as a "good" teacher, to be comfortable and knowledgeable in the job, to be of value to students
Discipline	5	Control (2), self-respect (2), self-preservation, respect for others, loyalty, preparation, respect from students and others, being organized and prepared, confidence in others, being liked by students
Wrong career choice	4	Unfair to students, expense for education, need to be fulfilled in career I choose, not unhappy for the rest of my life
Negative effect on student	3	Life, respect for others' lives
Lack of control and personal power	3	Leadership, ability to inspire, charisma, personal control, power, competence, integrity, autonomy
Student teaching grade	2	—
Student teaching placement	2	Security, organization, follow-through, time with husband
Not being prepared for class	2	Acceptance, preparedness, success, being prepared—to combat opposition, being truthful about what I like
Sexual harassment by males	1	Control
Looking foolish because of health condition	1	Avoiding embarrassment, control, classroom management
Lack of freedom	1	Respect, acceptance, approval
Looking foolish during observation by university supervisor	1	Respect of others
Getting a job afterward	1	Investment of time and money

Discussion of Fears

The written responses of all thirty-one students indicate that fears of student teaching are real. Two students wrote that they have frequent nightmares about student teaching. One sees student teaching archetypally as a "huge leap into a vast unknown jungle." Another wrote, "Anyone who does not have some apprehension towards their student teaching either does not care or is cold blooded." In addition to these and the fears listed in Tables 13-1 and 13-2, one expressed a common fear, that "My students will think I am stupid, or nerdy, or worse, just another run of the mill student teacher."

Students commonly listed a primary fear, such as "lack of knowledge," and then wrote extensively on that topic, mentioning other topics only briefly. Several also discussed concrete plans for addressing their fears as illustrated by one who wrote, "I value intelligence . . . and feel inadequate about my own knowledge [therefore, she continued playfully,] I shall persist until I have read the entire canon twenty times." Two students mentioned fears of intimidation by students who are "taller" and "bulkier" than they: "I have just begun to start handling these males who question my authority and test all kinds of boundaries. . . . My worst fear would be for several of the male students to begin harassing me [either verbally or physically] and refuse to stop when told." She mentioned her own small size as a contributing factor. Others similar in size and stature, however, did not mention harassment as a concern.

One student expressed fear of "what this hectic year will do to my children, [e.g.,] making them feel neglected . . . and turn to the wrong things." Another expressed similar concerns, projecting into her future roles—teacher and parent.

The Effect upon Students of Writing about Their Fears and Values

"To be able to be truly honest with students means confronting yourself in a way seldom done" (Backes 78). As one student in this study said, "It is rare that we sit down and think about the things that we are most afraid of" or "consider them from a positive angle" as another wrote. Table 13-3 summarizes the effects upon students' attitudes and perspectives of writing about their fears and exploring the opposites, their values.

Positive Change

Reframing changes experience. In written responses, twenty-four students indicated that the fears/values process changed attitudes toward fears in positive ways, giving a new perspective, turning fears which they had seen as negative into values and goals they saw as positive. One response seems to encapsulate the views of all twenty-four: "It reduced the power my fears have over me." Others said about the process: "It clarified my fears and desires and values in life," "made me realize that my fears are conquerable . . . less menacing to me . . . and gave me a chance to see why I value these things so highly"; "It helped to diminish my fears and increase my awareness of what it is that I

Table 13-3. Effects of Writing about Fears and Values upon the Attitudes and Perspectives of Thirty-One College Seniors

Number of Students	Indications	As Reflected by
24	Positive Change	Decrease in fear, greater sense of personal power and control over situations, more positive sense of self
3	Mixed Messages	Claims of "no change in attitude toward fears" or "more fear" (contradicted by written elaboration)
3	No Change	
0	Negative Change	Increase in fear and apprehension
1	No Response	Participated in fears/values process but did not write a response to the experience

want in my classroom"; "My fears seem to dissipate when I focus on positive values and goals." It made my fears "seem a little bit more trivial than before. For example, being 'liked' seems like something a kindergarten child would say." Others said, "We gained insight"; "It allowed me to be honest with myself, enabling me to search for ways of overlooking this fear and holding on to my value." It helped me "to understand my fears a little better and actually brought out fears I did not know I had before."

Through paradoxing and reframing, the act of writing about the fear/values analysis process itself, this last stage of analysis generated new insights for some, "made me realize all of my values come under the heading of 'self-respect'," as one expressed it. Another who had seemed to gloss (perhaps attempting to avoid) any real fears in the first stage, said, "Honestly, I'm really excited to be student teaching and I think I'm nervous about everything," but in writing about the fear/values process, the last stage, she expressed an unacknowledged fear: "I may not be good at teaching. . . . I don't want to disappoint (my family)—or myself." Another confronted a familiar pattern in the last stage: "I need to develop more trust in myself and my abilities and stop waiting to fail. It is a neurosis of mine that I feel eventually I will be exposed as a fraud, that I don't really know what I claim to know. Even though this has never happened, I still fear that it is just around the corner." One surprise finding was that only one student mentioned fear of the university supervisor's observation.

No Change

Three students claimed that the fears/values process did not change their attitudes toward their fears. They gave these reasons: "I have written about it before in journals and to friends"; "It did not change my attitude toward my fears but served to connect the two in my mind, my fears and some very positive points about my attitude toward teaching"; "Writing about them doesn't change them, doesn't make them less scary."

Medical literature offers overwhelming evidence that trauma affects mental and physical health. Most pre-student teachers view student teaching as traumatic to some extent. Clinical, social, and health psychology are making important discoveries about the positive effect of disclosure, through talking and writing about emotional trauma, upon psychological and physical health. If these students were avoiding disclosure, that is unfortunate because according to Berry and Pennebaker, the work we go through to avoid disclosure puts stress on the body that leads to illness (12). Yet, any masking of emotions should not be surprising. Teachers can easily observe the tendency among students of all ages to mask negative (or positive) affect through changing or controlling facial behavior in accordance with socially sanctioned display rules. This may be related to classroom personality and to individual temperament. It is also related to shared expressiveness within families according to Burrowes and Halberstadt (Halberstadt 16). Moreover, "people from families of low-expressive background refrain from using expressive skills because they have been taught to actively inhibit nonverbal displays of emotion" (14–16). In addition, a number of studies show that internalizers (those showing little if any emotional response to emotion-inducing stimuli) actively work to suppress emotional expression (Fowles 87–104). This behavior, however, has damaging consequences. These suppressed responses only go underground and are then expressed covertly through increased autonomic arousal which actively increases autonomic activity and places continual stress on the body (Pennebaker and Chew 1427–433). Much research documents the relationship of suppressed negative responses and health-related problems, whereas talking or writing about personal traumas produces short- and long-term mental and physical health improvements (15). Chronic worriers, for example, avoid processing the real source of their anxiety. According to Borkovec, Roemer, and Kinyon, chronic worriers, those with generalized anxiety disorder (GAD), experience greater health problems than those who worry about only a few major topics (e.g., family, finances, health); yet, ironically, they use chronic general worrying as avoidance of their own childhood memories—the real source of their anxiety disorder. The trauma of their past has been too distressing for them to think about directly. This avoidance provides immediate short-term physiological activation but long-term distress because it prevents emotional processing. Disclosure, on the other hand, facilitates emotional processing (51–53).

Such avoidance raises the question for us in the academy: "What past traumas within the academy might these students have experienced?" Jane Tompkins asserts that "School, by definition, conditions us to believe that there are others who know better than we do; it encourages and often forces us to give up our own judgment in favor of the judgment of those in authority . . . (and) militates against the very thing that education is for—the development of the individual" (xix). Have these students been so traumatized when they showed originality or when they showed weakness—when they didn't have the answer—or the teacher's answer that they continue to see the academy as a scary place where vulnerability and disclosing perceived weakness is dangerous?

Do assignments such as writing about their fears, therefore, throw them into immediate avoidance? Might their avoidance also be triggered by concerns over course grades or letters of recommendation? If the academy is to move beyond being the dangerous place Jane Tompkins describes, we must create environments which encourage risk taking and cognitive elaboration and restructuring, whether in writing about fears of student teaching, in offering original interpretations of literature, or in exploring writing topics around the students' concerns. Failure to do so at best maintains and at worst exacerbates the students' distress and physical and psychological symptoms of ill health.

In the study I had simply given the instructions without commenting upon the concept of paradoxing or reframing. Some responses may have been legitimate, others avoidance. Perhaps, at least after the study, I should have given these students information about the connection between emotions and intellect and the power of reframing one's experience. If they saw the experience only as writing without emotional engagement, they missed the important transformative potentiality of reframing or re-cognizing one's experience.

Mixed Messages

Three students wrote that the fears/values process resulted in no change in their perspective or attitude toward their fear; however, the elaborations they wrote suggested that they had, in fact, gained new insights. This suggests that reframing changes the experience even if we are not able to acknowledge the change: "Writing down the fears makes me feel worse because I can see them on paper, rather than just in my mind. On the other hand, writing down which values that counter my fears has made those fears seem a bit insignificant. Now that I know that love, accept-ance and success are so important, my fears are not." Another wrote, "My fear has not changed because it is fear of the un-known. Recognizing my fear and values forces me to admit that I want to be liked"; "It doesn't make me feel better, but . . . allows me to see that acceptance is imperative in my life."

Regarding class discussion after completing all writing for the fears/values analysis, one student wrote, "We gained insight into our personality differences as well as learned that we are not alone." Another professed, "It also helps to know that other people share my fears and have a few more of their own."

Conclusion

This study has implications for graduate assistants and new, non-tenured teachers and professors at all levels. It has implications for all human beings who face fear. As the study demonstrates, facing fear is a heroic act. It takes courage. But in the process of uncovering this shadow, we can reach enlightenment through the experience of paradoxing and reframing. Instead of fleeing from, denying, or judging the fear, paradoxing immerses us in the negativity of it, giving an unexpected degree of power over it. This process discourages just holding on to fear and, thereby, being limited, handicapped, or constrained by it. Instead, it re-quires that we suspend fear long enough to reframe it through a new lens of "values," which changes the way we see it and expe-rience it. This transformative process gives us a fleeting glimpse of what we can be in our personal and professional lives. It lets us see that solutions are not "out there" but can be within one's own perceptions. Through confronting fears in writing, we ac-celerate the coping process, a process characterized by discovery of insight, not mere catharsis (Pennebaker, Colder, and Sharp

536). Though self-expression has its own value and can be a powerful learning experience, the fears/values process does not stop at self-expression but consciously moves beyond it through paradoxing and reframing. In so doing, we move away from the age-old educational paradigm Jung warns against, a paradigm that favors reliance on external rules for guiding decisions, dismembering us from our own private experience and its potential value for informing personal decisions. Instead, by combining intellect and emotions, we increase our intelligence in both, as Goleman advises us to do, and liberate ourselves from solitary or total reliance on either.

Denying the shadow of fear has negative consequences in our lives and our professions. Yet, worrying about but not exercising control over fear can be immobilizing, locking capable individuals into the terror of the future, the confusion of "What if?"—"What if I don't get hired? Get tenure? Get respect? Get accepted? What if . . . ?" But facing fear and then reframing it allows the individual to expand the experience in an archetypal, heroic way, going beyond the chronology of past, present, and future to being inside the *now* of the experience. Reframing allows the individual to transcend the darkness of professional fear, moving beyond its debilitating terror or gnawing torment to achieve the enlightenment found in one's personal and professional values. Not coincidentally, the quest of the hero is always a search for something of value to be brought back and shared for the good of all. Looking beyond their fears of *personal ignorance*, students in this study saw their value for *knowledge*. Beyond their fears of *being discounted or treated with disrespect by students and cooperating teachers*, they saw their value for *integrity, human relationships*, and *professionalism*. Beyond their fear of *looking foolish*, they saw a value for *self-confidence, courage, and competence*. Ultimately, beyond most of their fears, they saw with dazzling new clarity that what they valued most of all was an image of themselves as good teachers, as caring human beings who could make a difference in the lives of their students, the way many of their own heroes, their teachers, had done for them.

In advising new teachers, Deborah Ann Forster-Sulzer says, "The secret to imaginative teaching is the ability to look within yourself, to question and reflect upon what you truly believe is important as an educator" (77). By so doing, participants in this study became important figures on a hero's journey, and many discovered enlightenment. As Joseph Campbell says, when we follow the hero's path, to risk authentic expression like the "heroes of all time who have gone before us . . . we discover where we had thought to find an abomination, we shall find a god. And where we had thought to slay another, we shall slay ourselves. Where we had thought to travel outward, we will come to the center of our own existence. And where we had thought [to] be alone, we will be with all the world" (124).

Note

1. John Florell, a practicing psychologist and director of Bromenn Counseling Services, Bloomington, Illinois, offers workshops throughout the Midwest and served as a guest speaker for students in my class after they had completed the assignments described in this essay.

Works Cited

Anderson, Chuck. "'Carry Me Forward . . . into the Future in your Heart': The Place of Narrative in Health Professions Education." *Medical Encounter* 11.3 (1994): 9–11.

Atwell, Nancie. *In the Middle: Writing, Reading, and Learning with Adolescents.* Portsmouth, NH: Boynton/Cook, 1987.

Backes, Anthony. "Be True." *English Journal* 84.2 (1995): 78.

Berry, Diane S., and James W. Pennebaker. "Nonverbal and Verbal Emotional Expression and Health." *Psychotherapy and Psychomatics* 59.1 (1993): 11–19.

Bishop, Wendy. "Writing Is/and Therapy? Raising Questions about Writing Classrooms and Writing Program Administration." *Journal of Advanced Composition* 13.2 (1993): 503–16.

Borkovec, Thomas D., Lizabeth Roemer, and John Kinyon. "Disclosure and Worry: Opposite Sides of the Emotional Processing Coin." *Emotion, Disclosure, and Health.* Ed. James Pennebaker. Washington, DC: American Psychological Association, 1995. 47–70.

Bourgeois, James A. "A Psychiatric View on Technical Writing Instruction (Therapeutic Benefits)." *Technical Communication*. 39 (1992): 382.

Campbell, Joseph. *The Power of Myth*. New York: Doubleday, 1988.

Campbell, Peter A., and Edwin M. McMahon. *Bio-Spirituality*. Chicago: Loyola UP, 1985.

Colt, George Howe. "The Healing Revolution." *Life* (September 1996): 35–50.

Darling-Hammond, Linda. *Teacher Supply, Demand, and Quality*. Washington, DC: National Board for Professional Teaching Standards, 1990.

Dossey, Larry, M.D. *Healing Words*. San Francisco: HarperCollins, 1993.

Elbow, Peter. *Writing with Power*. New York: Oxford UP, 1981.

Foehr, Regina Paxton. "Writing the Spirit: Interviews with Larry Dossey, M.D., John Bradshaw, and Thomas Moore." *The Spiritual Side of Writing: Releasing the Learner's Whole Potential*. Ed. Regina Paxton Foehr and Susan S. Schiller. Portsmouth, NH: Boynton/Cook-Heinemann, 1997. 44–69.

Forster-Sulzer, Deborah Ann. "A Letter to the Newest Members of Our Family." *English Journal* 84.2 (1995): 77–8.

Fowles, Don C. "The Three Arousal Model: Implications of Gray's Two-Factor Learning Theory for Heart Rate, Electrodermal Activity, and Psychopathy." *Psychophysiology* 17 (1980): 87–104.

Goleman, Daniel. *Emotional Intelligence*. New York: Bantam, 1995.

Graves, Cherie. "First Day of Student Teaching." *English Journal* 84.2 (1995): 71.

Halberstadt, A. G. "Family Expressive Styles and Nonverbal Communication Skills." *Journal of Nonverbal Behavior* 8 (1983): 14–26.

Hamilton, Candace. "A Student Teacher's Advice to Master Teachers." *English Journal* 84.2 (1995): 70–71.

Jung, Carl G. "The Problem with Evil Today." *Meeting the Shadow: The Hidden Power of the Dark Side of Human Nature*. Ed. Connie Zweig and Jeremiah Abrams. Los Angeles: Tarcher, 1991. 171–73.

Kahn, Beverly B. and Wallace J. "I Am the Author Books." *Elementary School Guidance and Counseling* 25.2 (1990): 153–57.

Levinson, Dan. "For the Man at Midlife." *Meeting the Shadow: The Hidden Power of the Dark Side of Human Nature*. Ed. Connie Zweig and Jeremiah Abrams. Los Angeles: Tarcher, 1991. 262–64.

Metzger, Deena. "Writing about the Other." *Meeting the Shadow: The Hidden Power of the Dark Side of Human Nature*. Ed. Connie Zweig and Jeremiah Abrams. Los Angeles: Tarcher, 1991. 299–301.

Pennebaker, James W. "Putting Stress into Words: Health, Linguistic, and Therapeutic Implications." *Behavior Research and Therapy* 31.6 (1993): 539–48.

Pennebaker, James W., and Carol H. Chew. "Deception, Electrodermal Activity and Inhibition of Behavior." *Journal of Personal and Social Psychology* 49 (1985): 1427–433.

Pennebaker, James W., and S. K. Beall. "Confronting a Traumatic Event: Toward an Understanding of Inhibition and Disease." *Journal of Abnormal Psychology* 95 (1986): 327–41.

Pennebaker, James W., Michelle Colder, and Lisa K. Sharp. "Accelerating the Coping Process." *Journal of Personal and Social Psychology* 58.3 (1990): 528–37.

Pennebaker, James W., J. Kiecolt-Glaser, and R. Glaser. "Disclosure of Traumas and Immune Function: Health Implications for Psychology." *Journal of Consulting and Clinical Psychology* 56 (1988): 239–45.

Rico, Gabriele. *Pain and Possibility: Writing Your Way through Personal Crisis*. Los Angeles: Tarcher, 1991.

Rose, Mike. *Lives on the Boundary*. New York: Penguin, 1990.

Stibravy, John, and John Muller. "Using Technical Writing to Enhance Self-Esteem." *Technical Communication* 39 (1992): 375–83.

Tompkins, Jane. *A Life in School: What the Teacher Learned*. New York: Addison-Wesley, 1996.

Wachtel, Paul L. *Therapeutic Communication*. New York: Guilford, 1993.

WRITING AND HEALING IN THE WORLD

Questions that open to voices not yet heard in our academic conversations test far more than our capacity to hear: they test more critically how we live in the world with others.

JAY ROBINSON, Conversations on the Written Word

CHAPTER FOURTEEN

Voices from the Line

The Clothesline Project
as Healing Text

LAURA JULIER
Michigan State University

L ike the Vietnam Veterans Memorial and the AIDS quilt, the Clothesline Project calls attention to a point of deep and epidemic woundedness in our cultural fabric that has been accompanied by a collective—some would say collusive—silence. In their concern with healing, each of these projects raises a number of significant issues in creative juxtaposition; each has enabled individuals to come to terms with their own grief and pain, and each has elicited countless stories of personal transformations and healing. At the same time, each project also points to the complex relationship between individual pain or grieving and a collective social responsibility for the problem. In thus calling on the wider human community to acknowledge the problem, each project has accomplished or contributed to a move from cultural silence to open conversation. Indeed, some claim that individual healing occurs *because* in these projects the individual experience is recognized as part of a larger social problem.

The Clothesline Project bears witness to victims and survivors of violence against women: Shirts of varied colors are strung on a clothesline, each created by an individual woman,[1] anonymously, about her experience of—or in memory of a woman who has died from—violence against her *as* a woman. Some shirts are inscribed with letters, some scream single words, some are not verbal. Though each is a powerful text of resistance, violation, and wholeness, the shirts become the Project only when

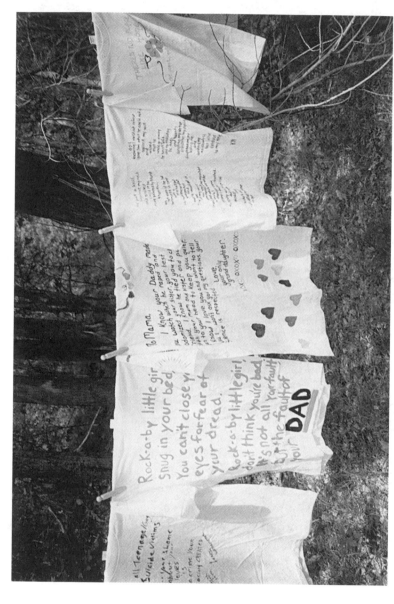

FIGURE 14-1. "At each display, women are invited to add shirts to the line, and thus the clothesline is both text and event, a witness to healing and a means of healing, a private act and a work of social activism."

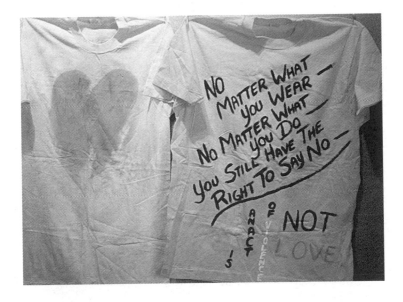

FIGURE 14-2. *"Some shirts are inscribed with letters, some scream single words, some are not verbal."*

they are hung on the clothesline together. The central design statement of the Clothesline Project, like the wall and the quilt, is the gathering of individual names or voices into a single visual metaphor. In gathering the shirts, the Clothesline Project transcends the isolation of individual experiences of violence, gathering them into a multivoiced witness to a shared cultural experience.

Those who work with the Clothesline Project speak repeatedly about the ways in which its displays accomplish personal and public healing in terms which contrast pointedly with dismissals of it as pop psychology or as an inappropriate airing of private matters of the kind dominating TV talk shows.[2] Rachel Carey-Harper (who conceived of the original Clothesline Project in 1990 while working with the Cape Cod Women's Agenda) writes that women make shirts to represent "their personal experience of violence" as well as "to celebrate their transformation from victim to survivor in a powerful statement of solidarity" (33). But more than transformation in the lives of individual women, Carey-Harper also envisions cultural transformation and global healing:

> The Clothesline Project works to reverse and transform the spiritually harmful effects of this violence on a global scale, an example of political action as sacred space. (33)

Another writer describes how the Project "extends the boundaries of healing" (Goldstein 34) in an image of global reach:

> There will be a time when our arms will be so wide that they will encircle and embrace the entire world. In this manner, we transform the places where the Clothesline is displayed into sacred space. (34)

What seems to lead both women to talk about the Project as space—and further, to reify that space as sacred—is precisely its power to heal: "The Project also speeds the healing process for the survivors of violence against women and serves to connect women across the United States and throughout the world" (Goldstein 33). Like the AIDS quilt (and unlike the Vietnam wall), the Clothesline Project is not a fixed public monument, and so its shape is constituted each time it is displayed, each display circumscribes a space, and thus its text is continually re-created and revised. Furthermore, at each display, women are invited to add shirts to the line, and thus the Clothesline Project is both text and event, a witness to healing and a means of healing, a private act and a work of social activism.

The rhetoric of the Clothesline Project assumes and asserts that healing comes in part from the *voicing* of what had been silent or silenced, or marginalized in significant ways. In a previous article, "Private Texts and Social Activism: Reading the Clothesline Project," I argue that the Clothesline Project, and the quilt and the wall, are thus unique sorts of texts. Each of them seeks to break through current discursive practices about its subject, and the ways in which each crosses or blurs traditional and expected boundaries between private and public speaking point directly to its power. In writing about his vision of a memorial for those who served in Vietnam, Jan Scruggs repeatedly insisted that the memorial, no matter what its design, not take a position about the war, not say anything political about it. He insisted it be a site for conversation and reconciliation to begin: that is, to enable the kinds of speaking about the war which, in the cultural climate at the time of the war, had not been safe or possible. The quilt, too, reconstitutes the images and stories of AIDS by reclaiming the language about AIDS and transforming it from "a single fearful view" often cast in binary opposites, to a "multivocal diversity," an "alternative heteroglossi[a] that leaves no one marginalized" (Elsley 193). Each voice speaks; each story is told on its own terms. "There are many ways to speak about AIDS," it proclaims, and "each one is valid" (193). Airing dirty laundry is, I claim, one critical way of understanding the Clothesline Project's conceptual metaphor and goes almost literally to the heart of the matter, challenging historical distinctions between what may be made public or must be kept private (i.e., silent) about women's lives. On the clothesline, each individual may, while honoring and voicing her own experience and pain, at the same time do the work of healing by placing her story in the context of and adding her voice to the larger social picture. The Clothesline Project makes room for—and invites women to create, find, or construct—a subject position alternative to what has been a dominant discourse about violence and women. By constituting space in which a woman has control over what is said and how her experience is represented, the Clothesline Project reconstructs the power relations within which the "text" of her experience is voiced. What has been spoken of only as personal is reconfigured as part of a social pattern—a socially produced conflict shared by many other women—and therefore subject to change through *collective* action. Each shirt—each individual act of "talking back," to use bell hooks's language—becomes "a gesture of defiance that heals" (9).

So what do women actually say when they choose to put themselves on the line? How do they represent themselves as victims, survivors, wounded, wounding, healing, or whole? In what ways do they represent their journeys from wounded selves to whole or healed selves, and what do they claim about the process of healing, and about the role that making and hanging the shirts plays in that process? Because issues of naming and silence, anonymity and speech, resonate in complex ways, especially for feminist theorists and activists, how may we understand the anonymity afforded by the shirts? If we are more inclined to understand it as a poignant testimony to the great risks for women in speaking openly, what implications do we see for ways women find to say what they must, and for the ways as a culture we persist in not hearing? How do the women who speak on the line negotiate and make sense of these apparent contradictions?

In writing this article, I wanted to examine the rhetoric and language of the Clothesline Project in order to see how it is that women voice themselves and their healing processes. I wanted to look more closely at what the language and images on the shirts reveal about how the women on the line see themselves and in what senses they talk about writing as healing. I especially wanted to examine the way in which the shirts refer explicitly to a movement from silence to speech, and how the Clothesline Project enacts or represents or enables that movement. In this analysis, however, I have carried an abiding worry that in writing about the shirts, I would be imposing my own voice onto the voices of the shirts, or adding another violation by presuming to analyze them. As one of the caretakers of the Mid-Michigan Clothesline Project (MMCP) has put it, "Often when I try to explain what the Project is I feel as if I am interrupting the voices on the line" (Esdale, MWSA). I remind myself that these are the problems of reading and interpreting any text; different interpretations are possible. My choice to put the texts of these shirts on the page—to talk about them at all—is, like hanging the shirts in a line for a display, necessarily an act of interpretation. So even as I have placed the shirts side by side and grouped them in order to talk about their language, as I have arranged them for this particular display, I have been reminded that these texts resist categories, and that this reading is only one among many.

Chapters of the Clothesline Project exist across the United States and in several other countries. Each chapter, although invited to register with a national office, exists more or less independently, forming mostly through the efforts of an individual who has seen the Project elsewhere, or as a result of a visit or display from a nearby chapter. Sponsorship and sources of money vary depending on the above factors. The national office has evolved hesitantly from discord among founders of the original project in Cape Cod, has sought corporate funding, and has tried to serve as a clearinghouse and point of contact for the various chapters. A newsletter has been published intermittently. Although at one time the national office distributed guidelines for creating a project (e.g., how to anchor poles in a temporary outdoor setting in order to hang the clothesline) and for publicizing and fund-raising, each chapter seems to make its own decisions about significant features of its individual project—such as whether or not to include shirts made by men, how to refer to the shirts, and when and where to display the line.

I describe the shirts of one particular chapter, the Mid-Michigan Clothesline Project. (For a history of this particular chapter, see King.) Shirts from other projects are likely to speak differently about and to the issues I examine in this study, and so it is important to emphasize that the Clothesline Project is a product of place and time, a text situated culturally and socially, voicing itself in ways that are shaped by the communities out of which it arises and to which it is connected. A chapter initiated and cared for by students on a college campus, with shirts contributed predominantly by members of campus survivor support or therapy groups, will necessarily speak with different language and in different images than one with beginnings in the church basement of a rural Midwest community. The social setting in which each project has been generated also includes a particular culture or set of practices of shirtmaking, evident most noticeably in the pieces of public rhetoric or familiar texts which appear on some of the shirts. When shirts are made at therapy groups, Take Back the Night rallies, or events for Domestic Violence Awareness Month, the language from posters, chants, and recovery group literature is also imported onto the shirts, shaping the tone and rhetoric of each Clothesline Project chapter.

This essay seeks to add to our understanding of how written language works for those who see themselves in need of healing, and how it constructs an intersection between individual healing and the social healing or transformation which is a part of it. What I find significant in this analysis of the rhetoric, the words, and the images of the Clothesline Project is the ways the shirts speak about the act of writing itself, of creating a text, which represents breaking silence, as the "official" logo of the national Clothesline Project reminds us. As all teachers of writing know, writing *is* an act of speaking out, and certain acts of speaking out can transform the world. The directive that Muriel Rukeyser gave her students and her readers about this kind of transforming speech act—"What would happen if one woman told the truth about her life? The world would split open"—is in all ways a risky one. And so I wanted to see what we could learn from texts which were created outside some of the key parameters of school writing: That is, these writings have no named authors, nor are they produced with assessment as any part of the process; in addition, a readership is not specified, and as with some but not many instances of school writing, the purposes, the audiences, and the "assignment" are not specified for the writer/creator. All that is specified is this: A woman will have complete control over her speaking, its form, its content, its audience, and its purpose, her speaking out will be protected, and her text will join others and will not stand alone.

Telling What Happened: "This is not touching. This is not poignant. This is true!" (#64)

Many of the shirts offer or reference narratives of "what happened," although it is not clear nor really possible to know how literal these are. Some seem allegorical; some, however, are journalistic and clearly verifiable, often quoting newspaper reports or headlines. The entire text of one shirt, for example, is a dated excerpt from the local newspaper; another uses the rhetoric of a police report to mark the unfolding event[3]:

> 10-22-91
> "A jobless truck driver
> who was persuaded by police officers not
> to jump off a bridge was charged Monday
> with strangling his estranged wife
> and smothering his three young daughters
> — *Lansing State Journal*   (#10)[4]

> A shirt for Suzzana. You will not be forgotten . . . March 10, 1988
> 9:00 pm . . . left my house to walk 5 blocks home, 10:35 pm . . .
> police called to inform her parents that an "incedent" happened
> 11:00 pm . . . her mother calls me to take me 5 blocks . . . to where
> she was murdered.   (from #68)

The autonomy in making her shirt gives each woman space to wrestle with naming her experience and finding language for it in her own voice and in her own way. The difficulty in giving a name to this violence is not only represented and indicated by the silences and the struggle for language on the shirts; often the reference to what happened is very brief, or elliptical:

> I've heard about it often . . .
> Rape
> . . . but it's not supposed to happen to my mom.   (#37)

> [below a drawing of a brown trick or treat bag:]
> have you ever been saved by the bell? 10-31-89   (from #77)

> Momma and Daddy—the Hutcherson Boys—
> Brian
> Basements Bedrooms Woods Blood
> Bruises Humiliation
> I survived despite what you did.   (from #82)

Telling what happened also may be a way to construct a story differentiated from the one imposed on the victim/survivor as a child. Telling her story makes tangible that difference. The "story" is often a narrative built up out of images, with very little chronology and no names.

>   a wooden spoon
> —it broke in ½
> —I fell to pieces
>   your brown leather belt
> stayed brown
> —I turned   purple, red, yellow blue
>   your big hand touched me
> —It was not gentle loving or caring
>
> Your voice hurts me "no one will love you"
>   "You're fat"
>   "your stupid"
>   "There's the door—Just leave no one wants
>   you here"
> This is what I experienced
> This is what I live with now   (from #32)

I was staring at the model airplanes
Hanging on the ceiling
I was lying on my back
on the cement basement floor
(cold as my skin)
my pants pulled down to my ankles
and I consented
and I didn't understand
There was no blood.
There was no evidence. Didn't I say yes
What's my problem?   (from #64)

In telling what happened, the shirtmaker makes clear that telling is always done within a net of relationships, sometimes indicating the ways that the violence has affected not only the victim. On the following shirt, the woman speaks out about what she knows happened, as if she were addressing her grand-mother; in doing so she also acknowledges the grandmother's need not to hear or speak about it. (See Fig. 14-1, center shirt.)

To Mama,
    I know your Daddy made you watch when he raped and sodomized your sister, your best friend. I know he tied you to chairs with your mom and sister and put a gun to your head to keep you quiet. I know I love you and want to tell you I won't ask you any questions. Your silence is respected.

Love, your only grand-daughter   (#85)

Her voiced decision to respect that need for silence is a way of claiming a bond, it seems, as well as a way of speaking out about the consequences of the violence and its contours. Clearly, telling what happened is a complex act. Like the granddaughter above, the women find ways to locate themselves in relation to the si-lences of others.

To my father,
You knew what was happening,
and still you even drove me
to his house and when I
wrote mom and told her that
Mr. Beyers held me down on
the ground with my arms pinned over my head and told me
that he *owned* me and she

– 366 –

called you and told you to keep that
man away from her daughter you said
"Yes. I think that would be a good idea."
(I listened to the call) You told me
"You can't see him anymore" and you never
apologized to me for your part or recognized
my pain and I hate you for that I hate
you for watching my abuse and ignoring it and
never considering my *pain* and *shame* and
humiliation . . .   (from #86)

A number of the shirts speak about the problem of remembering what happened — or allowing oneself to know — and then telling what has been remembered. Such a telling also needs someone who will listen or hear:

I meant to tell him to leave me alone
'cause what he was doing to me felt wrong
I meant to tell what he had done
but I didn't 'cause I had
          no one.   (from #52)

As in #85 above, a number of the shirts speak directly to the problematic intersection of speaking out and exposure, anonymity and isolation.

Now because of your choice
Is my life supposed to become
an open book? (from #93)

You told me you would kill me
You broke into my house
So I wouldn't testify
You told me you wouldn't
go to jail
and you were right.
I HATE you for the things   NO!
you did to me
I still can't tell anyone everything
And for the things you will do to others
because you are not in jail.   (from #91)

The shirts also frequently reference the inadequacy of language itself to tell what happened, or question the efficacy of telling:

I could fill this shirt with words and it still
won't go away but it feels good to share
I was raped
I couldn't make a pretty shirt—pain is
neither romantic nor pretty
How many times have you heard this story?

(from #62)

Of course this is fragmented
my life was fragmented
I've just put the pieces back together   (from #64)

WHAT CAN YOU SAY WHEN THE STREETS RUN
       WITH BLOOD?   (from #68)

I can't put into words
how much my life changed
after that night   (from #92)

The Wounded Self: "Shattered soul, closed to wonder" (#26)

The wounded selves on these shirts are haunted by memories,
living with shame, often with silence. They speak of dirty selves,
divided selves, hidden selves, and broken bodies. Many, like #92
excerpted above, speak of themselves as forever changed, having
lost something they see as irretrievable.

I am incubating a memory
A secret so foul and dread I
keep it hidden even from myself;
Within a shell of amnesia
But the stench of the shell's contents
Permeates my life . . .   (from #80)

Blood seeping from blood
I am wounded.
covered by breath I scream
In dream state I break free
but I leave behind my body
for you to condemn
my outer shell torn to shreds   (from #93)

Should I bow my head in shame or
should I try my
hardest to hold my
head up high and be
proud no matter how
difficult it gets. You
made me doubt who I
am. You the man whose
face I can no longer
remember took away
[back:] a big part of me
when you penetrated
me you penetrated my
heart, mind, and soul
You made me feel
dirty and now
nobody can erase that
feeling or memory.
It will always
haunt me.   (from #94)

and everyone, even the clerk at
the grocery store, sees my *shame* which
is with me still and
I DO NOT FORGIVE YOU
and never will   (from #86)

. . . they were sentenced to 2
months in jail. I
was sentenced to
a lifetime of
memories . . .
. . . I can never look
at a man anymore
without thinking,
that maybe, he & I,
might end up together,
where he can hurt
me . . .
. . . Sometimes I get
so sad, that I can't
even cry . . .   (from #113)

As information about how survivors of violence and abuse experience themselves, none of this is new or surprising. It is important to listen to not only how each woman sees herself, but also how each woman, at the point at which she has chosen to put herself on the line, situates that woundedness within a journey.

> For years I couldn't find the words. I blocked my feelings and my memories. I blamed myself for everything that went wrong. I was the class clown always desperate for attention and never understanding why—now I understand—*I remember Everything* and I want to hear, but all I hear is your voice telling me I'm evil—that this torment and pain is love—that no one will ever love me like you do—that love = death. I believed you—I was five—what else would I believe? And I took that voice as my own into all my abusive relationships. I thought that was all there was—I thought it was natural for men to hurt me. And when I was gang raped in college I believed their words over my own—when they said "Why does this always hurt you?" I searched for the reasons instead of pressing charges for this I blame you and I want you to know [reverse:] That I will not let you win—you will not destroy me. Somehow I will find a way to heal—to reclaim the hope you stole from me when I was just a baby . . .   (from #116)

> [written inside an image of wings]
> the angels kept me alive for
> a reason when I wanted to let go because
> death was the only way I knew how to say no—we wrestled
> The angels and I. But I didn't want to win. I only knew
> how to loose—I had lost to the angry words & the knife &
> the gun & the penis & the drugs AND EVEN WHEN HE WENT
> AWAY I FELT LOST
> I felt lost with a longing
> always reaching for the something missing   (from #101)

> The scars   The pieces   the pain
> no Love unable to love . . . For now (Hopefully)   (from #32)

On these shirts, the journey is represented as focusing on hope, or on searching for something missing, or at times on the reconstruction of a world view different from the one that was authored by the perpetrator, or one which made violence acceptable.

Speaking Back: "To my rapist—" (#72)

Often the shirts address the perpetrator, as if asserting a nonvictimized self is most powerfully—or necessarily—accomplished by speaking to the perpetrator himself.[5] On some, it seems the woman addresses the perpetrator in order to wonder about motivation and satisfaction, and about the inner life and logic of the perpetrator.

> What did you experience all those years ago . . .
> How do you live with yourself now?
>> (from #32)

> Was it worth it?
> I sure as hell hope so.   (from #26)

On some, speaking to the perpetrator—addressing the person directly—is clearly an act of speaking out and fighting back.

> If you *must*
> Take control
> Take control of
>> Yourself!   (from #2)

In a sense, this text represents an act of revision, re-imagining and re-scripting the interaction to which it refers, re-naming the issue at the heart of the matter. When the shirtmaker speaks directly to the perpetrator, whether dead or alive, it often seems a way to distance herself from the victimized self, and to describe and claim a self moving into a new, healed or whole state.

> This time I stood staring at you
> stunned with disbelief at what I see;
> your lifeless body in front of me
> I feel so confused and my eyes start to tear
> with tears of relief instead of fear
> No more secrets to hide what you've done
> I stand here firm, I will not run!
> Later today when they bury you
> I'll have something to bury, too
> The guilt and shame that I have carried today
> with your body will be buried.
> [reverse side:]
> I stand by your grave without
> guilt or blame
> Your life is over: mine will never be the same
> Yet I'll return to your grave before I'm through
> for I have pain that belongs to you
> So timely and symbolic the battle I've won

> Your life has ended Mine has just begun   (#42)

There is often a distinct tone of defiance on many of these shirts, as if speaking out is allied with speaking back. In the series of assertions with which the following ends, for instance, the shirtmaker keeps revising her language, as if to cover as many possibilities as she can imagine:

> The memory does not come easy
> it comes with screams
> that will not stop
> it comes with tears and terror
> it comes with shame that i felt this,
> shame that i feel this
> The memory does not come easy
> I tell you because I know
> I tell you because I will not be silent
> I tell you because I will not be
> silenced.   (#57)

In these shirts, the women assert a different reality, an interpretation of events, motives, emotions, consequences, and rights other than the ones asserted by their perpetrators.

> I know
> Now you
> were not
> friend.
> You seduced me with
> unasked for touch.
> you intimidated
> then terrorized
> me with your words
> and actions
> you exploited
> my trust.
> You had the
> power then
> I take back
> my power now!   (#81)

> I will dance
> again, but not
> your dance!
> I will dance gently with my sisters.
>   (from #102)

On the shirts, these women are able to re-see and revise their experience; they seem to see that language can be amended to re-shape experience. In each of the three shirts above, the final lines repeat a key term, recasting it, re-naming it. In #57, the speaker will be neither the agent nor the object of silence. In #81, power belongs to "you," then is reclaimed by the speaker. And in #102, the speaker's dance brackets, and thus subdues, the one imposed by her perpetrator. Indeed, as shirt #81 shows, whereas language was once used to intimidate and terrorize—to shape experience one way—now it may be used to claim the power to name and to shape, to be in the present, to assert a future.

Claiming Wholeness: "Someday when the shell cracks, I shall clean out the foulness and air out my soul" (#80)

The overwhelming sense on most of the shirts is of women trying to find a way to move from woundedness toward some vision of healing. It is possible in the following, for instance, to hear the shirtmaker talking to herself, catching herself, and countering herself with a directive she is still learning. It is also possible to hear it as the shirtmaker interrupting another woman, asserting and thereby perhaps teaching her an alternative way of being:

> If I was aware . . .
> If I wasn't there . . .
> Stop!!
> You don't have to be a victim   (#1)

> Memory/sensations of violating intrusions
> Between my legs, of blows about the head.
> The Brain has blocked but the Body
>   REMEMBERS
> And someday when the shell cracks, I shall clean
> out the foulness and air out my soul.   (from #80)

> Praying now to the angels that kept me alive for a reason
> that they might also
> fire my passion to
> burn clean now
> until the pleasure

comes in peace
and not in pain
and becomes not the enemy
(from #101)

Often on the shirts there is a powerful sense that the speech
act initiates the ability to imagine enacting a different future. In
the following, the speaker, "K," identifies herself, then juxtaposes
a statement about herself in the present tense with a statement
about her future:

Dear Daddy:
I am your beautiful
grown-up daughter!
Now I choose men who
treat me the way you did, and
the way you treated my mother.
For your future grandchildren
I will break the cycle!
I love you,
K.   (#106)

If this were not hanging on the clothesline, its meaning would be
quite ambiguous. It almost sounds like a sweet affirmation; it is
certainly not clear at all what actions are referred to when the
speaker describes men "who treat me the way you did and the way
you treated my mother." Read in the context of the Clothesline
Project, however, it becomes ominously unspecified, and only the
phrase "break the cycle" signals that this may be about abuse in
any way. "Daddy" has treated the speaker and her mother in ways
that the speaker continues to experience through her choice of relationships; the projected future and the changed self are ones in
which "K" claims the ability to act. She is the agent of that change,
and of that healing.

On the following shirt, the speaker is positioned within a tension: She is able to name and project a healed self—a state of "innocence"—and says she wants to "claim" it as her own, but she
is not yet able to:

The innocence you say is mine
I want so bad to claim
But in order to have room for it
I must resolve my blame.
(from #49)[6]

The ways in which the healed self is represented on these shirts is asserted most consistently with proprietary claims.

> This is my body
> This is my space   (from #2)

They speak about "taking back my life" (#109) or needing to "reclaim my life" (#112). Some seem to be taking inventory:

> I have strength
> I have control
> I have self-esteem
> I have Power
>
>   (#9)

> From the ashes
>   I am rising
> From the darkness
>   I emerge
> I take with me
>   knowledge and power
> And leave behind
>   the blame.
>   This one is for me.
>   (#108)

It is on the shirts which imagine and depict a healed self that a process of healing is most rhetorically visible, as they linguistically move from the past to the future. Over and over in these shirts, the moment of speaking is one which both asserts a healed self and represents a speaking self in the process of moving toward that state. At times, the use of present tense seems to suggest that healing is happening in the moment of speaking:

> I am so scared
>   and the
> memories come fast
>   and I
> can't claim them
>   and I
> cry in pain but
> no one hears and I
> am alone help me please
> I need you but the distance consumes
> me and my soul longs for flight

and it goes on and on please
                make it *stop*

back: I can not let them
destroy me I must
reclaim my life and
I fight and fight the darkness
for a way back from this hell
I need to love, trust
                live
They will not win
I will become whole again
Together we can find the way.
                                (#112)

    Asserting a different kind of future and an active self seems
to change the present even in the act of speaking.

Been through hell
and halfway back again
I will not quit
I will get out
I am getting out   (from #105)

April 10, 1984
You took me
—my lover
in the middle of the night—
in a foreign country and
_____^{7} me FOREVER!
You KIDNAPPED me
You TERRORIZED me
You RAPED me
But . . . I survived!
And I am taking back my life.
And I will forever remember.
And I will forever be strong.

Because . . . I am a
strong   brave
honest _____ _____
_____ _____   SURVIVOR!
                            (#109)

This text begins by addressing the perpetrator, telling what happened and when, and interpreting the event(s) in a way that al-

lows her to move to the middle line: "But . . . I survived!" This is a statement about her present; she talks about the process of "taking back" her life, a process she is in the midst of as she speaks, and then envisions the future where she "will forever be strong," which somehow enables her to come back to present tense to assert that she is "strong" *now*.

The language on these shirts over and over depicts rebirth or the creation of a new self, and in this creation, the speaker herself is the active agent:

> I have replaced what
> they took with a
> more beautiful, durable,
> 'take time to smell
> the roses' ME. (from #113)

This self-creation is also often done in the company of others—almost always other women, almost always called "sisters." In these scenarios and metaphors, the future and the healing include collaboration with others. In the following, for instance, the surviving self is washed clean of the wounding and can thus give hope to her children.

> I will forever live to wash away your words of hate, the words
> you brainwashed me with.
> My life will be a testimony to my children of strength and hope.
> (from #79)

Often the acts of creating a different self and a different future are claimed to be for others, for children, sisters, or other women. In the following, for example, these all come together, although the speaker visibly hesitates before articulating the future she might be able to bring about with the act she cannot yet quite name:

> I will not let you win—you will not destroy me. Somehow I
> will find a way to heal—to reclaim the hope you stole from
> me when I was just a baby and my love was so complete and
> trusting. I will come together with my SISTERS to fight for
> other children, other women, so their cries do not go unheard
> as mine were. And one day, maybe, maybe . . . My little girl will
> finally be FREE to play and trust and love again.
> (from #116)

Whether in this text "my little girl" is understood to refer to the writer's own self, as the child she once was—a reading which only occurred to me as I listened to others talk about the text of this shirt—or to the writer's biological child, she is nonetheless imagining a future in which a different scenario is possible.

Providing a Safe Space for Speaking Out: "I tell you this because I will not be silenced" (#57)

Each shirt is a voice, a story. Each act of making a shirt is an act of re-presenting a voice and a body. Radka Donnell, in what she calls a "quilt poetics," writes about the ways in which cloth references "the person as a body and the body of a person" (116–17). Clothing is that which caresses with its intimate touch, as well as that which stands for the disembodied self, a sign of the body as object. One way for a woman survivor of violence to begin reclaiming the language of the body is to have the body speak in her own voice, reinscribing the body with stories of her own making.

From the shirts on the line, we learn that the wounded self is isolated, and in the grip of others' interpretive story lines. She has managed to voice what has been seen or felt to be inaccessible, self-referenced, inappropriate, or singular and isolated. The healed self is surviving, and sees survival as a way to counter the assault. She speaks out and speaks back, uses assertions and commands, is connected to others whom she perceives to be vulnerable like her, is active on her own behalf and sometimes on behalf of others. She speaks to the perpetrators of violence and to other victims, others like herself. She envisions, voices, and dreams about a world where violence does not happen.

Attending closely to the language of the shirts on the clothesline suggests, among other things, that the move from private language into public discourse is seen by many of the shirtmakers as an act of healing. This need to speak out is voiced on the shirts most often as an individual need. Rarely on individual shirts is there a mention that it will join others in the collection that is the Clothesline Project, although they do reference other women: sisters, family members, friends, women they read about in the newspaper, women in therapy groups. While the individual shirts speak repeatedly about the necessity—as well as the dangers and difficulties—of speaking out, those who view or only hear about the Clothesline Project often question the efficacy of the Project, asking, "What good does it do?" Sometimes it is a question about how speaking out "helps" the individual women who make their shirts and speak their truths, but often it is a question about social or global change. One woman who has viewed the MMCP more than once writes,

> there are other voices in me. one says that the project is an incredible witness to women's strength and isn't it great that some of them have found this space to speak. and then this other voice says, well, there's the vietnam wall and the aids quilt and the clothesline, but there's still war and aids and violence against women so . . . what's the point. (Gelbart)[8]

Those who care for the Clothesline Project, however, speak more about creating and protecting the space in which the voices are heard, space to share stories, to join with other women, to image the size of the problem, to draw courage from numbers, and to give each woman what she has not had. Writes one caretaker of the MMCP:

> It is not enough for us to drown in statistics, in theories and psychological hypotheses about such violence, to talk battered women's syndrome, institutional oppression, origins of patriarchy, campus safety issues; we must hear women's voices and know that they are ours. We must never forget, for every statistic, for every theory, a woman, a life. (Cairns)

And another:

> The CP for me has always been . . . [a] place where women can come together in support of one another. A place where women's everyday experiences are validated. A place where women can reclaim themselves and lay shame to rest. The shirts embrace each other and the women who come close to listen.
>
> It isn't like the CP and other "women's only" type spaces were just *there* for women. We have had to fight to secure these spaces for ourselves. (Esdale, MWSA)

My study of the rhetoric of, on, and about the Clothesline Project suggests that it is the way the Project creates a radical intersection between public and private speaking, between individual witness and collective transformation, and the ways in which individual identity is both absorbed and yet preserved, which is the site of the dynamic tension of the Project. Those who create their shirts speak as individuals (and in doing so may represent themselves in a social context or identify themselves as part of a group, be it as survivors, victims, or women). Those who view or read the Project are the audience, removed from the production of text in one sense, drawn into it in another, their questions perhaps heard as attempts to traverse that separation. It is those who care for the shirts and the Clothesline who most vividly and concretely bridge that space between author and reader, speaker and audience, by stringing the shirts together, holding the line, often helping to hang the shirts with their makers, listening to, monitoring, and answering questions from those who view it. From their words, their own speaking, pondering, theorizing, their passionate commitments, we hear something slightly different. It is the caretakers who over and over see and hear the shirts as they hang them, who in repeatedly juxtaposing them hear echoes and threads, and who outline and create that space in which the voices of the women's shirts may be heard together.

The caretakers of the Clothesline Project repeatedly talk about not interfering with or distorting what the shirts say, even for instance in refusing to display the project in spaces which do not allow for both sides of the shirts to be seen and read, or where they have been asked to choose for display only shirts that aren't offensive or disturbing. They talk about letting shirts speak for themselves.

> The shirts are a collection of women's voices and experiences which relay messages so strong that whenever I try to speak about the CP my initial reaction is to clam up because I feel that the shirts speak for themselves. Often when I try to explain what the Project is I feel as if I am interrupting the voices on the line. (Esdale, MWSA)

And in fact, they have been adamant about also insisting that they do not "make" the space for the women, but rather protect it. In an ongoing conversation about the protectiveness felt by the caretakers for the "women on the line," one member of the Mid-Michigan Clothesline Project wrote:

> i cannot effectively articulate how invaded i feel when men are even close to the shirts. and at one display when a man marched right up to a basket of shirts and began hanging them i felt so violated. i do feel that it is important for men to see the project, however, i want them to keep their hands off of the shirts. (Esdale, Personal electronic communication)

And in the following, another caretaker of the MMCP testifies to her sense of the interwoven strands of individual and communal, body and shirt, shirt and woman, brokenness and wholeness, which is the tapestry of the Clothesline Project:

> As a caretaker, I feel that displaying the shirts is freeing the women and sharing their stories all over again. Every shirt is a woman and she is alive and before your eyes. She is not a statistic sitting lifelessly on a page in black and white. She is here, almost in the flesh standing with hundreds of other women together. People viewing the Project cannot ignore or deny violence in women's lives when an army of women is in front of their faces. . . . The shirts come to life and I am her or she is all of us, and I can feel and see and sense everything she is describing. In certain moments all I can feel is the torture and abuse and killing of women and girls. I feel as if I constantly watch a part of each woman die. But the part that remains most powerful is the strength and courage of every woman on the line. Walking down the line is a true testament to what all women face every day, and more amazingly how we all survive it. Beyond her pain and shame are messages of rebirth and resolve to continue building where she was destroyed or torn apart. (Hauze)

The individual need to remember, the difficulty in remembering, the need to counter cultural denial and amnesia—all these impulses are evident in the Clothesline Project as a design statement which gathers and makes space for the many. As such, it is a statement against the depersonalizing impulse of traditional public monuments in which one representational figure stands for the many. Acts of witnessing such as these—like the reading of names at each display of the AIDS quilt, like the ringing of bells at each display of the Clothesline Project to signify how often a woman is raped or assaulted, like the "¡presente!" cried after the name of each Latin American *desparacido* read aloud—have become recognized in the late twentieth century as necessary in order to sustain public awareness and public memory. In part because of this need to bear witness, we see the emergence of new forms of public speaking and their recognition as significant works of social action and public art. The Clothesline Project is thus one of a growing number of texts which blur traditional boundaries between public and private speaking, and enable us to talk in new ways about the efficacy of language to heal. To those who ask how this particular rhetorical strategy "helps," one of the shirts replies:

> We have to tell the truth. We have to hear the truth
> We can't solve problems we can't hear.
> All I can tell you is that together we learned to support each other.
> Tell the truth.
> Keep breathing.   (from #88)

In writing this article, I am indebted to the following women for their questions, responses, and commitments: Julie Bevins, Amy Gilmore Cairns, Celia Esdale, Suzanne Gagne, Kimberly Hauze, Malika King, Colleen Tremente, and Elaine Yakura.

Notes

1. At every display of the Clothesline Project, space and materials are offered for women to make shirts on site. Often the shirts are created in private, but just as often, especially at outdoor displays, they are created in the open, among a circle of women, both those on the line and those caretakers and others sitting around in the middle of the display. These shirts are usually completed and hung for the first time during that display.

2. I am referring here not to published critiques of the Clothesline Project but to the accumulated experience of caretakers of the Mid-Michigan Clothesline Project, at displays of their own Project and at other regional displays, conferences, presentations, workshops, and

talks in which they have taken part. Among the themes that have emerged from the MMCP's habit of reflecting upon and theorizing from their experience—documented in archival material being collected by the Michigan State University Library's Special Collections—are repeated comments and questions about the educative function of the display, the usefulness of displaying violence, whether the Project isn't more self-referential whining than something positive. Caretakers of the MMCP report that these comments and questions come generally but not exclusively from those who have not spent time at a display.

3. Numbers refer to shirts in the Mid-Michigan Clothesline Project. Each shirt is given a number when it is first hung on the line. The number, date of inclusion in the Project, and the full text, including notations about colors, graphics, and the part of the shirt on which the text appears, are recorded in the MMCP's archives, compiled and preserved by its current caretakers. Although the shirts are different colors and a color scheme for the kind of violence represented on the shirts is suggested, not all shirtmakers adhere to the scheme, and it is not possible to "verify" that the shirtmaker chose the color of the shirt to correspond to the scheme.

4. I have endeavored to reproduce as closely as possible the texts of the shirts, preserving spelling, punctuation, capitalization, line breaks, and the visual arrangement of lines in relation to one another. When I have reproduced only a portion of the text of a shirt, other than in subheadings, I have indicated so in the citation, *not* with ellipses; any ellipses in these texts appear in the originals.

5. When perpetrators are named or referenced on the shirts in the Mid-Michigan Clothesline Project, they are almost always male.

6. This exact text also appears on shirt #34 in the Mid-Michigan Clothesline Project. For neither is a date recorded indicating when it was made, and no other text appears on either shirt. I note all this because I have not been able to find a public or already-published source for the text of these shirts and have no way of explaining the repetition.

7. Blank lines refer to segments of the texts that are not readable due to degradation of the materials, in this case ink which has disappeared.

8. When I quote women who work and speak as caretakers of the MMCP, I have used the names by which they call themselves and are known. When I refer to and quote women who have viewed a display of the MMCP or have made shirts for the MMCP, I have used pseudonyms.

Works Cited

Cairns, Amy Gilmore. "Mid-Michigan Clothesline Project Roundtable: Surviving Violence." Michigan Women's Studies Annual Conference, East Lansing, 8 April 1995.

Carey-Harper, Rachel. "The Clothesline Project: Bearing Witness to Violence against Women." *Woman of Power* (Winter 1994): 33.

Donnell, Radka. *Quilts as Women's Art: A Quilt Poetics.* North Vancouver, B.C.: Gallerie Publications, 1990.

Elsley, Judy. "The Rhetoric of the NAMES Project AIDS Quilt: Reading the Text(ile)." *AIDS: The Literary Response.* Ed. Emmanuel S. Nelson. New York: Twayne, 1992. 187–96.

Esdale, Celia. "Mid-Michigan Clothesline Project Roundtable: Surviving Violence." Michigan Women's Studies Annual Conference, East Lansing, 8 April 1995.

———. Personal electronic communication. 27 February 1995.

Gelbart, Janine. [Pseudonym]. Personal electronic communication. 11 February 1997.

Goldstein, Honora. "The Clothesline Project National Network." *Woman of Power* (Winter 1994): 33–34.

Hauze, Kimberly. "Mid-Michigan Clothesline Project Roundtable: Surviving Violence." Michigan Women's Studies Annual Conference, East Lansing, 8 April 1995.

hooks, bell. *Talking Back: Thinking Feminist, Thinking Black.* Boston: South End, 1989.

Julier, Laura. "Private Texts and Social Activism: Reading the Clothesline Project." *English Education* 26.4 (1994): 249–59.

King, Malika. "From Darkness into Light: A Clothesline Project Chronology." *Re-visions: Journal of the Women's Studies Program at Michigan State University* 8 (1995): 28–31.

Rukeyser, Muriel. "Käthe Kollwitz." *A Muriel Rukeyser Reader* Ed. Jan Heller Levi. New York: Norton, 1994. 217.

Scruggs, Jan C., and Joel L. Swerdlow. *To Heal a Nation: The Vietnam Veterans Memorial.* New York: Harper, 1985.

CHAPTER FIFTEEN

"The More I Tell My Story"

Writing as Healing in an HIV/AIDS Community

EMILY NYE

New Mexico Institute of Mining and Technology

What is the usefulness of our thoughts and our theories? What is their reach toward students in classrooms, toward students whose differences from one another and from us test the comprehensiveness and humanity of any thoughts we think, any theories we manage to construct? . . . Questions that open to voices not yet heard in our academic conversations test far more than our capacity to hear: they test more critically how we live in the world with others. (Robinson 5)

Early in the psychologist Carl Rogers's career, he observed that as he broached particular issues in therapy and classwork, his patients seemed to pick up intuitive signals that he was ready to help them. In the same way, early in my career I found myself asking questions about my work and personal interests. As I became more comfortable with and knowledgeable of the importance of writing as a personal outlet and means of expression, students and colleagues approached me with incidental confessions about how journal writing had helped them through various hardships. The dialogue became increasingly familiar to me. Yet the thoughts and theories I pondered had not yet been spoken in academic conversations.

At some point, I reconsidered a telephone conversation that had haunted me for several years. One of my girlhood friends had called from New Mexico with the news that her father had just died of AIDS. In addition to the shock of the news, a nagging worry hit me. Mary and I share many parallels in our lives; one is the fact that I also have gay family members who might be at risk for AIDS. That was the first time that an AIDS death reached close to home, although now there are many more. The impact of AIDS was evident in the gay community of Denver, where I was living at the time, and in the mainstream Denver community as well. Representations like the AIDS quilt and movies and books drew my attention and interest and led me to the study of writing and AIDS. Personal experience (including my observations of and commitment to work with the gay community) combined with a more political motivation, to help people find their voices in writing and "speak" out. Robinson's test of "how we live in the world with others" was, for me, personal, political, and professional, resulting in a project inscribed with personal relevance, as well as academic interest.

After a lengthy search, I found two AIDS groups to work with in Denver, Colorado. One was the Caring Center, part of the Denver Nursing Project in Human Caring. I volunteered at the center for seven months, and worked with a writing group for six weeks in the winter of 1994. I also ran a daylong writing group at the center in April. In addition, I volunteered for the same length of time at Our House, an independent boarding house for people with AIDS, though I did not work with writers there. I needed to immerse myself in the subject I was studying, to make it familiar and understand as much as I could about what living with AIDS meant. Only then could I observe how the added factor of writing affected people's lives.

Writing about AIDS

Much has been written by and about people with AIDS. In an article entitled "Testimony," Timothy Murphy examines the pros and cons of narratives about people with AIDS. These narratives praise the dead, conveying the idea that those who die from AIDS deserve better than silence. Murphy writes, "The personal narratives of those dead and dying of AIDS may have ultimate designs on social reformation and medical advance, but they all begin as the story of an individual life" (319). The act of writing and the writing produced are ways "to resist the absurdity of suffering and death" (316–17). Such narratives help interpret the meaning of a person's life.

But writing about AIDS is not just eulogy. "I gradually found my way out of my screaming room by sorting out and writing down all that happened to us," writes Barbara Peabody in *The Screaming Room,* the narrative of her son's death (253). In *Borrowed Time,* Paul Monette wrote "to offer a small measure of power over the nightmare" (178). Monette's other recent works, *Becoming a Man* (nonfiction) and *Halfway Home* (fiction) give readers insight on living with AIDS. Elizabeth Cox wrote *Thanksgiving,* the account of her husband's death, to help her make sense of what she could not explain. She also wrote to help overcome social indifference to and ignorance of AIDS. Andrew Holleran, in *Ground Zero,* is critical of writing about AIDS. He writes that "the act of writing seemed no help whatsoever. The only conceivable function of writing about It seemed to be to relieve the writer's own anxiety and depression; but who needed that?" (16). Murphy, on the other hand, favors writing about AIDS, calling it "a necessary voice and one that has moral import even where it reveals only the homely truths that we deserve better than we get, that we mourn more than the world can know, that we are each other's only refuge" (319).

Scholars and students from across disciplines are contributing to the theoretical literature about AIDS (McMillen). Simon Watney, in his book *Practices of Freedom: Selected Writings on HIV/AIDS,* argues that many narratives are extreme and overdone, and stratify the concept of "victim" who is either innocent or guilty. Such narratives do not enlighten the public; rather, they contribute to stereotypes and prejudices. Scholars like Douglas Crimp (*AIDS: Cultural Analysis/Cultural Activism*) and Watney focus on examining narratives associated with AIDS. Watney is critical of many narratives, such as some of Randy Shilts's work, claiming that some writing does not contribute to a wider understanding. Some narratives are, according to Watney, "emblematic. . . . They condense together strands of fact and fantasy, in such a way that they come to represent what people often think of automatically as both typical, and truthful" (in McMillen A20). Watney believes that analyzing narratives and other representations of AIDS can be useful, but such scholarship has its limits. It may, in fact, become a dangerous kind of voyeurism. Other new theorists, such as Daniel Harris, believe that "AIDS theory" serves to "ghettoize the American university." Academic AIDS theory, he maintains, "promotes the illusion that American intellectuals are engaged with social issues—without really requiring engagement" (McMillen A20). From my standpoint as a composition teacher and writing group facilitator, the act of writing about AIDS does constitute engagement. But the writing group facilitator must be committed to serving the group and to engaging with the people involved and the stories expressed.

While I was interested in reading what professional writers were publishing on their AIDS experiences and what critics were saying about those publications, I was even more interested in what "nonprofessional" writers were writing. These were the people with whom I would be dealing. My work with students and nonprofessional writers revealed that often these individuals had the most pressing stories to tell, and they often found creative, albeit roughcut, ways to express themselves. One published collection by non-professional writers was *Unending Dialogue: Voices from an AIDS Poetry Workshop,* which was compiled by poet Rachel Hadas. Hadas facilitated a poetry writing workshop under the auspices of the Gay Men's Health Crisis in New York City in 1990. Hadas cited the Italian writer and social critic, Primo Levi, who sounds a bit like Paulo Freire when he says: "one can and must communicate, and thereby contribute in a useful and easy way to the peace of others and oneself, because silence, the absence of signals, is itself a signal" (in Hadas 109). Hadas calls for "the courage to fill the white sheet; if we can do that, then the harsh mirror will give us back something" (110). The men she worked with created and revised stunning and polished poems. The writers in her group capture the anguish of AIDS. Many examples show use of symbolism and attention to meter as well as format and line arrangement:

> The secrets of war—a love willing to die for—music and
> media conspire to seal a kiss with pictured victory in
> another land.

The words, I love you, spoken in the youthful voices of the
stars, and music, masterful as a modern symphony in
imageland's perpetual moment, emerge as drama and release.
Memory flies in space ships, off to save another day.

JAMES TURCOTTE (HADAS 45)

Hadas also includes poems she wrote in response to the workshop
experience. Hadas's work reveals the composition of masterful
poetry; but the polished nature of the writing seems to have dulled
the poetry's impact on the reader. Her belles-lettres approach
lacks a more complex understanding of the many layers of AIDS
discourse, politics, and psychology. Still, I appreciate Hadas's efforts, and particularly her concern that people with AIDS speak
out. If AIDS is a language, she says:

> we are tragically far from running out of speakers. . . .
> Not the paucity of speakers, but the multitude of sufferers
> threatens and overwhelms everyone with silence, and it is this
> threat that I am concerned to combat. (119)

Equally compelling evidence of writing with AIDS patients is
seen in less well-endowed publications. I was impressed by the
numerous lower-cost newsletters and leaflets which many AIDS
organizations produce, such as Irene Borger's ongoing writer's
workshop at the Los Angeles AIDS Project. While the language
is not as well-sculpted as that of Hadas's writing group, I was
more powerfully moved by these "rougher" publications, which
illuminated the economic and social differences of various communities of AIDS writers.

Throughout AIDS organizations and support groups, the literacy and education levels of writers vary, but people still write.
In "The Phoenix," a newsletter for Continuum, an AIDS group in
San Francisco, the poems are shorter, and with simpler sentence
structure and vocabulary. There is a different self-consciousness,
and less of a belles-lettres effect:

> But as I am moved by
> my brave friends who seek to make
> Their final voyage
> Clean and easy,
> Still I am not comforted.

When I have felt like this I used to
Laugh at my tears and mutter
"Back to Philosophy:"
But in my deepest meditation,
Still a voice within me insists:
Fuck it. I think AIDS is
awful.

DOSSIE EASTON

Perhaps it isn't fair to compare different collections; yet it is significant that Continuum, which services a population of drug
users as well as gay men, photocopies and staples its publication
while the Hadas collection is a paperback published by a major
Boston publishing house.

Preliminary reading, interviews, and observations led me
to see the complexity of studying writing as healing, especially
within the AIDS community. Professional writers, as well as many
teachers, understand what Robert Coles calls "the call of stories"
or the impulse to express oneself in words. Writers like Hadas
are concerned with an aesthetic experience of writing. I take the
idea of writing and AIDS in a different direction, to examine what
the writers' words mean to them, and I read *in* the word "heal" as
a possible outcome. Some of the published narratives I have mentioned, such as Peabody's *The Screaming Room*, and Holleran's
Ground Zero, also suggest that healing occurs through writing.
In the pages that follow, I will show how both the process and
product of writing do in fact correlate with a notion of health for
the people with whom I worked.

Writing and Healing: Toward a Definition

Educational psychologist Jerome Bruner studied works of literature to understand the psychological role of narratives, or stories, on human consciousness. He claimed that literature, viewed
as art, opens individuals to solving dilemmas, to the hypothetical,
and to a range of possible worlds. Those who tell stories experience the power of structuring perceptual experiences and organizing memory. The products of written discourse, texts, are
affected and constructed by culture. Thus, the narratives we tell

come to stand for more than just an individual's story. Ultimately, according to Bruner, narratives join the writer to "possible worlds that provide the landscape for thinking about the human condition" (128).

Indeed, every narrative told constructs a world of its own. I compare Bruner's "landscape" with a more theatrical metaphor, a backdrop, or setting of a play. As I tell the narrative of, say, my Aunt Edna, other stories unravel. I see my mother's older sister; an immigrant family in Manhattan; Grandfather Moishe, a tailor who really wanted to be a rabbi. Others may read this story and recognize parts of their own landscape or backdrop. They may connect my Aunt Edna to their Aunt Edna, or Tia Rosa, or Cousin Hosei. In addition to the details of these narratives, themes emerge: love and devotion to family, exile from homeland, religious and cultural discord. Such narrative linkages connect people and help explain our experiences. They help us to reconstitute ourselves as part of the larger humanity and restore us to "health," which can best be defined as both a personal and collective or communal wholeness.

In the field of education, increasing interest has been focused on the power of narrative in human lives. *Stories Lives Tell: Narrative and Dialogue in Education,* edited by Carol Witherell and Nel Noddings, focuses on the self-constructive and healing effects of narrative. The collection includes essays by scholars in education and other disciplines, such as anthropology and composition. These essays reflect the growing trend of exploring the narratives of our lives and explain how we can use narrative to teach others and to learn about ourselves. "Stories invite us to come to know the world and our place in it," write Witherell and Noddings (13). Narrative asks us to consider what we know and whom and what we care about:

> Through telling, writing, reading, and listening to life stories—one's own and others'—those engaged in this work can penetrate cultural barriers, discover the power of the self and integrity of the other, and deepen their understanding of their respective histories and possibilities. (4)

According to education scholar JoAnn Cooper, who has studied the effects of journal and diary writing, listening to our stories helps us "to nourish, encourage, and sustain ourselves, to enter into a caring relation with all the parts of ourselves" (97). Through writing, we "receive ourselves, our feeling, our beliefs" and we hear our own voices as they tell our stories in ways that help us grow (105):

> As chroniclers of our own stories, we write to create ourselves, to give voice to our experiences, to learn who we are and where we have been. Our diaries become the stories of our journeys through life, stories that are both instructive and transforming in the telling and listening. These stories, these myriad voices, then serve to instruct and transform society, to add to the collective voice we call culture. Diarists, then, both as researchers and research subjects, begin to heal themselves and the split society has created between subject and object. (111)

This split is an example of what keeps us from being whole, from "health." It is useful for writers to become or own themselves as both the subject of their writing, as well as the object of examination. Maxine Greene points out that writers, along with other expressive artists, open new ways of seeing that blur the boundaries of subject and object. The result is an intersubjectivity that brings people together so that they may "invent projects for transformation, for re-invention of some aspect of the world" (242). We may remake a world without a crippling pain or scar. We may write ourselves into a story where we once were absent.

Barbara Myerhoff and Deena Metzger view journal writing as an opportunity "for reflection and reflexiveness. As such, it is at once a journey and a record, an activity and a genre" (342). In journal writing, the writer observes the self, sees it, shapes it, and "acquires self-knowledge by beholding the self at a little distance" (348). Such self-reflection through journal writing does for us now "what ritual and myth once did for others. It is the liminal genre, without conventions, limits, or boundaries, used to travel into liminality where the unknown parts of self and the environment are glimpsed. Journals allow one to construct a self, with a cogent design, a set of symbols, a history" (351). Journal writing enables writers to hold on to some core of self, and keep at bay triviality, anonymity and madness (353). Such writing helps make sense of experience and "may serve as a basic healing activity. The healing process for the poet is not involved in the cultural accomplishments of the poem. It is in the reflexive aspect of art that self is constructed" (354). This constructed self mirrors one's experience, yet is also a powerful step into claiming and crafting a voice for the future.

In medicine, the importance of narrative is argued by nursing theorist Margarete Sandelowski, who asserts that narratives are an expression of human consciousness. She attributes the increased interest in narrative to a sense of loss as "patients and their biographies have receded from view and even disappeared, upstaged by histories and nosologies of disease and by the promise and perils of technology" (24). Some nurses are coming to revalue narrative as a way of knowing. They use it to discover knowledge, and to recover the art of nursing. Sandelowski writes, "Narrative knowing is a means to know again what nurses have always known: whether nurse or nursed, we are the stories we tell" (25). Sandelowski argues that nurses must listen to patients as they tell the stories of their illnesses or crises. Such telling represents much more than a tracing of events. Rather, it represents patients' efforts to explain events, justify actions, come to terms, make transitions, and maintain a certain self-image. Looking at narrative in this way, listening is an interpretive, moral, and political act. Nurses "read" in these stories the source of diagnosis and treatment from the patient's point of view. When patients relate narratives to nurses, "these narratives are formulations of the patient-as-text that nurses read and interpret, or they are the products of a joint authorship between the nurse and patient" (28). Sandelowski contends that when nurses think of their work in narrative terms, healing means constructing stories that patients can live by and with. A narrative-sensitive nurse can help a patient see the structure and meaning of his or her life/stories. The nurse can also help a patient construct a more unified narrative, or assemble a useful interpretation of past events.

Nurse theorist Jean Watson's theory of human caring is based on the assertion that "Society needs the caring professions to help restore humanity and nourish the human soul in an age of technology, scientism, loneliness, rapid change, and stress, an age without moral or ethical wisdom as to how to serve humanity" (*Nursing* 49). In Watson's view, through the *caring* relationship, a patient may gain a higher degree of harmony. This harmony generates increased self-knowledge, self-reverence, and self-healing

("New Dimensions"). As this happens, both nurse and patient engage in a healing process where both individuals become more whole. "Both bring with them to the relationship a unique life history, and phenomenal field, and both are influential . . . affected by transaction . . . which becomes part of a person" ("New Dimensions" 58). Watson says the caring process responds to a subjective inner world "in such a way that the nurse helps individuals find meaning in their existence, disharmony, suffering, turmoil—promotes self-control, choice, and self determination" (49). The values underlying Watson's theory are respect for the wonders and mysteries in life, acknowledgment of a spiritual dimension in life and internal powers of the human care process, and growth/change ("New Dimensions" 34). Ultimately, caring theory facilitates a healing process. This process is fostered by the understanding, love, and concern of those who care. This is important in nursing, because caring is necessary where curing has failed.

Other healthcare practitioners provide additional definitions. I cite the book *Healers on Healing* (Carlson and Shield), a collection of essays by physicians, nontraditional healers, and scholars. John Upledger, a physician and researcher on chronic illness and pain, believes that healing is a process leading to self-discovery. Rachel Remen, a physician and director of the Commonweal Cancer Help Program, sees the healing process as a movement toward wholeness. And Elisabeth Kubler-Ross, medical doctor and scholar on the death and dying process, states that the healer's role is to help people get in touch with "unfinished business" so that they can return to a state of emotional wholeness. Gadow suggested that perhaps it is healing for people to define for themselves what *they* believe healing is.

Scholars from across disciplines ponder writing as a means toward "healing," yet understand and do not flinch at such descriptors as "resolving" and "working through" used to describe processes associated with writing. Language in all three cases (healing, resolving, working through) becomes a tool for assimilating experiences, as summarizing information reduces cognitive work. Once a thought or story is written down, its memory and value are preserved, and one's mind is at peace.

James Pennebaker states that writing encourages structure and organization of thoughts, and it results in slowing down one's thought process. In fact, writing clears the mind of unresolved trauma and helps people to foster problem-solving abilities. In addition, writing about thoughts and feelings associated with difficult events forces people to synthesize many overwhelming memories. Translating a memory into language thus may alter one's perspective, according to Spiegel, Hunt, and Dondershine. Stamatelos and Mott worked with developmentally disabled people to show that writing could enhance self-esteem. Through writing, people learn to sort out and order their experiences and to discover that they share universal feelings.

Another branch of the literature on writing and healing takes a more psychological and empirical approach. James Pennebaker draws a clear parallel between writing and therapy. He claims that both yield measurable improvements in physical and psychological health; both encourage self-reflection and greater insight about words and thoughts; and both promote understanding and acknowledgment of emotions. Therefore, writing can lead to therapeutic benefits which stem from releasing inhibition. Holding back information requires physiological effort. Psychologists David Watson and Lee Anna Clark found that inhibition serves as a cumulative stressor which increases the probability of illness.

Having immersed myself in reading about HIV/AIDS and having constructed a preliminary definition of writing and healing that accommodated theories from composition, psychology, and the medical community, I was ready to begin gathering data that might allow me to examine and to understand the writing group members' work and perceptions of what made them feel better as they composed their pieces. My experience as a journal writer, writing teacher, and writing group facilitator led me to realize that I needed to experience or participate in the writing—and the healing—and use myself as part of the "research instrument." To accomplish this, I chose a methodology called "Grounded Theory."

Grounded Theory

Grounded theory, according to Anselm Strauss and Juliet Corbin, is "a qualitative research method that uses a systematic set of procedures to develop an inductively derived grounded theory about a phenomenon (24). The researcher explores a hunch (or hunches), allowing questions to evolve and shape the study even while the fieldwork is ongoing.

Grounded theory allows social scientists to develop or generate theories (ways to explain phenomena) that explain particular empirical situations, and are understandable to lay people as well as social scientists. Grounded theorists study how theory can be uncovered, or discovered, from data. Their research emphasis rests more on generating new theory than verifying old theory, which is a central concern of traditional scientific method. Such traditional methodology overemphasizes verification of theory. This, in effect, de-emphasizes the prior steps of discovery. Glaser and Strauss believe that a theory's adequacy cannot be separated "from the process by which it is generated"(5). Grounded theory allows theory to emerge from the data collected. As such, it is a way of "arriving at theory suited to its supposed uses" (3).

Grounded theory is not a usual practice in composition research. Sociologists traditionally use it to detect and illustrate basic social processes—of prime importance to sociologists, but not as relevant to composition teachers. Because grounded theory deals with many facets of a phenomenon (its social processes, the individuals involved, institutions, media, and language, to name a few), it is possible to lose the details and richness of the textual data collected. I allowed for these possibilities by collecting ample writing samples from the individuals with whom I worked and allowing their words to convey the power of their emotions. Clifford Geertz called this "thick description." Such description requires a careful and concrete account of events and often uses the words of the subjects of study themselves. I was concerned with recording specific features of context; I wanted to capture how my "informants" experienced AIDS and dealt with it.

Glaser and Strauss did not intend for researchers to follow the methodology as a cookbook formula. Although they wrote broadly about grounded theory, and taught many students how to use it, they meant it to be an evolving framework, a tool so that researchers could ask and answer their own questions (similar to the teacher-research movement in education). In my case, the choice to use grounded theory influenced how I approached my research sites. Grounded theory made me more aware of the social processes and patterns all around, as well as more conscious of my own role as researcher. Because of its roots in the social sciences, much of the background reading on grounded theory emphasizes the relationships between members of groups, as well as the relationships of groups to each other. For example, as I approached the Caring Center, I saw it as a part of a much larger whole (AIDS care in Denver). As I spent time at the center, I became interested not only in the administration's direction, but also in the interactions among clients, nurses, and volunteers.

As a scholar of language and writing, I was particularly interested in how words were used at both research sites. Grounded theory enables the study of language in the context of social behavior. This awareness of language and behavior helped anchor me (as a researcher) in the data. As noted, the researcher is as much a tool of perception as is any other person observed. My actions and reactions became part of the research. For example, when I visited Our House or the Caring Center, I was always conscious of myself and each movement I made, almost as though I was watching a movie of my life. I saw not just the brick building which is the headquarters of Our House, but the history of the neighborhood, including my own history and memories of experiencing this Denver neighborhood years earlier. I achieved a similar bigger picture of the Caring Center by imagining it within a figurative organizational chart so that I could understand where the power (funding) structures were positioned. This social and self-consciousness created a holistic—and accountable—approach to research.

Coding the Data

As I collected data, I had to develop a coding scheme. Charmaz describes coding as the first phase of the analytic method. It is the process of sorting and categorizing data. Codes "serve as shorthand devices to label, separate, compile, and organize data" (111). The codes become conceptual categories. I followed Charmaz's advice on how to scrutinize the data for these categories. She advised looking for connections between people and situations. She also suggested constructing codes to record inconsistencies and conflicts in the data. She recommended asking oneself: "What kinds of events are at issue? How are they constructed? What do these events mean" (113)? By asking these questions, I saw common themes emerge from the data. Strauss and Corbin call these "conceptual labels."

Coding was a tedious task. I typed up my research journals, as well as a synopsis of the many interviews I conducted. Following Chesler's method, I read the raw text carefully, and with a yellow highlighter, I underscored repeating words, as well as any mention of healing or writing. Next, I restated the seemingly significant underscored phrases.[1] This journal entry from February 19 illustrates:

Apprehension/Apology
it came through me
what would come next

outside communication

kill younger self
well-done/dramatic

facilitator's doubt

contradiction: murder as love?

expectations of criticism

poignant and sensible

hidden talents
mistakes are treasures
surprise
compassion
affirmation from the group

As we turned to read what people had brought in, Josh volunteered to go first. First he said, "*No one arrest me. This is just how it came through me. I didn't know what would come next.*" Kay said, "He called me and read it to me last night over the phone."

Josh had taken the photo (from the previous workshop) and ended up *killing his younger self.* The piece was *well-done* and *dramatic*, but he was rattled. Katlin [the nurse who had been observing] was rattled too. I wondered later if I should have *done something else* with his response, or if I should have behaved differently. His piece reminded me of the book *Beloved* and how the woman kills her child to keep her from a *life of abuse.*

Then Allister read. His meeting with his younger self included a Souza accompaniment. In the confrontation, his younger self said, "Go ahead. I know you're going to *criticize me.*" "Oh no, I don't want to," was the answer. Allister went on to give *poignant and sensible advice:* "Nothing is prohibitive if you truly want it. *You have hidden talents. Our mistakes are treasures.*

Once again, he *surprised* me. He was truly *compassionate* with his younger self. Everyone praised his work.

By the time I had performed this initial underscoring of the entire body of data, I had counted more than 600 conceptual labels. Some of these labels were repeated, others collapsed into similar codes, and some were not relevant to my study. I reworded some of the key phrases and attempted to reassemble the data into clusters. This is called "constant comparison," the purpose of which is described by Chesler:

> Since the articulation of one cluster as distinct from another cluster involves making comparisons, only a constant series of comparisons enables the coder to feel secure about the creation of a conceptually distinct category. (10)

I designated nine general areas: the Caring Center, Our House, the writing group, Josh, Kay, Rodney, Allister, Gideon (the five writers with whom I worked the most), and miscellaneous. Many of the conceptual labels described in the example above were in the "Writing Group" area. They were part of a cluster that contained codes expressing how people felt about themselves. These codes included the following restatements, or verbatim phrases:

mechanical: didn't tap emotions   take self too seriously

go ahead and criticize   surprise

compassionate and sensible advice   nothing is prohibitive

hidden talents   mistakes are treasures

they liked it   sounds like everything is okay

As I reread the clusters, I noticed the high number of statements with positive connotations. It occurred to me that the writers were expressing good feelings about themselves. No exercise specifically asked for such writing. The category became more distinct as I recoded, and I officially named it "Feeling Good About Oneself." It eventually had thirty-seven codes in it. By "dialoguing" with the field notes and noticing the prevalence of repeated words and concepts, I discerned twenty-four emerging categories:

Family/Support (49)   Acknowledgment (19)

Telling Your Story (43)   Resignation (18)

Reckoning/Making Sense of Life (42)   Dichotomy (15)

Feeling Good about Oneself (37)

Healing (30)

Shared Survival Tips/Info (29)

Wishes/Regrets (26)

Self-Knowledge/Self-Perception (24)

Anger (23)

Self-Criticism (20)

Humor (19)

In Control (19)

Turning Point (13)

(Self) Destruction (12)

Present Moment/Now (7)

Responsibility (6)

Commitment (6)

Process (6)

Pride (6)

Guilt (4)

Fear (3)

I evaluated these categories according to Strauss and Corbin's criteria. Most seemed conceptual to me, although a few, like "commitment" or "process" were abstract. My list was comprehensive; it covered important major areas. As for being grounded in the data, I could find direct links between the words of the writers and how these words found their way to my list. I continued to sample data once these categories were established; I reviewed data collected earlier until I was persuaded that the categories were in fact saturated. I placed corresponding codes in their appropriate categories and "ranked" them. The number in parenthesis above indicates how many codes belonged to each category. While these findings might be of interest to many healthcare workers and researchers, I found it necessary to consolidate and collapse the categories into those dealing with writing and discourse. When I did this, I was able to draw a few conclusions. At this point in my research, I was beginning to tell *my* story of what I saw happening. As I began to analytically explain this story, or develop a "story line," core categories emerged, as well as other categories which I believed to be relevant, although they did not contain many codes.

For example, almost every writer exhibited some form of anger toward AIDS. After observing writing group members and reading their work, it was apparent that writing was a flexible outlet for anger. Group members expressed anger in different ways. Kay was angry at society. A heterosexual woman with a young daughter, Kay was infected with the AIDS virus through a one-night stand. She felt angry about a speaking engagement where she encountered a hostile response from high school students. She wrote a letter to the school afterwards and received no reply. Later, she composed an article for *Resolute,* a local AIDS newsletter, and said that she "felt much better afterwards." Gideon's anger took the form of frustration and resignation. Gideon was a heterosexual former drug addict from New York. He seemed dismayed about his condition and by his powerlessness. His anger was visible in his sarcasm. He suggested that in earlier years he might have acted on his anger; now he writes about his feelings in his journal. Josh found his anger to be "motivational"—i.e., it led to his action as a speaker and educator. A heterosexual who contracted AIDS from a girlfriend, Josh tried to work through his many conflicting feelings. In his private writing, he wrote poison-pen letters to his mother and to the woman who infected him. He also directed his anger at society (stemming back to his years of service in Vietnam). Allister expressed a great deal of anger at his family, society, and the church. Allister was an older (over sixty) homosexual male who had been HIV+ for more than a decade. He told me once that his writing "came out angry." He explained that his drafts were too emotional and angry; he toned them down as he revised and made them public.

Other Caring Center clients expressed anger at society, and at AIDS in general. Rafael found *Out Front* (a Denver gay newspaper) to be an appropriate outlet for his angry, poignant, and sometimes irreverent ruminations. Helga, whose hemophiliac husband, Elmo, had AIDS, was angry and frustrated with the suffering and death she experienced in the course of Elmo's disease. It was clear that AIDS functioned to separate segments of society and even family members.

Two other categories merit attention: time and humor. Every writing group member—unprompted by me—mentioned the importance of living in the present moment. Having HIV, or perhaps any terminal illness, changes one's sense of time. Writing was a means of directly focusing on and experiencing the present. As Allister wrote, "Now is the beginning." Rodney, who lived at Our House, had both HIV and Parkinson's Disease. He developed a philosophy about time in which death was a place without beginning or end. Kay wrote about the importance of creating "positive, happy moments" (away from HIV).

Finally, the writing group members strongly suggested that humor was a mechanism for coping with AIDS. There is, in fact, a body of literature exploring the healing value of humor (Klein).

Humor provided levity and release. It was also a useful coping strategy, ice-breaker, and educator. Laughter results in unity and catharsis. Though the majority of out-of-class writing was serious, humor was welcome. It was for the most part incidental (such as the language of Gideon's younger self or Kay's luggage handler story about the bomb squad being called when someone's vibrator was accidentally turned on inside a suitcase), but upon hearing one's writing out loud, if something was funny, the group laughed. Sometimes chaos resulted from my own facilitation of a particular exercise, and again, laughter was an appropriate response.

Humor was evident everywhere. Adam, from the Caring Center, wanted to write down his "hysterical" story about a mandarin chicken. At Our House, jokes were commonplace. Rodney shared with me a tape of his stand-up comedy routine. People sometimes described themselves in a humorous way, such as Gideon's view of himself as "a higher-class junkie." Humor also posed irony in several stories that people told. The last line of Josh's serious testimonial about AIDS, published in the Caring Center newsletter, *Resolute,* reads: "I wait for death . . . I rollerblade." Allister informed me on several occasions of the humorous shock tactics he would sometimes use with young male AIDS patients who were feeling sorry for themselves. While AIDS is a decidedly *unfunny* disease, humor emerged repeatedly, and in many helpful ways.

As I continued combing the data for relevant categories, I observed how many times storytelling or narrative surfaced throughout the data. I compared categories and characteristics of stories told, and saw that these stories served different functions. The most pertinent labels were: Telling Your Story; Reckoning/ Making Sense of Life; Wishes/Regrets; Shared Survival Tips/ Information. I combined these to distinguish four different types of discourse: Life Stories (in general), AIDS Stories, Sharing AIDS Information (usually clinical), and Survival Tips (often emotional and spiritual). These types of discourse construe AIDS as an empowering condition, as well as a kind of educator.

As I "teased" the storytelling codes apart, I distinguished subtle differences in types of narratives and their uses. From the first day of the group, several people said they would like to tell the stories of their lives. In early writing assignments, such life storytelling did not mention AIDS. It was only a setting down of dates and facts—a kind of life review that is common in people with life-threatening diseases or old people looking back on their lives.

Telling one's story from this perspective allows a retrospective of life. In Lamendola and Newman's 1994 study of HIV/AIDS as expanding consciousness, the authors asked individuals with HIV or AIDS to tell about meaningful events and people in their lives. The participants' life stories revealed a pattern including stages of alienation, breaking away, aloneness and searching, and a turning point. This turning point marked an individual's discovery of new meaning. Through their writing, each group member expressed such a turning point. Allister experienced several turning points, most notably becoming a monk ("Meditations and teachings at the monastery were a new life"). About his life with AIDS, he wrote, "Now is a beginning." AIDS was the turning point for Kay, and acquiring Skeeter, her horse, was a later turning point. "He is meant to live with us," she wrote. For Rodney, developing Parkinson's Disease was his turning point, compounded by his HIV diagnosis. Like Allister, living in the present is his goal. Becoming a DJ was both the beginning for Josh (as he actualized his lifelong dream), and the beginning of the end. HIV saved Gideon, or so he says. His relationship with Janine, a woman who did not leave him when he was diagnosed, marks another turning point.

But another kind of life story was also evident: the telling of one's AIDS story. These were obvious in their oral form, as Kay and Josh made numerous speaking engagements in Denver. Allister had also been an active AIDS spokesperson in Texas. The same effect came through in their written works, such as Kay's essays in *Resolute,* and several of Josh's pieces. The audience for an AIDS story seemed more likely to be a person without AIDS, which very much changed the rhetorical stance and message. The speaker had a sort of privileged position of authority. The goal was not to gain pity, but rather to educate—Josh wrote that his goal was to "save one life."

Reviewing the other emergent categories about storytelling, I distinguished two labels: Shared Survival Tips/AIDS Information to arrive at a total of four categories of narrative. A large part of discourse at the Caring Center and Our House concerned survival strategies. Given the specialized nature of America's healthcare system, in addition to the stigma that accompanies AIDS, a person with HIV might well feel unempowered and overwhelmed by the bureaucracy of healthcare delivery systems. Sharing AIDS information was the exchange of practical advice. Kay often called up a friend who was "a walking pharmacy." She asked him if he had tried a particular drug, and if so, what the effects had been like. Kay trusted her friend's direct experience much more than her doctors, "who had never tried anything. It was kind of a scary thought." In writing about AIDS information, as writers did, the audience (others with HIV) learned about new medication and research. At the same time, the individual speaker or writer benefits by building self-esteem. AIDS makes people experts. Some AIDS information shared was technical; other information was more personal. Individuals realize that they are knowledgeable and helpful to others. By "owning" information about AIDS, individuals gain something they seldom experience: control. They also gain empowerment as they are not as dependent on their doctors. In other words, the writers with whom I worked used literacy to help each other, and to help themselves.

While Sharing AIDS Information was included in the same category, it was distinctly different from its partner discourse, Survival Tips. Like the Reckoning and Wishes codes, this type of discourse had a more emotional tone. Allister frequently took the opportunity in his writing to share survival tips. In the notebook he shared with me at the conclusion of the group, I found one piece directed toward people who have just learned they have AIDS. He wrote: "You can't feel sorry for yourself. You can't talk to old friends [they don't want to hear]. Make new friends in your support groups. Don't dwell on AIDS. Turn to your higher power, but beware of religion." Allister truly was a wealth of information and advice, and he had a certain confidence in his words. By contrast, Gideon also used writing to review how he was surviving and to teach others. His advice was usually to reiterate that "Dealing with emotions is part of the healing process," and "Forget about control." His words were more tentative than Allister's or Kay's.

Writing and Healing: Some Conclusions

Several conclusions regarding writing and healing among people with HIV/AIDS can be drawn from my study. First, people found it healing to make sense of their lives. Writing their life stories, particularly key moments and events, helped them to become more aware of their lives and to reckon with their pasts. They developed a sense of the whole of their lives by marking points along the time line of their existence. Second, teaching others about AIDS posed a different healing function. Because teaching requires knowing, this narrative posture allowed writers to accept an authorial stance which is adversarial. The writers found it healing to "fight back" by sharing their stories. The narratives of people with AIDS, similar to the narratives of Holocaust survivors, may shock or frighten outsiders into confronting the reality of the epidemic. Intersubjective connections occur. As Josh told a class of community college students at one of his speaking engagements: "I'm the other guy; I'm the person who thought it would never happen to him." Such realizations of "otherness" bring to light one's own mortality. As Kay put it, "AIDS has no boundaries and can enter their lives as easily as it did mine." Finally, sharing information and survival tips among members of the AIDS population strengthens support within a community. In effect, such support nurtures the creation of caring communities. It is healing to care and caring to heal. It is also empowering to claim experience and survival.

Another conclusion addresses healing through group writing. The writing we did involved two stages: private writing, followed by public reading. My orientation as a journal writer influenced the private writing. Yet the group process required making the private public. I contend that this shift of private to public constitutes a healing process for three reasons. First, writing is a vehicle to record "untold stories." As many scholars agree, such storytelling helps individuals to unburden themselves, to make sense of experience, or to reconstruct themselves or the events in their lives (Polkinghorne; Schafer; Butler). Second, in a writing group, the group dynamic of sharing with one another evokes compassion, caring, and a sense of belonging. These lead to growth and transformation on both individual and social levels. Finally, being acknowledged is part of the healing process. Being heard, or acknowledged, is being cared for.

In journal writing or private writing that is not shared, individuals acknowledge their own thoughts and feelings. There is certainly great value in becoming more self-aware and conscious. Yet here I focus on the value of public acknowledgment by a facilitator and other group members. The writing group members, in their interviews, mentioned the desire to be acknowledged and heard. An audience's acknowledgment lessens the individual's feeling of aloneness. Writer Frank Ostaseski, of the Zen Hospice Project in San Francisco, explains the value of acknowledgment in the context of his work with death and dying. He says that telling stories is a way of preparing for death: "Telling our stories can give us distance and help move us through the process. Often this is the way we make sense of our lives and discover meaning. But every story needs someone to listen" (14). I would argue that telling stories is also a way of preparing for life, and *decreasing* distance between ourselves and others. Social worker Ruth Campbell, who has facilitated a writing group at the University of Michigan for more than fifteen years, cites the words of an elderly writer who explained, "We are a very caring group." Another group member described what acknowledgment meant to her:

> The group membership turned out to be so miscellaneous, such honest genuine people and so sincere, that I never want to give it up. We are very different, but perfectly integrated and I love every one of the others. (556)

In being acknowledged, an individual becomes part of a "whole"—a community—even if it is for a moment. Such a literally holistic view clearly falls under the definition of healing posed earlier: to become or feel whole.

A personal example illustrates the "healing" effect of being acknowledged in the writing group. For the second group meeting, members brought in a photograph of themselves and wrote about it for homework. I brought in a photo of myself and my sister, taken the previous summer. I wrote:

> I like this photograph because my sister and I are clowning around again the way we used to as children. We are both

> smiling and silly, but really we were both exhausted and re-
> lieved, having both recently found our ways out of unhealthy
> relationships. There's some tension in the photo. You can see
> it in my sister's neck and how the tendon bulges. . . .

At the mention of leaving a relationship, a phenomenon nearly
everyone at the table had experienced, a chorus of "Ahhhhhh"s
went around. I felt touched that people acknowledged my pain.
I realized I had been holding in that part of myself. I felt less alone
in my experience, knowing that other people understood my
feelings.

In terms of acknowledgment among the writers with AIDS,
gay and straight alike expressed stories of stigmatization. After
Kay's *Resolute* article about a bad response from high school students at a speaking engagement, she received positive feedback.
Friends and readers affirmed that they also had experienced in-
sensitive audiences. Acknowledgment helped heal her hurt feelings, and although she still shies away from giving talks at high
schools, she resumed her busy tour of speaking engagements. Acknowledgment in this case entails a nonjudgmental response.
She wrote about such acknowledgment in her relationship with
her horse, Skeeter. "He recognizes us," she wrote, "He listens."

Different kinds of acknowledgment exist. Josh and Kay repeatedly mentioned their desire to tell their stories (in written as
well as oral form) in the hopes they could help or "save" someone.
Allister said he would share his work "if someone would find it
useful." Local newsletters became vehicles for acknowledgment,
as did the group.

Rodney presented an exceptional case study of being acknowledged. Of all the writers who participated in this study, he
was the most physically challenged and limited in his physical
movement because he had both HIV and Parkinson's Disease. Yet
he wrote for many different audiences and found acknowledgment in many ways. His family viewed him as a writer and poet.
He was asked to help write the funeral programs for his mother
and grandmother. He also received an important form of acknowledgment from writing letters to his girlfriend. He shared
with me some of the poems and songs he wrote for her; and when
he discovered that she also liked to write poetry, they began to
collaborate. A reciprocal form of acknowledgment occurred,

which I imagine was healing to both of them. In addition, Rodney submitted some of his work to a national song publisher. Sometimes when Rodney writes, he thinks of himself differently and signs his name "Sly" or "Slick" for his hero, Sly Stone.

Back to the Group: "You've Touched on Just about Everything"

In June, several months after the writing group ended, I contacted its members, explained my process of data analysis, and showed my list of coding categories. I then summarized my preliminary findings for each individual and asked for their feedback on my conclusions. Kay responded, "This is a very good list. You've touched on just about everything." The group members commented on several of the findings. They were surprised at the low incidence of fear and guilt in the results. Kay said, "Guilt was top for me at first, but I worked through it in therapy. I realized that I was just human. It took a long time . . . one and a half years." About fear, Josh and Gideon both agreed that much had happened since the writing group ended, and if the group were running again, fear would probably be more present in people's minds. In fact, each member of the group in some way had experienced his or her mortality: Josh had surgery; Gideon had his first bout with pneumonia; and Kay lost a close friend.

Josh was particularly interested in the finding about the high incidence of anger. He suggested that it is difficult for people to consciously write about anger: "It has to incidentally come out." Kay said, "I get more angry with time—fed up. I'm more angry at society than anything, with the blinders people wear. I've never been angry at myself. . . . I'm far more guilt ridden than angry." Gideon agreed that anger was important to express. "It's a big part of it," he said. "I write to my virus once a month. Some letters are angry, and some aren't. That's just another stage, but it [anger] does come back."

Concerning humor, everyone agreed that it was a good defense mechanism and coping device. Gideon said, "It makes you feel good. When it comes to when I can't joke around and laugh, it's time for my demise. It's important to keep a sense of humor.

It's really healing." Kay also stated that it was essential in speech as well as writing. "When you speak, you need it. You can see sadness [in nurses]. The humor breaks it up. I always try to do something to break up the heaviness of the subject."

Josh disagreed with my finding that the people at the Caring Center who seemed most knowledgeable had a higher "rank." "I don't see that as different from normal life," he said. He suggested that long-term survivors have the most "rank" at the Center. As far as "owning" information, and being or feeling in control, Josh said "Doctors don't know. *I* know what's going on in my body. No matter what they [the VA] tell me, I know whether it's good or bad for my body. It's an intuition, and I'm right every time." Kay was equally adamant. She said that doctors are not nearly as informed as people with AIDS. "For once," she said,

> there's an illness where people can really have control. I think I really scare my doctor. I tell her no, I'm not going on antivirals, I don't believe in them. I've learned from PWAs [People With AIDS]. From Bob and all the stuff he was on. I saw him go through it. That information will help me one day. My friend Cecil has been on everything. I call him and say, "Cecil, can you tell me the side effects?" I felt better and was able to take it (rather than follow the advice from doctors who have never taken it). It's really scary.

Finally, I asked writing group members why most of the stories they told were positive or happy stories. I prefaced this by explaining that my private journals contained a mixture of positive and negative writing. Josh became philosophical as he responded. "The more I tell my story," he said, "the less the bad stuff has power over me. It changes me as to how I look at the disease. As I change the story, I change myself. I'm evolving. It's like I'm on speed or something." This reaffirms Josh's view, represented in other writing, of coming to terms with a new self that surprises him very much. His sense of self with AIDS may still seem alien and "other." I probed the question, asking Josh, Kay, and Gideon why it was that people expressed positive thoughts and feelings, when sometimes I wasn't sure that they really felt that way. Josh said, "There's so much negativity going on that we're forced to be happy-faced. The little things do mean a lot. In a writing group, the people are all willing to share the good." This implies that "good" is a cherished resource, unlike the "bad" or negative thoughts and feelings which he may be writing privately but not sharing. Kay said that she would much rather write about pleasurable things. She said that she enjoyed writing about the past. To the contrary, Gideon said, "I want to forget that part of my life, but I can't." In response to the question of why writing reflected mainly positive feelings, he said:

> It's not just writing, or disease. It's people in general don't want others to know their feelings, how fucked up, insecure and emotional you feel. You don't want support and don't think that you deserve it. You try to avoid that closeness stuff.

Classroom Implications

"That closeness stuff" evolved into the core of my study. Untold stories become told stories whose words both revealed and changed worlds. It was clear to me that my interactions with each writing group member, as well as with others I met, were among the most important parts of my study. It became equally clear to me that writing was not the focus of those relationships; caring was. The writing group members' work led each individual on a healing voyage, depending on how each writer defined healing. The writing charted the healing, just as a river's height is marked by the walls of a stone canal, but it was not the healing. As Mary Rose O'Reilley, in her collection of essays, *The Peaceable Classroom*, puts it, "Most of the healing that goes on in English class (and maybe everywhere) is self-healing. The teacher's job is not so much to counsel as to provide an atmosphere of safety and to keep out of the way of the process" (47). Group members care for and comfort each other. The writers know where they hurt, and what it is they need to heal.

In "The Heart of the Matter," an essay in the Brand and Graves collection, *Presence of Mind*, Gabriele Rico explains what she hoped to achieve in her earlier book, *Pain and Possibility: Writing through Personal Crisis*, what I saw happening in the lives of the writers with whom I worked:

> I wanted people who do not ordinarily write to discover writing as a tool, enabling them to move from passive suffering to active participation in healing—the word hål clearly sharing the connection to a process of whole-making. . . . Writing as a whole-making activity reflects the basic need to story our lives. (200–1)

Rico's interesting invention of the verb "to story" creates a helpful linguistic space to actively explore writing as healing. As we write our stories, we listen to ourselves speak, and we listen to the stories of others. With the insight and awareness we gain, we change. We (re)construct ourselves through narrative, and the writing makes us whole. Among HIV/AIDS writers, writing produced and shared with others opened just this dimension of healing: a social healing for people with HIV disease and a more general healing message for anyone who has ever experienced the emotional pain of being stricken, ostracized, and oppressed.

The need exists for writing with people in the AIDS community. However, as I've tried to suggest, persons must locate themselves first, including their own bias and their fears. They must learn to listen to the multiplicity of voices and stories speaking out about AIDS. They must consider the desired degree of engagement in the writing group. I didn't know these things until I was well into the Caring Center writing group. Each writer had a different reason for writing and a different story to tell. My findings suggest that writing group facilitators, working with people who have HIV/AIDS, should offer exercises that evoke the kinds of stories that people wanted to write: stories that allow general life introspection; AIDS stories for people who do not have AIDS; stories that share information about AIDS with other members of the AIDS community; and more personal and emotional stories about AIDS for others in the writing group and the AIDS community. These were the stories that, in James Moffett's words, brought writers from "chaos to cosmos" and that restored them to wholeness.

I have become a better teacher through my work with HIV/AIDS writing groups. They have shown me that there is much to learn from the stories that my future "students" will write. They have taught me about sensitivity, compassion, patience, courage, and history. They have shown me a way to address my goal of bringing together personal and professional writing. On very good days, these parts of myself harmonize, and I feel whole.

Note

1. There are many qualitative research computer programs now on the market to make this process easier.

Works Cited

Borger, Irene, ed. *Witness*. Los Angeles: AIDS Project Los Angeles Writer's Workshop, 1990.

Brand, Alice G., and Richard L. Graves, eds. *Presence of Mind: Writing and the Domain Beyond the Cognitive*. Portsmouth, NH: Boynton/Cook, 1994.

Bruner, Jerome. *Actual Minds, Possible Worlds*. Cambridge: Harvard UP, 1986.

Butler, Robert. "The Life Review: An Interpretation of Reminiscence in the Aged." *Psychiatry* 26 (1963): 65–76.

Campbell, Ruth. "Writing Groups with the Elderly." *Individual Change through Small Groups*. Ed. M. Sundell, P. Glasser, R. Saari, and R. Vinter. New York: Free, 1985. 546–59.

Carlson, Richard, and Benjamin Shield, eds. *Healers on Healing*. Los Angeles: Tarcher, 1989.

Charmaz, Kathy. "The Grounded Theory Method: An Explication and Interpretation." *Contemporary Field Research: A Collection of Readings*. Ed. Robert M. Emerson. Prospect Heights, IL: Waveland, 1983: 109–26.

Chesler, Marc. "Professionals' Views of the 'Dangers' of Self-Help Groups: Explicating a Grounded Theoretical Approach." Working Paper #345. Ann Arbor: Center for Research on Social Organization, 1987 (May).

Coles, Robert. *The Call of Stories*. Boston: Houghton, 1989.

Cooper, JoAnn. "Telling Our Own Stories: The Reading and Writing of Journals or Diaries." *Stories Lives Tell: Narrative and Dialogue in Education*. Ed. Carol Witherell and Nel Noddings. New York:

Teachers College Press, 1991. 96–111.

Cox, Elizabeth. *Thanksgiving*. New York: Harper, 1990.

Crimp, Douglas, and Leo Bersani. *AIDS: Cultural Analysis/Cultural Activism*. Cambridge: MIT P, 1988.

Gadow, Sally. Personal Interview. March 1994.

Glaser, Barney, and Anselm Strauss. *The Discovery of Grounded Theory: Strategies for Qualitative Research*. New York: Aldine De Gruyter, 1967.

Greene, Maxine. "Toward Possibility: Expanding the Range of Literacy." *English Education* 18.4 (1986): 231–43.

Hadas, Rachel. *Unending Dialogue: Voices from an AIDS Poetry Workshop*. New York: Faber, 1991.

Holleran, Andrew. *Ground Zero*. New York: Morrow, 1989.

Janoff-Bulman, Ronnie. "Victims of Violence." *Handbook of Life Stress, Cognition, and Health*. Ed. Shirley Fisher and James Reasons. New York: Wiley, 1988. 101–10.

Klein, Allen. *The Healing Power of Humor*. New York: Putnam, 1989.

Lamendola, Frank P., and Margaret Newman. "The Paradox of HIV/AIDS as Expanding Consciousness." *Advances in Nursing Science* 16.3 (1994): 13–21.

McMillen, Liz. "AIDS as Metaphor: The Epidemic Spawns a Growing Body of Scholarship on Its 'Signification'." *The Chronicle of Higher Education* (19 October 1994): A20.

Moffett, James. *Coming on Center*. Portsmouth, NH: Boynton/Cook, 1981.

Monette, Paul. *Becoming a Man: Half a Life Story*. New York: Harcourt, 1992.

———. *Borrowed Time: An AIDS Memoir*. New York: Avon, 1988.

———. *Halfway Home*. New York: Crown, 1991.

Murphy, Timothy. "Testimony." *Writing AIDS: Gay Literature, Language, and Analysis*. Ed. Timothy Murphy and Suzanne Poirier. New York: Columbia UP, 1993. 306–20.

Murphy, Timothy, and Suzanne Poirier, eds. *Writing AIDS: Gay Literature, Language, and Analysis.* New York: Columbia UP, 1993.

Myerhoff, Barbara, and Deena Metzger. "The Journal as Activity and Genre." *Remembered Lives: The Work of Ritual, Storytelling, and Growing Older.* Ed. Barbara Myerhoff. Ann Arbor: U of Michigan P, 1992.

Noddings, Nel. *Caring: A Feminine Approach to Ethics and Moral Education.* Berkeley: U of California P, 1984.

O'Reilley, Mary Rose. *The Peaceable Classroom.* Portsmouth, NH: Boynton/Cook, 1993.

Ostaseski, Frank. "Stories of Lives Lived and Now Ending." *Inquiring Mind* 10.2 (1994): 14–29.

Peabody, Barbara. *The Screaming Room.* New York: Avon, 1986.

Pennebaker, James. *Opening Up: The Healing Power of Confiding in Others.* New York: Morrow, 1990.

The Phoenix. Newsletter for the Continuum Community. San Francisco, California. Spring 1993.

Polkinghorne, Donald. *Narrative Knowing and the Human Sciences.* Albany, NY: State U of New York P, 1988.

Rico, Gabriele. "The Heart of the Matter: Language, Feeling, Stories, Healing." *Presence of Mind: Writing and the Domain Beyond the Cognitive.* Ed. Alice G. Brand and Richard L. Graves. Portsmouth, NH: Boynton/Cook, 1994. 199–214.

———. *Pain and Possibility: Writing Your Way through Personal Crisis.* Los Angeles: Tarcher, 1991.

Robinson, Jay. *Conversations on the Written Word: Essays on Language and Literacy.* Portsmouth, NH: Boynton/Cook, 1990.

Sandelowski, Margarete. "We Are the Stories We Tell: Narrative Knowing in Nursing Practice." *Journal of Holistic Nursing* 21.1 (1994): 23–33.

Schafer, Roy. *The Analytic Attitude.* New York: Basic, 1983.

Shilts, Randy. *And the Band Played On: Politics, People, and the AIDS Crisis.* New York: Penguin, 1987.

Spiegel, David, T. Hunt, and H. E. Dondershine. "Dissociation and Hypnotizability in Post-Traumatic Stress Disorder." *American Journal of Psychiatry* 145 (1988): 301–5.

Stamatelos, Theodore, and Donald Mott. *Writing as Therapy: Motivational Activities for the Developmentally Delayed.* New York: Teachers College Press, 1983.

Strauss, Anselm, and Juliet Corbin. *Basic Qualitative Research: Grounded Theory, Procedures, and Techniques.* Newbury Park, CA: Sage, 1990.

Watney, Simon. *Practices of Freedom.* Durham, NC: Duke UP, 1994.

Watson, David, and Lee Anna Clark. "Negative Affectivity: The Disposition of Experience Aversive Emotional States." *Psychological Bulletin* 96 (1984): 460–65.

Watson, Jean. "New Dimensions in Human Caring Theory." *Nursing Science Quarterly* 1.4 (1988): 175–81.

———. *Nursing: Human Science and Human Care.* Norwalk, CT: Appleton, 1985.

———. "Transpersonal Caring: A Transcendent View of Person, Health, and Healing." *Nursing Theories in Practice.* Ed. M. E. Parker. New York: National League for Nursing, 1990. 277–88.

Witherell, Carol, and Nel Noddings, eds. *Stories Lives Tell: Narrative and Dialogue in Education.* New York: Teachers College Press, 1991.

Chapter Sixteen

Las Madres, Upstairs/Downstairs

From Soul Maps and Story Circles to Intertextual Collaboration

Sandra Florence
University of Arizona

L as Madres was housed in an old two-story white building at the edge of the Armory Park/Barrio historic neighborhood, a mix of Anglo and Hispanic working-class families, artists, upwardly mobile residents and business people, and transients. A huge mural is painted on one side of the building. The mural's Black and Hispanic faces stare down on Sixth Avenue, where cars whiz past and transients hang out on the corners panhandling for cigarettes and spare change. On the opposite side of the building was once a playground with swings, jungle gyms, and plastic toys. The interior space was cheerful with plants and posters, with a small lobby area that opened onto the children's classrooms. Just off these rooms was the kitchen where Cuka, the Mexican cook, made delicious healthy lunches for mothers, children, and staff. The mothers attended classes upstairs.

I had wanted for some time to conduct a writing group with women at risk, believing that writing can be a healing and empowering experience. I've been in many writing groups myself and have seen that sitting in a room and simply writing with others can have a very powerful effect on people, transformative, even life-changing. I hoped to bring some of the healing effects to the women of Las Madres, whose lives were at best unstable and insecure and at worst were shattered by drug abuse, domestic violence, and poverty.

I started on that first day with some fear of the women I'd be working with. Most of the women had been assigned to Las Madres by the courts. Most had drug and alcohol problems.

Many of them had been in abusive relationships with men, many had abused their children, and some had lost their children to Child Protective Services. The women didn't have parenting skills, were poor, living on welfare, with little education. Some of the mothers had managed to regain custody of their children by committing themselves to a program like Las Madres. I wondered at first if these women would be interested at all in a writing group. Would they really be interested in two hours of writing? What could I possibly have to offer them? And yet, I believe and have seen for myself that writing can open people up to parts of their lives that have been shut off before and that this process of writing and sharing might help them reach a greater understanding of themselves and others.

Time at Las Madres was always hard to come by. It was packed full of activity. While their children were downstairs in preschool classrooms, the mothers were upstairs working on GEDs, taking parenting classes, or attending seminars on family issues. Every minute of their day was scheduled with activities. This proved to be a barrier to extended work with the women because I often had to cancel the writing group for other activities, activities at times that seemed to run counter to the kind of reflective, quiet work that our writing group required. And this seems to be a fact of life in all community education programs where so many conflicting needs must be met.

I knew that Las Madres used some forms of writing, forms that might be perceived as punishment. For example, the women were asked to sit on the pew (a bench in the lobby used for reflection time when they had broken rules), and often they were asked to write about what was going on for them. This did seem to help them reflect on their actions and motivations. At one point we discussed the possibility of doing a collection called *Stories from the Pew*, although in the end nothing came of this. Journal writing was required on subjects such as mother/daughter relationships, and parenting.

But I wanted to offer them a peaceful time to write, time outside their hectic schedule of parenting and educational activities, when they could come together for two hours and simply focus on themselves and write out of that experience. I wanted to share with them the use of writing as a tool for growth, insight, healing, and transformation, and a way of being with other women that was supportive and nonthreatening.

During my work, I kept a journal, reflecting on our sessions together and planning the next group. What I also found I needed to do at this time was to think about how my own experience was touched by theirs and to deal with some of the tougher emotions that overwhelmed me as I listened to their stories about losing their children, fighting addiction, and trying to survive in abusive relationships. What follows is the journal I kept while working at Las Madres, part of it recorded during the time of my work, part of it reflection after. I offer it not as a theoretical statement about writing and healing, but as an entry in the lore of healing.

> People with no other art forms have three;
> They can tell their past, they can find humor,
> They can tell their dreams. (Sexson 101)

Upstairs: Meeting 1

I met the group for the first time yesterday. There were four mothers in the group and another woman identified as a "demonstrator." She has been in the program at Las Madres for almost two years and is considered a success. Therefore, her role is to demonstrate to others what they can achieve. She was helpful in encouraging the other women to talk and write. Most of these women are referred to Las Madres through the courts or CPS (Child Protective Services). Most have drug addiction problems and a history of abusive relationships with men and in some cases of abusing and abandoning their children. Many of the children were exposed to drugs prenatally and have considerable emotional and behavioral problems. There were five women on that first day. After talking to the mothers and explaining my reasons for being there, they shared small pieces of their stories.

Vicky B was Native American, early thirties, with four children, two attending the program with her. She was there because of her alcohol and drug problems. She had a quiet, intense energy about her, and when she spoke about her love for her children and her need to do well in the program, it was with a quiet dignity and grace.

Vicky H was African American, late twenties, with two children, also attending the program because of drug addiction problems, and domestic violence. She was very articulate, lively, strong, able to say very clearly what she wanted and how she was going to achieve it. She said she did not think of herself as a victim.

Vicky M was Anglo American. Vicky didn't say too much during our first check-in. She was very cautious at first, but I didn't let it bother me and I understood her need for that.

Cynthia was African American, early thirties, three children, involved in the program because of her alcohol problems. She had a beautiful round face and smiled at me when she spoke, which was hard for her at first; her voice would quaver, and I could see tears in her eyes, and then a troubled look would cross her brow as she talked about her life.

Bobbie was Anglo Hispanic, mid-thirties, four children, one she'd given up for adoption many years ago. She was in the program with a variety of problems such as drug addiction, poverty, homelessness. She'd been involved with Child Protective Services. Bobbie was a "demonstrator" because she'd managed to attend Las Madres for two years, an achievement in itself.

While they seemed interested in doing the writing group, they were not overly enthusiastic. We began with the Soul Map, a journal technique developed and discussed by George Simons in his book, *Keeping Your Personal Journal*. The Soul Map asks that a writer draw a visual representation of her life at this moment in time, using any images that seem to fit her interior landscape. I had to explain and give them several examples before they would start. They clearly wanted to do it "right."

At first they seemed reluctant, hesitant to move their bodies, to clasp their hands around the markers and begin. I would experience this passivity, this weight that they must throw off before they could begin writing, many times during our work together. This was a "silence" that was hard for them to give up, to climb out of. I'm not talking about the kind of meditative silence that would come when we were writing together, when the children were quiet downstairs, and the mothers could turn their attention inward. But the silence that they had been locked in because of fear, ignorance, and abuse. This movement out of silence was the first step in a movement out of isolation for them.

I had provided large sheets of paper and colored pens. I did a map as well. After a while, we were all completely quiet and sitting on the floor or in soft chairs; we gave our full attention to the maps. This took about thirty minutes, and I could see that several of the maps were very elaborate and intricate. Then I asked them to identify the landmarks on the map either with metaphors, similes, or other words—to label the significant places on their map. Then I asked that they select a word, phrase, or image that expressed what they saw in the map. Then they wrote again about what they liked in the map and what they would change.

This initial drawing activity that then led to the writing really opened them up to some of the difficult emotions that they carry around inside them. After the drawing and writing, they were much more open to discussing their lives and talking about their problems. In some small way, by naming the problem, they were relieved of its burden. For most of them the words that describe what is going on in their lives are *frustration, loneliness, obstacles.* One woman used *life* as her word and explained that everything has a good and bad side and that is just life. She went on to say that she didn't want to dwell on her mistakes but to see them as a way to learn. It sounded good, but I felt there was a kind of smoothing over of her real feelings.

During our discussion Cynthia asked, "Is it wrong to feel what I feel?" The other mothers immediately responded to her and said that all feelings were okay. She seemed relieved with their support, and I began to understand Cynthia a little better as someone who, despite her beauty and outward strength was very fragile when it came to her sense of self.

Throughout this time, there were constant interruptions. People came into the room without knocking and then excused themselves. Once or twice a staff member came in and rummaged through a desk for a piece of paper, or she interrupted one of the writers to ask where an item was. I felt very angry at these intrusions. It seemed as if there were no boundaries or sensitivity to the actual work that was going on. But the participants didn't seem to be bothered by these interruptions; they took them in stride as though they were the most normal thing in the world. They seemed used to this constant fracturing of their daily lives and activities. They looked at me after each interruption though. My irritation must have been visible. Finally, Vicky H said, "that bothers you right?" I nodded. She looked down at her nails distractedly and said, "me, too." I realized I would have to talk to the director and ask for more secluded or private space to work in, and to emphasize the importance of our writing group as refuge. I didn't want to be negative about the arrangements at Las Madres, so I changed the subject and after a brief discussion, we went around the circle, and each woman explained her map.

A Description of the Soul Maps

VICKY B: Mountains, trees, a bridge, and steep path going up the mountain with many boulders and obstacles in her path. Vicky said, "I feel like turning around and going back down the mountain and not even trying." (Her word was *frustration*.)

VICKY H: A deep black pit and an opening out onto the surface of the earth and a large body of water. Vicky H said, "The water can be calm and healing, but it can also rage just like I can." A huge orange and yellow sun in the corner of the drawing. (Her word was *life*.)

VICKY M: Three circles representing her relationship with her children—Vicky M said, "I feel like I just go around and around and never get anywhere. And this fat person at the bottom of the page represents my body which I don't like." An enclosed area with grass and some protective rocks represented her aloneness. (Her word was *isolation*.)

CYNTHIA: A desert island with a coconut tree on it. Bleak, lonely, and Cynthia said, "I hate coconuts." There were rocks, obstacles to overcome, and a line representing a roller coaster and at the end a drop of blood. The roller coaster ends abruptly. Cynthia said, "I feel sometimes like just going over the edge." But she also said that someday she would complete the roller coaster ride. (*Loneliness* was her word.)

BOBBIE: She used the entire paper to draw a beautiful picture of mountains and trees and a stream rushing downhill with a waterfall at the end. There were trees and mountains that represented family—some children whom she has abandoned and has never tried to get back. She is closer to certain friends than she is family. There were a couple of trees right along the bank of the river. One represented a son and the other a friend, both of whom she is worried about and feels they might be swept away in the river. Bobbie said, "I'm worried about my son because of his gang membership, and my friend because she is still using drugs." (*Nature* or *family* was her word.)

After the maps and discussion, everybody was feeling open and happy, although I'm not sure why. At first I thought that opening up and focusing on writing about problems would only bring the women down more, but that was not the case. The energy in the room had really picked up as each woman shared her troubles and fears, and even some of her hopes. Their ability to articulate what was going on in their lives had already been elevated several notches by the act of giving image to their feelings and then putting those images into words.

We decided to do four five-minute writings on different subjects. I chose the first topic—*fear*. Then the mothers took turns calling out subjects—*anger, men, children*. The two topics that seemed to really spark some heated writing were *men* and *anger*. They all wrote freely and by the last topic were eager to share their writings. I return Friday to do the second group. The same women will be in the group and two staff members will join us.

Reflection: Your Story Is in Mine, Mine in Yours

Before the group started, I had a momentary urge to take a drink. I don't know where the urge came from, but I am someone who has ten years of sobriety.

> Standing in the small room upstairs that we would use for our writing, waiting for the women to finish having lunch with their children, the dense stuffy air packed with emotional pain, the occasional sound of children's laughter and crying from downstairs hits me hard. I feel like crying. As if I can feel all their

pain and yet I know I am feeling my own. I can feel that emptiness that wants to drag me back down into addiction.

The danger and the reward of doing this kind of writing with people is to realize that each of their stories is also in my own story, even when I think I am so different, so far removed in my experience and values from them, so safe and secure in the world I have built for myself. I had felt the sadness of the place, and yet if I let myself, I could also see that each of our stories could serve as maps for the rest of us. As it turned out that first day, they all worked hard the full two hours and it felt very safe to be there. The two-hour time frame seemed not so long as dense, as though time were loaded and compressed, as though we were in another dimension together created out of the writing and talking. I forgot time as I always do when I allow myself to sink, perhaps searching for some kind of oblivion or open space, and yet at the same time, neither tears or laughter but understanding. Is it possible to reach understanding through this process?

The themes that emerged from our writing and discussion that day were frustration, isolation, loneliness, obstacles, fear. The five-minute writings came out of the Soul Map exercise, and the women easily focused on the relationships in their lives and their roles as mothers/wives/lovers/friends. They were already beginning to see their lives in a picture that they could imagine how to change, or they could see how they had changed and that certain views of themselves no longer fit or worked. In sharing their feelings with each other in this structured way, they noticed a pattern that seemed to affect all of them—their relationships with men were obsessive and abusive at times, and the obsession with the men in their lives often led them into addiction, crime, and neglect of their own children. This made me ponder my own relationships, which had at times threatened my stability and even my connection to my daughter. Their willingness to talk openly about these things brought back my own earlier shortcomings and mistakes, my obsessiveness in relationships. It was not pleasant for me to think of myself in these terms. Later that night I went back to some writing I had done fifteen years earlier that revealed elements similar to what these women were beginning to reveal in their writing: dependency in negative relationships, sacrificing one's own beliefs for someone else's, and being stuck in an addictive cycle:

> I exchanged air
> for a picture of you
> your face etched on every leaf
> tried copying your breathing
> a closeness I couldn't afford
> tried following directions
> you had given
> that only led in circles
> like a clock
> I found
> all that passed between us
> was time.

I immediately felt a kind of interdependence with them as we told our stories, as we began to create the place to tell them. And it was as if their stories were in mine, and mine in theirs, and while I believe there is no such thing as a completely objective observer—I had not come to Las Madres simply to observe—I did not expect to be pulled so strongly into these women's stories. As we tell our stories, as we write them, we begin to see that we touch edges with everyone else in some way.

We discussed the following take-home exercises as good ways to keep the writing they do in the group ongoing. A journal of unexpressed emotions and a dream journal. We agreed that probably the most important and interesting exercise would be the Journal of Unexpressed Emotions. Since they had all indicated that they wanted to work on feelings, this seems like a good place to start. They talked about repressing and squelching their "real" feelings, both positive and negative in most situations in their lives. So the challenge became how to recognize these moments and change them. How to express honest feelings fully in order to learn from them. I asked them to write emotional events down during the following week, how they felt at the time, what they did or didn't say, and what they would like to have said. At the end of the week, they should look over their writings to see how many of their emotions went unexpressed. We would then share this in group.

Downstairs: Why Are You So Blue Today?

Marcus, a four-year-old Indian boy with waist-length black hair, was very sad. He sat in the circle with his head down as the other children, ten of them, sang the song, "Why are you so blue?" Their voices were scratchy and soft; some of them didn't know all the words but they hummed and muttered through the song to the end, pleased that they were participating. One of the pre-school teachers, Brittney (known as "Bit" by her class), asked if someone would like to give Marcus a cookie. Annika, a three-year-old black girl, raised her hand and offered Marcus a cookie. He smiled and took it; then Annika gave Marcus a hug.

Then they began singing the song to the next child in the circle, Marissa, a tiny little girl with beautiful black hair tied with red ribbons. But Marissa was not blue. She was happy because she was at school, and her "nana was visiting." The song "Why are you so blue?" was just one of the activities the children participated in to help them express their feelings: Through songs, dreams, drawing, and circle time, they were being encouraged to share their experiences with one another—their sad moments, their happy times and to get support from each other. The children were using fundamental forms of literacy to express feelings and to contribute something to each other's lives. Many of the children had been badly abused; many had seen their mothers beaten. Sometimes the children intervened in a violent episode in their homes. Joey was one of these children, a sad-faced five-year-old who had tried to protect his mother from her boyfriend by hitting and kicking the man beating her. Whenever Joey tried to hug his mother, she would push him away and say, "Get off me, boy, you're too old for hugs." Joey was five. His four-year-old brother Robbie, never spoke.

Britt said of her work with the children, "There was a lot of pain running through the children at Las Madres. We were trying to give them a sense of wholeness in their lives, giving them some of the most basic things in life like affection, and teaching them simply to share and be kind to each other." At times there seemed a natural inclination on the children's part to do this—something inside them had not yet been broken by their difficult lives.

Upstairs: Meeting 2

I met with the mothers today. The group consisted of Cynthia, Vicky H, Vicky B, and two new members—Vera, a staff member who's been in the program for several months, and Cassandra, a newcomer to the program.

Vicky M had a doctor's appointment and Bobbie had a meeting. I realize I'm always disappointed when anyone misses the group, as though (odd as it seems) a strange spell has been broken. Today we talked a little first and then we did some freewriting. Then we discussed the writing. Cassandra, a newcomer to the program and the writing group, didn't write very long. She is nine months pregnant; the baby is due any day. She seemed very tired and sad, her stringy blonde hair almost covering her face and her eyes red and swollen from crying. At first she lay on the sofa behind our circle and refused to participate, but as the rest of us began to talk, I could feel the weight in the air dissipate. The voices of the mothers seemed to clear a path, and she joined in. The others wrote quite a bit and were very talkative and lively.

Vera seemed to be in a good place. Her husband was getting out of prison and coming home. She would begin to have custody of her daughter, who is in foster care, every other weekend. She was happy, but said she was also afraid of the good things that were happening, afraid that they would disappear or that her husband would not be able to stay clean.

Vicky H was also in a good place. She is a bit guarded when she shares, but she is very articulate about what she wants out of life: education, a good relationship, success, money. She is never lacking for words, a kind of bravado that may be concealing other fears. She seems to be taking charge of her life quite well. But I believe the writing stops her and makes her more reflective and sensitive to her needs. Several of the moms confronted Vicky about leaving by simply looking at her and asking, "Are you sure you're ready to go?" She shrugged good-naturedly and said, "I know I can do it."

Vicky B seemed much more positive today than during our first meeting. She came right in and was smiling and ready to work. She had more to say and wrote much more in her journal.

I felt hesitant to call time after we had been writing for thirty minutes.

Cynthia said that she was tired but she also wrote more today. I noticed how much better she was connecting her thoughts and being clear. She was making complete sentences when she wrote and talked. This was new for Cynthia, who usually wrote in fragments and spoke in choppy half-finished sentences that trailed off into silence, as though no one really cared to hear what she had to say. She usually becomes teary whenever she starts to speak, but today there were fewer tears. But the real change has been in the writing.

Is there a healing going on? Pieces, fragments of Cynthia's life and language coming together. All of us trying to understand and respond to the pieces of our lives. We've created a place to speak and write, a place where everyone's voice can be heard and valued.

We did a Soul Genealogy, a return to the map to look for the raw material. We used the Soul Map to identify people who had been supportive in their lives, people who had nurtured and cared for them and provided positive support. I told them this did mean family members, but it could be anyone, role models, friends, famous people they admired, whom they considered part of their support group. I asked them to create a list of these people or a cluster of names.

Then I had them do another cluster of the anti-heroes/heroines, those people who may have been charming and even lovable but who were harmful and dangerous to them. Vicky H asked if the same person could be on both lists, and I realized how acute her awareness was of the complexities involved in this kind of work. This exercise was difficult for me. In the middle of it, as the mothers were sharing, I began to feel anxious. Most of my anti-heroes were ex-lovers, and this self-awareness stopped me from revealing too much about my own anti-heroes. I felt my own wall go up, and I pulled back. *How much should I tell them about my life? They are all so embroiled in their own relationships. They might find my experience threatening or intrusive, but my unwillingness to reveal very much about my life might also hinder our work together in the long-run.* I did share with them that I was a recovering alcoholic. Somehow this piece of information made them warm up to me. They were skeptical at first. "You're in recovery?" they asked, and later, "that's cool." But they were also relieved it seemed. Suddenly we were kindred spirits and our lives not completely separate and distant. They still put me in the role of "expert," but now some of the guardedness began to dissolve.

This whole writing exercise turned out to be a powerful one for them and for me. We shared some of the people from the lists, and then Cassandra really started talking at this point. She is angry at Carlos, the father of her unborn baby. Essentially he has abandoned her and is living with his old girlfriend. She began crying, but there was much anger underneath those tears. All the mothers talked with her and gave advice and encouragement. I let them do it, and I stayed out of it, to see if the writing and the talk that comes from it could just be the tool that led them to insight and answers. When things calmed, I asked them to pick someone on their list to write a letter to. We took fifteen minutes while they wrote their letters. I was amazed at the power in the letters, at their clarity in the face of emotional intensity.

Vera wrote to her mother who had introduced her to drugs and prostitution when she was very young. Her letter went over the early years with her mother and sister as she asked her mother questions about their life and why she had chosen to live that way. But her letter was not condemning.

Cynthia wrote to the father of her children from whom she's separated now, in an attempt to understand that relationship more clearly and to try to set boundaries with this man. She wrote in a voice that was still unsteady, rocky, vacillating between a hard demanding tone to a more soft-spoken one. But I could hear the shape of her voice and a new persona that was beginning to emerge through her writing.

Vicky H wrote to the father of one of her children. While Vicky B did not want to share her writing, she volunteered that writing the letter had helped her see some things about one of her anti-heroes that she'd never considered before.

Cassandra wrote to Carlos who has abandoned her for another woman. The letter expressed her pain and her strength. Once again I was amazed at the eloquence. Cassandra had moved from inarticulate blubbering, overwhelmed by feelings she could not make sense of, to an eloquent expression of her anger and pain. By the end of the group, Cassandra had laughed, cried, and said she felt better. She sat in our circle for the rest of the group.

Reflection

Again during the session, we were interrupted several times. A staff person walked in and told Vera she had a telephone call. Vera got up and left the room and was unable to complete her list. The noise in the small office next to the room we met in made it difficult to concentrate because of continuous phone calls, talk from staff members, and people walking through our room to get to the other room. It was odd, but the interruptions seemed indicative of these women's lives in general: chaos, constant interruption, lack of respect for people's endeavors. I made a mental note to speak to the director again about the poor arrangements. At the same time, this was one of our best sessions because every member was fully engaged in both writing and sharing. I felt that we were making progress. At the same time, I felt uncomfortable with some of the very strong emotions that came up in the group, as though I ought to have had therapeutic training. I worked through it—and talked to Kathy Davis, the director, about it. She said letting the group members do the work with each other was the most valuable and if the writing was getting them to talk openly and honestly with one another that was best. She promised me that the group would not be interrupted anymore.

Thinking over the activities of this past week, I wanted to try to make our writings as complete as possible, not simply to focus on "problems" but also to look at the good. I had been reading *A Blue Fire* a selection of writings by James Hillman, a Jungian psychologist who describes himself as a member of a community of people who are at work re-visioning things. I liked much of what he says, particularly the idea of "living life backwards," to identify the stellar moments in our lives and to reflect on them. By stellar I don't necessarily mean the high points but also the beautiful dark and low points that have their own song and voice. So we were looking for experiences, memories, catalysts, dreams, images, figures, and people who populate the memories and dreams. And our stories, however fragmented, are the material that can coalesce into a landscape of meaning, a meaning that can be healing.

> Know Thyself is revelatory, nonlinear, discontinuous; it is like a painting, a lyric poem; biography thoroughly gone into the imaginative act. We may fiction connections between the revelatory moments, but these connections are hidden like the spaces between the sparks or the dark seas around the luminous fishes' eyes, images Jung employs to account for images. Each image is its own beginning, its own end, healed by and in itself. So, Know Thyself terminates whenever it leaves linear time and becomes an act of imagination. A partial insight, this song now, this one image; to see partly is the whole of it. (Hillman 59)

Perhaps the connections between revelatory moments are only interpreted and fabricated; however, our real connections come in the form of relatedness to others as we share these revelatory moments in our writing.

Upstairs: Meeting 3

I haven't been able to go to Las Madres for several weeks. Conflicts kept coming up for the women. So we had our third meeting Friday. Two of the original women were in the group—Vicky H, and Cynthia, and Vera from last time.

We began with freewriting—and then discussed what was going on. My own writing that day revealed my insecurity about what I was doing at Las Madres, about the confusion and interruptions and lack of continuity:

> I hope the moms are enjoying this group. Sometimes it seems like I have to work too hard all the time. Like everything I choose to do is hard, hard. Like writing with hard-core, angry, dysfunctional, sometimes violent and criminal, addicted, homeless, poverty stricken, maybe mentally ill women. And yet I'm here because I drove over here and asked to do this, to write with these women whose lives have hit a low point. Am I crazy or is it overly busy here? Everybody seems to be rushing

around all the time. Why am I feeling depressed? The lack of completion to things. Women disappearing from the program, "missing in action" as Bit calls it, the constant state of dissolution, things coming apart, tiny pinpoints of recovery and healing, then relapse and the plunge back into despair. I'm the kind of person who likes to be in long-term projects, and to see those projects to a satisfying conclusion. Here, our efforts are continuously thwarted, things are left undone, activities interrupted for others, projects abandoned and left unraveling. When we come here for these two hours to write, when I finally get all the women in the room and they're scratching away in their notebooks, and I see the quiet, almost serene looks on their faces, or even when I see a worried look crossing a face, I feel relieved; and sometimes when they look up at me and smile briefly, my heart hurts and I feel like crying for them, with them. And I wonder, what's next? Where do we go from here?

This was the crucial point in how we moved into the writing, what feelings came up and how much energy the mothers had. Some days I can tell they're too burned out, too angry from living in constant crises, although this makes our writing group all the more important, to move them beyond what is hard and far too literal in their lives to a kind of re-visioning of their lives through their storytelling, through a constant reimagining. This reimagining is hard work, for it is not just about one individual's story but is a means by which each person's story can shed light upon others, open a passage, create an aperture through which others can pass in and through. I was conscious of us "listening" to one another and our "listening" being a form of acknowledgment that is often lacking in our lives. Here we are reaffirming one another's lives and the possibility of those lives changing.

In *Conversational Realities,* John Shotter states that we construct reality as we talk in daily conversation. Our ideas, our motivations usually remain at the subconscious level. However, writing requires an act of will and consciousness and takes us beyond merely constructed reality to a consciously and deliberately constructed relatedness to other. Writing is the vehicle through which we can manifest these daily constructed realities. To re-vision and to reimagine are to dream. To listen is to acknowledge and honor. "Listening too must be responsive, in that listeners must be preparing themselves to respond to what they are hearing" (Shotter 51).

Vicky H didn't feel challenged by Las Madres anymore and was thinking of doing something more, attending school or getting a job. She sounded good, but I wondered if she wasn't moving too fast. Cynthia asked her if she thought she was ready to be on her own without the support of Las Madres. Vicky said yes, but seemed to be rethinking her decision. Again, I felt that the writing slowed her down, inviting her to re-vision her choices in the light of the common experiences of the group.

Vera smiled but was dark-eyed and on edge. Her husband has been home for a month and is already using. Vera is once again disappointed and stuck in what seems a very abusive relationship.

Cynthia talked about being rushed and hating that feeling of having to leave one task for another. Her ability to express these specific needs was significant. I could see her moving back and forth between anger and sadness. She has a gentle, languid quality about her, but a controlled anger is taking shape as she writes and talks more.

After the check in, I decided to shift gears, to move us into less painful territory away from the "literalness" of daily problems. We took turns reading out loud in a circle, Gary Soto's poem, "Elements of San Joaquin":

(excerpts)

Field	Wind
The wind sprays pale dirt into my mouth	A dry wind peeled over the valley peeled mountains, grain by grain
Stars	Sun
At dusk the first stars appear	In June the sun is a bonnet of light
Rain	Fog
When autumn rains flatten sycamore leaves	If you go to your window you will notice a fog drifting in
Daybreak	
In this moment when the light starts up	

At first, they waited for me to tell them what the poem meant, but I knew they already had responded to the poem and were simply reluctant to express themselves. All the life experiences they've had have given them a deep understanding of and value for what is beautiful, what can be captured on the page and savored. As we talked more and I encouraged them to look for associations and connections to their own lives, they became more animated and began writing down ideas and expressing their own inter-pretations. I asked them to record the "elements" of a place they remembered that was significant for them and that nourished them and to use those elements in writing to recall their past in poems and stories. We shared the elements of our "places" with one another before we began to write: "rippling water," "ashes," "solitary part of my being," "flowers and fruit," "a full moon flooding the pond with light," "hot sand," "cry at night." Two of the writings were like poems. Vera recalled a visit to Rocky Point as a child. Cynthia described a trip to another beach in Florida. Vicky wrote about her once-beautiful neighborhood that has turned into a slum. She described the streets where she used to play as a child now filled with prostitutes and drug dealers.

Reflection

It seemed risky to ask them to talk about poems, that they might feel inadequate or bored. They had expressed this feeling many times in our discussions, and they tended to place me in the role of "expert." Whenever I tried to shed that role, they put me right back into it. In interacting with the text of the poems on their own terms, they immediately found their own elements to work with. These elements became the ingredients of their poems and stories and we all listened to one another's writing; there were jokes about stealing lines and ideas from each other. They began to recall and then to texture the beautiful elements into their writing. I guess the trick to becoming who we are is to use the in-gredients we have. Someone in the group remarked that between them they might have enough ingredients to make a whole and decent life.

Downstairs: Stone Soup

Joey and Robbie, Andrea and Lucero, Stephanie, Sabrina, and Nesha were out on the sidewalk with their teacher, Bit, looking for a good stone to start the soup with. Nesha held up a tiny broken pebble and Stephanie said, "that's too small." Nesha tossed it back into the gutter. Joey shouted, "It has to be a good rock." Lucero lifted up a big round grey stone; it took almost all the energy in her small five-year-old body. Yes, that was it, the good rock, the perfect beginning of stone soup. Back in the kitchen under Cuka's guidance, the children added their individual ingredients. "Bit" read the book, *Stone Soup*, as each child stepped up and took his or her turn tossing in celery, carrots, tomatoes, onions, corn, cilantro, cabbage, till everyone had contributed something to the pot. It would boil and steam and the vegetables would intermingle to create a rich soup. Later, the children would invite their mothers downstairs to share their stone soup.

> Dreams can tell us who we are (divine) or
> how to become who we are (heal). (Sexson 103)

Upstairs: Meeting 4

Today Vicky and Cynthia were in the group, and Bobbie. Bobbie seemed very agitated and her energy was disruptive. She didn't write for more than a few minutes and kept doing distracting things, dropping papers, getting up to get a drink, combing her hair. The other women picked up on that energy and I think found it difficult to concentrate. We were all feeling fragmented and edgy. I had been looking forward just to sitting and writing with the mothers. Sometimes our freewriting seems to produce a state of grace, a calm inside the storms of our lives, but today it wasn't really working. During our sharing Bobbie interrupted and said she wanted to talk about a dream she had written about. She had been keeping a journal of her dreams, when she could remember them, and wanted to ask others what they thought of it. She shared her dream, but would only be specific about a little bit of the dream—she was in a hospital and parts of her body were being amputated. She said she found it too disturbing and though she wanted to know what it meant, it frightened her to talk about it out loud.

I knew I was way out of my depth here, but I asked her what she thought it meant. She shrugged, and looked pained. I told her one way to interpret the dream was to think of each element or person in the dream as herself. In this way maybe she could feel less trapped and victimized by the dream by giving it her own meaning. She said she would keep writing about it and thinking about the dream in this way. Others began remembering dreams they had—pieces of dreams that stood out for them, but Vicky asked, "How do I use them even if I figure out a meaning? I had a dream book once, and I'd look up my dreams but their explanations seemed bogus. I couldn't figure out what to do with it." We decided to make up our own dream interpretations, to imbue the images and elements and figures of the dreams with our own meanings. "It's my dream; nobody else's," Vicky said. I asked them to write down some dream images they could remember and to spend some time focusing on the images, to let the images themselves contain the meaning or the message for them. This is what they came up with.

> A baby is kissing my forehead = success in a difficult undertaking.
>
> My Aunt Mattie is in the water, and I'm trying to get her out. I ask her, "Can you get out?" = good news; help when you need it.
>
> A garden. It's hard to pass through = When things are good, I get stuck.

This renewed an interest in the dream journal. Although everyone had been excited about it in the first place, homework assignments rarely got done. "I'm too busy getting up with my baby at night to be writing down my dreams," one mother complained. But Bobbie had done this on her own, and it had rekindled the group's interest as a whole. This was one of the aims for the mothers in Las Madres—that each person could help others stay in touch and avoid despair and disappointment.

We've formed a community here through our sharing and confiding of stories; in spite of the crises and chaos, we have things to say to each other and to write about that seem to come from our community and that go beyond the community as defined by its problems and dysfunction. What I notice now is that the mothers seem to be writing beyond the labels and definitions of themselves as abused, dysfunctional, addicted. They want to move beyond "crisis" narratives and into new forms of writing.

Upstairs: Meeting 5

Today during our check-in we returned to the freewriting. They are writing much more during this time and perhaps we should start the series of dialogue journals. Pass our writing along to each other to comment on. We've been working together long enough to have built a bond of trust, although I'm never quite sure. The bond is new and fragile and at any given moment might break. But I'm proud of these women and even a little proud of myself for sticking with this and letting my own mask dissolve a bit. Sometimes I don't feel like a teacher at all, just a mother, a daughter, a woman who has had addiction problems, struggled with her role as a young parent, been a bad parent at times, and even experienced domestic violence. And this was the hardest for me to admit, to relive these experiences through these other women's lives. I had left an abusive relationship before things became really bad, but I had had more options than these women. What had been so different for me? Maybe it was the writing, my need to turn the painful events of my life into the raw material of art. And to use the stories and poems I'd created, not so much to analyze my life, but to perceive my life as it really was and then to write my way through it. Hearing the women in our group write about these experiences brought me right back into my own story.

Putting Our Lives Back Together

A key issue in the work of the group was a movement toward wholeness. Many of the women said very clearly they wanted to work on feelings. When I worked with newcomers in the program they usually cried after they wrote, and in one case—a Native American woman who came to the group only once—I had to read her writing for her. However, they had no hesitation about their work being read. There seemed to be immediate breakthroughs for them once we started writing, once their words were actually voiced. They opened up and began to define the problems in their lives. As we wrote about some of the problems, we began to find solutions as well. It is clear that because their lives are so complicated and fragmented, the writing time gave them an opportunity to begin to write past the "literal" conditions of their lives and experience toward a kind of wholeness within themselves. The masks dropped. This includes my own "teacher mask." When I was there writing with them, I felt tired, sad, and yet safe and comforted by the awareness of those feelings.

> However much we are affected by the things of the world, however deeply they may stir and stimulate us, they become human for us only when we can discuss them with our fellows. . . . We humanize what is going on in the world and in ourselves only by speaking of it, and in the course of speaking of it we learn to be human. (Hannah Arendt qtd. in Bauer 55)

My experience with the two parts of Las Madres, one upstairs and one downstairs, working in groups to communicate human feelings of joy and pain, was a profound one, giving me ideas from which to work and develop ways to promote healing and communication within larger community contexts. I could see how this sharing and confiding, this participation in a community built through writing, was beginning to move them out of some of the isolation, emptiness, and loneliness they felt. Something really started moving. Their writing became a prelude to critical action:

> Bobbie wanted to write letters to the court and to her landlord.
>
> Vera began to write as one step in a process of getting her nine-year-old daughter out of foster care.
>
> Vicky H was composing letters to her counselor, persuading her that she was ready to leave Las Madres.
>
> Cynthia began writing down her feelings in a journal of unexpressed emotions as practice for the real confrontation with her ex-boyfriend and family members. She wrote more each time we met and began to speak with less hesitation and without tears.

All of them expressed the desire to write stories and poems and continue with the journal.

Although we did not work together for a long time, in the three months that we did, the women began to learn ways to speak for themselves and to practice saying what they needed to on their own and their children's behalf.

After Las Madres: The Intertextual Collaboration

At Las Madres, we experienced an "intertextuality" by working off one another's stories. The sharing of stories produced an awareness of our interconnectedness and our responsibility to one another within the writing group. Such connectedness and responsibility seemed a perfect antidote to a certain distance and alienation I felt between myself and my students, between myself and other members of the community, and between the academy and the community. What emerged from my work at Las Madres and my sense of alienation and distance were the elements of a writing process that would become the Intertextual Collaboration (ITC).

While the ITC has many aspects and elements, a central feature directly related to the Las Madres experience is that it demands that writers listen to and value every voice. In the postmodern conversation that results, a play of voices replaces the attempt of one voice to dominate all others. Here, briefly, is how the ITC works:

1. Together participants brainstorm a broad theme (neighborhood, family, work), and then select five to six subthemes around which to structure the conversation.

2. Participants select the subtopic with which they wish to begin. They go home and write a draft of their first paper.

3. The following week, they bring this draft and three copies to the group. In small groups, each person reads aloud, and discussion follows, which is guided by the writer. The focus is on the ideas, not the writing specifically. In other words, participants use the writing as a vehicle to exchange ideas on the theme. Each person takes a turn reading and sharing.

4. At the end of the first session, each participant takes home copies of all group members' writing. During the following week, participants select something from each draft (a phrase, a word, an idea, a style) and integrate it into their work, producing a second draft. In addition, each writer must create and keep an acknowledgments page citing the source of the borrowed material and explaining the reason for using it.

5. Participants bring a second draft to the group, meet in small groups with different writers, and repeat the process—reading aloud, discussing and listening to the ideas that arise from the writing, integrating those ideas into subsequent drafts, and acknowledging them.

6. This pattern is repeated throughout the ten weeks that a group meets, until each person has worked with everyone in the large group and borrowed something from each to produce texts that reflect the multiple voices and perspectives of the group.

Now I want to stop here and examine what I think makes the ITC a unique experience, what is particular about it as a collaboration, and what it can teach us in terms of creating and healing community. While the postmodern dimension is somewhat obvious—the play of voices and the affirmation of diverse perspectives—the ITC does not invalidate existentialist or humanist positions. Both have their place within the process. The ITC contains both individual expression and the interface with and experience of community that most individuals cannot escape. While each writer joins this community and must work within its boundaries—stealing language and ideas from the other participants as a way to sustain and re-examine experience—he or she also has complete freedom in terms of how this is carried out. A writer may adopt a very minimalist approach to the intertextual community, choosing to use as little of the language of the other group members as possible.[1] Such an alienated individual can choose to remain alienated, can keep any stance he or she wishes, but not without an intensive examination of that position brought about by the continuous movement back and forth between individual perspective and the joining of voices with others through both spoken and written conversation. The acknowledgments page serves as an important record of the influence others exert on each writer's work and illustrates how we are always influenced by those around us, whether we accept or reject one another, how we make gestures toward one another, and how we reshape other people's ideas and make them our own. The acknowledgments page is thus one of the most important aspects of the ITC process because it allows each writer to honor each voice, to see his or her own voice honored in the written landscapes of others, and to retain his or her individual position within this community. In the ITC, we are not after consensus but an integration of diverse perspectives in a revelatory moment. And this revelatory moment, however fleeting, can be healing.

The Intertextual Collaboration in Action

In 1995, Peggy Erhardt-Gray, of Pima County Adult Education, and I began a project called Finding A Place in America: A Collaborative Conversation. The project, supported by the NEH under its special initiative, the National Conversation on American Pluralism and Identity, is intended to bring Americans from diverse backgrounds into conversations about what it means to be American. We have used the Intertextual Collaboration to have these conversations (thirteen in all) and discovered that it is a powerful tool for developing understanding of and empathy with diverse points of view. The division between people and contexts begins to close as we traverse boundaries, writing our way into and through each others' stories. The Intertextual Collaboration, gives us a way to admit difference and to use this difference in ways that can build, heal, and rebuild community bonds.

For the first University of Arizona/Community conversation groups, which we called the Communiversity Writes and Talks, we chose "community" as our broad theme. We were experimenting to see if a diverse group of people with very different educational backgrounds and experience could actually work together in a sustained exploration of ideas. The features of ITC such as interconnectedness, the practice of listening and acknowledging others, the sense that your story is in mine and mine in yours, had developed out of Las Madres, where everyone was similar in experience and educational background, where they shared traumatic, addictive lives that had led to violence and poverty, and where they expected to "serve" one another in their recovery and healing. But how would the features of the ITC play themselves out in a setting intentionally composed of very different people—homeless men; second-language speakers; a woman on welfare in the JOBS program; a professor from Judaic studies; an undergraduate from the Spanish department; a mix of teachers, staff, and students, young and old, with diverse ethnicities from two very different educational settings—even antagonistic ones, adult education and the university? Would the participants be able to do justice to each other's work in a choreographed collaboration of listening, speaking, writing, reading, stealing, incorporating, and acknowledging the other as primary and instrumental in the movement toward common understanding? Or would, as Jeffrey Nealon describes, "a single subject . . . demand social recognition and submission of others" (Nealon 131), which is still the case in so many public contexts from the Town Hall meeting to the peer writing group? We feared these "differences" and "disparities" among participants might remain so firmly entrenched as to produce an atmosphere of distrust that would make our writing together impossible. What we found was just the opposite. The ITC showed us how democracy can work in community groups and the classroom:

> One of the best—and one of the most unique—aspects of the project was that there was a strong element of equality. Though staff and students from both the U of A and Pima County Adult Education collaborated on this process, there was no sense that participants from one institution were superior to the other, nor any sense that the staff was superior to students. This made for an ideal environment that promoted safety and honesty.
>
> PEGGY ERHARDT-GRAY, *Pima County Adult Education*

> I feel like I've been writing to know, and my companions in this project have been writing to know, and we've been sharing what we have come to know with each other. In these activities, the world shows itself to be various and interesting and affecting. Incorporating into my writing the words and thoughts and images of other people honors those words as their words at the same time it transforms them into mine. This has been a writing project, and one which has enacted numerous acts of human gift-making and giving.
>
> SUSAN BOULDIN, *University of Arizona*

Honoring and listening to every voice demonstrates that we may not only tolerate differences in others but that we can find ways to use difference as a resource for building and strengthening our ongoing relationships with one another, to heal the connection with one another, and to strengthen the community we want to have with others, which must be created over and over again, reshaped and re-visioned as we engage in the experience of it. This process of re-creation and re-visioning is supported by the ITC, where each person is asked to keep the writing, and therefore the thinking, open to the influence of others.

As we compose with others, taking ideas, words, phrases into our own mental landscapes, as we not only *hear* the voice of the other, we *bear* the voice of the other into our own work, healing the fractured sense of self and other through a continuous collaborative revision. It is a kind of "undoing" of beliefs and misconceptions that then opens us to a whole sense of ourselves in community with others.

Undoing and Becoming

The ITC allows participants to wrestle with biases and prejudices that we don't always recognize. In an ITC, we get to confront our own limited thinking about ourselves and others. Such thinking stands in the way of both intellectual and emotional growth and may in turn stand in the way of community and responsible participation in it. We meet and reach out to these limitations, shine a light on them, and then reach beyond to our writing partners and fellow citizens and allow them entrance into our mental and physical landscapes. The text—the intertextual text of identities, souls, beliefs, experiences, and values—becomes a creation we share through our ongoing confrontation. In this sharing, we discover, for example, that the belief that the homeless man or welfare mother will never do anything productive in society mirrors our own fear of failure and loss. When another participant can hear a homeless man's or a welfare mother's story voiced and see it on the page, and subsequently find value in the language and experience of it, then a real change in consciousness and attitude can occur.

In our first group, using "community" as a theme, John Ferrante wrote about addiction and homelessness which lead to death. Below, an excerpt from his story is followed by a series of responses to his text from members of the writing group, which in turn is followed by his own acknowledgment of two of his writing partners. The passages, while lacking the full context of an ITC community, do give a taste of the interactive and collaborative nature of the ITC, as well as the way in which it supports changes in perspective and understanding:

> It's funny how all the regular people seem to disappear when you're on a mission. Like they become just part of the scenery. Maybe it's because I don't need 'em right now. My world has gotten pretty small and they'd rather not have me in theirs. Well, that shit works both ways. Nothin' I ever learned in school ever taught me about livin' like now. No survival value. People get broke, get hungry, get desperate and all that good shit ya learn goes right out the fuckin' window. You'll do any fuckin' thing when you're desperate and can't figure an angle.
>
> All these fine folks comin' in and out of the store; with their nice clothes and their new cars and money in their pocket. They stare when they think your not lookin'. I hate the way they treat ya when you ask for some change. Either tryin' to act like you're not there or treatin' you like dirt.
>
> JOHN FERRANTE, *Homeless Education Project*

> I used John's idea about being treated as though you're invisible when you're on the street because it reminded me of the student who has come to believe that he/she doesn't count, that he/she is invisible to many adults. As I listened to what John had to say about homeless addicts, I'd have to say that I grew up a little bit. Even though you might read extensively about current events and consider yourself to be open-minded, unless you speak to the source of difference, you don't really understand it as well. Just to sit at a table with people who live in Tucson, my home, people I would probably never see, much less meet, that was gratifying for me. It's odd how the city is so segregated by earning power and opportunity. We all stay in our designated areas and never see or meet each other. This project gave me a new opportunity to be part of something larger.
>
> PAM TIETIG, TEACHER, *Tucson Public Schools*

I used Pam's passage to develop and briefly illustrate how education and real life don't always mesh—how education can be a poor preparation for reality. The concept of using other people's ideas for something I'm writing seemed foreign at first. But now I see the possibilities that open up. Talking and listening to others' writing shows me how different my experience has been. Questions are posed that I can answer and answers are made clear to questions I had.

JOHN FERRANTE, *Homeless Education Project*

[This passage was written in response to an entry by Cindy Meier, who was writing about her mother's death.]

This was a death week once again, the finality of death only here coupled with memories—this helped me to write the final pages of my story where the homeless man dies. The depth of feeling that comes from hearing what Cindy has written is incredible. Working with the author of a piece makes it that much more personal and strong.

I began to see how my background gave me something to share with others that they didn't know about—that they were interested in. In other words, I had a story to write, from my experience, that others wanted to hear, read about. This writing project has helped me to change the way I look at myself and my capabilities.

JOHN FERRANTE, *Homeless Education Project*

The assumption that a university professor cannot have compassion for or communicate with those with little or no formal schooling can keep us locked into a fractured view of society. Such a view keeps us from seeing how to value and utilize difference as a resource rather than a weapon. In the following sequence from an ITC entitled Notes Towards a Communiversity, John Bormanis, a University of Arizona professor, responds to John Lair, a homeless man:

Being an academic and UA instructor, I come to this aspect of community thinking: the two are totally separate. And the whole enterprise of higher education is anathema to community because it focuses so much upon individuals and their careers. And as John read his writing about the death of his father and his lack of sadness at the event, I opened up to another level of understanding my problems with the University: my fear of a lack of community, of being alone, in an atmosphere where everyone is either too busy or too overworked to engage in community building.

John's writing evoked in me a great sadness over the fact that my father was so caught up in his own work that I seemed to him a secondary concern. . . . [T]his process of Intertextual Collaboration worked at both a creative and social level. . . . I was astonished at how liberating an event this writing project was for me. I'd never really gotten to work so directly with people on my writing and theirs on a regular basis. And to be able to do so as a community where we were all acting to work together, rather than just to take from the others for the sake of ourselves, was a true joy. When I tried to incorporate others' writing into my own, I thought about them as people I cared about, not just as texts that could or could not highlight my own arguments. I cared about what they thought, and whether or not how I represented their words would be meaningful to them. I don't think I've ever focused as intensely on the desires of others in the course of my writing. And that, strangely enough, has brought me back to myself in ways that have been quite fulfilling.

JOHN BORMANIS, *University of Arizona*

The ITC engages individuals in a confrontation with their own attitudes, assumptions, and ways of remembering experience that may no longer work and can be revised through the intertextual process.

It was so interesting being in a group with what I imagined to be "university-types." Talk about buying into a stereotype. How soon I discovered that we shared the same desire to be in the class and the same desire to make it a wonderful gift to ourselves.

PEGGY ERHARDT-GRAY, *Pima County Adult Education*

Before entering into this new world of self-thoughts, ideas, and writing methods that I was unaware . . . I most certainly was in doubt because I didn't know what to expect. I knew I wanted to write. But I didn't know how. I was surprised by the willing and earnest feedback and suggestions from the group. The writing pieces I've read gave me a springboard on how to use parts of stories and interlace them into mine. At times, the feelings that I received from the group were mixed with sorrow and joy, awe and surprise, humor and heightened insight. I'm glad that I made the right decision to enter into this new and different writing project, and if I'm ever asked what was the determining factor that influenced me most, it would be the human factor of the collaboration of the group as a whole unit.

JOHN LAIR, *Homeless Education Project*

The Intertextual Collaboration process helps us confront the limitations we place on ourselves and our achievements and can push us into new creative territory, new relationships and arrangements with others. It can help us feel part of something larger and expand our view of what and who can be a part of *our* community.

> It is always a good thing when I really listen to what people are saying. This writing experience was a wonderful one because each week I really listened to other members' points of view. And it became clear early on, that we each brought our own gifts and that these gifts were worth sharing. As much as I learned from others' work I also learned a great deal about myself. From my place on the fringe, if I chose to, I could look around me and see others close by, and some of them would be the members of this group. That's pretty good company. I am glad that I came to share this experience with the people here. It provided me with ample opportunity to connect with people that I wouldn't know otherwise. It may be that my current, static circle is no longer static and has grown some.
>
> PEGGY ERHARDT-GRAY, *Pima County Adult Education*

Conclusion

What we discovered through the Intertextual Collaboration was that most of us, whether we are university professors or homeless persons, feel limitations of one kind or another in our lives and want to reach for greater creativity and more participation in community. Greg Hart, the director of Pima County Adult Education, observed that

> university professors and the homeless have written about and shared their life experiences and values. Immigrants and military veterans have found their common ground. The barely literate and the super-literate, through the process of Intertextual Collaboration, have discovered that competencies come in

many guises, and that discrepancies in competencies often obscure what is universal and lasting in our shared humanity.

Amazing things began to happen for the writers in our intertextual groups. In one "family" group, with subthemes including, mothers/fathers, home, siblings, neighborhood, extended family, participants began to report on the encounters they were having with their families. One woman called her sister up to share one of the stories she was writing about their childhood. Another man reported hearing from an uncle he hadn't seen for many years. Several other participants reported making special contact with family members to ask about their writing, to read their stories to parents, to check on specifics. I had a similar experience, when my brother made contact with me—we had not spoken for almost a year at the time. Something in our work together reverberated and resonated beyond the writing circle. We learned something about revision not only of our writing, but also of our lives. And as we collaborated with one another, we became both the initiators of and the witnesses to our revisions and transformations, our healings. As Peggy Erhardt-Gray eloquently put it,

> We worked together to create an extraordinary voyage to some places I'd never been. How intimate we became—mourning this one's mother and that one's youth. We peered into some shadows that became less daunting with more light. We wrote about family from the broadest sense to the most narrow; from fiction to the most personal; from rage to the most forgiving. How different our families were. Yet they united us with such force.

I do not claim that the Intertextual Collaboration is the answer to all the problems we face in our attempt to build, to deepen, and to maintain workable communities of diverse individuals at the beginning of the twenty-first century. But I do claim that it is a mechanism by which we, like the mothers of Las Madres, may come to serve each other through the words we speak and write. In those words and in that serving, we may find a way to live through and beyond the differences that have bent and broken us, a healing, a wholeness.

Note

1. Ty Bouldin, a teacher who has used the ITC in his advanced composition courses, describes the minimalist approach of one alienated student: "This writer used only *articles* from other writers' texts in his piece, stating that there simply was nothing in other people's work that he could relate to; however, in both conversation with his peers and in the acknowledgments to his paper, the writer clearly articulated both an appreciation of the work and values of his peers and of the ways in which his own experience contrasted with theirs. Because his own text was the only one in the class that explored negative experiences of family, this student's work played an important role in the classroom community. It was as though he had taken on the burden for everyone of facing painful and negative dimensions of family life."

Works Cited

Bauer, Susan. *Confiding: A Psychotherapist and Her Patients Search for Stories to Live By*. New York: Harper, 1994.

Brown, Marcia. *Stone Soup: An Old Tale*. New York: Aladdin, 1987.

Hillman, James. "Healing Fictions." *A Blue Fire: Selected Writings of James Hillman*. Ed. Thomas More. New York: Harper, 1991. 59.

———. *Kinds of Power*. New York: Doubleday, 1995.

Nealon, Jeffrey. "The Ethics of Dialogue: Bakhtin and Levinas." *College English* 59.2 (1997): 129–48.

Sexson, Lynda. "The Inward Text." *Ordinarily Sacred*. New York: Crossroad, 1982. 101–18.

Shotter, John. *Conversational Realities: Constructing Life through Language*. Newbury Park, CA: Sage, 1993.

Simons, George F. *Keeping Your Personal Journal*. New York: Paulist Press, 1978.

Soto, Gary. "Elements of San Joaquin." *19 Poets of the Golden Gate*. Ed. Philip Dow. San Diego: Harcourt, 1984. 440–43.

INDEX

Ocean Power: Poems from the Desert (Zepeda), 53
O'Connor, Flannery, 42
"Ode to a Nightingale" (Keats), 313
O'Donnell, Thomas G., 12
Ohio State University, 167
O'Keefe, John, 205, 206
On Becoming a Person (Rogers), 100, 101, 107–8
Ong, Walter, 91, 94, 96
Opening Up (Pennebaker), 167
Orality, 91, 94, 95, 96
O'Reilley, Mary Rose, 410
Ornstein, Robert, 183–84
Orwell, George, 185, 191, 250
Other
    critical dialogue between self and, 116
    discourse with, 62, 67–68
    educational institutions as, 8
    encounter with, 104
    Lacan on, 60
    Rogers on, 101, 105
    and self-nonself distinction, 212–13
    and sense of self, 80
    speaking with, about trauma, 197
"Outlaw emotions," 133, 137, 140, 148, 151

Pace, Diana, 117–18, 150, 155n.9
Pain, 163
Pain and Possibility (Rico), 339, 410–11
Panger, Daniel, 235
Papez, J. W., 204, 205
Paradoxing, 341–42, 346–47, 350–52
Parker, Patricia, 321
Pascal, Roy, 226, 232
Passive voice, 76
Pathography. *See also* AIDS/HIV;

and other diseases
    battle myth of illness in, 233, 234, 234–38
    case history contrasted with, 224
    death and rebirth myth in, 233
    definition of, 222
    examples of, 234–40
    and formulation, 231–34
    journey myth in, 229–30, 233, 238–40
    mythic thinking in, 228–41
    and personal story as construct, 225–28
    process of, 241–42
    as voice of patient, 222–25
Payne, Michelle, 17–18, 115–55, 453–54
Peabody, Barbara, 387, 390
Peaceable Classroom (O'Reilley), 410
Peavey, Fran, 227–28
Pedagogy
    Bruner on, 97–100, 102–4
    confrontational teaching, 14
    critical pedagogy, 121
    discovery learning, 323–24
    and Freire, 112n.4, 121
    and informed practice, 16–17
    innovations in writing courses, 251–57, 287–88
    and lived experience, 9, 14–16
    postmodern pedagogies, 14, 121–22, 151–52, 153–54n.1
    process model in writing instruction, 194
    and self, 11–17
    traditional approach to writing instruction, 249–51
    "wild pedagogy," 154n.1
Pennebaker, James W., 167, 197, 282, 308, 340, 342, 348, 350, 394–95
Penrose, Roger, 202, 218n.4

EDITORS

Charles M. Anderson is professor of rhetoric and writing at the University of Arkansas at Little Rock. He teaches courses in rhetorical theory and expository and technical writing. He also teaches medical ethics and literature and medicine at the University of Arkansas for Medical Sciences. He has published articles in *Literature and Medicine,* chapters in anthologies on writing and rhetoric, and a book entitled *Richard Selzer and the Rhetoric of Surgery.* In 1996, he was awarded his university's highest teaching award. He is currently working on a collection of personal essays entitled *Journey Time.*

Marian M. MacCurdy, a writer, teacher, and singer, is currently associate professor and chair of the writing program at Ithaca College, where she teaches both creative and expository writing. She has published scholarly articles as well as personal essays and poetry in such journals as *Raft, Ararat,* and the *Journal of Poetry Therapy.* An article, "The Four Women of the Apocalypse: Polarized Feminine Images in Magazine Advertisements," is included in an anthology entitled *Utopia and Gender in Advertising: A Critical Reader.* Her essay "From Image to Narrative: The Politics of the Personal," which began her exploration of the relationship between writing and healing, was published in the spring 1995 issue of the *Journal of Teaching Writing.* She is a frequent speaker at national conferences of organizations such as the National Council of Teachers of English, the Conference on College Composition and Communication, the National Association for Poetry Therapy, the Women's Studies Association, and the Associated Writing Programs. She holds a Ph.D. in Humanities from Syracuse University.

CONTRIBUTORS

Guy Allen is professor in the professional writing program at the University of Ontario at Mississauga. He served as coordinator of the Psychoanalytic Thought program at University of Toronto from 1992 to 1998. From 1977 to 1998, he taught in the university's transitional year program. He works with the Humanities and Psychiatry Interest Group at Mt. Sinai Hospital in Toronto, where he and a group of psychiatrists explore narrative as an educational and therapeutic tool. He has collected and edited several prose collections (including student narratives), works as managing editor for a small press devoted to new writers, and co-hosts a community radio program that broadcasts autobiographical narratives by new writers. He is also the founder of the popular Totally Unknown Writers Festival in Toronto.

Jeffrey Berman is professor of English at the University at Albany. He is the author of *Joseph Conrad: Writing as Rescue, The Talking Cure, Narcissism and the Novel, Diaries to an English Professor,* and *Surviving Literary Suicide.*

Alice G. Brand is professor of English at State University of New York College at Brockport. While serving as director of composition for twelve years, she published several scholarly works: *Therapy in Writing, The Psychology of Writing: The Affective Experience,* and *Presence of Mind: Writing and the Domain Beyond the Cognitive* (co-edited with Richard L. Graves). These interests led her to study the brain and emotion, out of which came an article in *Rhetoric Review* and the piece in this collection. Her *Writing-Across-the-Curriculum Guide for Disciplinary Faculty* was recently printed for campus use. Three collections of her poetry have also been published.

Jerome Bump is former Associate Chair of the NCTE Assembly for Expanded Perspectives on Learning (1997–1998), and has held fellowships from the National Endowment for the Humanities and the Woodrow Wilson Foundation. He is the author of *Gerard Manley Hopkins* and fifty articles and book chapters, as well as editor of *Gerard Manley Hopkins: A Centenary Celebration* and former editor of *Texas Studies in Language and Literature* (1986–1992). He currently serves on the advisory boards of *Victorian Poetry* and *The Hopkins Quarterly*.

Sandra Florence teaches writing at the University of Arizona and runs writing groups in the community. Her special interests include writing to promote community dialogue and writing and healing. Recently, she received a grant from the NEH for a project called Finding A Place in America: A Collaborative Conversation, which brought together community and university participants to write on themes in American life. The project has produced fifteen texts on subjects such as family, children, work, literacy, community, books, generations, spirituality, education, and art.

Regina Paxton Foehr, Chair of the NCTE Assembly for Expanded Perspectives on Learning, teaches writing and English methods courses at Illinois State University. She co-edited *The Spiritual Side of Writing: Releasing the Learner's Whole Potential.* Her current research topics, which include archetypes and writing and facing the shadow in education, reflect her interest in the role of the unconscious and other forces that affect how we write, how we think, and how we learn.

Anne Ruggles Gere is professor of English and professor of education at the University of Michigan, where she directs the joint Ph.D. program in English and education. A past chair of CCCC, she is the incoming president of NCTE. Her recent publications include *Intimate Practices: Literacy and Cultural Work in U.S. Women's Clubs, 1880–1920* and articles in *Signs* and *College English*. She and her daughter Cindy are currently working on *Woman of the King Salmon*, a book about their shared experience with fetal alcohol syndrome.

Anne Hunsaker Hawkins is associate professor of humanities at Pennsylvania State University College of Medicine. Her publications include articles on literature and medicine and literature and medical ethics as well as two books: *Archetypes of Conversion* (on spiritual autobiography) and *Reconstructing Illness* (on autobiographies about illness). She is co-editor of *Teaching Literature and Medicine* and is currently writing a book about children with HIV and their caregivers.

Karen Holt first discovered the power of healing through writing during her college course "Advanced Expository Writing." She is working on a collection of essays to complete her M.A. in writing. She currently resides in Little Rock, Arkansas, with her husband and her cats and makes her living as a hairstylist. She reads for relaxation and writes for self-exploration.

T. R. Johnson is assistant professor of English at the University of New Orleans, where he directs the Writing Center. He researches the experience of composing from the standpoints of composition theory, the history of rhetoric, American cultural studies, and the philosophical work of Gilles Deleuze. His work has appeared in *Hypatia, The Composition Journal,* and a variety of other publications.

Laura Julier is associate professor of American thought and language at Michigan State University, where she teaches American literature, writing, and women's studies, and is also associate director of the Writing Center. She has published another article on the Clothesline Project in *English Education,* as well as several publications on service learning pedagogy in the teaching of writing, and articles on voice in writing and in teaching. She is currently at work on a book on the rhetoric of representation in Indian captivity narratives.

Patty McGady is a writer who lives in Little Rock, Arkansas, most of the time. She writes essays and proposals and works with writers on medical subjects, particularly those promoting support for persons with liver disease. Her children are doing well, and the grandchildren are more fun than she can manage. She is working to calm the dragon of her own liver disease.

Emily Nye is associate professor of English at the New Mexico Institute of Mining and Technology in Socorro, New Mexico, where she is also director of student services. She established the university's first writing center and coordinated the composition program for three years. Her dissertation served as the basis for her chapter in this volume as well as the root of her subsequent research. She has facilitated more than a dozen writing groups with various populations, but mainly with senior citizens. She and her colleague Cheryl Learn are currently examining the use of narrative in the well-being of senior citizens.

Michelle Payne is assistant professor of English and the assistant director of composition at Boise State University. She teaches undergraduate courses in writing, critical theory, and women's studies, as well as graduate courses in composition and rhetoric. Her publications include an article on Zelda Fitzgerald in *The Bucknell Review* and a chapter on gender, authority, and teaching writing in *Taking Stock: The Writing Process Movement in the '90s.* Her forthcoming book, *Bodily Discourses: When Students Write about Sexual*

Abuse, Physical Abuse, and Eating Disorders in the Writing Classroom, considers why students write about these issues, how they write about them, what assumptions inform teachers' responses, and what cultural contexts shape students' representations and teachers' responses.

Jonathan Schiff received his Ph.D. from the University at Albany in 1997, his dissertation focusing on the theme of mourning in F. Scott Fitzgerald's writings. He is currently an adjunct lecturer at the University at Albany. His book, *Ashes to Ashes: Mourning and Social Difference in F. Scott Fitzgerald's Fiction,* is forthcoming.

Tilly Warnock is associate professor of English in the program in rhetoric, composition, and the teaching of English at the University of Arizona. She has been director of a writing project, a writing center, and a composition program. Currently, she is working on a book, *Kenneth Burke's Rhetoric: Lessons in Reading, Writing, and Living,* and a novel, *Goldfish in My Head.* She has published articles on rhetoric, composition, and literature, as well as a composition textbook, *Writing as Critical Action,* and she has edited an anthology with Joseph Trimmer, *Understanding Others: Cultural and Cross-Cultural Studies and the Teaching of Literature.*

This book was typeset in Sabon
by G&S Typesetters, Inc.
Typefaces used on the cover include Serlio,
Antique Olive, and Shannon Book.
The book was printed on
50-lb. opaque paper
by Versa Press, Inc.